Absolute
Beginner's
Guide to
Networking

Third Edition

 que® 201 West 103rd Street,
Indianapolis, Indiana 46290

Absolute Beginer's Guide to Networking, Third Edition

International Standard Book Number: 0-7897-2545-2

Library of Congress Catalog Card Number: 00-111683

Printed in the United States of America

First Printing: June 2001

04   03   4   3   2

Trademarks

Warning and Disclaimer

Associate Publisher
Dean Miller

Senior Acquisitions Editor
Jenny L. Watson

Development Editor
Mark Reddin

Managing Editor
Thomas F. Hayes

Senior Editor
Susan Ross Moore

Copy Editor
Bart Reed

Indexer
Sheila Schroeder

Proofreader
Jeanne Clark

Technical Editor
Bill Morter

Team Coordinator
Cindy Teeters

Interior Designer
Kevin Spear

Cover Designer
Trina Wurst

Page Layout
Heather Hiatt Miller

Contents at a Glance

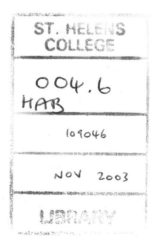

Table of Contents

About the Author

Joe Habraken is a computer technology professional and best-selling author with more than 15 years of experience in the information technology field. His recent publications include *Microsoft Office XP 8-in-1*, *The CCNA 2.0 640-507 Routing and Switching Cheat Sheet*, and *Practical Cisco Routers*. Joe currently serves as a Technical Director at Reviewnet, a B2B Web-based company. He also teaches computer certification courses at the University of New England in Portland, ME.

Dedication

To all those who work with computers, I hope this book helps you. I also hope that you will let your screensaver come up once in a while so that you can go out and enjoy the non-binary wonders of Nature.

Acknowledgments

As you will find with computer networking, networks (like Rome) are not built in a day. And the same goes for a book like this. It really does take a team (sometimes it seems like a village) to create a book that covers a subject matter that seems to change on a daily basis.

First of all, I would like to thank Kim Rich, who took time out from her busy schedule to shoot many of the photos that appear in this book. I would also like to thank Chad Zook, who reviewed the proposal and outline for this book and made a number of excellent suggestions related to the book's content.

I would also like to acknowledge the very hard-working Jenny Watson, my acquisitions editor, who assembled the team that worked on this project. Jenny showed the patience of the Buddha and made sure the project stayed on track. Jenny certainly receives a heart-felt thanks for making this book project a reality.

A big thanks goes out to Mark Reddin, the development editor, who burned the midnight oil to make sure this was the best book possible. Also, I would like to thank my former teaching colleague, Bill Morter, a fantastic computer instructor and curriculum designer, who verified the technical aspects of the text and made many useful suggestions for improving the book's content.

I would also like to thank Bart Reed, our copy editor, for cleaning up the text and finally, a big thanks to the Project Editor, Susan Moore, who ran the last leg of the race and made sure this book got into print (and into your local bookstore). Thank you all very much!

Tell Us What You Think!

As the reader of this book, *you* are our most important critic and commentator. We value your opinion and want to know what we're doing right, what we could do better, what areas you'd like to see us publish in, and any other words of wisdom you're willing to pass our way.

As an associate publisher for Que, I welcome your comments. You can fax, e-mail, or write me directly to let me know what you did or didn't like about this book—as well as what we can do to make our books stronger.

Please note that I cannot help you with technical problems related to the topic of this book, and that due to the high volume of mail I receive, I might not be able to reply to every message.

When you write, please be sure to include this book's title and author as well as your name and phone or fax number. I will carefully review your comments and share them with the author and editors who worked on the book.

Fax: 317-581-4666
E-mail: feedback@quepublishing.com
Mail: Dean Miller
          Associate Publisher
          Que
          201 West 103rd Street
          Indianapolis, IN 46290 USA

INTRODUCTION

Computer technology has evolved in a truly explosive fashion over the last 20 years. Computers have become hundreds of times faster and at least two times less expensive seemingly overnight. Even the smallest companies now see a computer network as an indispensable part of their business infrastructure. And with the Internet and World Wide Web bringing massive amounts of data right to your desktop, no one can dispute that we are living in an information age.

A big issue for companies both big and small is getting network resources and Internet information to the desktop of each and every employee. This means having an understanding of how networks work and knowing what kind of technologies are available for moving data between two computers in the same room or two computers separated by a thousand miles. Networking is also no longer just the domain of companies and business—even the home user now can see the advantages of networking computers and other devices in the home.

When I sat down to write this book, I took a quick look back at my network administration experiences and thought about the things I had learned on the job and the things I wish I had known (things that certainly would have saved me some overtime and grief in certain situations). I wanted to put a body of information together that would be useful for someone new to networking but also provide enough depth to be an excellent starting point for someone who plans on learning more and maybe eventually working in the computer networking field. You are now holding the result.

The *Absolute Beginner's Guide to Networking, Third Edition* will help you bridge the information gap related to information technology and computer networking. Although this book covers a wide breadth of information, it also provides you with enough detail that you won't be lost as you further explore the subjects covered.

Although this book takes its subject matter very seriously, the material itself is approached in a straightforward, conversational manner that should help you digest the information without dozing off or developing a horrible migraine headache. Technology can be very intimidating, but this book will show you that the right information can go a long way as you explore networking technology, network operating systems, and the hardware devices that make networking possible.

Conventions Used in This Book

Certain conventions have been followed in this book to help you digest all the material. For example, new terms appear in *italics*. These terms can also be found in the Glossary, which supplies a short definition for each term.

At the beginning of each chapter, you'll find a quick-view list of the major topics that will be expounded upon as you read through the material that follows. The end of each chapter provides a list of summary points, reiterating some of the important information covered in the chapter.

You will also find several icons used throughout this book. These icons are accompanied by additional information on a subject, supply asides that provide useful insight, or give warnings that can help you steer clear of problem areas related to a certain subject or technology. These icons are as follows:

These sidebars include additional information related to the current topic, but they do not have to be read in order for you to have complete understanding of the information provided in the regular text.

These sidebars contain higher-level information and additional insight into a topic that expands on the material provided in the chapter.

These boxes attempt to reach out and grab your hand before you press that red destruct button. Warnings point out major problems or issues related to technologies or network practices.

How This Book Is Organized

This book has been completely updated for its third edition. It covers many cutting-edge technologies and also attempts to provide some hands-on insight into certain operating systems and hardware devices.

The book is divided into four parts; each part provides you a body of information that covers a particular area related to computer networking. Part I, "Networking Basics," provides an overview of computer networking and information on network hardware, network cabling, and the protocols that are used for network communication.

Part II, "Getting the Network Up and Running," covers the various aspects of configuring peer-to-peer and server-based networks. It includes information on configuring network client computers and network servers running different network operating systems, such as Windows 2000 Server and Novell NetWare. This section also discusses the different ways to deploy applications and communication software on the network.

Part III, "Expanding Your Network," discusses how to use WAN technology to expand and connect LANs at different locations. This part of the book also discusses how to connect a network to the Internet and develop a company Web site.

Part IV, "Keeping the Network Running Smoothly," discusses how to protect network data using strategies such as RAID arrays and backups and also discusses how to troubleshoot network problems. This part of the book provides a primer on network security, which includes information on protecting the network from viruses and outside attacks. Allowing users to connect to the network infrastructure remotely using dial-in connections and personal digital assistants is also discussed. This part of the book concludes with a discussion of some of the technological advances that are on the horizon in the networking field.

To help you keep track of all the new terminology that is introduced in the book, Appendix A provides a glossary. Appendix B, "Online Networking Resources," provides you with a number of links to informational and product sites related to computer networking that will allow you to continue your study of the networking field and read about specific networking products mentioned in this book.

PART I

NETWORKING BASICS

COMPUTER NETWORKING OVERVIEW

In this chapter

- Defining the computer network
- Reasons for networking personal computers
- Understanding Centralized Computing
- The evolution of the modern PC
- How PC networks got their start
- Transferring data from the computer to the network
- Understanding the role of the Network Administrator

I do not fear computers. I fear lack of them.

–Isaac Asimov

It is certainly safe to say that computers have become as integral to modern life as fast food, cell phones, and sport utility vehicles. And although these trends may seem a little alarming, even scary (especially to anyone who has had a near miss with a massive SUV piloted by a driver who is preoccupied with his cell phone and a greasy box of French fries), the personal computer has evolved from a standalone device reserved for business applications into a device that can provide everything from real-time communications between users, to streaming audio and video, to the sharing of facts and figures across the length and breadth of our planet.

Computers are no longer just number-crunching business tools; they have become integral to communication, entertainment, and education. All the incredible possibilities offered by personal computers are in most part based on the simple notion that we can connect computers together into networks.

What Is a Network?

Before we plunge headlong into a discussion of how networks actually operate and what it takes to get them up and running (a discussion that will lead you through the other chapters of this book), we should probably first define what a network is and then discuss why you would want to connect computers into a network. A *network* can be anything from a simple collection of computers at one location that have been tied together using a particular connectivity medium (such as copper wires) to a giant global network, such as the Internet, that uses a number of different connectivity media, including satellite technology. The network can then be used to transmit data, voice, even video between users on the network.

Networks consist of the computers, wiring, and other devices, such as hubs, switches, and routers (which are all discussed later in the book), that make up the network infrastructure. Some devices, such as network interface cards, serve as the computer's connection to the network. Devices such as switches and routers provide traffic-control strategies for the network. All sorts of different technologies can actually be employed to move data from one place to another, including wires, radio waves, and even microwave technology.

Networks are not networks just because they contain highly complex connectivity strategies. Two computers running the Windows ME operating system can be joined together by their COM ports (also known as *serial ports*) by a single serial cable. Is this a network? Sure, it allows you to share resources between the two computers and therefore meets the basic definition of what a network is.

In our discussion of computer networks, we will be looking at two distinct entities: LANs and WANs. A *local area network (LAN)* is a collection of personal computers and other peripheral devices connected at one location. A *wide area network (WAN)* is a collection of LANs at different locations connected together using various WAN technologies (discussed in Chapter 10, "Expanding a LAN with WAN Technology.").

Why Network Your Computers?

There are actually some very compelling reasons why someone (someone being a person, small business, or mega-institution) with more than a couple computers would want to connect those computers into a network. What the network will actually be used for will, of course, vary depending on the needs of the person or organization creating the network. Networks can be used for simple tasks, such as sharing a printer, or they can be used for more advanced applications, such as a complex point-of-sale system and worldwide video conferencing.

All networks, whether big or small, are typically created so that users on the network can share resources and communicate. The list that follows breaks down some of the reasons for networking computers:

- *File sharing.* Networking computers makes it very easy for the users on the network to share application files. Files on a particular user's computer can be shared on the network or files can be placed on a file server, which provides a central location for all files needed by the users on the network.

- *Hardware sharing.* Users can share devices such as printers, CD-ROM drives, and hard drives. Once networked, computers can share their own local devices, such as CD-ROM and hard drives, or take advantage of high-speed printers or other devices that are provided by a particular server on the network.

- *Program sharing.* Applications such as spreadsheets and word processors can be run over the network. This allows you to keep most of the files that make up the application on a special application server on the network. This makes installing the software on a computer easier (because it can be done over the network). It also makes upgrading an application easier because the upgrade only has to be performed on the server itself.

- *User communication.* Networks allow users to take advantage of communication media such as electronic mail, newsgroups, and video conferencing. Because voice, pictures, and video can be moved across the network as data, network communication is certainly not limited to just text messages.

- *Multiplayer gaming.* While this certainly isn't a reason for networking computers in a business environment, individuals who set up home-based peer-to-peer networks can take advantage of a large number of computer games that provide support for multiple players on a network.

In networks that consist of more than just a few computers, you will have two different types of computers operating on the network: clients and servers. *Client computers* supply users with a connection to the network. *Servers* actually serve up the resources that are available on the network—everything from files to electronic mail post offices. A more detailed discussion of clients and servers is offered later in this chapter.

Not only does a network provide the ability to share resources found locally on the network (such as a printer shared by several users in a small office), but the fact that the network exists means that the local network can be connected to other networks. Most networks, big and small, are also now connected to the Internet, meaning that the potential for sharing resources and communication is almost endless. One of the most compelling reasons for a company to decide to network its computers is to have all its users "plugged in to" the global network that is the Internet.

A Look at Mainframes and Minicomputers

Although this book concentrates on helping you understand, create, and then manage your own networks, we should first place personal computers and PC networking into an appropriate context by taking a moment to investigate how computer technology has evolved and where it is today—an environment where personal computers can be easily linked together into both small and large networks.

Let's begin our quick historical survey with a look at mainframes and minicomputers.

There Be Monsters

Computing and the advances that led to modern computing go as far back as the human race itself. Devices such as the abacus (500 B.C.) and the Jacquard loom (a nineteenth-century mechanized loom that used a series of punch cards to create a particular weave) always enter into the discussion, but let's forgo some of the preliminary facts and jump ahead to the 1950s.

Although there were a number of super computers created prior to 1950, the early mainframe market (which was not all that huge because of the size and cost of these computers) was dominated by International Business Machines (IBM). The IBM Model 701, which used vacuum tubes, was created in 1952. IBM also led the field in mainframe innovations and introduced the first computer disk storage system, as well as developed the FORTRAN programming language. By the end of the 1950s, computers were being built with transistors rather than vacuum tubes; this decade also saw the creation of over 200 programming languages.

Although many of the early mainframes were called *super computers*, the average PC user now packs more computing power on his desktop than was offered by these vacuum tube leviathans.

Minicomputers Take the Stage

As computer technology continued to develop at a breakneck speed in the 1960s and 1970s, mainframe computers were made smaller and more affordable—affordable being a relative term; minicomputers (or miniframes) were still very pricey—by the use of circuitry boards and chips. Magnetic storage also took a leap forward when IBM introduced the floppy disk in 1971.

As was the case with mainframes, the early days of miniframe computing did not provide the level of intimacy that we experience when working on our individual personal computers today. Users typically interfaced with this highly centralized computer through an intermediary: an Information Science (IS) administrator or programmer. As computer technology evolved further, mainframe and miniframe users were able to communicate directly with these computers using dumb terminals. A *dumb terminal* is really nothing more than a monitor and keyboard that allow a user to interface with a centralized miniframe computer. A dumb terminal has no hard drive, and only minimial processing power.

In the 1970s, the miniframe gained dominance in the computing world, making computer technology accessible to a larger number of companies and organizations (even though these companies paid a premium for their ability to compute).

With a larger market for miniframe sales, this meant that new players appeared in the computer manufacturing arena. For example, Digital Equipment Corporation (DEC) developed one of the first miniframe computers and became a force in the miniframe market (see Figure 1.1).

A Centralized Computing Model

One point that should be made in relation to mainframes and miniframes is that, by design, all storage and computing power was centralized. This meant users (on dumb terminals) accessed centralized, shared information and used centralized applications provided by the miniframe (see Figure 1.2). In many cases, some type of messaging system was also available to users on a mainframe or miniframe so that they could communicate.

FIGURE 1.1
DEC became a force in the miniframe market with the introduction of the DEC PDP-8 minicomputer.

Technologies to connect mainframe and miniframe computers at different physical locations were also developed in the 1970s. For example, the X.25 protocol offered wide area connectivity over existing phone lines (X.25 is still used as a WAN strategy and is discussed in Chapter 10).

So, this mainframe/miniframe centralized computing model offered many of the "perks" (such as shared resources and shared hardware) that were mentioned as benefits of networking personal computers (in the previous section "Why Network Your Computers?"). In essence, the practice of centralizing computer data and sharing computer resources among users was already something that network administrators and users took for granted. That is, until the personal computer made a big splash in the business world of the 1980s.

FIGURE 1.2

Minicomputers
provided users
with shared
computer
resources
because all
resources were
centralized on
the miniframe.

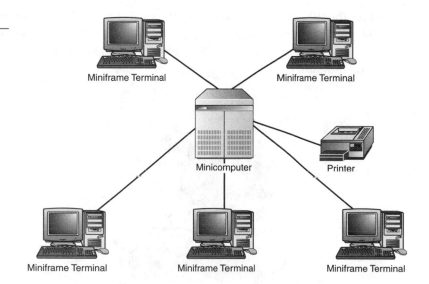

FIGURE 1.2

Minicomputers
provided users
with shared
computer
resources
because all
resources were
centralized on
the miniframe.

The Advent of the Personal Computer

Many techno-historians would debate which of the personal computers that
appeared in the late 1970s and early 1980s really captured the imagination of early
PC computer users and led to the personal computer revolution. You would certainly
have to say that, for the most part, these early PC aficionados were adventurous folk
with both extra disposable income and time on their hands.

An illustration: In 1975, *Popular Electronics* featured the Altair 8800 personal computer on its cover. Created by Micro Instrumentation Telemetry Systems (MITS), the
Altair was a kit computer; it had to be assembled by the user. This cover story, however, led to a huge increase in orders for the Altair.

The Altair boasted an Intel 8080 processor, 256 bytes of memory, and a toggle-
switch-and-LED front panel. But there was no monitor or keyboard. To make the
computer "work," you had to program the Altair using the toggle switches, entering
binary code one bit at a time. If you made a mistake, you had to start over. You had
to really want to compute when you sat down in front of your Altair.

Although the Altair certainly wasn't embraced by all PC users (by 1980, Apple actually owned half the PC market), this early PC did indirectly help create a software
giant. Bill Gates and Paul Allen developed BASIC for the Altair on punch paper
rolls, and thus Microsoft was born.

In August 1981, the IBM PC was released. Although not the only heavy-hitting PC
available in the 1980s (the Apple Macintosh was released in 1984), the IBM PC
(see Figure 1.3) quickly became the standard for businesses. Because the operating

system for the IBM PC, DOS, was not wholly owned by IBM (Microsoft made MS-DOS available to other PC manufacturers), clones of the IBM PC quickly appeared in the marketplace. This made the PC a tool that even individuals and the smallest of businesses could afford.

FIGURE 1.3

The IBM PC became the standard desktop computer for businesses.

The development of software applications for DOS-based machines exploded in the 1980s, cementing the PC's role as the business-computing workhorse. However, the fact that PCs were standalone devices meant that users could not readily collaborate and share resources. The PC basically isolated its user.

Note

One of the first techniques widely used to share information between PCs was dubbed *sneakernet*. Basically, if users wanted to share information or print documents, they would have to save information to a diskette. They could then share this information with a colleague by sharing the diskette, or they could walk over to a computer connected to a printer and print their work from the diskette.

PC Networking: How It All Began

Given that IBM brought a standalone, decentralized computing device—the PC—to the business marketplace in 1981, one would think that the theory, hardware, and software used to network PCs together had yet to be developed. In fact, though, the issues related to networking PCs had been worked out prior to 1980 by the ingenious researchers at the Xerox Corporation's Palo Alto Research Center (PARC). Not only did they create the Alto, a computer with a graphical user interface (GUI) and a mouse, but they also developed the hardware and software necessary to connect computers and printers together into a LAN.

Oddly enough, Xerox never capitalized on many of the discoveries made at PARC. Apple was actually the first company to introduce a computer with a GUI interface and a mouse when it unveiled the Macintosh in 1984.

In 1976, PARC researchers Robert Metcalfe and David Boggs (Metcalfe's assistant) published a paper titled "Ethernet: Distributed Packet-Switching for Local Computer Networks." Ethernet (discussed in detail in Chapter 4, "Building the Network Infrastructure") was further developed by Xerox, Intel, and DEC and is still the most popular PC networking architecture in the world.

As the PC gained dominance in the computing world, other network architectures were developed (such as IBM's Token Ring, which is discussed in Chapter 4). Many new companies, such as 3Com and Cisco Systems, surfaced in the 1980s and 1990s and grew rapidly as the need for networking interface cards and other network connectivity devices expanded in parallel with the evolution and sales of the personal computer.

Clients and Servers: What Does It All Mean?

Although a number of the PC operating systems now available (such as Windows and the Apple OS) provide for peer-to-peer networking (discussed in the next chapter), in most cases one thinks of a network as being made up of clients and servers. A *client* is a computer that allows a user or users to log on to the network and take advantage of the resources available on the network. A client computer will run a client operating system (such as Windows 2000 Professional or Windows Me). The purpose of the client is to get a user onto the network; therefore, client computers don't usually have the processing power, the storage space, or the memory found on a server because the client does not have to serve up resources to other computers on the network.

Because client and server computers both have processing capabilities, the workload on a PC network can be distributed between the client and the server. This differs from the centralized computing provided by mainframes and minicomputers, where the central computer provides all the processing power for the users logged on via dumb terminals.

A *server*, on the other hand, is typically a much more powerful computer that runs a network operating system (NOS). The server provides centralized administration of the network and serves up the resources that are available on the network, such as printers and files (the NOS provides the server with these capabilities). The administrator of the server decides who can and cannot log on to the network and which resources the various users can access.

Most LANs consist of many clients and a few servers. While one server always controls user logons, other servers can specialize in providing certain types of resources (such as print servers and file servers, which are discussed in the next chapter). Figure 1.4 provides a diagram of a "typical" PC network.

Obviously the scale of a network will depend on whether the network is used by a huge corporation or has been set up for a home business. For example, a home network and a business network will probably both make use of hubs as a way to physically connect the computers. But a home network won't necessarily have network servers and print servers that are required to provide services to the large number of users found on a corporate network.

FIGURE 1.4
PC networks
consist of clients
and servers.

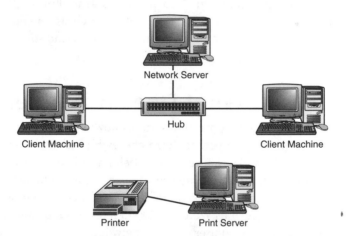

You may hear the term *workstation* used interchangeably with *client* in reference to the computers used by network users to access the network. In reality, *workstation* more commonly refers to higher-end client machines that require more memory and processing power to run more complex software, such as the design software used by engineers.

Network Players: Users and Administrators

The fact that two different types of computers—clients and servers—exist on the network means that the people on the network will also play different roles. Users make up most of the folks you find on a PC network. They are there to access network resources. A user requires a user logon and password to gain access to the network.

The person who serves as the caretaker of the network is the network administrator. The administrator controls the network servers. So, this means that network access and the level of access is controlled by the administrator using the tools provided by the NOS.

Most network operating systems supply the network administrator with the ability to monitor network use, including user logons. Tools for monitoring hardware parameters such as memory and processor usage on a server are also typically available. The administrator is also responsible for disaster planning and securing the network resources from outside attack and virus infestation.

One of the most difficult aspects of being a network administrator is convincing users that the access levels and security policies used on the network are there for a purpose—and that purpose is to protect the valuable corporate resources found on the network. Although network administrators are typically thought of as dime-store dictators or control freaks by the users, administrators are typically faced with long hours and a great deal of hard work to keep their networks up and running. They certainly don't wear beepers as a fashion accessory.

Understanding LAN Data Transmission

Before we delve more deeply into the nuts and bolts of PC networking, we need to discuss how data is transmitted on the network. The way data travels on the network media (such as copper wire and glass fiber-optic cable) differs from how data flows between the different components in a computer.

First, let's define the bit. A *bit* is the smallest unit of data found on a computer; bits are represented by either a one (1) or a zero (0). When you type a letter or create a spreadsheet, you see your data as words in paragraphs or numbers in a column. Your computer sees this information as binary data—ones and zeros.

On a computer, data in the form of a bit stream travels in parallel across wires arranged on the motherboard. These parallel wires on the motherboard as referred to as the *data bus*. When data is required by the computer's processor from the computer's hard drive, the data moves along the bus, which is very much like a multi-lane superhighway, allowing several bit streams to move simultaneously.

To actually move data from one computer to another on the network, there obviously needs to be some kind of network medium; copper wire is actually the most often used network medium (the topic of network media is discussed in Chapter 4, in the section "Choosing a Network Connectivity Strategy"). Unfortunately, no matter what type of network medium you choose, the data can only travel along it as a single bit stream, which is referred to as a *serial transmission*.

A device is needed to take the parallel data from the computer, which is like a multi-lane super highway, and condensed it into a serial transmission, which is the equivalent of a one-lane road. This device also provides the connection between the PC and the network media.

The device I'm talking about here is a *network interface card*, or *NIC*. The NIC contains a transceiver (a transmitter and receiver) that is able to convert data from parallel to serial, and vice versa. A NIC can come in the form of a separate card that you install in the computer (there are a large number of different NIC manufacturers). The NIC must be compatible with the bus slot that you wish to install it in. Some personal computers, such as the Apple iMac, come with a built-in NIC that's ready to go. Figure 1.5 shows two different kinds of NICs.

FIGURE 1.5

Network interface cards provide the physical connection between a computer and the network.

So it's the NIC that supplies the physical connection between a computer (client or server) and the network media, and it's the network card that supplies the translation of data from parallel to serial. As you can see, the NIC is a very important component of networking PCs. The network interface card is discussed in Chapter 3, "Networking and PC Hardware," in the section "Working with Network Interface Cards."

Networking Does Not Require the "All Knowing"

Now that we've gotten a quick survey of computer evolution out of the way and defined some of the general aspects of computer networking, such as clients and servers, I'd like to take a moment to give you a pep talk. Although some incredible minds have worked long and hard on developing the software and hardware that is used to create a computer network, it is not required that you have the collective intelligence of all the network pioneers to be a network administrator.

Being a network administrator is the same as being a bricklayer or a concert pianist. They both understand the basics of their medium—the brick and the piano—but neither of them could necessarily create a brick or a piano from scratch. However, they both understand the tools of their trade. Even being the administrator for a small network used in a home office will require a knowledge base related to PCs beyond that of the average user.

You will need to understand how computers work and be able to add devices to PCs, such as network interface cards and new hard drives, but you are not necessarily required to build computers from scratch. You are also not required to know all the intricacies of every piece of software running on the network.

Anyone willing to develop a good understanding of computer hardware, networking devices (such as hubs and the various choices for networking media), and network operating systems (especially the network operating system you will use on your network) can build a solid and usable LAN. Although this book is not going to make you a network expert, it is certainly a good first step as you accumulate the knowledge base that will allow you to create and manage your own networks. Just remember, it's not rocket science, just computer networking. So, fear not and read on.

Chapter Summary

In this chapter we had the opportunity to sort out some of the important technology milestones that lead to the introduction of the personal computer. We also had an opportunity to define networking and take a look at why you would want to network PCs.

- Strictly speaking, a network is two or more connected computers. The larger the network, the greater the variety of network devices (such as hubs or routers) that will be required to connect the networked computers together.

- Computers can be networked to share resources such as printers and files. Networked computers can also provide a communication medium for network users.

- Mainframes and minicomputers provided a centralized computing model in which all resources are supplied by the mainframe or minicomputer and accessed by users accessing the computer using dumb terminals.

- The IBM PC, launched in August of 1981, began the PC revolution. It became the standard for the desktop business computer.

- Networking hardware and software was developed at the Xerox Palo Alto Research Center in the 1970s. The networking standard developed at PARC was further developed by Xerox, Intel, and DEC into the Ethernet networking architecture, which is still the most popular PC networking architecture in the world.

- Networks are made up of client and server computers. Client computers are used by network users to gain access to the network. Server computers are used to supply the resources that are accessed by the users on the network.

- Network user access to the network and its resources is controlled by the network administrator. The network administrator controls both the access level of the users and the resources that they can access. This ability to control access is provided by the network operating system running on the server.

- Computers process data in parallel, whereas data is moved across the network in serial. The network interface card (NIC) is used to translate data from parallel to serial, and vice versa, and it provides the computer with a connection to the network media.

- Being a network administrator does not mean that you can build a computer from bear skins using a stone knife or that you can make data move through the air using only the power of your mind. To be a network administrator, you need a good grounding in PC hardware and software and a very good understanding of the intricacies of the network operating system that you use to control your network.

2

DIFFERENT NEEDS, DIFFERENT NETWORKS

In this chapter

- Understanding peer-to-peer networks
- Operating systems that provide peer-to-peer networking support
- Working with peer-to-peer network limitations
- Understanding server-based networks
- Deploying specialized network servers
- Understanding network topologies
- Assessing your networking needs

There are three kinds of death in this world. There's heart death, there's brain death, and there's being off the network.

–Guy Almes

In the last chapter we took a quick look at computer evolution and discussed some of the compelling reasons why you would want to network personal computers. Now, we can concentrate on two main approaches to networking: peer-to-peer networking and server-based networking. Each of these networking approaches offers advantages and disadvantages.

You will find that deciding on a particular approach to networking will be directly related to the number of users you have and the types of services your network needs to offer to these users. For example, if just a few users need to share a printer, a peer-to-peer network will probably get the job done.

Peer-to-peer networks work particularly well in homes or small office situations where only a few files and possibly a printer need to be shared. Setting up a peer-to-peer network in a home also makes it easy to share a single connection to the Internet (connecting a network to the Internet is discussed in Chapter 12, "Connecting a Network to the Internet").

In cases where you have a lot of users and want to make the sharing of files or other network resources more secure and centrally controlled, a server-based network would better meet your needs. After discussing the two different approaches to networking and the basics of networking topologies, we will take some time to sort out how you can assess your own networking needs and then plan your own network.

Understanding Peer-to-Peer Networking

Peer-to-peer networking provides a simple, low-cost method for connecting personal computers in situations where you want to share files and other resources such as a printer. Peer-to-peer networking does not require a server, meaning the added expense of a powerful computer to act as a server and a network operating system for the server is avoided in this approach to creating small networks.

In a peer-to-peer network, the computers on the network function as peers. A *peer* computer basically acts as both a client and a server computer. Peer computers can access resources on the network, and they can supply resources to other peer computers (the same as a server does on a server-based network).

A peer-to-peer network is also commonly referred to as a *workgroup*. This is because the term *workgroup* connotes collaboration without central control, differentiating the peer-to-peer network from the larger-scale server-based network.

The only real requirements for building a peer-to-peer network include installing an operating system on the PCs that supports peer-to-peer networking and then physically connecting the PCs (this means outfitting the computer with a network interface card and then cabling the PCs together; in the case of Macintosh computers, you don't even need the network interface card). Before taking a look at where we are today with peer-to-peer networking and the pros and cons of peer-to-peer networking, let's take a quick look at how peer-to-peer networking has changed over the last decade.

Peer Products Come and Go

Peer-to-peer networking has been around almost as long as the PC. On the IBM PC/clone side of personal computing, the DOS operating system did not provide for peer-to-peer networking. Add-on products were required to provide the functionality for sharing files or printers over a small network. Products such as Artisoft's LANtastic and Novell's NetWare Lite (Novell no longer markets NetWare Lite or a follow-up peer-to-peer product named Personal NetWare) provided workgroup networking in the late 80s and very early 90s.

The fact that you had to actually purchase the peer-to-peer networking software obviously increased the cost of creating a small workgroup. In many offices, where only a few users shared a printer or files, *sneakernet* (meaning no network at all) was still the low-cost choice.

Artisoft quickly became a huge player in the peer-to-peer networking market and built a multimillion-dollar business. LANtastic is still sold today by SpartaCom, Inc., an Artisoft spin-off. Artisoft itself is still around but now concentrates on software-based telephone systems for small- to medium-size businesses and corporate branch offices.

In 1992 Microsoft launched Windows for Workgroups 3.11. This desktop operating system, which actually ran on top of DOS (you had to have DOS installed on your computer before you installed Windows for Workgroups), offered built-in workgroup networking. This meant that printers and files could be shared by users without buying additional software.

Subsequent client versions of Windows, such as Windows 9x (Windows 95 and 98), Windows NT Workstation, Windows 2000 Professional, and Windows Me, are also workgroup ready. Figure 2.1 shows the browser window of a computer running Windows 2000 Professional (Dobby), which is part of a three-computer workgroup called HABRAKEN. As Microsoft Windows became the dominant operating system for PCs, this really signaled the end of the need for additional software to add workgroup functionality to a personal computer.

FIGURE 2.1

Microsoft
Windows makes
it easy to config-
ure and use
peer-to-peer
workgroups.

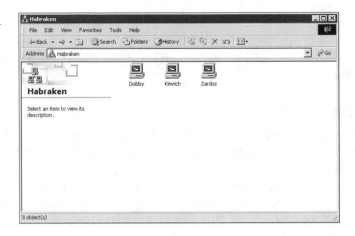

 With the launch of Windows 95, Microsoft offered a client operating system that no longer required an initial installation of DOS. Although DOS is still certainly not dead (the Windows 9x and Me operating systems still have some DOS code floating around inside them), the Windows NT and Windows 2000 operating systems were built from the ground up and will actually not run a great deal of the applications built for DOS-based computers.

On the other side of the personal computing fence, the Macintosh OS offered peer-to-peer networking capabilities from the get go. Not only did the Mac OS have the software side of workgroup computing covered, but Macintosh computers were also built with a hardware interface that allowed you (with just the purchase of a couple special cables) to connect two Macintoshes and a printer (for quite some time the only printers available for the Mac were Apple printers). The built-in networking language (or protocol) in the Apple Macintosh OS was called *AppleTalk*. The actual hardware devices, such as the built-in ports on the back of Mac computers and the special *shielded twisted-pair cables* (shielded twisted-pair is a special cable that contains pairs of wire that are shielded by a covering and twisted to reduce interference) that made up the physical connection for the networked computers, were referred to as *LocalTalk*. Network cabling types are discussed in detail in Chapter 4, "Building the Network Infrastructure."

 With Ethernet networks and the Internet Protocol (IP) becoming dominant forces in personal computing networking, Apple's newest personal computers, such as the iMac, come with a built-in Ethernet interface. The Mac OS still offers built-in workgroup capabilities. The network functionality in the Mac OS has also gone through an evolution and now provides better support for *Transmission Control Protocol/Internet Protocol* (or *TCP/IP*, a suite of protocols developed for the Internet) and other network protocols. (We will discuss network protocols, such as AppleTalk and TCP/IP, in Chapter 5, "Network Protocols: Real and Imagined.")

Peer-to-Peer Networking Today

With Microsoft Windows and the Mac OS dominating today's personal computing market (because of availability, usability, and acceptance as standards in the business world), peer-to-peer networking is certainly an easy-to-configure, low-cost avenue for sharing files and printers at home or a small business. Once the computers and printers in the peer-to-peer network have been physically connected, actually setting up the sharing of files and printers in either OS is a very straightforward matter (which we discuss in Chapter 6, "Configuring Peer-to-Peer Networks").

I would be certainly remiss if I didn't mention Linux and its possible use as a client operating system on personal computers configured for peer-to-peer networking. You can, with a little work, configure nearly any of the many flavors of Linux to support file and printer sharing for a workgroup environment (Linux also supplies many options in the server-based environment, such as file and printer sharing as well as Web hosting). Not only can the personal computers running Linux share files and printers with each other, but they can also be configured to share printers and files with Windows-based computers. Figure 2.2 shows the Explorer window of a Linux workstation that has been configured to be part of Windows workgroup (we will look at Linux and Windows workgroup configurations in Chapter 6). Don't be alarmed by the question mark icons used for the different Windows shares. The Linux interface uses that icon for any item, even applications, that are not native to the Linux installation.

Note Linux is a Unix-like operating system (which in its early incarnations meant working with a command-line interface somewhat like DOS) that was originally developed by Linus Torvalds. The operating system uses no proprietary code, meaning the source code for Linux is freely available to anyone. Having an open source code for an OS means that any programmer can freely create add-on utilities or programs for the OS. They can even develop their own version of the Linux OS. This has lead to many different flavors of Linux, such as Red Hat, SuSE, and Caldera. You can download many of these different versions of Linux for free (different licensing agreements are involved, depending on how and where you will use the operating system). Although GUI interfaces for Linux have been developed, Linux is still not an operating system for the beginner. There are, however, millions of people worldwide who do use Linux for software development, networking, and as an end-user operating system.

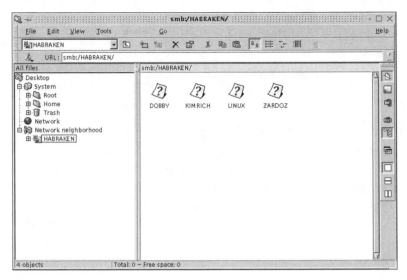

Pros of Peer-to-Peer Networking

The pros related to peer-to-peer networking revolve around cost and ease of installation. Depending on the operating system you are running on your computers, peer-
to-peer networking does not require the purchase of additional software or a
computer to act as a dedicated network server. Most operating systems that support
peer-to-peer networking also make it very easy for you to configure your computers
so that they will communicate in a workgroup.

In a nutshell, here are the overall advantages of peer-to-peer networks:

- They are relatively cheap as far as hardware outlay goes. You don't have to
  buy any additional computers, such as a server.
- They are pretty easy to set up.
- All the software that you need is typically included in your operating system.
- Centralized administration is not required and individual users can configure
  the sharing of resources.
- The peer computers don't depend on a central server machine for their
  resources or to log in to the network; therefore, they can operate even when
  other peer computers are not available.

Even though peer-to-peer networking is cheap and fairly simple to set up and configure, it is not scalable, meaning that around 10 computers at the most can live
together in a peer-to-peer situation. What's more, you will still have to outfit the

computers with network interface cards and connect them. If you use twisted-pair cabling, you will need a hub. If you go with coaxial cable, you will need T-connectors and terminators. Other connection strategies, such as wireless communication, will require the appropriate hardware.

Connecting computers in a peer-to-peer network is really no different from creating a small server-based network. All the computers must be connected by some connectivity scheme. Chapter 4 discusses the different connectivity media in the section "Choosing a Network Connectivity Strategy."

Cons of Peer-to-Peer Networking

Although peer-to-peer networking appears to be the perfect networking solution in situations where you don't want to go to the trouble to install and configure a network server (or can't afford a server and the network operating system software), it does have a number of limitations. First of all, it is extremely limited as far as the number of computers you can connect together. This type of networking is really reserved for very small installations of 10 computers or less. Many experts recommend that a peer-to-peer network not include more than five peer computers; this limit is recommended because the greater the number of peers accessing information, the greater the performance hit on the peers that are providing that information. Since peer networking distributes resources across the network, having many peer shares (which each potentially require a different password) can make accessing files confusing.

Desktop operating systems that have been configured for peer-to-peer networking typically will limit the number of connections they allow to a resource. For example, Windows 2000 Professional allows 10 simultaneous connections.

Peer-to-peer networking also does not provide any centralized security on the network. Users don't have to be authenticated by a network server to actually view and potentially use the resources on the network. This is related to how resources are shared in a workgroup.

Each resource that is shared (such as a drive, folder, or printer) can potentially require a different password for access. If a lot of resources are shared across the network, you will have to remember the password for each resource. This type of security is referred to as *share-level security*; each drive, folder, or printer that is shared is referred to as a *share*.

A summary list of peer-to-peer network shortcomings follows:

- There's an increased performance hit on computers because of resource sharing. If users access your printer, your computer's processing resources are used as they print.

- No centralized location of shared files makes it difficult to back up data.

- Security must be handled on a resource-by-resource basis.

- Decentralization of resources makes it difficult for users to locate particular resources.

- Users might have to keep track of numerous passwords.

Peer-to-peer networking definitely needs to operate in an environment of cooperation. If your users can't play well together, you will have problems because the users themselves control the various resources. Peer-to-peer networking is, however, a good way to share resources on home networks and small, single-office business networks. If you simply want to share a printer between a few computers or build a gaming network, peer-to-peer is the way to go.

Server-Based Networks

Server-based networking provides you with the ability to build large networks that offer a greater range of resources to users (when compared to peer-to-peer networks). This is because a number of different, specialized server types (such as mail and database servers) can be included on the network.

Server-based networks also provide you with greater centralized control of resources and make it easier to add additional computers, users, and resources (again, when compared to peer-to-peer networks). Server-based networks are *scalable networks*, meaning they are easily expandable.

One requirement for a server-based network is a computer running a network operating system; this computer is known as the *server*. As already mentioned in Chapter 1, "Computer Networking Overview," a server computer is basically a special-purpose machine that logs in users and "serves" up resources, such as files and printers, to the users. Because the server verifies users and determines the level of access the users will have to the various network resources, server-based networks provide a more secure environment than peer-to-peer networks.

Server-based networks typically employ a more powerful computer (in terms of processor speed, RAM, and hard drive capacity) to act as the server. Network operating systems such as Microsoft Windows 2000 Server and Novell NetWare both have baseline hardware needs for the computer that will run the operating system. We will discuss computer hardware issues related to networking in Chapter 3, "Networking Hardware." Network operating systems will be discussed in Chapter 7, "Working with Network Operating Systems."

Actually accessing resources on a server-based network is also easier than in the peer-to-peer environment because one username and one password get a user onto the network and provide that user access to any resource he or she has the appropriate permissions for. This is in sharp contrast to a peer-to-peer network, which may have a different password for every resource on the network.

Pros and Cons of Server-Based Networking

As is the case with peer-to-peer networking, server-based networking has its pros and cons. The upside of server-based networking revolves around the fact that this type of network provides central control of resources and makes it easier for users to actually find resources. For example, the network operating system (NOS) Microsoft Windows 2000 Server manages resources such as shared folders and drives, printers, and even users in a tool called the Active Directory, shown in Figure 2.3 (this is how the Active Directory tool would appear to a network administrator).

Active Directory is used to add and remove users from the network and can even be used to place users that access the same resources into groups. Management tools like Active Directory provide the administrator with the ability to control network access and the different levels of access that are given to users or groups of users. Information on configuring user accounts for network access is discussed in more detail in Chapter 16, "A Network Security Primer," in the section "Administrators and Users."

This ability to manage network users and resources centrally comes with a high price tag, however, and one of the major cons of server-based networking is the cost of the dedicated server computer and the NOS that you must run on it. Server-based networks also require a network administrator—someone who is well versed in the NOS being used. This usually means an additional employee on the company's payroll, which is another cost associated with server-based networks.

However, the overall cost of network operating system software and computer hardware is lower today than it ever has been, and the server-based network has become the standard for networking in even relatively small companies. Security features built into the NOS allow the network administrator to protect the company's data from outside the network, and they also provide a great deal of control over sensitive data and its access from inside the network.

FIGURE 2.3

Network operating systems such as Windows 2000 Server provide for the central management of users and resources.

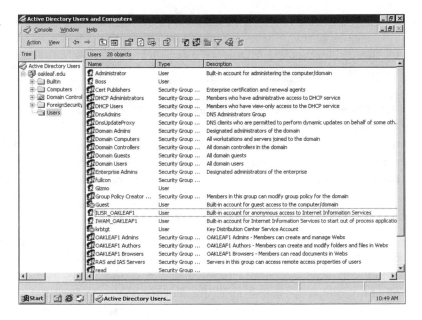

Let's break the pros and cons of server-based networks into two lists, with the pros first:

- Users log on using one username and password to access network resources.
- The network security is centrally controlled, as are the network resources.
- Resources such as folders and files can easily be backed up because they are centrally located.
- Dedicated, high-powered servers allow users faster access to resources.
- Server-based networks can be easily expanded.

Now let's look at the cons:

- For small companies, the cost of the server equipment, the network operating system, and the appropriate client licenses can be a con.
- Although not a con if you are the network administrator, someone must be charge in setting up and controlling the resources on the network. This typically means a dedicated network administrator's position.
- If the main server goes down, so goes the access to network resources.

The local area network (LAN)—another name for a server-based network in one location—is really the rule rather than the exception in today's business world. Even small LANs can use different types of servers to provide users with the resources they need. Let's take a look at the possibilities.

Types of Network Servers

We've already discussed the fact that a LAN uses a server to validate users as they log on to the network. If a user's login name and password don't match up, the server doesn't let him or her on the network. In large networks, this "central computer" (for lack of a better name) can be kept quite busy logging users on to the network as they fire up their client PCs. Rather than overburden this server with additional duties, it's not uncommon to distribute the workload among other specialized servers.

Tip

> Even though various network services can be spread out over several special servers, the access to these servers is still controlled by the user's logon name and password. The central server not only lets the user onto the network but also determines the resources that the user can actually access. You will (in general terms) learn how users' access of resources is controlled on a LAN in Chapter 8, "Sharing Resources on the Network."

File Servers

A file server's job is to serve as a home for the files that are needed by users on the network. This can include files that a number of users share. These files are typically held in what is called a *public folder*, which can include private folders that are specific for a particular user. The great thing about using a file server is that important files reside in one place, making it very easy to back up the data periodically. The downside is that if the file server goes down, users can't get at their files.

Print Servers

A print server is used to host a network printer. It is basically the control conduit for the printer. Because print jobs need to be spooled (placed on the computer before they are sent to the printer) before they are printed, the print server supplies the hard drive space needed. The print server also queues up all the print jobs being directed to the printer. The network administrator can also delete print jobs and change the queue order of print jobs by accessing the print server.

Communication Servers

A communication server runs specialized software that allows users on the network to communicate. It provides services such as electronic mail and discussion groups to allow users to share information. Two of the most popular communication packages for a LAN (and each need to be set up on a server on a LAN) are Microsoft Exchange and Lotus Notes (both of these communication packages are discussed in Chapter 9, "Working with Applications on the Network").

Application Servers

Application servers host various applications such as specialized databases. Even typical desktop applications such as word processors and spreadsheet software can also be stored on an application server. This makes updating software applications much easier because the software doesn't actually reside on every client workstation; users start these applications from their local computers, but the application software is actually stored on the server.

Web Servers

Web servers provide you with the ability to create a Web site that can be accessed internally by your employees (this is called an *intranet*) or by folks surfing the Internet. Web servers aren't for everyone, and many companies still use Web-hosting companies to get their Web sites up and running on the Internet. A number of different software packages can be used to set up a Web server, and they vary in ease of use and stability. Microsoft Windows 2000 Server ships with Internet Information Server 5.0 (IIS5), a Web server software package. Figure 2.4 shows the IIS5 management console that is used to configure a Web server on a Microsoft network.

FIGURE 2.4

Web servers are used to host corporate or personal Web sites.

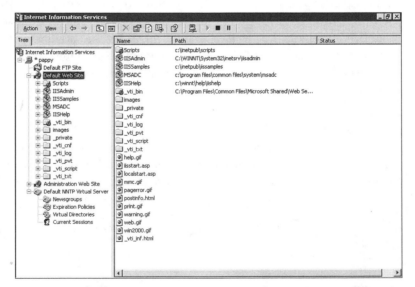

With security on the Internet becoming more of a concern every day (or so it seems), setting up your own Web server can open up your company to a direct attack from the outside. The security issues related to protecting a company's Web site are certainly beyond the scope of this book, but some general security issues related to Web servers and the Internet are discussed in Chapter 13, "Hosting a Web Site."

Other Specialized Servers

There are also other types of servers that can reside on the network that don't actually provide any resources to the LAN users, but they are needed to make the network run properly or more efficiently. For example, on larger networks that use the TCP/IP network protocol, each computer must be configured with a unique Internet Protocol (IP) address (which is much like a person's Social Security number) to communicate on the network (IP addressing is discussed in detail in Chapter 5 in the section "TCP/IP"). This means that the network administrator might have to configure hundreds of computers, one at a time. However, a server running the Dynamic Host Configuration Protocol (DHCP) can actually automatically assign IP addresses to computers as they are started up on the network.

The Dynamic Host Configuration Protocol (DHCP) can be run on your main network server or other server on the network. Windows 2000 Server has a built-in version of DHCP. This means any server running Windows 2000 Server can be configured to provide IP addresses (this range of addresses is called a scope) to the computers on the network dynamically. This saves you a lot of time having to statically configure the IP address for each and every computer on the network.

Other specialized servers you might need on a LAN relate to the fact that operating systems all assign some kind of friendly name to a computer. For example, think about the World Wide Web; when you want to go to a Web site, you type the Web site's name (also known as a *Uniform Resource Locator* or *URL*) into your Web browser. You don't typically enter the actual numerical address of the site (which is an IP address). Special servers on the Internet, called *DNS servers* (they run the Domain Name Service), are used to resolve that friendly name you entered into an actual address. It is not uncommon to also set up DNS servers on LANs to provide this same type of service.

Understanding DNS and how DNS servers work wasn't always an issue that network administrators had to deal with. Only recently, when everyone decided that his or her LAN also needed to be connected to the Internet, did issues related to name resolution and the TCP/IP protocol arise. We will try to make some sense out of TCP/IP and how IP addresses are used on a network in Chapter 5, and then we will look at how the Internet works (which includes some information on DNS) in Chapter 11, "How the Internet Works," in the section titled "Understanding DNS."

You've probably noticed that the needs of your users and the size of your network dictate how many of these specialized servers you have to set up on your LAN. The larger your LAN is, the greater the need to distribute the day-to-day workload among different servers on the network. In contrast, a small network might use just one server that logs on users and supplies printer and file services.

Understanding Network Topologies

Now that we've completed a general overview of the two types of networks you can build (peer to peer and server based), we can discuss some of the basics related to the actual physical layout of LANs. Different topologies have been defined to characterize a LAN's layout (a *topology* is just how the network's cabling maps out).

Although these topologies do in some respects reflect the type of cabling (coaxial cable versus twisted-pair cable, both discussed in Chapter 4) that is used and the network architecture that is deployed (network architectures are also discussed in Chapter 4), they are just models and in many cases a LAN might use a hybrid of a couple different topologies.

Bus Topology

A *bus topology* is characterized by a main trunk or backbone line with the networked computers attached at intervals along the trunk line, as shown in Figure 2.5. This topology type is considered a passive topology because the computers on a bus just sit and listen. When they "hear" data on the wire that belongs to them, they accept that data (they actually listen using their network interface cards). When they are ready to transmit, they make sure no one else on the bus is transmitting and then send their packets of information.

FIGURE 2.5
A bus topology provides one of the simplest ways to connect a group of computers.

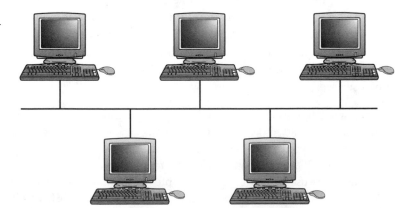

Bus networks typically use coaxial networking cable (it looks like the same coaxial cable used for cable television, but it is actually slightly different) hooked to each computer using a T-connector. Each end of the network is terminated using a terminator specific to the cable type (if you use 50-Ohm cable, you use 50-Ohm terminators). Because the bus network is really just a collection of cable, connectors, and terminators, there is no amplification of the signal as it travels on the wire. This means that the size of the network will be limited by the maximum distance the cable type can actually move the signal that holds the data.

Although a number of different cable types can be used for LANs, copper-based twisted-pair wire has really become the standard. In fact, most network interface cards now only come with a port for a twisted-pair connector and not the T-connector used with bus networks. It is fairly inexpensive and easy to work with because it is flexible (it bends around corners). The different wiring possibilities for your network and wireless connectivity are discussed in Chapter 4.

Bus networks are easy to assemble and are easy to extend. They require a fairly limited amount of cabling when compared to other topologies. Bus networks are prone to cable breaks, loose connectors, and cable shorts that can be very difficult to troubleshoot. One physical problem on the network, such as a detached connector, can actually bring down the entire bus network. Although at one time a bus network would have been the cheapest and easiest way to connect a small group of computers for peer-to-peer networking, the drop in the price of hubs (discussed in the next section on star networks) and the ease of using twisted-pair wire have really pushed the coaxial cable bus network to the edge of extinction. The main reason for knowing about bus networks is that there are still many bus installations found in small and medium-size companies. Remember that troubleshooting this type of network will typically require an inspection of all the cabling and their connections. As far as building a new network using a bus technology, you are far better off going with a star configuration using a hub (the star topology is discussed in the next section).

Star Topology

In a *star topology*, the computers on the network connect to a centralized connectivity device called a *hub*. Each computer is connected with its own cable (typically twisted-pair cable) to a port on the hub, as shown in Figure 2.6. Star LANs also use the same type of wait-and-listen strategy to access data or send data as characterized by the bus topology.

Because the star topology uses a separate cable connection for each computer on the network, star networks are easily expandable, with the main limiting factor being the number of ports available on the hub (although hubs can easily be daisy-chained together to increase the number of ports available). Expanding a start topology network is also very unobtrusive: adding a computer to the network is just a matter of running a wire between the computer and the hub. Users on the network will be pretty much unaware that the expansion is taking place.

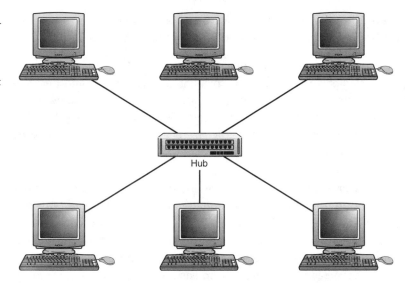

Hub

Disadvantages of the star topology revolve around cabling needs and the hub itself. Because each computer on the network requires a separate cable, cable costs will be higher than a bus topology network (although twisted-pair, the cable type used for star networks, is the least expensive cable type). Having to purchase a hub or hubs for your network does add additional costs when you are building a network based on the star topology, but considering the benefits of this type of topology in terms of managing the physical aspects of your network, it is probably well worth it.

The greatest benefit of using the star topology is that you can easily add new computers to the network without disrupting service to the computers already on the network. As well, if one computer goes down on the network, it does not negate the ability of the other computers on the star to communicate with each other. Obviously, the most crucial failure point on a star network would be the central hub.

Ring Topology

A *ring topology* connects the LAN computers one after the other on the wire in a physical circle, as shown in Figure 2.7. The ring topology moves information on the wire in one direction and is considered an active topology. Computers on the network actually retransmit the packets (*packet* is a generic term for the data that is being moved along the network) they receive and then send them on to the next computer in the ring.

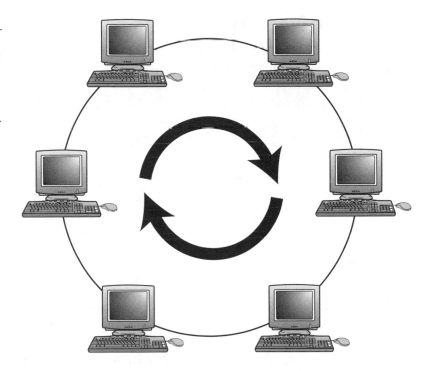

The ring topology is considered an active topology because the computers in the ring actually pass a *token* around the circle. The token is a special packet of data, sort of like your ATM card, that gives the computer with the token special abilities. If a computer wants to send data onto the network, it has to wait until it has possession of the token. This is how the IBM Token Ring network architecture operates (which is discussed in Chapter 4).

True ring topologies can be difficult to troubleshoot, and the failure of one computer on the ring can disrupt the data flow (because data circulates around the ring in one direction). Also, adding or removing computers from this type of topology can disrupt the operation of the network. On most small LANs, you won't run into the ring topology because IBM Token Ring and some other high-speed network technologies that use a ring are more typical of larger networks.

Since Token Ring hardware is expensive and Token Ring networks require a substantial knowledge base to administer, ring topologies are only used on larger corporate networks. You would not use this type of topology for a home or small office network. The star topology is the cheapest and easiest to deploy in a small office situation.

Assessing Your Network Needs

Now that we've gotten some of the prerequisite basic theory out of the way, we need to take a moment to discuss assessing your own network needs. The type of resources that your users need to share and the number of users, as well as their physical locations, will really dictate how you use the rest of the information in this book to choose the type of network you build, the network operating system you use, and the type of servers (if any) you place on your network.

Let's break the process into a list:

■ How many users do you currently have and do they each have their own PC? A very small user base with only a couple of computers could really get along just fine on a peer-to-peer network. More users and more client machines may dictate that you go with a server-based network.

■ What type of resources do your users need to share? If you are looking at a situation where only a printer and a few files need to be shared, you are again probably in the realm of the peer-to-peer network. In cases where specialized resources such as databases and multiple printers or file servers are required, you will definitely be working in a server-based networking environment.

■ Where are your users? If all the users work in close proximity, you can typically select an easy-to-deploy network media type, such as wire (or you might be able to use existing electrical or phone wire, as discussed in Chapter 4). If your users are on different floors of a building or in different buildings, this will complicate issues related to getting all the users connected. In cases where you have users that telecommute, you can use special servers, such as remote access servers (called RAS servers), to allow users to dial into the network. We cover remote access in Chapter 17, "Networking on the Run."

■ How will your network grow over time? If you expect growth in your user base and the type of resources that they need to access, a server-based network is really the only way to go. A star topology also provides the easiest type of network topology for expanding the number of computers on the network.

■ What does your budget look like? Even if you determine that you need a number of specialized servers on your network, you have to be able to afford the physical aspects of the network (such as the cabling and the topology). How many specialized servers you can set up is also going to be limited by your budget. Although it might seem to be very exciting to plan to implement the latest and greatest technologies, budgeting constraints might require that you build a simpler network that provides you with the ability to expand in the future.

Although these are just some general guidelines, you should probably do a serious needs analysis before jumping into the network arena. There is nothing worse than miscalculating your needs and ending up with a network that just isn't usable or ending up with a network that is under utilized.

Planning the Network

You should hold off on creating your network plan until you have truthfully assessed your networking needs. Once you have that information available, you can start the task of determining what kind of client machines you need to purchase and what kind of servers you will have to set up on your network.

Your best first step is to completely read this book. It provides basic information related to hardware, network media, network protocols, and client and server operating systems. Because this book does not profess to be anything more than an introduction to the world of networking, you will need to do some additional research. The World Wide Web is an incredible resource for the novice network builder. It provides information on products, networking theory, and even allows you to purchase the hardware and software that you need to get your network up and running. Take a look at Appendix B, "Online Networking Resources," which provides a number of Web links to sites that provide information related to networking.

In situations where you will be involved in the building of large networks, you might want to go outside your company and hire a consultant to help you plan the network infrastructure. In the case of smaller networks, a little research and some careful consideration should help you put together a network that will meet your needs.

Chapter Summary

- Peer-to-peer networks are best used in situations where a few users need to share a few resources.
- Peer-to-peer networks use share-level security, which means that each resource could have a different password.
- Server-based networks provide for centralized management of the network.
- Server-based networks log on a user with one password. The user can access any resources that he or she has been given the appropriate permissions for.
- Server-based networks can distribute the workload among specialized network servers, such as file and print servers.
- Special servers, such as Web servers, can expand the ability of the network to communicate outside its physical location.

- The bus topology is the simplest topology and uses a passive methodology for computers accessing the network.

- The star topology is the most common network topology and also the easiest to expand. The star topology is also considered a passive topology (like the bus topology).

- The ring topology is an active topology because computers on the ring pass a token. To send data onto the network, possession of the token is required.

- It is extremely important that you assess your networking needs before actually planning your network. Take future growth into account when assessing your LAN needs.

3

NETWORKING HARDWARE

In this chapter

- Working with network interface cards
- Selecting and installing a NIC
- Using hubs
- Working with PC motherboards
- Understanding processors and PC RAM
- Working with hard drives
- Differentiating server and client hardware

Our Age of Anxiety is, in great part, the result of trying to do today's jobs with yesterday's tools.

–Marshall McLuhan

Now that we've discussed the different kinds of networks and looked at network topologies, we should spend some time discussing the hardware involved in networking. This chapter will concentrate on the connectivity devices that define the network topology—the most important being the network interface card. We will also take a look at hubs, routers, and switches.

Another important aspect of building your network is selecting the hardware for your client PCs and your network servers. There are many good primers on computer hardware—for example, the *Absolute Beginner's Guide to PC Upgrades*, published by Que. Also, numerous advanced books, such as *Upgrading and Repairing PCs* (by Scott Mueller, also from Que), are available, so we won't cover PC hardware in depth in this chapter. We will take a look at motherboards, RAM, and hard drives because of the impact these components have on server performance. We will also explore some of the issues related to buying client and server hardware.

Let's start our discussion with the network interface card. We can then look at network connectivity devices and finish up with some information on PC hardware.

Working with Network Interface Cards

As far as networking is concerned, the network interface card (NIC) is one of the most important PC devices. Each computer on the network (including servers and clients) requires one, and it is the NIC that provides the connection between the PC and the network's physical medium (such as copper or fiber-optic cable, both of which are discussed in the next chapter).

An IBM PC (or compatible PC) typically requires that a NIC be added to it (unless you buy your network clients and servers with a NIC as their standard hardware configuration). Even Macintoshes and Apple PowerPCs require NICs. In most cases, newer Apple computers, such as the iMac, have built-in Ethernet NICs. Figure 3.1 shows a PCI NIC from 3Com, which provides the RJ-45 female port for the CAT 5 twisted pair that connects the computer to a hub or switch (more about these connectivity devices later in the chapter).

Not only does the NIC provide the computer with a connection to the network, but it also handles an important data-conversion function. Data travels in parallel on the PC's bus system; the network medium demands a serial transmission. The transceiver (a transmitter and receiver) on the NIC card is able to move data from parallel to serial, and vice versa. This is not unlike automobiles moving on a multi-lane superhighway that must all merge into one lane of traffic.

FIGURE 3.1
Network inter-
face cards pro-
vide the
connection
between the PC
and the network
cabling.

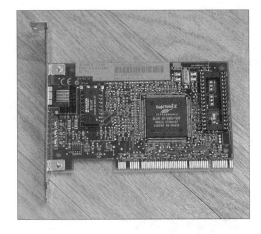

Network interface cards also supply the basic addressing system used to get data from one computer to another on the network. This hardware or MAC address is burned into a ROM chip on the NIC. It is referred to as the *MAC address* because the Media Access Control (MAC) layer is actually a sublayer of the OSI model's Data Link layer (the OSI model is discussed in detail in Chapter 5, "Network Protocols: Real and Imagined," in the section "Understanding the OSI Model").

The hardware address on the NIC actually provides the definitive address for a computer on the network. Different protocol stacks, such as TCP/IP, use a logical addressing system (in the case of TCP/IP, it is IP addresses). In this case, the logical address must be resolved to the NIC's hardware address before the data can actually be received.

Selecting a NIC

NICs come in different types, depending on the network architecture being used on the network (such as Ethernet or token ring, which are both discussed in the next chapter). NICs also differ in the type of motherboard slot they fit into. PCI NICs fit into a PCI slot on a motherboard. ISA NICs fit into an ISA slot. Figure 3.1 shows a PCI card (PCI cards are shorter than ISA cards, as are their respective slots on the motherboard).

When you select a NIC, it needs to be compatible with the architecture of the network. The Ethernet network is, by far, the most common network architecture type and is used for both peer-to-peer networks and large-scale corporate networks. Ethernet connectivity devices, such as hubs, are also much cheaper than the connectivity devices deployed on a token-ring network.

Note
Token-ring networks are typically found in larger corporations. The token-ring architecture does offer some advantages over Ethernet (particularly on high-traffic networks, where bandwidth is at a premium), which we discuss in the next chapter.

The NIC that you select must also fit in an empty expansion slot on your computer's motherboard. On an IBM or compatible PC, you have a number of choices, such as an ISA, PCI, or EISA slot. The slots available will depend on the motherboard (motherboards are discussed later in the chapter). Figure 3.2 shows a motherboard that provides both ISA and PCI expansion slots.

FIGURE 3.2

Your motherboard will typically provide ISA and PCI expansion slots.

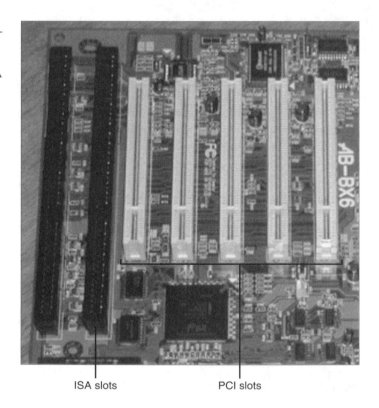

ISA slots   PCI slots

The Industry Standard Architecture (ISA) bus (a *bus* is the internal wiring system on the motherboard) was the standard used on the IBM PC and the IBM XT class of personal computers. This slot type supported 8-bit throughput for expansion devices. The ISA bus speed was increased to 16 bits in 1984. A large number of devices, such as modems, sound cards, and NICs, are available for this bus type. Even some new motherboards provide ISA slots. However, a day will come when the ISA slot is considered obsolete and only the higher-throughput PCI slots will be available on motherboards.

The PCI bus, on the other hand, was introduced by Intel in 1993 and has really become the industry standard. PCI provides a 32-bit bus, and PCI version 2.1 supports 64-bit and faster bus specifications. As with ISA, PCI cards support a large number of peripheral devices.

Note

There is a slight chance you might run into three other computer bus architectures: EISA, VESA, and MCA. Extended Industry Standard Architecture (EISA) was developed by Compaq and other PC clone manufacturers as a suggested PC slot standard (it never became the industry standard) when IBM rolled out PCs embracing Micro Channel Architecture (which is now nothing more than a footnote in bus architecture literature). EISA provided 32-bit bus throughput as well as ISA compatibility. The Video Electronics Standards Association (VESA) bus provided support for 486 processors. This 32-bit bus system has been abandoned by motherboard manufacturers in favor of the PCI bus. Micro Channel Architecture (MCA) was a new bus system launched by IBM for its PS/2 family of computers. MCA was not compatible with ISA, and the availability of MCA peripherals was limited when the PS/2 family was first introduced. MCA expansion cards were also extremely expensive. The MCA bus was eventually abandoned by IBM in favor of the PCI bus.

Although ISA NICs are generally going to be cheaper than PCI NICs, PCI NICs are obviously going to provide better overall performance because of their potential for faster throughput. You can get some other enhancements with a NIC that improve the transfer of data from the NIC to the computer's processor:

- *Buffering*. Memory chips are actually placed on the NIC. This RAM is used as a buffer. It can hold data that is awaiting services provided by the computer's processor. It can also hold data waiting to be broadcast out onto the LAN medium.

- *Direct Memory Access (DMA)*. Computers that support DMA allow devices such as network interface cards to transfer and accept data directly from the computer's RAM. This means that the processor does not have to become involved in the process of moving data to or from the NIC and RAM.

- *Bus mastering*. NICs can be designed to directly access computer RAM without using the computer's processor as an intermediary. Bus mastering (which is similar to DMA) allows the NIC to control the bus and send and receive data to and from the computer's RAM.

NICs that provide buffering and support DMA or bus mastering are going to be more expensive than NICs that do not. However, when selecting a NIC for a mission-critical server, you will probably want to buy one with all the performance bells and whistles.

Installing a NIC

You certainly don't need an engineering degree to install a network card in a PC. However, before you tackle the job, you need to be aware of one thing: You need to have a handle on a subject area that an old colleague of mine referred to as "static awareness." Static electricity can actually produce enough voltage to ruin a motherboard or expansion card, such as a NIC. This means that you should use some sort of antistatic wristband that attaches to the PC case or do your work while standing on an antistatic mat. The bottom line is that you should avoid working on the computer in a room that is carpeted.

You will also want to be sure you have a couple of decent screw drivers. These screw drivers should not have magnetized tips. Now, here are the steps to follow:

1. Open up the case on the computer and install the NIC in an open expansion slot.

2. Close up the case and attach the network medium (typically twisted-pair cabling).

3. Boot up the computer. If you purchased a plug-and-play network card and are using an OS that supports plug-and-play technology, the most you will have to do is provide a disk or CD-ROM that contains the driver for the NIC.

4. If you are using an operating system that does not detect new hardware devices, you will have to manually install the NIC. If the card came with installation software, use that software to install the necessary drivers.

Because most new computers and the operating systems that they run embrace plug-and-play technology, installing a NIC in a computer is really just a matter of placing the NIC in an empty motherboard slot and then restarting the computer. Plug-and-play NICs will be recognized by the operating system and the appropriate software driver will be loaded on the system. Figure 3.3 shows the Windows 2000 Professional OS identifying a plug-and-play NIC.

FIGURE 3.3

Operating systems that embrace plug-and-play technology make it easy to add a plug-and-play NIC to the system.

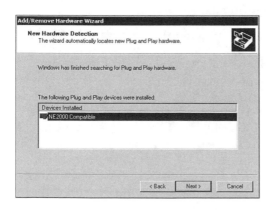

Not all operating systems embrace plug-and-play technology, however, and these types of operating systems will require that you select an IRQ (or *Interrupt Request*) for the new NIC. Each device in your computer, including the mouse, keyboard, and NIC, is assigned an Interrupt Request line that the device uses to alert the microprocessor (CPU) that it needs data processed. Each device must be assigned a unique IRQ; otherwise, you will have an IRQ conflict. Although PCI motherboards do allow devices to share an IRQ, common practice is to have a unique IRQ for every device on the system.

Finding the available IRQs is not that difficult, and each operating system (including PC operating systems and network operating systems) provides you with a tool to view the used and available IRQs on the system. For example, Figure 3.4 shows the Windows 2000 Device Manager, which displays the IRQs on the system.

Note

If you are using Windows 2000 Server, getting to the Device Manager is very straightforward. Right-click the My Computer icon on the desktop and then choose Properties. In the Properties dialog box, select the Hardware tab. Then click the Device Manager button.

FIGURE 3.4

An operating system provides a utility that allows you to examine the IRQ configuration of a system.

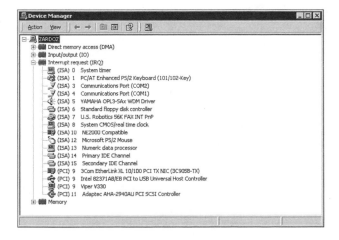

Table 3.1 shows the standard IRQ settings for a PC. As you can see, a number of the IRQs are reserved for particular system devices.

Table 3.1 IRQ Settings

IRQ	Use
0	System timer
1	Keyboard
2	Cascade to secondary IRQ controller
3	COM port 2 and 4 (serial port)
4	COM port 1 and 3 (serial port)
5	LPT2 (printer port)
6	Floppy disk controller
7	LPT1 (printer port)
8	Real-time clock
9	Free
10	Primary SCSI adapter (or free)
11	Secondary SCSI adapter (or free)
12	PS/2 mouse
13	Floating-point math coprocessor
14	Primary hard disk controller
15	Secondary hard disk controller (or free)

Obviously, in cases where the computer does not have a second COM port or an LTP2 port, these IRQs will be available. Each computer's hardware configuration will vary, so you will have to determine the available IRQs for each computer in which you are installing a NIC.

Most operating systems do a pretty good job of helping you get a newly installed NIC up and running. Windows 2000 Server and Windows 2000 Professional both embrace Microsoft's Plug and Play scheme for plug-and-play hardware devices. This means that both of these operating systems will, in most cases, identify and install the appropriate drivers for a number of the network interface cards available on the market. And although you can't call what they do "plug and play," Novell NetWare 5, Sun Microsystems Solaris OS, and the various Linux clones do a pretty good job of helping you set up the appropriate network card in your network server or client machines.

Working with Network Connectivity Devices

Depending on the type of topology your network uses and the type of cabling you use (cabling is discussed in Chapter 4, "Building the Network Infrastructure," in the section "Choosing a Network Connectivity Strategy"), your LAN might require some sort of connectivity device to connect the various network computers, printers, and other devices together. In cases where you need to extend your LAN (say, to the second floor of an office building) or add a large number of new users to the LAN, other connectivity devices might be required. Some of these connectivity devices merely serve to connect devices; others are used to boost the data signal traveling on the network medium, and still others actually participate in determining how data traffic should flow on the network.

Let's start our discussion of network connectivity devices with the hub, which is a device you would use on a small network, or even in a peer-to-peer networking situation, to connect computers. The other devices that we will look at, such as repeaters, switches, and routers, are often lumped under the blanket term *internetworking devices*. An *internetwork* is a network of LANs, meaning that some sort of connectivity technology is used to extend a LAN beyond its typical size or to connect different LANs together into one large network.s

Hubs

Hubs are commonly used LAN connectivity devices. They serve as the central connection points for LANs (hubs are used on LANs that embrace the star topology discussed in Chapter 2, "Different Needs, Different Networks"). A basic hub contains no active electronics and therefore cannot be used to extend a LAN (that is, extend it past the cabling distance specifications discussed in the next chapter). It basically organizes your cables and relays data signals to all the computers on the LAN.

Hubs are most commonly used on networks that use twisted-pair cabling. Ports available on the back of the hub provide the connection points for the devices on the network. Computers and other devices are attached to the hub by individual network cables. Hubs come in many sizes and shapes and supply different numbers of ports.

In cases where the LAN outgrows the size of the hub, a new hub can be attached (the hubs are "daisy chained" together using a short connection cable often referred to as a *rat tail*) to the current hub, thus providing greater port density. Figure 3.5 shows two different types of Ethernet hubs.

FIGURE 3.5
Hubs provide
the central con-
nection points
for LANs.

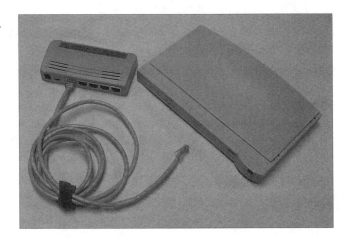

Hubs come in all sizes and shapes and are available in a wide range of prices.
Typically, the more ports on the hub, the more expensive the hub. Hubs that support
faster varieties of Ethernet, such as Fast Ethernet (which we discuss in the next chapter in the section "Understanding Ethernet"), will also cost more.

Repeaters

As you will find out in the next chapter, the different types of network cabling all
have a maximum distance that they can move a data signal. In cases where a LAN
must be extended beyond the maximum run for a particular cabling type, repeaters
are used. A *repeater* takes the signal that it receives from computers and other
devices on the LAN and regenerates the signal so that the signal maintains its
integrity along a longer media run than is normally possible.

Repeaters don't have any capabilities for directing network traffic or deciding the
particular route certain data should take; they are simple devices that just sit on the
network, boosting the data signals they receive. The problem with repeaters is that
they amplify the entire signal that they receive, including any line noise. So, in
worst-case scenarios, they pass on data traffic that is barely discernable from the
background noise on the line.

Bridges

A *bridge* is an internetworking device used to help conserve the bandwidth available
on the network. When LANs really start to grow, network data traffic can begin to
overwhelm the available bandwidth on network media.

One strategy for conserving network bandwidth is to chop the network up into smaller segments. These segments are connected to a bridge. Bridges are smarter than hubs and repeaters and actually use some software to help get the job done. A bridge is able to read the MAC address (also known as the *hardware address*—remember it's burned onto the NIC in each computer on the network) of each data packet circulating on the network segments connected to the bridge. By learning which MAC addresses live on each of the network segments, the bridge can help keep data traffic that is local to a particular segment from spreading to the other network segments that are serviced by the bridge.

Switches

A *switch* is another internetworking device used to manage the bandwidth on a large network. A switch, which is often referred to as a "bridge on steroids," controls the flow of data by using the MAC address that is placed on each data packet (which coincides with the MAC address of a particular computer's network card). Switches divide networks into what are called *Virtual LANs* or *VLANs*. The great thing about a VLAN, which is a logical grouping of computers on the network into a sort of communication group, is that the computers don't have to be in close proximity or even on the same floor. This allows you to group computers that serve similar types of users into a VLAN. For example, even if your engineers are spread all over your company's office building, their computers can still be made part of the same VLAN, which would share bandwidth.

Switches use a combination of software and hardware to switch packets between computers and other devices on the network. Switches have their own operating system. Figure 3.6 shows the status of a VLAN (VLAN1) on a Cisco 2900 switch. Understanding what is being shown in this figure requires an understanding of the switch's OS. Basically, this particular screen shows the hardware/MAC address of the switch and the IP address of the switch. Other statistics relate to the number of packets sent and received by the switch (which are all at 0 because the switch has just been placed on the network).

Because switches can offer a high density of connection ports, they can even replace the hub on a network. This means that each computer on the network can be connected to its own port on the switch. When PCs are directly connected to a switch, it can supply each PC with a dedicated amount of bandwidth. For example, users on a 10Mbps Ethernet network can realize bandwidth of 10Mbps. The computers don't compete for the bandwidth the way computers do on a network that is connected via a hub.

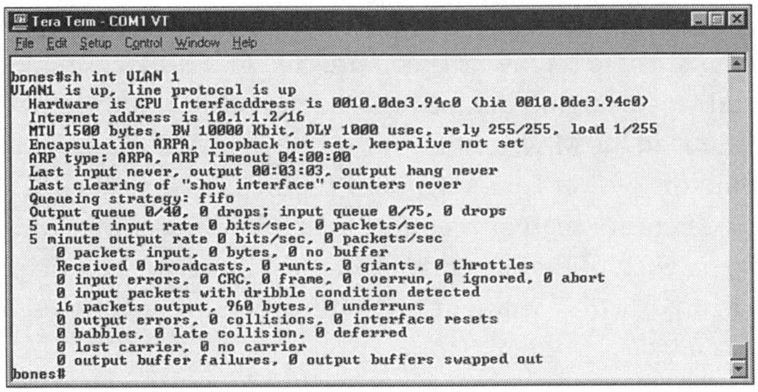

FIGURE 3.6

An operating
system is used to
configure and
monitor a
switch.

Switch hardware can also take advantage of full-duplex access to the network media, which allows for the sending and receiving of data simultaneously on the network. This provides network access on an Ethernet network that would essentially be collision free (Ethernet networks experience data collisions pretty much as a rule; Ethernet is discussed in the next chapter). A computer on a Fast Ethernet network, which runs at 100Mbps, would actually realize a net total of 200Mbps throughput because sending and receiving can take place simultaneously on the full-duplex media.

Switches (because of the aforementioned reasons) are becoming very popular on large networks. They have all but replaced bridges as the internetworking devices for conserving network bandwidth and expanding LANs into larger corporate internetworks.

Routers

Routers are even smarter than bridges and switches (routers operate at the Network layer—a higher level in the OSI conceptual model than bridges and switches, which operate at the Data Link layer; we discuss all the layers of OSI in Chapter 5). A *router* uses a combination of hardware and software to actually "route" data from its source to its destination. (By *software*, I mean an operating system.) Routers actually have a very sophisticated OS that allows you to configure their various connection ports. You can set up a router to route data packets from a number of different network protocol stacks, including TCP/IP, IPX/SPX, and AppleTalk (protocols are discussed in Chapter 5).

Routers are used to segment LANs that have become very large and congested with data traffic. Routers are also used to connect remote LANs together using different WAN technologies.

Figure 3.7 shows a Cisco 2516 router. This router has a built-in hub and three different WAN connection points. Notice the BRI port marked in the figure. *BRI* stands for ISDN *Basic Rate Interface*, which allows this router to connect to a remote network using an ISDN connection (ISDN and other WAN technologies are discussed in Chapter 10, "Expanding a LAN with WAN Technology").

BRI interface

FIGURE 3.7

Routers are used to segment networks into logical subsets.

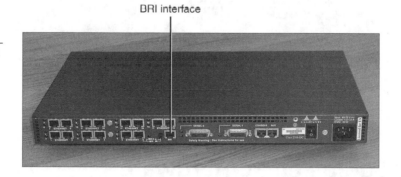

Routers divide large networks into logical segments called *subnets*. This division of the network is based on the addressing scheme the network uses, such as IP addresses. Data traffic related to a particular subnet is kept local. The router only forwards data that is meant for other subnets on the extended network. This routing of network data helps conserve network bandwidth.

Routers decide how to forward data packets to their destinations based on a *routing table*. Routers use protocols built into their operating system to identify neighboring routers and their network addresses (such as IP addresses). This allows routers to build a routing table. Figure 3.8 shows the command-line interface used on a Cisco router. This figure also shows the IP routing table for a small network that consists of two connected Cisco routers. Each of the subnets shown at the bottom of the table (notice the list of IP addresses) represents a different router interface. 10.2.0.0 and 10.3.0.0 are on the router that supplied this screen. The subnets 10.1.0.0 and 132.1.0.0 were discovered by the router (using the RIP protocol) on a connect router.

Note

No matter what operating system you use, computers use pretty much the same strategy to identify themselves on the network. This strategy involves *broadcast messages*, meaning that a message will go out to every other computer on the network, proclaiming a computer's identity or requesting information related to the identity of another computer on the network. Broadcast messages create what is called *broadcast traffic*, and broadcast traffic can suck up valuable network bandwidth that otherwise could be used to move LAN data. Routers keep broadcast traffic from spreading beyond a particular segment, thus conserving a lot of potential network bandwidth.

```
Tera Term - COM1 VT
File  Edit  Setup  Control  Window  Help

Alice>sh ip route
Codes: C - connected, S - static, I - IGRP, R - RIP, M - mobile, B - BGP
       D - EIGRP, EX - EIGRP external, O - OSPF, IA - OSPF inter area
       E1 - OSPF external type 1, E2 - OSPF external type 2, E - EGP
       i - IS-IS, L1 - IS-IS level-1, L2 - IS-IS level-2, * - candidate default
       U - per-user static route

Gateway of last resort is not set

     10.0.0.0/8 is variably subnetted, 4 subnets, 2 masks
C       10.2.0.0/16 is directly connected, Serial0
C       10.2.1.1/32 is directly connected, Serial0
C       10.3.0.0/16 is directly connected, Ethernet0
R       10.1.0.0/16 [120/1] via 10.2.1.1, 00:00:18, Serial0
R    132.1.0.0/16 [120/1] via 10.2.1.1, 00:00:18, Serial0
Alice>
```

Some Thoughts on PC Hardware

Now that we've discussed NICs and some of the connectivity devices you will run
into when you network computers, we will finish out the chapter by looking at some
other critical pieces of PC hardware—specifically, motherboards, processors, hard
drives, and RAM. We need to discuss these hardware components because they
inherently affect a PC's overall performance. Understanding how these hardware
components fit into the overall PC hardware puzzle will help you when it is time for
you to select hardware for network clients or network servers. Since this book serves
as a primer to networking and network hardware, you should consult a heavy-duty
reference such as *Upgrading and Repairing PCs* by Scott Mueller, published by Que.

First, let's take a look at some issues related to motherboards. Then we can take a
look at processors, hard drives, and memory.

Motherboards

The *motherboard* is the main system board for a PC, and it provides the data highway (or *bus system*) that moves data between components on the motherboard and
the PC's processor. The speed of data moving along the bus is measured in megahertz (MHz). Although 66MHz was the standard for PCs running a Pentium (or
Pentium clone) processor, motherboards can now operate as fast as 100 to 133MHz
(and faster bus systems from a number of motherboard manufacturers are just
beyond the horizon). A motherboard is specific to the type of processor run on the
computer. An IBM/PC clone motherboard using an Intel processor will be designed
differently from an Apple iMac motherboard, which uses a Motorola processor.

Motherboards have different designations, such as ATX and LPX. These designations refer to the footprint of the motherboard as well as the overall design of the motherboard and will therefore determine certain hardware choices.

The motherboard also provides all the slots for the computer's processor and memory. Areas to connect hard drives (and drives such as CD-ROM drives) with ribbon cables are also present on the motherboard, as are expansion slots (PCI and ISA) for other devices, such as sound cards and network interface cards.

Motherboards are also characterized by the type of connection provided for the processor. A Socket 7 motherboard uses a processor that is typically a small square attached to a socket on the motherboard with a bunch of little pins. Intel, AMD, and Cyrix make processors for Socket 7 motherboards.

Slot 1 and Slot 2 motherboards provide a larger "slot" for the processor, and the slot processor is typically a rectangle (it looks like a very small brick). Figure 3.9 shows an Abit slot-1 IBM/compatible motherboard (Abit is the manufacturer of the motherboard).

FIGURE 3.9
Motherboards come in a number of different configurations and sizes.

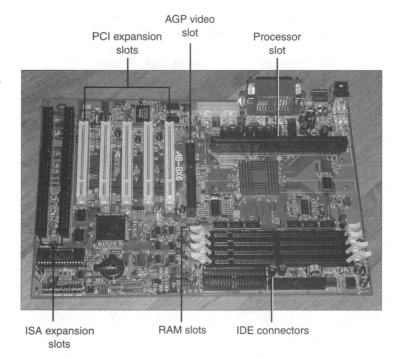

A number of the Slot 1 motherboards available on the market also supply space for dual processors. This makes the Slot 1 motherboard appropriate for high-end client workstations or network servers.

Although how fast a computer can work with data is really ultimately decided by the computer's processor, deciding on a particular motherboard should probably be determined, in part, by the features the motherboard's chipset provides. The chipset determines the ceiling for the bus speed. Chipsets provide DMA support (discussed earlier in this chapter in the section "Selecting a NIC") and other features, such as an Accelerated Graphics Port (AGP provides faster video response). These features will also boost the overall performance of the computer.

Processors

The processor is really the brain of the computer. It processes binary information input by the user or received from other devices on the computer, such as the network interface card. Processor speed is measured in megahertz (MHz). The Intel processor used on the original IBM PC ran at 8MHz. Processors are now available that run in excess of 1,000MHz (that is, 1GHz or *gigahertz*). Figure 3.10 shows an Intel Celeron 400MHz processor (on the left) for use on a Socket 7 motherboard and a Slot 1 Intel 300MHz Pentium II processor.

FIGURE 3.10
Processors are built to fit into a particular place on a motherboard.

Processors are manufactured by a number of different companies, including Intel, Motorola, Cyrix, and AMD. The selection of the processor type and speed, as far as networking is concerned, will depend on whether you are configuring a client machine or a network server. Faster (and even multiple) processors are a must on a server that needs to process a large number of calls for data from users on the network.

Basically, you should choose the processor you want to use for a computer and allow that choice to determine the motherboard you use for the computer. This helps narrow the choice of motherboards down to those that support the processor.

Memory

There seems to be as many memory types for personal computers as there are types of apples. Computer memory or *RAM (Random Access Memory)* is the working storage area. It is used by the processor and other devices to temporarily store information, and it's also accessed by software as we work on our computers.

You can't just install any type of RAM on your motherboard; it is actually dictated by the chipset the manufacturer places on the motherboard. This means you need to know the type of RAM that is compatible with a particular motherboard.

RAM comes in two basic formats: SIMMS and DIMMS. A *SIMM (Single Inline Memory Module)* is a epoxy-coated silicon wafer that contains a number of memory chips. The SIMM fits into a slot on the motherboard. SIMMs must be placed on the motherboard in identical pairs (there are typically four SIMM slots on a motherboard). This means that to have 64MB of memory on the motherboard, two 32MB SIMMs would be installed.

A *DIMM (Dual Inline Memory Module)* contains memory chips like a SIMM but actually provides a greater density of memory chips and therefore more RAM. DIMMs do not have to be installed in pairs, and there are typically three DIMM slots on a motherboard. This means that a computer with 128MB of memory would only require the installation of one 128MB DIMM. All the newer motherboards use DIMMs (although you might find some motherboards that have slots for both DIMMs and SIMMs).

RAM speed has been historically measured in nanoseconds (ns). The lower the nanosecond rating for the RAM, the faster the RAM. For example, 10ns RAM would be faster than 30ns RAM. The speed of newer RAM memory is now measured in MHz. Currently, 100 and 133MHz RAM is available. These two RAM speeds are roughly equivalent to 12ns and 8ns, respectively.

As mentioned earlier, a number of different RAM types are available, and the type used is dictated by the motherboard used on the computer. Although memory has changed dramatically since the advent of the PC, the RAM types listed here are all types you might find on a motherboard designed for a Pentium processor (clone processor motherboard):

 - *Fast Page Mode (FPM) memory.* This type of RAM is mounted in SIMM modules of 2, 4, 8, 16, or 32MB and is the traditional RAM type. FPM RAM is typically found in 60ns and 70ns versions. You cannot mix different speeds on the same motherboard.

- *Extended Data Output (EDO) RAM.* This RAM type is an improvement of FPM RAM that provides for the faster reading of data. EDO RAM is usually sold in 60 and 50ns versions. The 50ns version is available at a higher cost. EDO RAM is mounted in SIMM modules.

- *Synchronous Dynamic RAM (SDRAM).* This RAM type is a newer memory type and is used in most new PCs. This memory type is typically called *PC100* or *PC133 RAM*, depending on its speed. SDRAM comes in DIMMs and has an access time of only 12 to 8ns (PC100 and PC133 RAM, respectively) This type of RAM is called *synchronous* because it's actually able to synchronize itself with the speed of the motherboard.

- *Double Data Rate-Synchronous DRAM (DDR-SDRAM).* The newest RAM type, which is still only supported by a few motherboard manufacturers, is DDR-SDRAM. This type of RAM is actually able to transfer data twice during the motherboard's clock cycle (which is measured in MHz). This means that this type of RAM can be twice as fast as other RAM types. DDR-SDRAM comes in DIMMs.

Bottom line, the more RAM you have on a system, the better the system's performance. Adding RAM to any computer will increase system throughput. The addition of RAM, in many cases, will even provide more of a performance jump than switching to a faster processor.

Note Another RAM type that you may see in the near future is Rambus DRAM (RDRAM). RDRAM was developed by Rambus, Inc. RDRAM is a very fast type of DRAM that can run as fast as 600MHz. RDRAM is currently used in some graphics accelerator cards. However, Intel has a licensing agreement with Rambus to use RDRAM technology on future Intel motherboards.

Hard Drives

The first hard drive available for the original IBM PC boasted a capacity of 10MB (10 million bytes). Now it is common for hard drives or fixed disks to have capacities in excess of 30GB (that's 30 billion bytes).

Hard drives come in two flavors: IDE drives and SCSI drives. An *Integrated Drive Electronics (IDE)* drive is a hard drive (or other device such as a CD-ROM) where the controller for the drive is built into the drive itself. An IDE drive is connected to the motherboard using a ribbon cable. Each motherboard IDE connection supports up to two IDE drives. Motherboards typically have two IDE connections, meaning a maximum of four IDE drives (this includes hard drives and CD-ROM drives) could be installed on the computer.

> **Note**   The newest drive standard available is Enhanced IDE (EIDE). It provides faster data rates and can support larger storage devices than the IDE standard.

Small Computer System Interface (SCSI) hard drives are attached to a SCSI controller card (placed in one of the motherboard's expansion slots or built right onto the motherboard, in the case of servers). SCSI controllers allow for the attachment of more drives (up to seven); therefore, SCSI drives are pretty much the standard for server computers. Figure 3.11 shows an IDE drive (on the left) and a SCSI drive; note that the attachment pins are different (due to the fact that different ribbon cables are used to attach these drives to the motherboard or SCSI controller card, respectively).

FIGURE 3.11

Hard drives can be IDE or SCSI drives.

In terms of server hardware, SCSI hard drives are preferred over IDE drives because SCSI drives boast a 12% performance boost over their IDE counterparts. Also, only two IDE drives can be connected to the motherboard via the same ribbon cable (limiting a computer to a maximum of four IDE drives connected to the motherboard). On the other hand, one SCSI controller will support up to seven drives, which makes it easier to deploy multiple-drive configurations, such as a RAID array (RAID is discussed in the section titled "Working with RAID," in Chapter 14, "Protecting Network Data").

> **Note**   Network storage capacity is no longer limited to the hard drives you have on your network servers. The recent introduction of network attached storage (NAS) provides a way to add storage capacity to a network without adding an actual server computer. An NAS device is really just a box of hard drives that is directly connected to the network. NAS

devices, such as the Quantum SnapServer, run their own proprietary OS and can be configured for file sharing using remote management software that can be run from a network client or server. NAS devices don't need a monitor or keyboard because you remotely configure them over the network. NAS devices provide an easy way to add hard drive storage capacity to a large network or even a peer-to-peer network without the expense of a network operating system and dedicated server hardware.

Network Server Considerations

Network servers require large storage capacity, fast processors, and ample memory. Server tower cases also are larger than client computers and provide much more space for additional hard drives and other peripherals.

Server computers often have motherboards that provide space for more than one processor. Most network operating systems are built to take advantage of multiple processors. In fact, some network operating systems (such as Windows 2000 Advanced Server) support up to 32 processors.

Servers also typically contain many more hard drives than you would find on a client machine and usually contain SCSI hard drives rather than IDE drives (which you would typically find on a client computer). This is not only to provide adequate storage space but also to build in some redundancy for storing files. We will talk about how drive redundancy can be used to help keep important data safe in Chapter 14. The SCSI controllers are also typically part of the server's motherboard rather than an add-on card.

Note
Servers often will contain drive bays that contain "hot-swappable" drives. This means a drive can be added or swapped while the server is running. These drive bays allow you to access the drive by sliding the drive out of the case; it's not unlike opening a drawer. This means that you can deal with drive issues without powering down the network server or opening the server case.

The hardware configuration for a server will, to a certain degree, be dictated by the network operating system running on that server. Each network operating system provides a baseline configuration for a server that will run that NOS.

For example, the recommended baseline server configuration for Microsoft Windows 2000 Server is as follows:

- Processor: Intel Pentium 166MHz
- RAM: 128MB (256 recommended)
- Hard drive: 2GB

- CD-ROM drive: 12X
- Monitor: Super VGA capable of 800×600 resolution

Novell NetWare 5.1 also has similar hardware requirements as a baseline for a NetWare 5.1 server. Keep in mind that the baseline configuration is often the hardware that is needed just to run the NOS properly and doesn't necessarily take into consideration how many clients you have on your network or the type of resources that will be accessed on a particular server.

Network operating systems are also generally less forgiving when you attempt to run them on computers with odd configurations or atypical hardware. NOS software companies often provide a hardware compatibility list that allows you to view what types of server hardware have been tested with the particular operating system.

Before you actually finalize your server configurations, you need to do some research on the NOS you will be running. Novell, Microsoft, Sun Microsystems, and other NOS providers typically provide white papers and other material that allow you to look at case studies and performance data related to a particular NOS and various hardware configurations.

Microsoft, Sun, and Novell all provide the hardware requirements to run their network operating systems. Check out these sites:

- www.microsoft.com
- www.sun.com
- www.novell.com

Network Client Considerations

Network clients don't typically need the processing power and storage capacity required by a server computer. Network clients do need, however, to be able to properly run the client operating system they have been configured with. Be sure that a client machine has at least the minimum hardware configuration to run the client operating system.

Because there are tons of different computer configurations out there (for standalone PCs, with most being quite satisfactory as a network client) and operating systems such as Windows 9x and Windows Me have been created with that fact in mind. They run on many different hardware configurations. Higher-end client software, such as Windows 2000, will be supported on fewer configurations. As is the case with network operating systems, some client operating systems will provide hardware compatibility lists you can review. These lists allow you to choose a compatible configuration for your client computers.

> **Note** To buy or to build? That is the question. Although the relatively low price of computer components may seem like a fairly seductive reason to build computers for a network, prebuilt PCs are configured with components that the computer manufacturer knows (or *should* know) work well together. Also, the prospect of building 100 computers for a network is an extremely daunting task, even if you've thrown a few computers together yourself. Adding RAM or hard drives to a PC is one thing; building a computer is something else entirely.

Chapter Summary

- Network interface cards (NICs) supply the connection between the computer and the network's physical medium.

- The NIC supplies the MAC or hardware address that is used to identify a computer on the network.

- Operating systems that embrace plug-and-play technology automatically install and configure plug-and-play NICs.

- In cases where the operating system does not configure a NIC that you've added to the system, you will have to identify an available IRQ for the NIC to use.

- A motherboard is the main circuit board for a PC, and it provides the connection point for the processor and peripheral cards. The motherboard also supplies the data bus used to move data from various devices to the computer's memory and processor, and vice versa.

- Computer memory speed and capacity have changed dramatically as the PC has evolved. The Dual Inline Memory Module (DIMM) is pretty much the rule for outfitting and upgrading PCs with RAM.

- Hard drives come in two basic flavors: IDE (or EIDE) and SCSI. SCSI drives are typically used on network servers because a SCSI controller can support up to seven drives.

- A hub is used as the central connection point for network devices that use copper wire, such as unshielded twisted pair (UTP).

- Bridges can be used on large networks to segment the network and preserve valuable network bandwidth.

- Switches can be used to segment large networks in logical VLANs. Dedicated bandwidth can also be provided to client and server computers connected to a switch. Switches can also support full-duplex data transfers, which allow a computer to send and receive data on the network simultaneously.

- Routers are used to divide networks into logical subnets, which keeps local traffic on each of the subnets. Routers also have the ability to determine the route that data should take as it is moved on the network.

- Network servers require more processing power, RAM, and storage space than network clients.

4

BUILDING THE NETWORK INFRASTRUCTURE

In this chapter

- Understanding network architectures
- Working with Ethernet
- Becoming familiar with IBM Token-Ring
- Understanding the IEEE standards for networking
- Differentiating network cabling types
- Creating a phone-line network
- Using wireless networking strategies

What goes up must come down. Ask any system administrator.

–Anonymous

Now that we've sorted out the differences between peer-to-peer networks and server-based networks and looked at some of the hardware considerations for network clients and servers, we can concentrate on issues related to actually setting up a network's infrastructure. The word *infrastructure* is probably one of those words that is both overused and misused by network administrators. For example, when something goes wrong on the network, it is very convenient to tell management that there is "an infrastructure problem," which actually means "I have no idea what the problem is."

However, if you think about an infrastructure like our U.S. highway system, two things stand out: An infrastructure is both a physical construct (such as miles and miles of roads) and a place where certain rules have been devised for users of the infrastructure (such as speed limits, stop signs, all those things that drivers west of Ohio completely ignore).

Networks are no different; their infrastructure will consist of some kind of network medium such as copper cabling or radio waves. Rules for how computers and other devices actually access the network infrastructure will also be set in place. The first thing that we will look at in this chapter is network architectures. The network architecture you use for your network defines how network devices access your network medium.

Once we have the difference between network architectures such as Ethernet and token ring sorted out, we can then take a look at the different network media available. So let's get going!

Understanding Network Architectures

In Chapter 2, "Different Needs, Different Networks," we took a look at the different physical topologies used to describe how devices are physically laid out on a LAN. Topology is a fairly broad way to discuss how a particular LAN is organized. A *network architecture*, on the other hand, provides more specific information on not only physical layout but also the cabling specifications that can be used and the actual method that the computers and other devices use to access the network media. Network architectures are defined by strict specifications provided by the Institute of Electrical and Electronics Engineers (IEEE), an international organization whose mandate is to develop and share electrical and information technology specifications worldwide.

In Chapter 5, "Network Protocols: Real and Imagined," we will take a look at the OSI model, which provides a theoretical look at how network communication takes place between a sending and a receiving device. Although the IEEE standards relate to real-world network functionality, these specifications have actually been grouped at the Data Link layer of the OSI theoretical model. Now, having said this, we will save the theory until we discuss OSI and LAN protocol stacks in Chapter 5. Just be aware that for the purpose of discussion and development, the IEEE folks have placed their actual network architecture specifications into a model that explains network interaction in a purely theoretical manner.

As with any technology, network architectures have come and gone. For example, ARCnet (Attached Resource Computer Network), the oldest network topology (*old* is a relative term because this architecture was created in 1977), used a ring topology in which an electronic token was passed from computer to computer. The computer with the token could access the network and send data.

You would have to look far and wide to find an ARCnet network (although, I'm sure they are out there); other network architectures such as Ethernet (the most popular in the world) and token ring have replaced this early network architecture. What's more, new architectures, such as Fiber Distributed Data Interface (FDDI), have been developed to provide faster throughput on networks that use fiber-optic cable.

 Any technology evolves (except maybe hula hoops and scissors), and during this evolution certain standards (once considered incredible advances) fall by the wayside. Look at calculating devices: There was the abacus, then the slide rule, and now the electronic calculator (and calculators are all solar powered or have been replaced by personal digital assistants that include calculators, which is discussed in Chapter 18, "PDAs and the Network"). You don't see too many abacuses (or is that abaci?) on people's desks.

Before we take a look at the commonly used network architectures (as of today) and how even these architectures are continuing to evolve, we need to discuss the terms *data transmission speed* and *bandwidth*. Data transmission speed is measured in bits per second and noted as *bps*. A *bit* is one binary digit, either a 1 or a 0 (it is the smallest unit of data; 8 bits actually make up a byte). All the architectures that we will look at provide data transmission speeds in excess of a million bits per second, which is noted as *Mbps*.

In terms of networking, *bandwidth* is considered the number of bits that can be sent across the network medium at a given time. So, the terms *data transmission speed* and *bandwidth* are often used interchangeably when discussing an architecture's data throughput.

Another issue related to these different architectures is the actual distance that data can be transmitted along a particular medium type. For example, Ethernet has a limitation of 100 meters over copper twisted-pair wire (without using any type of amplification device such as a repeater, which is discussed later in the chapter). If fiber-optic cable is used, an Ethernet run can be up to 2,000 meters (that's 2 kilometers—a meter is slightly longer than a yard, so 2,000 meters would be more than 20 football fields long).

We will be discussing bandwidth and maximum cable lengths as they relate to each of the network architectures we discuss. Now, let's take a look at the LAN architectures themselves.

Understanding Ethernet

As with many of the PC and network technologies that we use today, Ethernet got its start in 1972 at the Xerox Palo Alto Research Center (PARC). Xerox actually released a commercial version of Ethernet in 1975 that provided a transmission speed of 3Mbps.

Ethernet was a big hit, and Xerox, Intel, and the Digital Equipment Corporation (DEC) worked together to modify the Ethernet specifications and produced a version that provided a data transmission speed of 10Mbps. It is this 10Mbps flavor of Ethernet that was standardized by the IEEE in its 802.3 specifications (which we look at later in the chapter).

Ethernet is the most commonly used network architecture in the world. Let's look at how Ethernet controls the access of computers and other devices to the network.

Ethernet Network Access Strategy

Ethernet is a passive, wait-and-listen network architecture. Computers must contend for transmission time on the network medium. In fact, Ethernet is commonly described as a *contention-based architecture*.

Ethernet provides access to the network using Carrier Sense Multiple Access with Collision Detection (CSMA/CD). This strategy of network access basically means that the devices (such as computers) on the network listen to the network and wait until the line is clear; they "sense" when the line is clear and they can transmit data. The computer then sends its packets out onto the line. If there is more than one computer transmitting, collisions result. Sensing the collisions, the computers stop transmitting and wait until the line is free. One of the computers will then transmit, gaining control of the line and completing the transmission of the data.

To receive data, computers just sit and wait, listening to the line. When they sense that a particular transmission is meant for them, they receive it on their network card.

Believe it or not, collisions are very common on Ethernet networks. Devices such as hubs (which we discussed in Chapter 3, "Networking Hardware") have a collision light on their front panel, and you will see it blink fairly often, letting you know that collisions have taken place on the LAN. Collisions are only a problem if they become excessive.

The main advantage of Ethernet is that it is one of the cheapest network architectures to implement. Network interface cards, cabling, and hubs are fairly inexpensive when compared to the hardware required for other architectures such as token ring (which we discuss shortly). A major disadvantage of Ethernet relates to collisions on the network. The more collisions, the slower the network will run, and excessive collisions can even bring down the network.

> As I've already said, collisions are a common occurrence on an Ethernet network. Collisions are only an issue if they become excessive. Excessive collisions could be caused by a malfunctioning network card or other device on the network. Cable runs that exceed the maximum length requirement can also lead to excess collisions because computers are not able to sense the activity of computers at the far end of the network. Also, the more devices there are on an Ethernet network, the more collisions will increase. There are strategies for cutting down on the number of collisions on an Ethernet LAN, such as using routers and switches (which we discussed in the last chapter).

As far as network topologies go, Ethernet networks typically will be found in a bus or star configuration, depending on the type of cabling used. With twisted-pair cabling becoming more and more popular and hubs becoming very affordable, most Ethernet networks will be configured in a star topology, as shown in Figure 4.1.

FIGURE 4.1

Ethernet LANs are typically arranged in a star topology, with a hub at the center of the star.

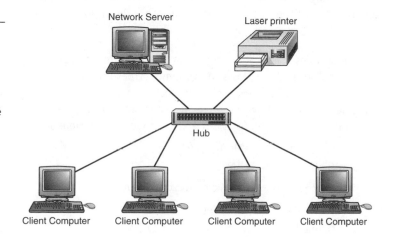

Higher-Speed Versions of Ethernet

Faster versions of Ethernet have been developed: Fast Ethernet and Gigabit Ethernet. *Fast Ethernet* is so named because of its "faster" throughput speed (when compared to the original 10Mbps flavor of Ethernet). Fast Ethernet provides a bandwidth of 100Mbps. This faster throughput is due to the fact that the time it takes to transmit a bit of information over the Ethernet media has been reduced by a factor of 10. So, Fast Ethernet is able to run 10 times faster than 10Mbps Ethernet, thus providing 100Mbps throughput.

Fast Ethernet cannot run over the same network cards and hubs used for a 10Mbps Ethernet network. Fast Ethernet network cards and Fast Ethernet hubs (and Fast Ethernet versions of other network devices) are required.

An even faster version of Ethernet is Gigabit Ethernet, which uses the same IEEE Ethernet specifications and the same data format as the other versions of Ethernet. Gigabit Ethernet provides a data transmission speed of 1,000Mbps.

Whereas Fast Ethernet is being used on LANs using both twisted-pair and fiber-optic cabling, Gigabit Ethernet is still currently restricted to fiber-optic–based networks and requires high-speed switches and specialized servers. This means that Gigabit Ethernet is primarily used as a high-speed backbone that connects LANs together. Cost issues and the hardware required still make it prohibitive for just any network.

Ethernet IEEE and Cable Specifications

Ethernet is defined by the IEEE 802.3 specifications and operates at the Data Link layer of the OSI conceptual model (discussed in Chapter 5). A number of different flavors of Ethernet and Fast Ethernet exist, depending on the type of cabling used on the network (we will discuss cable types in more detail later in the chapter, in the section "Cabling Options").

The IEEE provides specifications for a number of the technologies related to networking computers. The list that follows shows some of these specifications. You don't have to know the ins and outs of every specification to be a network administrator, but a general understanding of how these specifications define the actual technologies that we work with is a good thing (as Martha Stewart would say). Here are the specifications:

- 802.3 Ethernet (CSMA/CD) LAN
- 802.5 Token-Ring LAN
- 802.7 Broadband Technical Advisory Group
- 802.8 Fiber-Optic Technical Advisory Group
- 802.9 Integrated Voice and Data Networks
- 802.10 Network Security
- 802.11 Wireless Networks

These types of Ethernet and Fast Ethernet are designated by three-part names, such as *10BASE-T*. The first part of the name (which will be 10 or 100) designates the transmission speed. For example, 10 indicates 10Mbps Ethernet.

The second part of the name, which will be "base" for all the types of Ethernet, specifies that the Ethernet signal is a *baseband* signal. This means that the data flows in a stream in a single signal. This type of transmission cannot carry multiple channels of information as can the alternative, *broadband* (we discuss broadband technologies such as the T-Carrier system in Chapter 10, "Expanding a LAN with WAN Technology," and we look at broadband Internet connections in Chapter 12, "Connecting a Network to the Internet").

The final part of the Ethernet type name designates the kind of cable used. For example, in the type name 10BASE-T, the *T* specifies twisted-pair cable wire, and it is assumed that this is unshielded twisted-pair cable (it's also assumed that you would use Category 5 unshielded twisted-pair wire for networking—more about cabling later in the chapter). Now that we've sorted out the naming conventions, we can take a look at the Ethernet and Fast Ethernet standards available. These different varieties of Ethernet are summarized in the list that follows:

- *10BASE-T.* This type of Ethernet uses twisted-pair cable (it's *unshielded twisted pair*, or *UTP*). The maximum cable run (without any signal amplification) is 100 meters (328 feet). 10BASE-T uses a star topology.

- *10BASE-2.* This type of Ethernet uses a fairly flexible coaxial cable (RG-58A/U is its designation, and it is often referred to as *thinnet*), with a maximum cable run of 185 meters (185 is actually rounded to 200, thus the *2* in 10BASE-2). Using T-connectors (and no hubs) to connect the cabling to the computers' network cards, 10BASE-2 takes on a bus topology. Although 10BASE-2 has always been the cheapest implementation of Ethernet, 10BASE-T setups are now the norm.

- *10BASE-5.* This type of Ethernet uses a large-gauge coaxial cable (called *thicknet*), and the computers on the network are connected to a main trunk line. The cables from the computers are connected to the main trunk cable with the use of vampire tabs, which actually pierce the main trunk cable (pretty cool, huh). You won't find too many 10BASE-5 networks out there, although this type of Ethernet was popular in manufacturing environments at one time.

- *10BASE-FL.* This type of "slow" (meaning it only runs at 10Mbps) Ethernet runs over fiber-optic cable. The maximum cable run is 2,000 meters (2 kilometers).

■ *100BASE-TX*. This type of Fast Ethernet uses the same Category 5 UTP cabling found on 10BASE-T Ethernet. This implementation can also use 100-Ohm shielded twisted pair. The maximum cable distance without a repeater is 100 meters.

■ *100BASE-T4*. This type of Fast Ethernet can actually run over Category 5 cabling, as can 100BASE-TX, but it can also run over lower-grade twisted-pair cabling such as Categories 3 and 4. The maximum cable length is the standard twisted pair reach of 100 meters.

■ *100BASE-FX*. This type of Fast Ethernet runs over fiber-optic cable. The maximum cable distance with no signal enhancement is 412 meters.

You will find that many of the network cards and hubs you buy now support both 10Mbps and Fast Ethernet (the devices are switchable). Also, just about anyone putting together a new Ethernet network would use Category 5 (CAT 5) twisted-pair wiring. Most new network cards only support RJ-45 connectors—the male connector type used on twisted-pair wiring. Larger companies may use some fiber-optic cabling as a high-speed backbone between floors, but copper-base cable such as CAT 5 is still the norm.

Understanding IBM Token-Ring

IBM Token-Ring was developed by IBM in the middle 1980s with an interest in supplying a fast and reliable alternative to Ethernet. Although IBM Token-Ring (or Token-Ring as we will refer to it in this chapter) networks are wired in a star configuration, Token-Ring actually operates in a logical ring, meaning the central device that connects the computers (a *Multistation Access Unit*, or *MAU*) hosts an internal ring (more about these devices in a moment), where access to the network media is handled by possession of a token that is passed from computer to computer on the ring.

The MAU is the equivalent of the hub used in Ethernet networks. It provides the central connecting point for the computers on the LAN. MAUs, however, are more sophisticated (and expensive) than Ethernet hubs. The MAU provides the logical ring that supplies the ring topology used by the computers on the LAN as they pass the token.

Token-Ring hardware (network cards and MAUs) is generally more expensive than Ethernet hardware, but Token-Ring networks are considered more reliable in high-traffic situations because the way that computers gain access to the network medium does not produce the collisions that can take place in the Ethernet environment. Let's take a close look at the Token-Ring media-access strategy.

Token-Ring Network Access Strategy

As already mentioned, Token-Ring networks are wired in a star configuration, with a Multistation Access Unit (MAU) providing the central connection for the devices on the LAN. A MAU on a Token-Ring network is the equivalent of a hub on an Ethernet network, but the MAU is a much more sophisticated (and expensive) device. Token-Ring uses a ring topology, where data travels in only one direction. However, the actual ring on which the token is circulated is a logical ring inside of the MAU. Figure 4.2 provides a diagram of a Token-Ring network and the logical ring provided by the MAU.

FIGURE 4.2

Token-Ring LANs are wired in a star topology but operate as a ring.

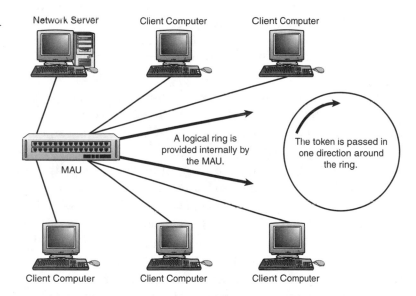

Network Server   Client Computer   Client Computer

A logical ring is provided internally by the MAU.

The token is passed in one direction around the ring.

MAU

Client Computer   Client Computer   Client Computer

Access to the network media is handled using a token. The token is passed around the ring until a computer wishing to send information out onto the network takes possession of the token.

A computer that passes the token to the next computer on the logical ring would be called the *nearest active upstream neighbor (NAUN)*. The computer receiving the token is the *nearest active downstream neighbor (NADN)*. Once a computer takes possession of the token and transmits data, it then creates a new token and passes it to its NADN. The token makes its way around the ring until a node on the network takes possession of it to transmit.

As far as receiving data on the network, data sent from a computer on the network moves around the logical ring. When the computer slated to receive the data sees the data on the ring, it accepts the data using its network interface card.

Token-Ring IEEE and Cabling Standards

The specifications for running IBM Token-Ring architecture have been defined by the IEEE and are designated as IEEE 802.5. Token-Ring, like Ethernet and the other network architectures (such as FDDI, which we discuss in the next section), operates at the OSI model's Data Link layer (covered in detail in the next chapter).

Because using a token-passing strategy means that computers can only broadcast data when they possess the token, Token-Ring is characterized by no collisions. Another plus of the Token-Ring strategy is that more-equal access to the network media is provided when compared to the strategy used by Ethernet (a device on an Ethernet network can actually dominate the network by flooding it with data). The fact that Token-Ring networks provide equal access for sending data has typically made them popular in certain industries, such as banking, because they provide a more guaranteed real-time delivery of important information (such as bank deposits and withdrawals).

Typical Token-Ring networks are slower than Ethernet (particularly Fast Ethernet). Token-Ring comes in two different flavors: a 4Mbps type and a 16Mbps type.

However, faster Token-Ring implementations are becoming a reality. IBM and other token-ring hardware vendors, such as Olicom Inc., are now making 100Mbps Token-Ring NICs. This new 100Mbps flavor of Token-Ring is referred to as High Speed Token-Ring or HSTR. Olicom also has developed a high-speed switch to complement the use of HSTR NICs on a Token-Ring network. The high-speed NICs and switches can be used on existing Token-Ring infrastructures without a change of LAN cabling.

Gigabit Token-Ring is now also available and is being used for high-speed backbones to connect Token-Ring LANs. The 1000Mbps (1000Mbps is a gigabit) throughput on the network is possible because of Gigabit Token-Ring switches that have been developed by companies such as Madge. These switches basically allow an uplink to be created between two Token-Ring LANs using fiber-optic cabling as the link backbone.

Note

Token-Ring does provide a very neat feature that allows the computers on the Token-Ring network to help diagnose problems with the logical ring. This process is called *beaconing*. When the computers on the network are first brought online, the first computer powered on is designated as the *Active Monitor*. The Active Monitor sends out a data packet every 7 seconds that travels around the ring to help determine whether any of the nodes on the network are done. For example, if a particular computer does not receive the packet from its NAUN, it creates a packet containing its address and the NAUN's address and sends the packet onto the network. This packet provides information that the Token-Ring can actually use to automatically reconfigure the ring and maintain network traffic.

As far as cabling specifications go, Token-Ring uses an entirely different system for numbering and categorizing the types of cables used for Token-Ring networks. The two most common cabling types used are referred to as *Type 1* and *Type 3*. Type 1 is a twisted-pair cable that is encased in a braided shielding (this type of cable is known as *shielded twisted pair*, or *STP*). Type 3 cable is an unshielded twisted-pair cable and is less expensive than the Type 1 shielded cable. It is limited for use on 4Mbps networks, however.

Fiber-optic cable can also be used to link Token-Ring MAUs together. Because fiber-optic cable provides for greater cable run lengths (which we will discuss shortly), connecting MAUs allows the possibility to extend the LAN over a greater physical distance. This type of cable is referred to as *Type 5*.

Although there are many more Ethernet networks worldwide than Token-Ring networks, Token-Ring is not necessarily a dying technology. New switching technologies and faster versions of Token-Ring are in the works to speed network throughput (see the information on High Speed Token-Ring earlier in this section). It is estimated that there are over 12 million computers on Token-Ring networks worldwide.

Understanding AppleTalk

AppleTalk is the networking architecture used by Apple Macintosh computers. AppleTalk is not included in the standards provided by the IEEE. The networking hardware required is already built into each Macintosh (although if you want to connect Macs to an Ethernet network, you need a Mac Ethernet NIC). The cabling system used to connect Macintosh computers is called *LocalTalk* and uses shielded twisted-pair cables with a special Macintosh adapter.

Appletalk is similar to Ethernet in that it is a passive network architecture. AppleTalk uses Carrier Sense Multiple Access with Collision Avoidance (CSMA/CA). Basically, the computers sit on the network and listen to determine whether the wire is clear. After making sure the network is clear, a computer will send a packet onto the network, letting all the other computers know that it intends to transmit data. The computer then sends out its data.

The fact that a computer that intends to send data out onto the network notifies the other network nodes as to its intentions greatly reduces the number of collisions on a CSMA/CA network (especially when compared to Ethernet).

These announcement packets, however, do have a tendency to slow down the network, and Macintosh networks only have a transmission speed of 230.4Kbps (meaning the throughput on these LANs is less than 1Mbps). The fact that the hardware and software needed to network a group of Macintosh computers comes with each

Macintosh (other than the LocalTalk cable) makes it an easy and inexpensive way to network several workstations to share a printer or to share files.

AppleTalk supplies a very sophisticated group of network protocols for moving data over the network, and we discuss the AppleTalk protocol stack in Chapter 5. AppleTalk networks are typically found in situations where only a small number of Macintosh computers are connected together so that they can share printers and other resources. New versions of the Mac, such as the iMac, come outfitted with an Ethernet network card, and because most people want to connect to the Internet, they will use the TCP/IP stack on their Mac rather than the AppleTalk stack.

Understanding FDDI

Although we have been primarily looking at network architectures that you may see on small and intermediate-sized networks (as well as some large networks), we should discuss an architecture that you would typically only see on networks of greater size. The *Fiber Distributed Data Interface (FDDI)* is an architecture that provides high-speed network backbones that can be used to connect and extend the range of LANs. FDDI uses fiber-optic cable and is wired in a ring topology. FDDI uses token passing as its media-access method and can operate at high speeds (most implementations are 100Mbps, but faster data-transfer rates are possible).

FDDI does not have an IEEE specification but rather has a designation of ANSI X3T9.5, which has been formulated by the American National Standards Institute (ANSI). Because FDDI uses a token-passing media-access strategy, it is considered reliable and provides equal access to all the computers on a network. With FDDI, however, you can set priority levels, which means you can designate that servers be allowed to send data more often over the network than client computers.

Because FDDI uses a true ring topology, there is always the potential problem of a break in the ring. To combat this problem, FDDI installations consist of two rings. Each ring passes the token in a different direction, and certain key computers are connected to both rings. Then, if there is a break in one of the rings, the data can be rerouted in the opposite direction on the other ring. Since FDDI networks are typically used as high-speed backbones connecting a wide variety of LAN types, it is extremely important that they supply a consistent connection between the LANs. This is why the redundant rings are used.

FDDI is expensive to set up because the computers require a special network card and fiber-optic cabling is also much more expensive than copper twisted-pair wire.

Because most FDDI installations use a redundant second ring, twice as much cabling is required.

Choosing a Network Connectivity Strategy

Now that we have taken a look at the commonly used LAN network architectures, let's concentrate on the different connectivity strategies that can be used to link your computers and other devices together. As you can see from our discussion of the various network architectures, the standard connectivity medium is some sort of cabling. The most popular cabling type is still copper wire. However, other technologies that make use of wireless technologies and wiring systems that are already in place (such as the telephone or electrical wiring system in a building) are also available and are becoming increasingly popular.

Let's take a look at some of the standards for network cables. Then we can look at some of the other connectivity strategies and how they are being used in different LAN settings.

Cabling Options

Network cabling consisting of copper wire has been the predominant network connectivity medium since the very beginning of the local area network. Copper-based cable transmits the data stream along the wire as an electrical signal. The discrete changes in the electrical signal on the cable distinguish the 1s and 0s in the bit stream. You already know that the network interface card (which we discussed in detail in the last chapter) has the job of taking the PC's information and getting it out onto the network medium in a format that is compatible with that particular medium (for example, electrical information is placed on copper wire, and light information is placed on fiber-optic cable).

When you are dealing with a physical medium such as copper wire (or fiber-optic cable for that matter), properties of the medium itself will affect the distance that a signal can be sent and the integrity of that signal. Some physical phenomena you should know about when working with physical cabling (and some of the wireless technologies as well) are defined in the list that follows:

- *Attenuation.* The degradation of the data signal over the run of the cable or medium (this is why different cable types have a certain maximum length that can be used).

- *Impedance.* The resistance of a wire to data transmission. All cable types have impedance that is measured in Ohms. The greater the impedance, the more energy that is required to move the signal over the wire.

■ *Interference*. Signals from other nearby devices and noise from the wire itself (some of the energy on the wire is absorbed by the wire itself) can interfere with the actual transmission signal. In cases where two wires run closely together, they can interfere with each other's signal. This is called *crosstalk*.

Copper-based network cabling takes two major forms: coaxial cable and twisted-pair cable. Although the prices for fiber-optic cable (which does not experience interference because it uses light energy rather than electrical energy) are dropping and more fiber-optic LANs are popping up all the time, copper wire is still the predominant wire type. Figure 4.3 provides a look at thinnet coaxial, thicknet coaxial, Category 5 twisted-pair cable, and fiber-optic cable, respectively.

T-connector   RJ-45 connector

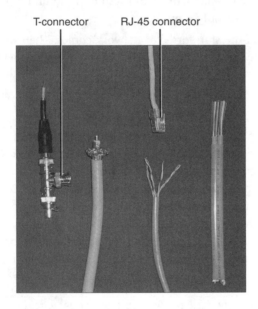

FIGURE 4.3

Copper-based and fiber-optic cables are used as the physical media for LANs.

Let's take a closer look at copper-based possibilities. We can then take a look at fiber-optic cable.

Coaxial Cable

Two types of coaxial cable are used for networking computers: thicknet and thinnet. *Thicknet* is a heavy-gauge coaxial cable that is fairly inflexible and requires special equipment (over and above a simple network card) to connect the computer to the network backbone.

Installations of thicknet (RG-8 and RG-11 coaxial cable) are dwindling but can still be found in certain settings, such as in manufacturing companies. This is because this thicker version of coaxial cable is well shielded (encased in a coating of material that looks somewhat like aluminum foil) and therefore doesn't suffer as much from interference as thinnet cable (a manufacturing environment with a lot of machinery in use can certainly produce potential interference problems when the cabling runs close to large electrical devices).

Thicknet networks are characterized by a cable backbone that is tied to servers and workstations on the network by vampire taps (the taps actually pierce the cable). Figure 4.4 provides a simple diagram of a thicknet LAN. The transceiver is actually attached to the tap (rather than the NIC, as we discussed in Chapter 3), and then the computer is connected to the transceiver/tap by a drop cable (which connects to the NIC on the computer).

FIGURE 4.4

Thicknet connects the computers on the network to a central backbone cable using vampire taps containing transceivers.

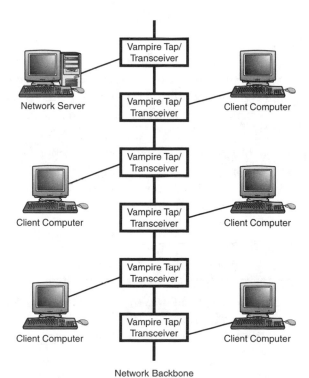

Thinnet (RG-58 coaxial cable) was the cable of choice at one time because of its relative ease of installation and its low cost. Thinnet LANs employ a bus topology, where a T-connector is attached to each computer's network card. The computers are then chained together using appropriate lengths of cable. Thinnet installations require that each end of the network be terminated, and terminators are placed on the downside T-connector of the computers that reside on either end of the network.

Although thinnet is still a very cheap way to connect a couple of computers (although it might be difficult to find network cards with the *British Naval connector*, or *BNC*, that can handle a T-connector), don't make the mistake of running out and buying some cable TV–grade coaxial. This type of cable, which is designated RG-59, is not the same grade as the RG-58 that is used for data communications. Yes, I know RG-59 cable works great for transferring data when you attach your computer to a cable modem that is connected to your cable outlet, but that's a different story. We discuss broadband Internet connections in Chapter 12.

Although it is valid for us to discuss coaxial cabling, in reality you are going to find that twisted-pair cable has all but replaced thicknet and thinnet LANs. Let's take a look twisted-pair wiring and how it works.

Twisted-Pair Wire

Twisted-pair wire comes in a number of different grades. Everyone is familiar with the twisted-pair wire used for the connection between your telephone and the phone wall outlet. Twisted pair is so named because the cable is actually made up of a number of single copper wires that are twisted together (take a look back at Figure 4.3).

Why are the pairs of wire twisted? You already know that copper wire is susceptible to interference (as discussed in an earlier Tip sidebar). Two copper wires running parallel to each other would actually interfere with each other quite a bit. Believe it or not, by twisting the wires together, the interference (or *crosstalk*) between the wires is minimized.

Twisted-pair wire comes in two major flavors: unshielded twisted pair (UTP) and shielded twisted pair (STP). The big difference between UTP and STP is that the STP wires are encased in a foil wrap that protects them from interference.

UTP is the most commonly used network wiring. It is inexpensive, flexible, and light, thus making it very easy to work with. UTP cable is terminated with an RJ-45 connector, which is kind of the big brother to the RJ-11 male connector that you find on a telephone cord.

UTP cable has been placed in different categories based on data-transmission capabilities. You will often hear UTP referred to as *CAT 3* or *CAT 5*. Table 4.1 provides a listing of these various UTP categories.

Table 4.1   Twisted Pair Categories

Category	Maximum Bandwidth Provided	Additional Information
1	None	Used in old telephone systems; this is not a data-grade cabling.
2	4Mbps	Provides enough throughput for use on LocalTalk/AppleTalk networks. Not really considered a data-grade cable, however.
3	10Mbps	Considered the minimum cable requirement for data networks running Ethernet.
4	16Mbps	Equivalent to the Type 1 Token-Ring cabling without the shielding.
5	100Mbps	Has become the standard for new LAN installations and has completely overshadowed all the previous categories.
6	1,000Mbps	Specifications have not been finalized for CAT 6. This may end up being the copper cable of choice for Gigabit Ethernet networks.

Note

Although Table 4.1 provides you with all the categories of UTP, you really only need to worry about whether to use Category 5 or maybe Category 6 for new Ethernet networks (which are by far the most common). The other categories only come into play when you are trying to take advantage of the wiring already in a building (or buildings) where you need to network computers. This is done quite frequently in situations where there isn't a big-enough budget to totally create a new wire infrastructure. I know of a small town that actually networked certain city buildings using the copper wiring in place for its outdated police callbox system.

Fiber-Optic Cable

Fiber-optic cable is a high-speed alternative to copper wire and is often employed as the backbone of larger corporate networks. However, the drop in the price of fiber-optic cable has started to make it a possibility for other LAN uses. Fiber-optic cable uses glass or plastic filaments to move data and provides greater bandwidth as well as longer cable runs (up to 2 kilometers, depending on the network architecture). With the need for network speed seemingly on the rise, fiber-optic installations are becoming commonplace.

Fiber-optic cable uses pulses of light as its data-transfer method. This means a light source is required, and lasers or light-emitting diodes are used. Fiber-optic cable is more expensive and more difficult to install than copper cable, but fiber-optic's ability to move data faster and farther makes it an excellent alternative to copper.

Copper wire can be looped, bent, and put through all kinds of gyrations and still carry an electrical signal. Just think about how tangled your vacuum cleaner cord gets when you are vacuuming; however, the vacuum cleaner keeps running. Fiber-optic cable, on the other hand, has to remain relatively straight to carry data as a light pulse. You can't bend fiber-optic cable in a 45-degree angle and you can't have kinks in it. Fiber-optic network installations require cabling professionals who understand the fragility and maximum bend of fiber-optic cabling. This is why copper cable still reigns as king (or queen, for that matter); it is easy to install and fairly forgiving when it is installed poorly.

A very interesting aspect of fiber-optic cable is that because it uses light to transfer network data, it is not susceptible to *tapping* (that is, the stealing of data off the line itself). Copper cabling, on the other hand, can be tapped because it uses an electrical signal to send data. On networks where security is an issue, fiber-optic cable provides a more secure environment.

Phone and Electrical Wire Networks

One option for connecting PCs in a small network environment, such as a home peer-to-peer network or a small business network with a limited number of computers, is to use existing phone lines. Because the data communications on the network operate at a different frequency than the phone, phone communication is not disrupted by using the phone lines for a dual purpose (phone calls and the movement of data).

There is actually an organization called the Home Phoneline Networking Alliance, which is attempting to create a standard for home networking products that use existing phone lines. Although many of the products available provide limited bandwidth, some supply 10Mbps throughput, which is as fast as the vanilla flavor of Ethernet. For example, Diamond sells a PCI Phoneline card (it looks a lot like an Ethernet PCI NIC) called the Diamond Homefree. It can be used to connect PCs at 10Mbps by attaching them to any phone jack using a cable with RJ-11 ends (the same ends you find on any phone cord). You will find that most of the phone-line products are compatible with the various Windows 9x, Me, and 2000 operating systems. Again, simple peer-to-peer networking is the aim of these products, as well as sharing a single Internet connection.

The specs for the Diamond Homefree 10Mbps PCI card claim that up to 50 PCs can be connected to a single phone-line network. This would actually make a peer-to-peer home or small office network somewhat scalable, meaning that it would be easy to add additional computers to the network. Just buy a Homefree card for them and plug them into a phone jack.

Other phone-line products take advantage of USB technology and use a small device that looks like a hub. The computers are attached to the device by a cable that runs from each computer's USB port. The hub-like device is then connected to the existing phone lines. Using USB technology makes it easy to create cross-platform networks, such as a combination of Macintoshes and Windows-based PCs that could then share the same Internet connection.

Your existing electrical lines also provide a source of wiring for connecting computers into a network. Again, a number of different companies make electrical or power-line networking products. This technology is considered to be another possibility for the home networking arena (as is phone-line technology) but could be used in some small business networking situations.

An example of a power-line networking device is the Passport Plugin made by Interlogis. It looks like a power adapter and plugs into any electrical outlet. The computer is then connected to the Passport Plugin by a serial cable. Interlogis goes one step further in that it includes a firewall with the Passport product, making it easy to protect a small network from intrusion when the shared Internet connection is either provided by a DSL or cable modem connection (firewalls are discussed in Chapter 16, "A Network Security Primer," in the section "Understanding Firewalls").

As with phoneline networking, this type of technology allows computers to share files and printers and also share a single Internet connection (which is discussed in more detail in Chapter 12). Power-line networks currently only offer bandwidth of around 350Kbps. This means that network communication is slower than some of the other alternatives (it is certainly not as fast as the phone-line alternatives).

Wireless Options

The options for creating wireless networks have seemingly exploded over the last couple years. Wireless network connections take advantage of radio signals, infrared light, or lasers. For longer distances, wireless communications can also take place through cellular telephone technology (as seen with any number of cellular devices, such as Web-ready cellular phones), through microwave transmission, or via satellite. Because the microwave and satellite technologies fall more into the realm of wide area networking, let's take a closer look at radio LAN technology and infrared technology. We will discuss cellular technology in Chapter 17, "Networking on the Run."

Radio Connectivity

Radio connectivity is used to extend the range of a LAN or make it easy for users with laptops to connect to the LAN without the use of cabling. Wireless radio LANs require that an access point be placed on the network for the computers that wish to connect to the LAN. For example, 3COM makes a wireless access point that attaches to an existing Ethernet network (Cisco also makes similar devices). It looks like a hub with an antenna on it. Computers outfitted with a wireless Ethernet card (these cards typically have a small antennae on them and otherwise operate like any other NIC using a transceiver) can connect to the access point. Figure 4.5 provides a diagram of a LAN that uses wireless technology for network access.

FIGURE 4.5

PCs outfitted with wireless network adapters connect to the LAN using a wireless access point.

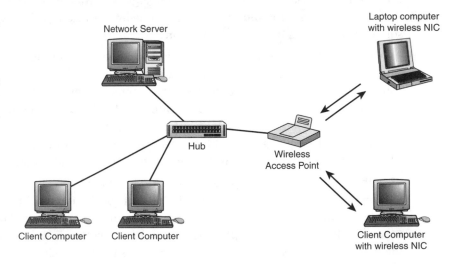

The distance that a computer can be from the access point and still connect to the LAN varies from wireless product to wireless product. The 3COM specs for its wireless access point device claim a throughput of up to 11Mbps and a maximum range of 300 feet.

Radio frequencies are regulated by the FCC in the United States. Therefore, to use most of the frequencies available in the radio wave spectrum, a license is required (for example, AM and FM radio stations must be licensed). Some frequencies, however, fall into an unregulated range. The FCC has reserved several frequency ranges for unregulated use (all measured in hertz): 902–928MHz, 2.4GHz, and 5.72–5.83GHz. Cordless phones and remote control toys have sucked up most of the 900MHz range, so wireless LAN technologies typically operate at 2.4GHz and above.

Wireless radio LANs are becoming increasingly popular in hospital settings (where nurses and doctors need to be mobile) and in business environments where a conference room must be quickly converted into a training room hosting multiple PCs connected to a LAN.

One issue related to wireless radio LANs is that it is fairly easy to intercept data. Although most radio LANs use one particular frequency, there are strategies for minimizing the possibility of data being intercepted (known as *eavesdropping*).

Some wireless communications will actually break the data up and broadcast portions on different frequencies, thus making it harder to eavesdrop. Another method of diminishing the possibility of eavesdropping is known as *frequency hopping*. This is where the transmitter and the receiver switch (or *hop*) frequencies periodically.

Infrared Connectivity

Another possibility for wireless networking is infrared. Infrared systems use very high frequencies, just below visible light in the electromagnetic spectrum, to carry data. Like visible light, infrared signals can be blocked by opaque objects. Therefore, this technology is not suitable in all situations.

Because infrared technology is fairly limited in respect to the distance that two communicating devices can be apart, it is primarily used as a way for a laptop user to connect to a printer (both devices are outfitted with an infrared eye). Infrared is also becoming a popular method of syncing up personal data assistants, such as two Palm Pilots (we discuss handheld computing devices in Chapter 18).

Chapter Summary

- Network architectures determine the physical layout of the network and the strategy used by computers to access the network medium.
- Bandwidth is the number of bits that can be sent across the network medium at a given time.
- Ethernet is the most popular network architecture.

■ Ethernet is a passive architecture and uses Carrier Sense Multiple Access with Collision Detection (CSMA/CD) as its network medium access strategy.

■ Ethernet runs at 10Mbps and is defined by the IEEE 802.3 specifications. Faster versions of Ethernet, such as Fast Ethernet and Gigabit Ethernet, are also available but require special network cards and network connectivity devices.

■ IBM Token-Ring, which is defined by IEEE 802.5, uses possession of a token (which is passed around the logical network ring) as the network medium access method.

■ AppleTalk uses Carrier Sense Multiple Access with Collision Avoidance (CSMA/CA) as its network medium access method. The hardware associated with AppleTalk is called LocalTalk.

■ The Fiber Distributed Data Interface (FDDI) is typically used as a high-speed backbone on networks and runs on fiber-optic cable.

■ The two types of cable options for network media are copper cable and fiber-optic cable.

■ Unshielded twisted-pair (UTP) cable is the cheapest and most often used cable type for new LANs.

■ Radio signals can be used to transfer data on wireless networks when an access point device is connected to the LAN and computers are outfitted with radio network cards.

■ Infrared is a wireless technology that is used to beam a signal between a laptop and a printer or to synchronize handheld personal data assistants.

5

NETWORK PROTOCOLS:
REAL AND IMAGINED

In this chapter

- Network protocols and data communication
- Understanding the OSI Conceptual Model
- The roles of the OSI layers
- Understanding real-world protocol stacks
- Networking with the TCP/IP stack and IP addresssing
- Understanding Novell's IPX/SPX network protocol stack
- Using NetBEUI on small networks
- Understanding the AppleTalk protocol stack

Any sufficiently advanced technology is indistinguishable from magic.

–Arthur C. Clarke

So far, we've taken a look at the types of networking, the hardware considerations for building a network, and the different aspects of network architectures and network connectivity media. In this chapter we will concentrate on issues related to how computers actually communicate on the network. We'll cover the theoretical side of network communication and then take a look at the different protocols that are actually being used to transfer data on a network.

"What is a protocol," you ask? Well, think about the word *protocol* itself. A protocol is really a set of rules or guidelines dictating behavior. One communication protocol that is often followed in the business world is the handshake. It typically means that a nonthreatening exchange of information can take place.

 Note

Although everyone seems comfortable with the handshake as a greeting (except for perhaps Donald Trump, who has a phobia related to shaking hands), you will also find that the term *handshake* pops up a lot in the networking world. It is often used as a term associated with different data communications strategies and refers to an agreement made between two computers to exchange data. For example, we'll talk about the three-way handshake when we discuss the Transmission Control Protocol (TCP) later in this chapter.

Also, everyone has heard of diplomatic protocol, which defines the rules of communication used when two diplomats meet to discuss various issues. In the computer world, a *protocol* provides the rules for how computers communicate. Network protocols are actually hard-wired into the programming used by the networking software you find on client and server computers.

Because data is created and saved on a computer in a particular format, that data will actually undergo some translation and modification before it can actually be sent out over the network to another computer. Again, think about diplomatic protocol; if two diplomats don't speak the same language, they use interpreters. Well, you will find that sometimes data must be translated before it can be sent over the network so that the original data arrives at the receiving computer in a format that is understandable.

So, just as communication between diplomats might have to move through several layers (in this case, translators) before a message is received, computer data must move through several intermediary layers before the data can actually be placed on the network media and then travel out over the network. This means that a number of small protocols actually are used as the data moves through these layers. A group of small protocols that work together to prepare data for the communication process is called a *protocol stack*.

A number of different protocol stacks, such as TCP/IP and SPX/IPX, can be used to communicate over the network. To understand how the protocols in the stack work together, we will look at a theoretical model that has been created to explain network communication and data transfer. The OSI model is used by network administrators, software programmers, and other Information Technology professionals to discuss the way network protocols manage the communication between computers on the network. Programmers also use this layered model to develop new protocols and tools for network communication.

Understanding the OSI Model

In the late 1970s the International Standards Organization (ISO) began to develop a conceptual model for network communications called the Open Systems Interconnection Reference Model. It is commonly known as the *OSI model*.

In 1984 the model became the international standard for network communications, providing a conceptual framework that describes network communication as a series of seven layers. In the model, each layer is responsible for a different part of the process that takes place when two computers on a network establish a connection and move data between them. Figure 5.1 shows the layers of the OSI model. Table 5.1 provides a brief description of the role of each layer.

FIGURE 5.1

The OSI model is used to describe how a protocol stack initiates and controls network communication.

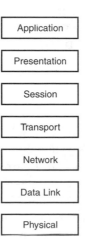

The OSI model is numbered from the bottom up. You will find, depending on what book or resource you are consulting, that the model layers are not always referred to by name. For example, the Network layer, which is the third from the bottom, is often referred to as *layer 3*.

Table 5.1 The OSI Layers

Layer Number	Layer	Function
7	Application	Provides the interface and services that support user applications and provides general access to the network
6	Presentation	Serves as the translator layer of the OSI model and is responsible for data conversion and encryption
5	Session	Establishes and maintains the communication link between the sending and receiving nodes
4	Transport	Responsible for end-to-end data transmission, flow control, error checking, and recovery
3	Network	Provides the logical addressing system used to route data on the network
2	Data Link	Responsible for the framing of data packets and the movement of the data across the physical link
1	Physical	Manages the process of sending and receiving bits over the physical network media (the wire and other physical devices)

If you are going to actually work in the computer-networking field, it is extremely important that you memorize the different layers in the OSI model and have a basic knowledge of what each layer does. A good way to remember the network layers from bottom to top is to use the following mnemonic: **P**lease **D**o **N**ot **T**hrow **S**ausage **P**izza **A**way.

How the OSI Model Works

The model actually is used to describe how data that's generated by a user, such as an e-mail message, moves through a number of intermediary forms until it is converted into a stream of data that can actually be placed on the network media and sent out over the network. The model also describes how a communication session is established between two devices, such as two computers, on the network. Because other types of devices, such as printers and routers, can be involved in network communication, devices (including computers) on the network are actually referred to as *nodes*. Therefore, a client computer on the network or a server on the network would each be referred to as a *node*.

When data is sent by a network node (for example, a computer sending an e-mail message, as already mentioned), that data moves down through the OSI stack and then is transmitted over the network media. When the data is received by a node, such as another computer on the network, it moves up through the OSI stack until it is again in a form that can be accessed by a user on that computer.

As you already saw in Table 5.1, each of the layers in the OSI model is responsible for certain aspects of getting user data into a format that can be transmitted on the network. Some layers are also for establishing and maintaining the connection between the communicating nodes, and other layers are responsible for the addressing of the data so that it can be determined where the data originated (on which node) and where the data's destination is.

An important aspect of the OSI model is that each layer is in the stack to provide services to the layer directly above it. Only the Application layer, which is at the top of the stack, would not provide services to a higher-level layer.

The process of moving user data down the OSI stack on a sending node (again, such as a computer) is called *encapsulation*. The process of moving raw data received by a node up the OSI stack is referred to as *de-encapsulation*.

To encapsulate means to enclose or surround, and this is what happens to data that is created at the Application layer and then moves down through the other layers of the OSI model. A header, which is a segment of information affixed to the beginning of the data, is generated at each layer of the OSI model, except for the Physical layer. This means that the data is encapsulated in a succession of headers—first the Application layer header, then the Presentation layer header, and so on. When the data reaches the Physical layer, it is like a candy bar that has been enclosed in several different wrappers.

When the data is transmitted to a receiving node, such as a computer, the data travels up the OSI stack and each header is stripped off of the data. First, the Data Link layer header is removed, then the Network layer header, and so on. Also, the headers are not just removed by the receiving computer; the header information is read and used to determine what the receiving computer should do with the received data at each layer of the OSI model.

It is with these headers that the sending computer is able to communicate with the receiving computer and either provide the receiving computer with information or actual instructions related to the disposition of the data at the various levels of the OSI model. Using the candy bar analogy again, the situation on the receiving computer would be like opening a candy bar enclosed in many layers of wrapping, with each individual wrapper providing important instructions on how to unwrap the candy further and eventually eat the candy bar.

Figure 5.2 provides a diagram of the encapsulation and de-encapsulation processes. The header information supplied at each layer of the OSI model by the sending computer will be used by the receiving computer as it massages the data into a format that can actually be accessed by a user on that computer.

FIGURE 5.2

Data is encapsulated on the sending computer and then de-encapsulated on the receiving computer.

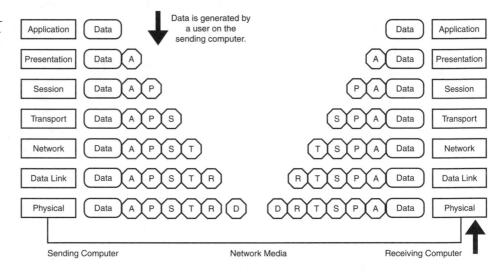

This concept of the sending computer placing messages or information in the various OSI layer headers that is then read and stripped off by the receiving computer is known as *peer communication*. Information placed in a header at a particular layer by an actual protocol operating at that layer is then read by a protocol operating at the same layer on the receiving computer.

One thing you should keep in mind as you review the different functions of the layers in the OSI model is that there are real protocols found in real network protocol stacks that actually perform the functions that we discuss in the sections that follow. Later in the chapter we will map a number of the LAN protocols in use today to the OSI model to show how the real protocol stack performs the functions that we have discussed in relation to each of the layers of the OSI model.

Now that we have some of the basic theory related to the OSI model out of the way, let's take a more detailed look at the various layers of the OSI model and how they relate to encapsulation and de-encapsulation.

Application Layer

The Application layer provides the tools that the user actually sees (but handles processes that the user does not see). Because it is at the top of the OSI model, it does not provide services to layers above it (because there are no layers above it), but it does provide network services related to user applications such as message handling, file transfer, and database queries. It also synchronizes applications between the client and server and makes sure that the resources are available for error recovery and to provide data integrity.

When a user working in a particular application, such as a spreadsheet program like Excel, decides to save a worksheet file to his home directory on the network file server, the Application layer of the OSI model provides the appropriate service that allows the file to be moved from the client machine out onto the appropriate network volume. This transaction is actually transparent to the user.

Presentation Layer

The Presentation layer can be considered the translator of the OSI model. This layer takes the data from the Application layer and converts it to a format that can be read by the Application layer of the receiving computer. The Presentation layer is also responsible for data encryption (if required by the application used in the Application layer) and data compression, which will reduce the size of the data.

You are probably already familiar with a number of the different file formats that serve as Presentation layer standards. These include standards for text, sound, graphics, and even video. Table 5.2 provides a summary of some of these file formats by standard category.

Table 5.2 Presentation Layer Standards

Data Type	Presentation Layer Standard
Text	ASCII, EBCDIC, HTML
Sound	MIDI, MPEG, WAV
Graphics	JPEG, GIF, TIFF
Video	AVI, QuickTime

So, the Presentation layer provides Application layer applications with a choice of data types for transmission over the network media. For example, if an application sends data in binary (pretty much the coin of the realm—it's recognized by every computer), no further action is required by the Presentation layer because the binary data can be read by the receiving computer. However, if the data is sent in another format, the Presentation layer will have to convert it to a more generic standard.

Session Layer

The Session layer is responsible for setting up the communication link or *session* between the sending and receiving computers. The Session layer also manages the communication session that is set up between these nodes.

The Session layer actually offers three different modes for the communication sessions set up between the network nodes: simplex, half-duplex, and full-duplex. *Simplex* transmits data in only one direction (such as your thermostat connecting to your furnace). *Half-duplex* allows for communication in two directions but only allows for the transmission of data in one direction at a time (such as a one-lane bridge). *Full-duplex* allows communication in both directions at the same time.

Another function of the Session layer is to place special checkpoints in the data stream as it moves from the sending computer to the receiving computer. These checkpoints can then be used in situations where the connection between the computers is lost. Only the data in the data stream that is found after the most recently received checkpoint will have to be resent by the sending computer.

Note | This idea of building features into software and hardware that aid in system or network communication recovery (such as the checkpoints in the Session layer) is lumped under the umbrella term *fault tolerance*. Fault tolerance simply means that some strategy is being used for quick recovery or to protect resources. For example, in terms of data fault tolerance on a network, one of the best methods is a regular backup of data (see "Backing Up Data," in Chapter 14, "Protecting Network Data").

Transport Layer

The Transport layer is in charge of flow control as the data moves from the sending to receiving node. Up to this point, we have referred to the information created by a user on a networked computer as data. When this data reaches the Transport layer, it is actually segmented into small data packages; each of these packages is referred to as a *packet*. A number of packets will make up the original data that was generated by the user (such as the e-mail message discussed earlier in the chapter).

As far as flow control is concerned at the Transport layer, the communicating computers will use acknowledgements to verify the receipt of data. These acknowledgements are sent from the destination computer to the sending computer when an agreed-upon number of data packets have been sent by the sending node. For example, the sending node might send three bursts of packets to the receiving node and then receive an acknowledgement from the receiver. The sender can then send another three bursts of data.

When packets are segmented at the Transport layer, they are sized according to the requirements of the protocols that will operate at the lower levels in the OSI model, such as the Network and Data Link layers.

The Transport layer also provides two different types of data delivery methods: connection oriented and connectionless. *Connection-oriented transport* uses a system of acknowledgements to ensure data delivery and defines a static route on the network so that the packets are delivered along the same route during the session. This is considered a reliable connection.

Connection-oriented protocols operate in much the same way that you establish communications over the telephone. You establish a session with the person you are calling. A direct connection is maintained between you and the party on the other end of the line. When the discussion concludes, both parties typically agree to end the session.

Connectionless transport at the Transport layer does not use acknowledgements or a static path for data delivery. Therefore, this is considered an unreliable method of data delivery. Connectionless transport does not require the network resources that connection-oriented communication requires, however.

Connectionless protocols operate more like the regular mail system. They provide appropriate addressing for the packets that must be sent, and then the packets are sent off much like a letter dropped in the mailbox. It is assumed that the addressing on the letter will get it to its final destination, but no acknowledgment is required from the computer that is the intended destination.

Both connection-oriented and connectionless methods of data transport are used on networks. For example, in the TCP/IP stack, the protocol TCP (Transmission Control Protocol) is used for connection-oriented transport. Another protocol in the TCP/IP stack, UDP (User Datagram Protocol), also operates at the Transport layer of the OSI model and is used for connectionless transport of data on the network. UDP requires fewer computer and network resources than TCP to move data.

Network Layer

The Network layer is charged with the duty of addressing the packets for delivery using a particular logical addressing strategy. For example, networks that use TCP/IP as their network protocol use IP addresses to address packets (every computer on the

Internet has a different IP address). Networks that use IPX/SPX (Novell's network protocol stack) use IPX addresses.

> How computers and other devices are identified on a network will depend on the network protocol that is being used. Each network protocol (as you will see later in this chapter) uses some sort of method for assigning logical (in many respects "made up") names or addresses to the various devices on the network.

The Network layer is also responsible for determining the path that packets will take as they are routed on a network from source to destination. The Network layer is where routers operate (routers were covered in Chapter 3, "Networking and PC Hardware"), using the logical addressing assigned to a packet to determine the route for that packet on the network.

Routers determine the route for packets with the help of a special kind of protocol, called a *routing protocol*. These routing protocols, such as the Routing Information Protocol (which is a protocol found at the Network layer in both the TCP/IP and IPX/SPX protocol stacks), build routing tables that are then used by the router for path determination.

Data Link Layer

We've already discussed the fact that as data on the sending computer moves down through the OSI layers, encapsulation takes place (the data is encapsulated with a header from each of the layers). At the Data Link layer, the data packet is actually placed inside a *data frame*. The frame type is defined by the type of network architecture that is being used on the network. For example, an Ethernet frame will be used on Ethernet networks, and a token-ring frame will be used on token-ring networks.

> The different frame types are actually defined by specifications devised by the IEEE (Institute of Electrical and Electronic Engineers). The IEEE also divided the Data Link layer of the OSI model into two sublayers: the Logical Link Control (LLC) layer and the Media Access Control (MAC) layer. The MAC sublayer is related to the hardware-addressing scheme that was devised by the IEEE. The LLC sublayer establishes and maintains the link between the sending and receiving computers as data moves across the network's physical media. The LLC sublayer also provides *service access points (SAPs)*, which are reference points that other computers sending information can refer to and use to communicate with the upper layers of the OSI stack on a particular receiving node.

The Data Link layer also is responsible for data movement across the actual physical link to the receiving node and therefore uniquely identifies each computer on the network based on its hardware address that is encoded into the network interface card. So that there is some mechanism for checking the validity of a frame sent over the network media, protocols that operate at the Data Link layer also will add a *cyclical redundancy check (CRC)* as a trailer on each frame (the trailer is placed at the end of the frame, whereas the header would be on the other end of the frame). The CRC is basically a mathematical calculation that takes place on the sending computer and then on the receiving computer. If the two CRCs match up, the frame was received in total and its integrity was maintained during the transfer.

Physical Layer

The duties of the Physical layer seem quite mundane, when you compare them to the rest of the OSI model. But they are certainly no less important. As the frames from the Data Link layer are passed to the Physical layer, they are converted into a single bit stream. This means that all the bits (a stream of 1s and 0s) are queued up one after another as they move out onto the network media.

The Physical layer is also responsible for the actual generation of a signal across the network media (this could be electrical, light impulses, or radio waves, depending on the type of network media the network uses). This means that the Physical layer defines the actual physical aspects of how the cabling (if actual physical cable is used) is hooked to the computer's network interface card.

Thoughts on Using a Conceptual Model

Now, having read about each of the OSI layers, you still might wonder why this conceptual model is even necessary. You will find that when we start discussing actual network protocols, many of them do not map perfectly to the various layers of the OSI model. First of all, a conceptual model for network communications is useful in that it provides a context for discussing how data is generated by a user and then moved from one computer to another on a network. Breaking the different events involved in network communication into subsets also makes it generally easier to discuss and understand the entire process.

Another good reason for using a layered model is that programmers can actually work on modular protocols that "hook" into the overall conceptual model without really having to worry about the protocols that exist above or below the layer that they are working at. They know that protocols exist at these layers that will get the job done.

For example, even though TCP/IP does not have an individual protocol in its stack that maps to each and every layer in the OSI model, programmers have used this modular concept of different layers as new TCP/IP protocols have been developed. The Hypertext Transport Protocol (HTTP) was developed by programmers who knew that protocols already existed in the TCP/IP stack that took care of the Transport, Network, and Data Link layer functionalities.

HTTP is the protocol that provides us with the ability to use Web browsers to access Web sites on the World Wide Web. Programmers designed it to plug into the protocols already available in the TCP/IP stack.

Now that we've spent some time discussing the theory and concepts of network communication, we can take a look at the protocol stacks that are actually used. We will start with TCP/IP, which, due to the Internet, has become the worldwide standard protocol stack for computer networking.

TCP/IP

The *Transmission Control Protocol/Internet Protocol (TCP/IP)* has become the common language for the networking world. It is the protocol suite (or stack) that serves as the foundation for the mega-network known as the Internet. Most network operating systems, such as Windows 2000 Server, Novell NetWare 5.x, and the many different flavors of Unix and Linux, now embrace TCP/IP as their default networking protocol.

TCP/IP was developed by the Defense Advanced Research Projects Agency (DARPA). It was originally developed as a wide area networking protocol suite that could be used to maintain communication links between sites even if certain sites became inoperable during a worldwide nuclear war; however, another underlying reason for the creation of the TCP/IP protocol stack was that the Department of Defense needed a protocol stack that could communicate across unlike networks. The unlike networks existed because the government uses a bidding system and suddenly found itself with different computer systems at various branches of the Defense Department: the army, navy, and so on. Therefore, TCP/IP is jokingly called the "protocol of low bid."

TCP/IP contains a number of "member" protocols that make up the actual TCP/IP suite. Because the TCP/IP protocol stack was developed before the completion of the OSI reference model, these protocols do not map perfectly to the various layers of the model.

The TCP/IP suite was actually developed using a different conceptual model, called the *Department of Defense (DOD)* model. The DOD model has four layers:

■ *Application layer*. This layer in the DOD stack is equivalent to the OSI Application, Presentation, and Session layers. This layer provides the user interface for the various protocols and applications that access the network, and it handles file transfer, remote logon to other nodes, e-mail functionality, and network monitoring.

■ *The Host-to-Host layer*. Equivalent to the OSI Transport layer, this layer provides flow control and connection reliability as data moves from a sending to a receiving computer. This layer takes the data from the Application layer protocols and begins the process of readying the data for movement out over the network.

■ *The Internet layer*. This layer corresponds to the OSI Network layer. It is responsible for the routing of data across logical network paths and provides an addressing system to the upper layers of the DOD stack. This layer also defines the packet format used for the data as it moves onto the network.

■ *The Network Access layer*. This layer is equivalent to the Data Link layer of the OSI model and consists of the protocols that take the packets from the Internet layer and package them in an appropriate frame type. The various frame types are described by the IEEE specifications we discussed in Chapter 4, "Building the Network Infrastructure."

We have been concentrating on the OSI model in our discussion of network protocol stacks, which is the accepted conceptual model for networking today. Figure 5.3 show some selected protocols from the TCP/IP stack mapped to the OSI layers.

FIGURE 5.3

The TCP/IP stack mapped to the OSI model.

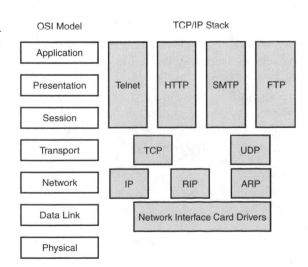

TCP/IP Protocols

A number of different protocols make up the TCP/IP stack. There are protocols that handle network access, data transport, and the logical addressing of data packets as they are routed over a network. Table 5.3 provides a brief explanation of some of the key TCP/IP protocols in the stack (including those shown in Figure 5.3).

Table 5.3 TCP/IP Protocol Stack Members

Protocol	Job
HTTP	The Hypertext Transfer Protocol defines the message format and transmission used by Web servers and Web browsers.
Telnet	The Telnet protocol is the terminal emulation protocol that allows you to connect a local computer with a remote computer or other remote device.
FTP	The File Transfer Protocol provides an interface and services for file transfer on a network.
SMTP	The Simple Mail Transport Protocol provides e-mail services on the Internet and IP networks.
TCP	The Transmission Control Protocol is a connection-oriented transport protocol.
UDP	The User Datagram Protocol is a connectionless transport protocol.
IP	The Internet Protocol is the basis for all addressing on TCP/IP networks and provides a connectionless-oriented Network layer protocol.
ARP	The Address Resolution Protocol maps IP addresses to MAC hardware addresses.
RIP	The Routing Information Protocol is a routing protocol used by routers to determine the best path for packets traveling on an internetwork.

As you can see from Table 5.3, the TCP/IP stack contains protocols that fulfill all the needs for data movement on the network as related to the OSI conceptual model. Protocols such as HTTP and FTP actually provide functions that operate at three layers of the OSI model (Application, Presentation, and Session). Although we refer to FTP as a *protocol*, it is actually a large protocol that provides a user interface and functions like a mini-application. FTP client software was used a great deal to transfer files on the Internet before HTTP became available.

Note

TCP/IP is the protocol of choice for routing data between networks. These large networks are best described as "networks of networks" (many LANs connected together) and are referred to as *internetworks*. Another term that is often used to refer to internetworks is *enterprise networks*. This describes the entire network infrastructure for a large company or institution that may be made up of multiple sites across a geographical area, a country, or even the world.

IP Addressing

Another important aspect of TCP/IP is the logical addressing scheme that TCP/IP uses at the Network layer of the OSI model. This logical addressing is provided by the IP protocol. Everyone with access to the Internet has probably run across an IP address. It takes the form of four decimal numbers separated by periods. This format is referred to as *dotted decimal*. Figure 5.4 shows the IP address for a computer running Windows 2000 Professional.

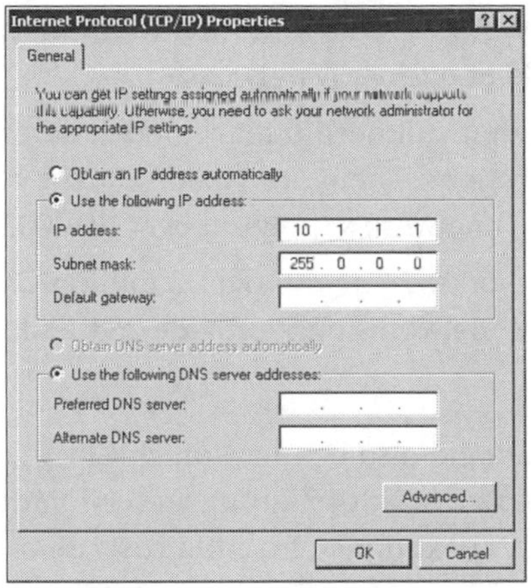

FIGURE 5.4

Each computer on a TCP/IP network needs a unique IP address.

This dotted decimal notation is actually showing us the address in a format we understand (a series of decimal numbers). Computers and other devices on the network actually see this address as a decimal stream of 32 bits. Each of the four parts of the address are referred to as an *octet*. That is because each octet contains eight bits of information (a bit being either a 1 or 0).

For example, the IP address 130.1.16.1 would be seen by devices on the network as this:

`10000010 00000001 00010000 00000001`

You can easily convert dotted decimal IP addresses to their binary equivalents using any scientific calculator, such as the Windows Calculator, that can be viewed in scientific mode. Be sure that the Dec (decimal) option button is selected and then enter the first octet's decimal number. Then select the Bin (binary) option button. Each binary number should consist of eight digits. You might have to add a leading zero or two to make up the eight positions. Repeat this procedure for each octet.

IP Address Classes

Because IP-based networks can be of varying sizes (very large, large, medium, and small), the architects of the IP addressing system set up different classes of IP addresses to accommodate different sizes of networks. Three classes of addresses for use on networks exist: Class A, B, and C. Here's more information on each class type:

- *Class A.* Used for very large networks and supplies over 16 million node addresses for the network. Due to the way IP addresses are structured, a Class A network can serve a huge number of host computers (nodes); however, there can only be 127 Class A networks. ARPAnet (built in the early days of the Internet) is an example of a Class A network.

- *Class B.* Used for networks that still need a lot of node addresses, such as for large companies and institutions. There are 16,384 Class B network addresses available, with each Class B network supplying over 65,000 host addresses.

- *Class C.* Used for small networks. There are over 2 million Class C network addresses available. Class C networks only provide 254 node addresses, however.

Two other classes of IP addresses should also be mentioned: Class D and Class E. Class D network addresses are used by multicast groups receiving data from a particular application or server service. An example of a multicast use of Class D addresses is Microsoft NetShow, which can broadcast the same content to a group of users at one time. Class E addresses belong to an experimental class, which is not available for use by folks like you and me.

You can quickly identify the class that an IP address belongs by looking at the decimal value of the first octet; each class (A, B, or C) has a specific first octet range:

- Class A (1–126)
- Class B (128–191)
- Class C (192–223)

Notice that 127 is missing from the range of numbers. It is used for special testing of the IP configuration of a computer.

The Subnet Mask

In the Old West, a cowboy was nothing without his horse. Likewise, IP addresses really don't mean anything without an accompanying subnet mask. Devices on a network need to be able to tell what part of the IP address is providing information related to which network the computer with a particular address is on and what part of the address actually refers to just the computer or node itself. This is determined by the subnet mask. Devices on the network use the subnet mask to "mask" out the portion of the IP address that refers to the network that the node sits on. If you look back at Figure 5.4, notice that a computer must be configured with both an IP address and the appropriate subnet mask.

Each class has a default subnet mask:

- Class A: 255.0.0.0
- Class B: 255.255.0.0
- Class C: 255.255.255.0

Without going into a lengthy and complex explanation of how computers and other devices use a subnet mask to determine certain information from an IP address, the default subnet masks provide some obvious visual clues. If you remember, a Class A network provides over 16 million node addresses. Also, there are only 126 Class A network addresses available.

If you look at the Class A subnet mask, you will notice that 255 only appears in the first octet. In binary, 255 would be 11111111, meaning that all eight bits are turned on. These "turned on" bits in the subnet mask actually mask out the first octet of any Class A IP address. This tells a computer that the first octet holds the network information.

Notice that all the other octets in the Class A subnet mask are 0—this would be 00000000 in binary—and would not mask out the information in the second, third, and fourth octets. This allows these octets to be used for node addresses. Each octet contains eight bits, so in a Class A network, eight bits are used to determine network information, and the other 24 bits are used for node addresses. This is why so many different possibilities are available for node addresses (again, over 16 million).

In the case of Class B networks, only the third and fourth octets are used for node addresses; this is because the first and second octets are masked out by the subnet mask and provide the network information. With only 16 bits available for node addresses, this means that Class B networks supply fewer node addresses (around 65,000).

Using this logic, you can see why Class C networks supply so few IP addresses (254). This is because only the fourth octet is reserved for node addressing, and the rest of the octets are used for network information. The subnet mask 255.255.255.0 masks out all the octets in a Class C address except for the last octet.

IP networks can be divided into subsets called *subnets*. Routers are used to connect subnets, as was discussed in Chapter 3. A mathematical process is used to take a particular range of IP addresses that have been assigned to a company and divide the class addresses into subnets. This math actually creates a new subnet mask for the network that tells nodes on the network what portion of the address refers to the network, what portion of the address refers to the subnet, and what portion of the address refers to the node. A number of Web resources are available that can teach you how to do the subnetting math. See Appendix B, "Networking Resources on the Web," for more information.

Configuring TCP/IP

You've already seen that each computer or other device, such as a router, switch, or directly connected printer, needs to be configured with a unique IP address and the appropriate subnet mask to be able to communicate on an IP network. We will discuss the ins and outs of actually configuring client and server computers running particular operating systems with different network protocols in Chapter 6, "Configuring Peer-to-Peer Networks," and Chapter 7, "Working with Network Operating Systems." Network printing is discussed in Chapter 8, "Sharing Resources on the Network."

Some other parameters are also typically configured when you set up a computer to use TCP/IP. These parameters relate to services that the computer uses to communicate correctly on the TCP/IP network:

- *Primary DNS server*. DNS or the *Domain Name Service* is used on the network to resolve fully qualified domain names (FQDNs) to IP addresses (we will discuss DNS in more detail in the section "Understanding DNS" in Chapter 11, "How the Internet Works"). Each TCP/IP network will have at least one DNS server. When computers are configured for TCP/IP, the IP address of the primary DNS server is specified in the TCP/IP settings.

- *Default gateway*. On IP networks that have been divided up into subnets, each of the subnets will use a router as its connection to the other subnets on the network. This router serves as the gateway to the other parts of the network (the "parts" being other subnets). For computers on a particular IP subnet to communicate with computers on other subnets, the IP address of the router (the *default gateway*) must be configured with the other IP settings for the networked computers.

- *WINS server*. In Microsoft networks that consisted of server and client computers running pre–Windows 2000 operating systems, computers were assigned friendly names known as *NetBIOS names*. Computers on IP networks would have to resolve NetBIOS names to IP addresses when they wanted to contact other computers on the network or move data on the network. It's not unlike matching a person's name to his Social Security number. To make a long story short, NetBIOS name resolution was initially handled by computers broadcasting requests to all the computers on the network to resolve a particular NetBIOS name to an IP address. This really cluttered the network with a lot of messages that sucked up valuable bandwidth on the network. The Windows Internet Naming Service (WINS) was developed so that a WINS server could be used to resolve these "friendly" NetBIOS names to IP addresses without the use of a lot of broadcasts. The IP address of a WINS server (if one is present on a network) can be configured as part of the IP configuration for clients and servers on the network (more about NetBIOS can be found later in this chapter in the section titled "NetBEUI").

Now, having said all this, a few words should be said about DHCP and its use to assign the parameters that we have discussed related to IP. In essence, a DHCP server can be used to supply computers on an IP network with an IP address, subnet mask, default gateway, DNS server, and WINS server automatically. On large IP networks, the use of DHCP servers can really cut down on the amount of configurations that a network administrator would have to set up to ready the computers for communication on the network. Figure 5.5 shows the IP configuration for a Windows 2000 computer that is set up to receive this information from a DHCP server.

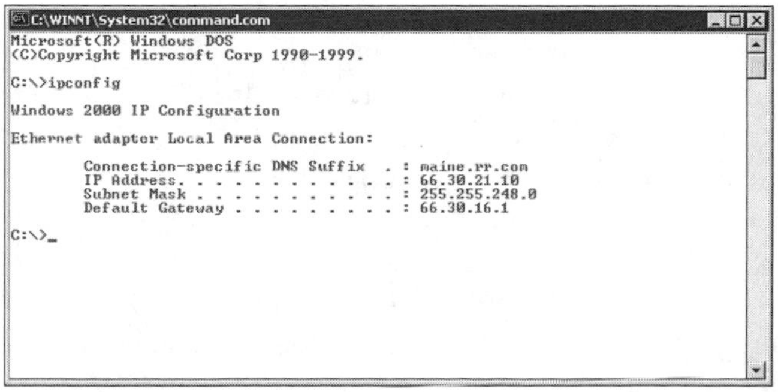

FIGURE 5.5
DHCP can be used to automatically configure IP parameters.

```
C:\WINNT\System32\command.com                                    _ □ ✕
Microsoft(R) Windows DOS
(C)Copyright Microsoft Corp 1990-1999.

C:\>ipconfig

Windows 2000 IP Configuration

Ethernet adaptor Local Area Connection:

        Connection-specific DNS Suffix  . : maine.rr.com
        IP Address. . . . . . . . . . . . : 66.30.21.10
        Subnet Mask . . . . . . . . . . . : 255.255.248.0
        Default Gateway . . . . . . . . . : 66.30.16.1

C:\>_
```

Tip

DHCP doesn't totally negate the need to configure certain computers on the network with static or fixed IP addresses (meaning you have to set up the IP parameters on the computer itself). The server running DHCP will require a fixed IP address, as will other servers, such as the DNS server.

You can see that configuring computers to run on TCP/IP networks is a pretty involved process, and all the details are certainly beyond the scope of this introductory-level book. We will, however, revisit issues related to TCP/IP networks when we discuss the Internet in Chapters 11, "How the Internet Works," and 12, "Connecting a Network to the Internet"). For now, let's move on to a discussion of some of the other network protocols.

You might be wondering, given that the number of computers connected to the Internet is growing on a daily basis, when we will run out of IP addresses. Networking professionals and engineers have also wondered this. Therefore, work is progressing on a new IP addressing system called *IP Version 6* (IPV6). We will discuss IPV6 in Chapter 19, "Future Networks: Where Is Technology Taking Us?"

IPX/SPX

IPX/SPX (which stands for *Internetwork Packet Exchange/Sequenced Packet Exchange*) is a network protocol stack developed by Novell for use on networks running the Novell NetWare network operating system. Novell NetWare is a popular network operating system (NOS) that has provided file and print server functionality to LANs since the early 1980s (we will discuss Novell NetWare in Chapter 7).

Novell NetWare was based on the XNS (Xerox Network Systems) network operating system that was created at the Xerox Palo Alto Research Center in the 1970s.

IPX/SPX, like TCP/IP, is actually a stack of protocols that perform different functions in the overall network communication process. Also like TCP/IP, IPX/SPX does not map directly on a layer-per-layer basis to the OSI conceptual model. IPX/SPX actually requires fewer resources (both from a computer and a network) than TCP/IP and therefore gained a strong foothold (as did Novell NetWare) in the early decades of the PC revolution, because computers with limited capabilities (limited in terms of the amount of memory and hard drive space, if any, on the computers) running the DOS operating system could be networked. IPX/SPX is suitable for small and large networks and is a routable network protocol suite (like TCP/IP).

As we discuss network protocols and networking in general, two terms that keep popping up are *resources* and *bandwidth*. A resource can be memory or hard drive space on a computer. The processor on a computer is also a resource in that it can only process so much information at any one time. On the network itself, bandwidth is probably the most important resource. I'm speaking of bandwidth in terms of the amount of data that can be pushed along the network media (the term *bandwidth* means something else entirely when you are discussing analog signals and their different amplitudes). Network administrators do everything they can to preserve the bandwidth on their networks. TCP/IP is generally considered more of a bandwidth hog when compared to IPX/SPX and therefore is one of the reasons why IPX/SPX was embraced early on for PC networking.

IPX/SPX Protocols

The IPX/SPX protocol stack is made up of a number of protocols that handle the various duties required for network communication on both a sending and a receiving node. Figure 5.6 shows a mapping of IPX/SPX stack protocols to the OSI conceptual model. Table 5.4 provides definitions of some of the more important protocols in the IPX/SPX stack.

FIGURE 5.6

The IPX/SPX stack mapped to the OSI model.

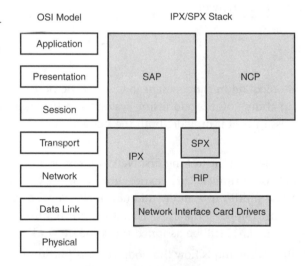

As you can see from Figure 5.6, IPX/SPX has protocols that handle the functionality of the Application, Presentation, Session, Transport, and Network layers. These protocols basically plug into the standards that operate at the Data Link layer of the OSI model and are defined by the IEEE standard discussed in Chapter 4. Novell NetWare can be used as the NOS on both Ethernet and token-ring networks.

Table 5.4 IPX/SPX Protocol Stack Members

Protocol	Job
NCP	The NetWare Core Protocol handles network functions at the Application, Presentation, and Session layers. It is responsible for providing the connection between clients and servers. It also handles packet creation when the sending of data is initiated by a computer on the network.
SAP	The Service Advertising Protocol is used by NetWare servers to announce the addresses of file and print servers on the network. This is how NetWare clients know how to find network resources.
SPX	The Sequenced Packet Exchange protocol is a connection-oriented protocol that operates at the Transport layer of the OSI model.
IPX	The Internetwork Packet Exchange protocol is a connectionless transport protocol that handles the addressing of nodes on an IPX/SPX network.
RIP	The Routing Information Protocol (the Novell flavor) is responsible for the routing of IPX/SPX packets on the network.

IPX/SPX Addressing

IPX/SPX also uses a logical addressing system to identify the nodes on the network. The IPX protocol is in charge of this addressing system. The IPX address is similar in theory to an IP address in that it provides both the network location and the actual node address of a computer.

Here's how it works: When you install the first NetWare server on the network, the server generates a network number. This hexadecimal number becomes the network number for the LAN, no matter how many additional NetWare servers (additional file and print servers) are added to the LAN. Therefore, all client machines (and additional servers) on the LAN will be assigned the same network number.

The clever part of IPX addressing is how the node address portion of the IPX address is determined. As you already know from Chapter 4, each computer has a MAC address, which is burned into a ROM chip on the NIC. The node portion of the IPX address is the MAC address of the computer (or other device).

Figure 5.7 shows an IPX address that was taken from a node on a NetWare network. The first portion of the address, as shown in the figure, is the network address, and the remainder of the address is the MAC hardware address for the device.

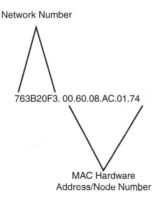

FIGURE 5.7

An IPX address is made up of a network address and a node address.

Network Number

763B20F3. 00.60.08.AC.01.74

MAC Hardware Address/Node Number

Configuring IPX/SPX

Novell NetWare is a good example of a client/server network operating system; a computer on the network either functions as a client or a server. Therefore, this means servers (such as the logon server and file and print servers) have to be configured and then clients configured so that they can access the resources provided by the various NetWare servers.

We will discuss some of the issues related to setting up and configuring NetWare servers in Chapter 7 in the section "Working with Novell NetWare." For now, I will say that actually installing the NetWare software on a server is very straightforward (as almost all network operating systems are now). However, even Novell now uses TCP/IP as the default network protocol for more recent versions of NetWare (5.x and newer), so during the installation, the IPX/SPX protocol stack must be enabled.

Configuring clients for NetWare is very straightforward because client software is included with the Novell network operating system that helps a network administrator in configuring the NetWare clients. NetWare can support DOS, Windows, Macintosh, and Unix clients. This add-on software for the client operating system sets up the computer with a NetWare logon so that users with user accounts on the NetWare server can log on to the network using their usernames and passwords.

Windows 9x, Windows Me, and Windows 2000 computers can all be configured as NetWare clients. You can use the WIN32 client setup software included with the Novell NetWare NOS, or you can configure Windows clients for a NetWare network using your Windows software. You'll learn more about configuring Windows clients for NetWare in Chapter 7.

Windows NetWare clients actually use a Microsoft clone of the IPX/SPX network protocol called *NWLink*, which stands for *NetWare link*—clever, huh?

Other Network Protocols of Note

With TCP/IP serving as the de facto network protocol and many legacy networks (another way of saying "old networks") running IPX/SPX, some very fast and clever network protocols have kind of fallen by the wayside. Let's take a look at some other network protocols that you can still use and that will certainly be found on networks running in certain environments.

NetBEUI

NetBIOS Extended User Interface (NetBEUI) is a simple and fast network protocol that was designed to be used with Microsoft's and IBM's NetBIOS (Network Basic Input Output System) protocol on small networks. *NetBIOS* is a protocol that allows computers to be identified on the network by a friendly name. Anyone who has ever set up a version of Microsoft Windows prior to the release of Windows 2000 has experienced the setting up of a computer name during the installation of the Windows software.

When you configure NetBIOS names on Windows computers, you are limited to 15 characters. With the introduction of Windows 2000, Microsoft has moved away from NetBIOS as the "friendly" naming system for computers on a network. Windows 2000 uses the *fully qualified domain name (FQDN)* as the friendly name on Windows 2000 networks. FQDNs are resolved to IP addresses by DNS servers. This shows how Microsoft has worked toward the goal of integrating internal networks with the big mega-network—the Internet.

Although it's an excellent transport protocol that doesn't require a whole lot of resources from a computer or the network to move data, NetBEUI is not a routable protocol; therefore, it cannot be used on large networks where routers are used to move data between the various segments or subnets. As far as protocol concepts go, NetBEUI operates at the Transport and Network layers of the OSI model.

NetBEUI and Its Friends

The fact that NetBEUI only provides the services needed at the Transport and Network layers of the OSI stack means that it needs help in performing all the requirements necessary for communication on the network and the movement of data. For example, it needs NetBIOS, which operates at the Session layer of the OSI stack. NetBIOS is responsible for setting up the communication session between two computers on the network.

Two other networking components that help NetBEUI along are the Redirector and the Server Message Block. The Redirector operates at the Application layer and makes a client computer see all the network resources as if they were local. The Server Message Block provides peer-to-peer communication between the Redirectors on client and network server machines. The Server Message Block operates at the Presentation layer of the OSI model. Figure 5.8 provides a look at how NetBIOS, NetBEUI, and the other components in the Microsoft networking stack map to the OSI model.

FIGURE 5.8

NetBEUI needs a little help in carrying out the various operations found in the layers of the OSI model.

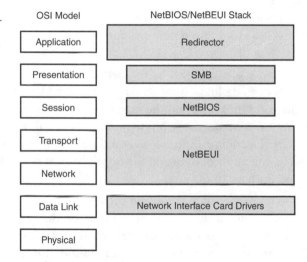

As mentioned earlier, although NetBEUI is an excellent transport protocol, it is not a routable protocol; therefore, it cannot be used on large networks (internetworks) where routing takes place. NetBEUI is fine for small, self-contained networks where a limited number of computers need to share resources. NetBEUI is very useful on peer-to-peer networks because it is extremely easy to configure on Windows-based computers (which we will look at in in the section "NetBEUI Issues" in Chapter 6).

AppleTalk

In the first decade or so of the PC revolution, the Macintosh computer definitely had a leg up on the DOS/Windows environment as far as networking was concerned because of the AppleTalk protocol stack. AppleTalk was (and still is) extremely easy to configure, and the hardware required for network connectivity (called *LocalTalk*) was built into each and every Macintosh (Mac computers, including the new iMac, still come with all the networking hardware required; however, their configuration is now slanted toward Ethernet and TCP/IP.)

AppleTalk is a routable protocol that allows large networks to be broken into logical subgroups called *zones*. A zone is a collection of certain users (which do not have to be located at the same physical location) and is similar to the concept of *workgroups* in Microsoft peer-to-peer networking (we will explore Microsoft workgroups in Chapter 6). Users in a zone typically share the same network resources, such as files and printers.

AppleTalk Addressing

AppleTalk also uses a two-part network addressing system (as does TCP/IP and IPX/SPX). This address is divided into a network portion and a node (or computer) portion.

The network number is actually specified by the network administrator. Because it is a logical addressing system, decimal numbers can be used to identify the different AppleTalk logical networks that reside on the actual physical network. For example, a logical network that takes up an entire physical network could be assigned the network number 10 by the administrator. If several different AppleTalk networks were to be assigned to one physical network, the administrator could designate them as a numerical range, such as 10–20.

Node addresses are extremely easy to configure because you don't actually configure them at all. When a Macintosh client is brought up on the AppleTalk network, it actually generates a random node number and broadcasts it out onto the network to let the other computers know that it is going to use that number. This serves as the node address for the computer. The logical network number created by the administrator (such as 10, as in the preceding example) and the random node address that is generated by the computer make up the complete network address for the computer.

If the node address generated by a computer on an AppleTalk network is already taken, the computer will generate a new node address and broadcast this to the other computers on the network.

AppleTalk and the OSI Model

The AppleTalk protocol stack is made up of a number of protocols that supply all the features required for network communication. Table 5.5 provides a list and brief definition of some of the AppleTalk protocol stack members.

Table 5.5 AppleTalk Protocol Stack Members

Protocol	Role
AppleShare	AppleShare provides services at the Application layer.
AFP	The AppleTalk Filing Protocol provides and manages file sharing on the network.
ATP	The AppleTalk Transaction Protocol works at the Transport layer and manages the connection between computers.
NBP	The Name Binding Protocol maps computer hostnames to Network layer addresses.
ZIP	The Zone Information Protocol controls AppleTalk zones and maps zone names to network addresses.
AARP	The AppleTalk Address Resolution Protocol maps logical Network layer addresses to Data Link hardware addresses.
DDP	The Datagram Delivery Protocol provides the logical addressing system for the AppleTalk network.

Note   Mac computers are now geared up to use TCP/IP as their network protocol. You can still use AppleTalk on networks that do not need to be connected to the Internet.

DLC

Before we completely end this discussion of network protocols, I should mention the *Data Link Control protocol (DLC)*. DLC was actually developed for communication between mainframes and Hewlett-Packard (HP) printers. You might run into DLC in situations where you have printers directly connected to a network (rather than connected to a computer on the network) using an HP Direct Jet box or HP Direct Jet card. Typically, printers connected using these devices will be assigned an IP address like any other node on the network.

However, if you are using HP Direct Jet–enabled printers on a network that is not using TCP/IP, you must use DLC for the printer or printers to communicate with the computers on the network. DLC can be configured on Windows-based computers. DLC is also configured on the printers using installation software that is provided with the HP Direct Jet box or card.

Chapter Summary

This chapter has provided a discussion of both conceptual network models, particularly the OSI model. We also had the opportunity to sort out the differences between different LAN protocols and how they relate to the OSI conceptual model.

- Network protocol stacks are used by computers to communicate on the network.

- The OSI model provides a conceptual model for network communication and data transfer.

- The OSI model is divided into seven layers; each layer takes care of specific duties related to network communication.

- The TCP/IP protocol stack has become the standard for computer networking because of the Internet.

- TCP/IP is actually a stack of protocols, and each protocol takes care of certain processes involved in network communication.

- The IP protocol provides the logical addressing system used on TCP/IP networks.

- An IP address is a 32-bit, four-octet address.

- Three classes of address, A, B, and C, are available for assigning addresses to TCP/IP networks. Class A is used for very large networks, Class B for medium-size networks, and Class C for small networks.

- The subnet mask that is configured on a computer along with the IP address is used by devices on the network to determine what part of the IP address is network information and what part is the actual node address.

- IPX/SPX is another routable protocol stack; it is typically used on networks running the Novell NetWare NOS.

- IPX is the protocol in the IPX/SPX protocol stack that handles the logical addressing system for the network.

- IPX addresses provide both network and node information. The network portion of the address is generated by the NetWare server, and the node address is the MAC hardware address of the computer.

- AppleTalk is a protocol stack created by Apple and used on Apple Macintosh networks. AppleTalk node addresses are created by a Macintosh computer the first time it connects to the network.

- DLC is a protocol that can be used to communicate with Hewlett-Packard printers directly connected to the network. It is used in situations where TCP/IP is not in use on the network.

PART II

GETTING THE NETWORK UP AND RUNNING

6

CONFIGURING PEER-TO-PEER NETWORKS

In this chapter

- Choosing a LAN protocol for peer-to-peer networking
- Understanding NetBIOS names
- Configuring LAN protocols on peer computers
- Sharing resources in a Windows workgroup
- Sharing files and folders in a Macintosh peer network
- Configuring Linux to share with Windows
- Getting Windows and the Apple OS to talk

To err is human but to really foul things up requires a computer.

–Anonymous

Now that we've sorted out the differences between peer-to-peer networking and server-based networking and have taken a look at the different LAN protocols, we can concentrate on how one would actually set up and configure a peer-to-peer network (we will look at server-based networks and network operating systems in the next chapter). Any LAN, no matter how simple, requires that computers be configured with the appropriate hardware and software to allow communication across some sort of network medium.

If you are in a situation where a limited number of computers need to share resources, such as files and printers, you might be able to get away with a peer-to-peer network (which we discussed in detail in Chapter 2, "Different Needs, Different Networks"). Although setting up and configuring a peer-to-peer LAN certainly does not require an in-depth understanding of a particular network operating system, it does require that you understand the peer capability of the operating system you are using on your computers. Remember that peer networks are designed for 10 PCs or less. Many operating systems, in fact, will only allow a maximum of 10 connections. This means that a computer sharing a printer or a particular folder as a resource won't allow more than 10 peers to connect to that resource at the same time.

So, in this chapter, we will take a look at choosing and configuring network protocols on a peer computer (and explore how these settings are made in some different operating systems). Then we will take a look at how you actually get the computers talking together on the peer-to-peer network.

Selecting and Configuring Network Protocols

No matter what operating system you run on your peer computers, the computers participating in the peer-to-peer network need to be configured with at least one common LAN protocol. In the Windows environment, the simplest LAN protocol to configure for a small network is NetBEUI, because once you select it as a network protocol, no other configuration is required. However, if the network also will have a connection to the Internet, computers on the peer-to-peer network have to be configured for TCP/IP.

On a Macintosh peer-to-peer network, the AppleTalk protocol is easy to set up, but again, if an Internet connection is involved, the Macs also have to be configured for TCP/IP. Let's take a look at configuring LAN protocols in the Windows environment and then we will take a look at Mac LAN protocol configuration.

Windows and LAN Protocols

All the recent flavors of Microsoft Windows (9x, NT, 2000, and Me) all handle protocol configuration in pretty much the same way. In the Windows 9x and Windows NT environments, the process is begun by right-clicking the Network Neighborhood icon on the Windows desktop. In the shortcut menu that appears, select Properties. This opens the Network dialog box. In the Windows 9x environment, protocols are managed on the Configuration tab of the Network dialog box. In the Windows NT environment, the Protocols tab of the Network dialog is used to add, remove, and configure protocols. Figure 6.1 shows the Protocols tab of the NT Network dialog box.

FIGURE 6.1

Windows 9x and Windows NT provide the tools for configuring protocols in the Network dialog box.

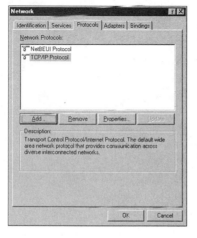

Adding a protocol to either Windows 9x or Windows NT clients is just a matter of clicking the Add button and then selecting the protocol from the list provided. Windows 2000 and Windows Me provide a similar set of steps for adding protocols, but each puts a slightly different spin on accessing the appropriate dialog box.

Note

Windows 98, Windows 2000, and Windows Me all configure TCP/IP as the default protocol. If you wish to use NetBEUI for peer-to-peer networking, you have to add the protocol.

Windows 2000 and Windows Me have replaced the familiar Network Neighborhood icon on the desktop with My Network Places. However, the dialog box where you install or configure protocols is actually only a couple of right-clicks away.

Tip

Because the Windows 2000 Professional operating system provides local security, you will have to log on to the computer as the administrator or log on with an account that is part of the Administrator group if you are going to change network settings for the computer.

Right-click My Network Places on the Windows 2000 or Me desktop and select Properties from the shortcut menu. The Network and Dial-Up Connections window will appear. In the window, right-click the Local Area Connection icon and select Properties from the shortcut menu. The Local Area Connection Properties dialog box will appear, as shown in Figure 6.2.

FIGURE 6.2

Windows 2000 and Me provide the Local Area Connection Properties dialog box for configuring protocols.

To add a new protocol, click the Install button (in Windows 9x and NT, the equivalent button is Add). The Select Network Component Type dialog box will appear, as shown in Figure 6.3.

FIGURE 6.3

Use the Select Network Component Type dialog box to add protocols and other components to the computer's network settings.

The Select Network Component Type dialog box provides you with three choices: Client, Service, and Protocol. Although this particular section covers adding and configuring protocols, let's take a moment to break down each of these components individually and then we can return to our discussion of protocols:

- *Client*. This choice allows you to select the type of client your computer will act as. In the case of peer-to-peer networking, you still have to have the Client for Microsoft Networks installed, even though you don't log on to a central server.

- *Service*. A service is an additional network feature such as File and Printer Sharing for Microsoft Networks or SAP Agent. Because file and printer sharing is very important in peer-to-peer networking, this service will need to be installed (which we do in the next section). The SAP Agent is related to SAP broadcasts on a NetWare network (SAP was covered in Chapter 5, "Network Protocols: Real and Imagined").

- *Protocol*. In a nutshell, protocols are the languages used for network communication between computers and other devices. As already mentioned, there must be a common protocol for the computers in a peer-to-peer network to communicate. Now, let's get back to the installation of a protocol in the Windows environment.

To add a protocol to the computer's configuration, click Protocol in the Select Network Component Type dialog box and then click Add. The Select Network Protocol dialog box will open, as shown in Figure 6.4.

FIGURE 6.4

Select a protocol to add to the computer's configuration.

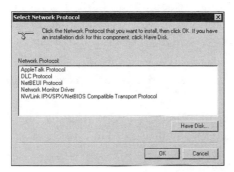

Select the protocol you wish to add and then click the OK button. The protocol will be added to the protocol list in the Local Area Connections dialog box. For your peer-to-peer network, you can use TCP/IP, NWLink (the Microsoft flavor of IPX/SPX), or NetBEUI.

You can actually use any of these protocols for your peer-to-peer networking. The most common choices, however, are typically TCP/IP and NetBEUI, although NWLink and IPX/SPX can also be used. Let's take a closer look at the configuration issues related to TCP/IP and NetBEUI.

TCP/IP Issues

TCP/IP is added to the network configuration of Windows 9x, NT, 2000, and Me by default. The TCP/IP settings are also configured on these Windows operating systems so that the IP address, subnet mask, and other TCP/IP settings, such as the default gateway and primary DNS server, are received automatically from a network DHCP server.

If you are putting together a peer-to-peer network where the computers are also connected to the Internet (through a DSL or cable modem connection), you can leave TCP/IP settings so that all the IP settings are configured by your Internet service provider's DHCP server. If you have multiple computers connected to the Internet (for example, using a DSL router or a cable modem), your Internet service provider will provide IP addresses in a particular range to the computers in your peer network. So the computers should be able to use TCP/IP to communicate locally as well. (We will discuss connecting multiple computers to a single Internet connection in Chapter 12, "Connecting a Network to the Internet," in the section "Sharing an Internet Connection.")

In cases where you are connecting your peer-to-peer network to the Internet using a single connection (discussed in Chapter 12) or are not going to connect the peer network to the Internet at all but still insist on using TCP/IP as your network protocol (NetBEUI would be a better choice in cases where no Internet connection is involved), you have two choices for coming up with the IP addresses for your computers:

- You can allow Windows 2000 or Windows Me to configure itself automatically.
- You can configure the computers' TCP/IP settings manually (which is something you will have to do if you are using Windows 9x or Windows NT Workstation computers on your peer-to-peer network).

Windows 2000 Professional and Windows Me both provide a new feature related to IP addresses called *Automatic Private IP Addressing (APIPA)*. Because Windows 2000 and Me are automatically configured to get their IP information (such as address and subnet mask) from a DHCP server, they will try to contact a local DHCP server. When they don't find one (because you wouldn't be running one on your peer-to-peer network), the APIPA kicks in and the computer assigns itself an IP address from the range 169.254.0.1 through 169.254.255.254 (Microsoft's private range of addresses, which are not used on the Internet) and a subnet mask of 255.255.0.0. Because the computers all end up with addresses in the same Class B range, they don't have any trouble communicating with each other using the TCP/IP protocol.

Now let's look at what you would do if you insist on statically configuring the computers with IP addresses. Because a peer-to-peer network won't have any specialized servers such as a DNS server (it won't have any servers at all), you won't have to configure any of the IP settings other than the IP address and the subnet mask. The question is, what should the range of IP addresses be and which subnet mask should you use for the computers in the peer-to-peer network?

The answer is pretty straightforward: Three ranges of IP addresses have been reserved to use for "private" addressing. These ranges of addresses have not been assigned to computers on the Internet, so if you use IP addresses in one of these ranges, your addresses will not potentially conflict with IP addresses already assigned to computers on the Net.

There is a range of addresses reserved in each of the three classes: Class A, Class B, and Class C. These ranges and the subnet mask you would use with each range are shown in Table 6.1.

Table 6.1   Private IP Address Ranges

Class	Address Range	Subnet Mask
A	10.0.0.1 to 10.255.255.254	255.0.0.0
B	172.16.0.1 to 172.31.255.254	255.255.0.0
C	192.168.0.1 to 192.168.255.254	255.255.255.0

Obviously, the Class A range gives you a very large number of available addresses (it's pretty much overkill for a peer-to-peer network), but you can set up your small peer-to-peer network as a Class A network if you like. You need to limit yourself to one class of private addresses, however, if you want the computers to talk to each other.

To manually configure the IP address and subnet mask, select Internet Protocol (TCP/IP) in the Local Area Connection Properties dialog box (or the Network dialog box of Windows 9x and NT clients) and then click the Properties button. Figure 6.5 shows the Internet Protocol (TCP/IP) Properties dialog box that opens.

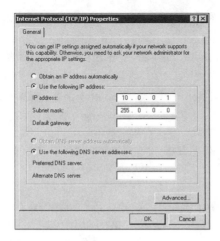

In the Internet Protocol (TCP/IP) Properties dialog box, click the Use the Following IP
Address option button and then enter the IP address and the subnet mask for the
computer. Then all you have to do is click OK and close the various open dialog
boxes. Some Windows clients will require that you restart the system for the new
networking configuration to take effect.

NetBEUI Issues

NetBEUI is probably the perfect protocol for peer-to-peer networks, as long as the
computers aren't going to be connected to the Internet. It's perfect in the respect that
you only have to install it as part of your Windows network setup; it doesn't require
any further configuration.

NetBEUI uses NetBIOS names as the computer identification system on the network.
The NetBIOS name is actually the friendly name that you assign to the computer
when you actually install the Windows OS on the machine.

Now, you are probably thinking that, with Windows 2000, the name you give the
computer is actually going to part of the fully qualified domain name (FQDN) for
the computer—and this is true because the Windows 2000 Professional operating
system was built with larger TCP/IP networks in mind, where there would be a DNS
server providing FQDN-to–IP address resolution. FQDN names (the client portion)
can be up to 63 characters. However, if you are going to use NetBEUI as your primary network protocol, you need to create computer names that are 15 characters
or less. This is the limit for NetBIOS names.

Windows 9x and Windows NT clients still use the NetBIOS naming standard for the
computer's friendly name, as does Windows Me. The one thing that you have to
remember, however, is that each computer needs to have a unique NetBIOS name,

because the name is serving to identify each of the computers on the NetBEUI network.

Therefore, if you set up several standalone computers and happen to give them the same computer name, you will need to change these to unique names before you string the computers together in your peer-to-peer network. This use of unique names for computers will also spill over into the names you use for your workgroups (discussed in a moment) and shared folders. This means that computers, workgroups, printers, and shared folders all need to be assigned unique names for the peer-to-peer network to operate correctly.

Even in situations where you will use TCP/IP as your network protocol, you may still want to limit the computers' friendly names to 15 characters or less. That way, if you attach a computer running an earlier version of Windows (such as 9x or even the ancient Windows for Workgroups), all the clients will be able to find resources on the network. Also, if you want to fall back to another LAN protocol, such as NetBEUI or NWLink, the computer names will already be configured for these other protocols.

You can easily change the computer's name in any of the Windows operating systems. For example, on a Windows 2000 Professional computer, right-click the My Computer icon and then select Properties. This opens the System Properties dialog box. Then all you have to do is select the Network Identification tab. To actually change the name of the computer, click the Properties button. The Identification Changes dialog box will open, as shown in Figure 6.6.

FIGURE 6.6

Computer names can easily be changed in any of the various flavors of Windows.

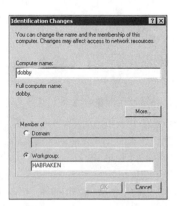

You can edit the name in the Computer Name field. After you complete the name change, the computer will need to be rebooted for the changes to take effect.

Now, with the understanding that we still need to look at Microsoft's version of the peer-to-peer network—the workgroup—and look at Windows File and Printer Sharing, let's take a quick look at how LAN protocols are configured in the Macintosh realm.

The Mac and LAN Protocols

The Macintosh OS makes it extremely easy to configure AppleTalk as the LAN protocol for a Mac peer-to-peer network. In fact, the AppleTalk protocol is installed by default on your Macintosh computers. AppleTalk is a much more complex protocol stack than NetBEUI, but it pretty much configures itself as NetBEUI does.

If you are using a Mac with a built-in Ethernet connection, the OS provides an Ethernet extension that allows AppleTalk to be used over a regular twisted-pair network outfitted with a hub. You can check to be sure that the Ethernet extension has been added to the AppleTalk configuration by checking the AppleTalk control panel.

To open the AppleTalk control panel, use the Apple menu to open the System Folder. Then open the Control Panels subfolder. You should find a icon in the Control Panels subfolder that you can use to open the AppleTalk control panel. Once you have the AppleTalk control panel open, just click the Connect Via drop-down list in the AppleTalk control panel and be sure that Ethernet is selected in the list.

Because you will be using AppleTalk to communicate to any printers that you have connected to your computers, it makes sense to go ahead and use AppleTalk as the LAN protocol for your peer-to-peer network. However, if you really insist, you can configure the computers with TCP/IP and assign IP addresses and subnet masks to each Mac that will be connected to the peer network.

To configure the Macs with IP addresses (and again, this is a Mac network that is not connected to the Internet), you can use any of the range of IP addresses discussed earlier in this chapter in the section "TCP/IP Issues." TCP/IP settings on the Mac are configured in the TCP/IP control panel. You must be sure that you configure each Mac with a different IP address and the appropriate class subnet mask (again, as discussed in this chapter in the "TCP/IP Issues" section).

Setting Up the Peer-to-Peer Network

Once you have the peer computers configured with a LAN protocol, you are ready to actually set up the peer network itself. This means that you need to physically connect the computers with some sort of network medium. Both Windows and the Mac OS allow you to directly connect two computers with a cable (we're talking a very small peer-to-peer network). The Windows computers would be directly connected using a serial cable that attaches to the computers' serial or communications ports. Beginning with the second release of Windows 98, the Windows OS provides you with the ability to configure this direct connection between the computers.

On the Macintosh side, you can use a standard Mac printer cable to connect the two computers. Alternatively, if the Macs have a built-in Ethernet RJ-45 interface (meaning they have a built-in Ethernet card), you can connect the computers with a special twisted-pair cable called a *crossover cable*. You can buy a crossover cable at just about any computer store.

> You can also use a crossover cable to connect two Windows-based computers that are outfitted with Ethernet cards. The crossover cable negates the need for a hub. If you want to try and make your own crossover cable, check out the GCC Web site at www.gcctech.com/ts/doc/crossover.html.

Let's assume, however, that your peer-to-peer network consists of several computers that have been connected using twisted-pair cabling and a hub (as we already discussed in Chapter 4, "Building the Network Infrastructure"). Now, we can take a look at how resources such as drives, folders, and printers are actually shared on the peer network in both the Windows and Mac environments.

Windows Workgroups and File and Printer Sharing

You need to configure two items in the Windows environment for the peer-to-peer network to work: a workgroup and Windows File and Printer Sharing (actually, you will also need to share folders and printers, which we will discuss in a moment). A *workgroup* is really just a logical grouping of computers that have been configured with the same workgroup name.

Specifying the name of the workgroup that a computer belongs to is configured on a Windows computer on the same dialog box tab that is used to specify the computer's name. For example, Windows 2000 Professional provides the Identification Changes dialog box (which is reached via the Properties button on the System Properties dialog box). Refer back to Figure 6.6 to check out this dialog box.

Windows Me can also be configured as shown in Figure 6.6 or you can get some help from a wizard. Windows Me actually provides the Home Networking Wizard to walk you through the process of creating a workgroup and sharing files and printers. The wizard is started in My Network Places, and it allows you to select the name of the workgroup that you will create, as shown in Figure 6.7. It also gives you the opportunity to assign the computer a unique "friendly" name.

> The Windows Me Home Networking Wizard can also create a home networking disk that you can use to quickly configure any Windows 95 and Windows 98 computers that you want to include in the workgroup created on the Windows Me computer using the Home Networking Wizard.

Once you have all the computers configured as part of the same workgroup, you need to be sure that File and Printer Sharing is turned on. File and Printer Sharing is a service that is added to the computer's networking configuration. It should appear in the list of protocols and services in either the Windows Network dialog box (for Windows 9x, as shown in Figure 6.8) or in the Local Areas Connection dialog box in the Windows 2000 and Me environments.

FIGURE 6.7

Windows Me provides a wizard for setting up a workgroup network.

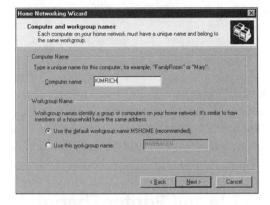

FIGURE 6.8

The Windows File and Printer Sharing service must be configured to share resources on the peer-to-peer network.

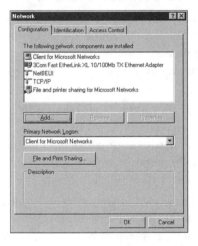

Windows Folder and Printer Sharing

Actually sharing folders and printers in the Windows environment is extremely straightforward (we look at sharing folders and drives on a server-based network in "Sharing Folders and Drives" in Chapter 8, "Sharing Resources on the Network"). In both cases, it's just a matter of right-clicking the folder or printer that you want to share.

In the case of folders, use Windows Explorer to locate the folder that you want to share with the other computers in the workgroup. Then right-click the folder and select Sharing. The Sharing dialog box will open. To share the folder, click the Share

This Folder option button. You can then specify a name for the *share*, which is what you call the shared folder. Figure 6.9 shows the Sharing tab of the Properties dialog box on a Windows Me computer.

FIGURE 6.9

Use the Sharing tab on the Properties dialog box to share the folder.

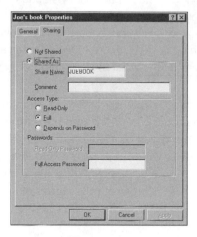

You can also specify a password and the access level for the folder (such as Read Only or Full). If you are using Windows 2000 Professional (or NT Workstation), you can actually set access levels based on local groups that you create on the computer.

In terms of printers, sharing is just as easy as sharing a folder. Open the Printers dialog box (in most flavors of Windows, click Start, point at Settings, and then select Printers). In the Printers dialog box, right-click any installed printer and select Sharing. The printer's Properties dialog box will open. Just click the Shared As option button and then specify a name for the printer. Windows 2000 Professional, as shown in Figure 6.10, even provides you with the ability to add drivers to the printer's configuration for down-level versions of Windows (such as Windows 95 and Windows 98).

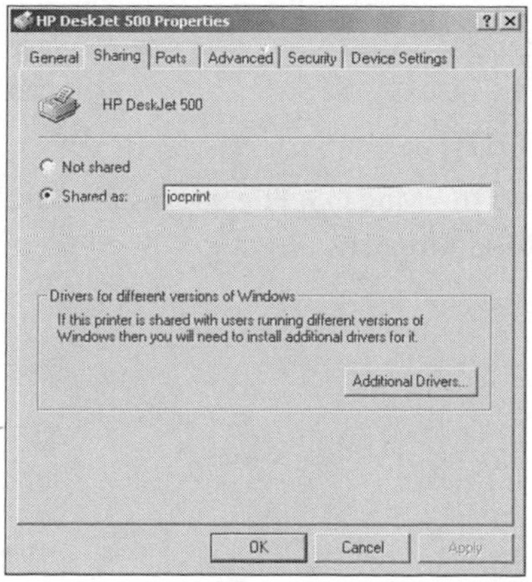

FIGURE 6.10

Printers are shared in the printer's Properties dialog box.

> **Warning**
>
> Windows NT Workstation and Windows 2000 Professional both provide local security. This means a local user has to have an account to log on to the computer. This also means that, in a peer-to-peer networking environment, users that will connect to resources provided by a Windows NT Workstation or Windows 2000 Professional peer computer will need to have an account on that computer. This gives them the permission to access the resource. For example, if Joe connects from a Windows Me peer computer to a resource such as a share on a Windows 2000 Professional computer, there will need to be a "Joe" account on the Windows 2000 Professional computer.

Once the shares and printers are available for the workgroup, the various users can access these resources. Workgroup member computers and the shares that they offer can be accessed using Network Neighborhood or My Network Places (depending on the version of Windows). Shared printers will also appear along with the shared folders and can be quickly connected to. Figure 6.11 shows a printer connection being created on a Windows Me computer that is browsing the shares of a peer called Zardoz.

FIGURE 6.11

Shares and printers can be accessed using My Network Places in Windows Me.

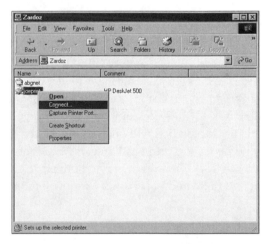

Macintosh File and Printer Sharing

File and printer sharing is built into the Mac OS. File sharing is configured in the File Sharing control panel, as shown in Figure 6.12.

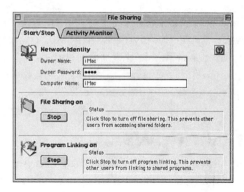

This control panel allows you to specify the network identity for the computer, including the owner's name, a password to protect resources (if you feel it's necessary in a peer-to-peer environment), and the name of the computer. To turn on file sharing, click Start in the File Sharing dialog box.

To share a file, folder, or drive, select the item on the desktop. Then access the File menu and select Sharing. A window displaying the sharing configuration of that particular file, folder, or drive will appear. To share the item, click Share This Item and Its Contents. Figure 6.13 shows the sharing info for a folder.

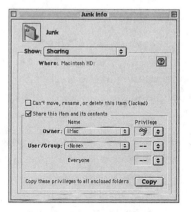

Privileges, such as Read Only and Read and Write, can be set for the resource, and groups can be created using the User/Group drop-down list, which allows you to assign privileges by user (as opposed to by resource, which is handled to the right of the Owner drop-down list).

Shared folders on the peer-to-peer network are accessed using the Chooser. All computers connected to the peer-to-peer network will appear in the Chooser when the AppleShare icon is selected.

Printer sharing on a Mac peer-to-peer network is extremely easy to configure. This is because you really don't have to configure anything. Any Mac-compatible printer with a LocalTalk or Ethernet port connected to the peer network will basically serve as its own print station, announcing its existence to all Macs on the network, and can be found by any of the peer Macs using the Chooser.

Combining Linux and Windows

Because peer-to-peer networks provide a way to connect a few computers together on "the cheap," we should also take a quick look at how Linux can fit into a Windows peer network. Linux is becoming an inexpensive alternative to other desktop operating systems (and also in the network operating system arena). This is particularly due to the fact that a number of Linux flavors can actually be downloaded from the Internet for free.

Linux-based computers can be made a part of a Windows workgroup by configuring an add-on program on the Linux computers called *Samba*. Samba derives its name from SMB or Server Message Block. SMB is an important part of the NetBIOS/NetBEUI protocol stack (which we discussed in Chapter 5) and supplies the data blocks that make requests between client and server or between peers on a Microsoft network.

Samba is able to simulate the operation of SMB and also provide NetBIOS over IP (TCP/IP being the protocol stack for Linux), which means that a Linux computer can actually pretend to be a Windows client. This means the Linux machine can share folders and printers or access folders and printers in the workgroup. Let's take a quick look at how Samba would be configured on a Linux computer, with the understanding that this is certainly not an exhaustive treatise on Linux or Samba.

 Note   Samba is actually made up of a suite of programs. For example, smbd is the Samba daemon that handles the SMB services. Another program, nmbd, handles the NetBIOS name issues.

Linux and Samba are not quite as user friendly as Windows and the Mac OS, but some recent improvements, particularly dealing with Samba, have made it less difficult to work with. A new tool called *SWAT (Samba Web Administration Tool)* allows you to configure Samba from any Web browser.

You will have to be sure Samba is installed as part of your current Linux configuration. Samba seems to be included as part of many Linux flavors, particularly if you purchased the product. If you download your version of Linux, you might also have to download and install the most recent version of Samba. Information related to

Samba and links for downloading the recent release of Samba can be found at `http://us1.samba.org/samba/samba.html`.

Once you get your particular flavor of Linux up and running and have Samba installed, all you need to do is open a Web browser window. Samba has been configured by default so that you can open the SWAT program in your Web browser by typing `http://localhost:901/` and pressing Enter. The number 901 is actually a port number that allows a TCP connection between Samba and your Web browser (the port number and the IP address provide the socket used as the communication avenue between TCP and HTTP on the Web browser). Figure 6.14 shows the Samba SWAT program running in Netscape Navigator on the Linux desktop (the desktop is provided by KDE because Linux itself is a command-line environment).

FIGURE 6.14

The SWAT program allows you to configure Samba from a Web browser.

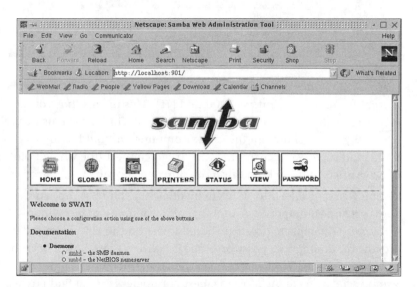

Once SWAT is up and running, you need to configure Samba so that it allows the Linux computer to communicate in the Windows workgroup. This is accomplished using the Samba Globals settings, which is reached by clicking Globals in the browser window.

The two most important settings in the Globals configuration is the name of the workgroup that the computer will belong to and how Windows peers trying to access shares on the Linux box will be validated. Figure 6.15 shows that the workgroup name has been configured for the computer.

FIGURE 6.15

Samba must be configured with the Windows workgroup name.

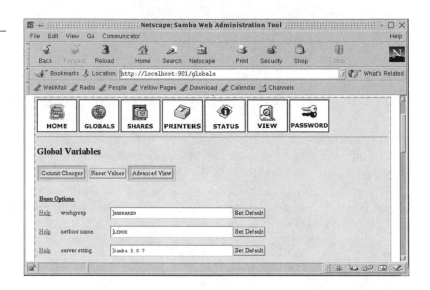

Linux actually has a lot more robust security than most of the flavors of Windows (except for perhaps Windows 2000 and NT). This means that you need some sort of mechanism that will dilute the security so that Windows clients in the workgroup can easily access shares on the Linux computer without having to provide a user-name and a password each time they try to connect (the whole point of peer-to-peer networking is to try to keep things as simple as possible).

Samba weakens the Linux security by allowing you to set up a guest account. The guest account is mapped to automatically when one of the Windows peers in the workgroup attempts to access a shared folder on the Linux computer but doesn't provide an appropriate password (this is because there hasn't been a user account established for the Windows user on the Linux machine). Figure 6.16 shows the Samba screen where the Map to Guest parameter is set to Bad Password and the guest account is specified.

For Samba to map incoming connections to the guest account, the guest account has to be created on the Linux computer (this is done using the administrator's root account). The guest account must also have access to the folders that you will share on the Linux box.

Shares are also created using SWAT. Directories on the Linux computer are mapped to a share name. This is done using the Shares screen (accessed by clicking Shares in the Web browser window). The Shares screen also allows you to set security options related to a particular share by specifying that the share is read or write. Access to specific hosts in the workgroup can also be allowed or denied using this screen.

FIGURE 6.16

Windows users accessing resources on the Linux box are automatically mapped to a guest account.

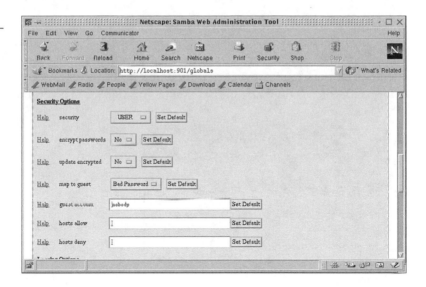

Once Samba is completely configured using the SWAT interface and the smbd and nmbd services are started using the Status screen of the SWAT utility, the Linux computer is ready to participate in the Windows workgroup. For example, Figure 6.17 shows the KDE Explorer (which is similar to the Windows Explorer) on a Linux computer where Samba has been activated and the Network Neighborhood is being browsed. The figure shows the Linux computer (Linux) and three Windows peers in a workgroup called Habraken.

FIGURE 6.17

Linux desktop navigation tools such as the KDE Explorer can be used to access the computers in the Windows workgroup.

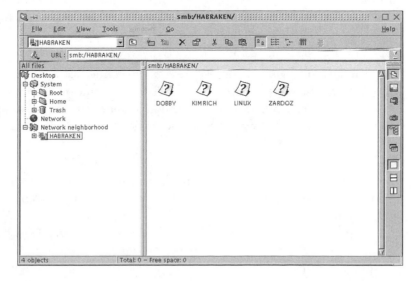

Likewise, when Windows computers use the Network Neighborhood or the My Network Places window to browse computers and resources in a workgroup, the Linux computer will appear as a member of the workgroup. Figure 6.18 shows the Windows network browser window showing the members of a workgroup named Habraken, which includes a Linux computer running Samba version 2.07.

FIGURE 6.18

Windows peers can access resources on the Linux computer running Samba.

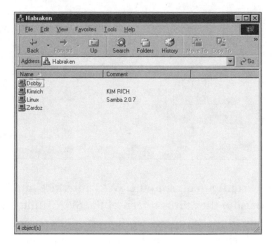

A Final Word on Peer-to-Peer Networking

Peer-to-peer networking is a pretty cost-effective way to hook up a few computers and share resources such as printers and files. What's more, there are products that allow you to connect computers running different operating systems together into the same peer environment. For example, we've already discussed Samba as a possibility for including Linux computers in a Windows workgroup.

Other products are available that you can use to connect computers running different operating systems. For example, Thursby Software makes a product called Dave, which allows you to connect Windows and Mac computers in the same workgroup. You can check out Dave and other products made for Mac-to-PC communication at www.thursby.com/.

Remember, however, before you start to develop grandiose plans for connecting a number of different operating systems into some giant peer-to-peer network that peer networks are meant to be kept small. If you have more than 5 to 10 clients, network performance will suffer greatly, as will individual computer performance, as all those peers begin to access resources on the various computers. Plus, peer-to-peer networking is supposed to be a cheap way to connect a few computers. Buying extra software to get different operating systems to talk to each other might start to approach the cost of what you would spend on a network operating system.

Therefore, if you find you need to connect computers running various operating systems and think your network might grow in the future, you're better off buying a server and a network operating system that will support the different client types and provide you with the ability to centrally manage the network.

Chapter Summary

In this chapter we sorted out the possibilities for peer-to-peer networking and looked at configuring TCP/IP and NetBEUI as the LAN protocols for our peer network. Peer-to-peer networking works best in situations where there are less than 10 computers. Other things that you learned in this chapter include the following:

- NetBEUI is the easiest LAN protocol to configure for a Windows peer-to-peer network.

- TCP/IP can also be used to connect Windows peer computers. Ranges of addresses in each IP class have been reserved for private networking.

- AppleTalk is installed by default on Macintosh computers and provides an easy-to-configure LAN environment.

- Windows workgroups identify the peer members by their computer names.

- Windows drives and folders can be shared by right-clicking the resource in Windows Explorer and selecting Sharing from the shortcut menu.

- Windows printers are shared in the Printers window by right-clicking a specific printer and selecting Sharing from the shortcut menu.

- Items selected on the Macintosh desktop can be shared by clicking the File menu and then clicking Sharing.

- Computers sharing resources on a Macintosh peer-to-peer network can be located in the Chooser when AppleShare is selected.

- Linux computers can be configured with Samba so that they can be part of a Windows workgroup.

- Other software products, such as Dave, allow you to connect Macintosh and Windows computers in the same workgroup.

WORKING WITH NETWORK OPERATING SYSTEMS

In this chapter

- Introducing network operating systems
- Understanding how client computers communicate with the server
- Matching client and server LAN protocols
- Understanding client and server licensing
- Installing a network operating system
- Working with Windows 2000 Server
- Working with Novell NetWare
- Considering Unix and Linux

Technology makes it possible for people to gain control over everything, except over technology.

–John Tudor

In this chapter, we take a look at the network operating system (NOS). Chapter 2, "Different Needs, Different Networks," discussed the major differences between peer-to-peer networking and server-based networking. One of the major advantages of server-based networking is the fact that this networking model provides centralized control of networking resources, such as files and printers. User access to the network is also centrally controlled on server-based networks.

It is actually the network operating system running on the server that supplies the network administrator with the ability to centrally control network resources and network users. Let's take a closer look at what an NOS is, and then we can take a specific look at some network operating systems such as Microsoft Windows Server and Novell NetWare.

What Is an NOS?

A *network operating system* is software that imparts special capabilities to a computer. These capabilities revolve around the fact that the configuration of the computer with an NOS makes that computer a *server* (a server being a computer that can "serve up" resources to computers requesting them). The NOS, in effect, makes the server the control center for all requests made by client computers as they attempt to access resources on the LAN.

Network operating systems come in two basic flavors: network operating systems that function as complete operating systems, such as the Microsoft Windows 2000 Server, and network operating systems that are added on top of an existing OS. For example, the Novell NetWare NOS is added to a computer that runs the DOS operating system.

Network operating systems have changed a great deal in the last 15 years. Early NOS platforms were basically designed to supply file and print services to users. This meant that deploying other server types, such as Web servers and application servers, meant you had to place a number of single-service servers on the network.

NOS software has become much more sophisticated and now supplies multiple services—one server might supply remote access and Web services and even serve as a router between two different IP subnets on a network. The NOS interface has also become somewhat more network administrator friendly.

For example, many of the NOS platforms now available, such as the popular Windows 2000 Server and Novell NetWare 5.1, provide a number of additional services over and above file and print services. These services include remote access and Web site management (remote access is discussed in Chapter 17, "Networking on the Run," and managing Web sites is discussed in Chapter 13, "Hosting a Web Site").

The NOS utilities used to manage the servers also provide a graphical user interface (GUI) rather than a command-line format, making it easier to configure and monitor the network.

Many NOS platforms also now provide utilities for monitoring server hardware resources and network traffic. In the past, having any decent monitoring capabilities meant you had to buy additional monitoring software. We discuss the use of these types of utilities in Chapter 15, "Network Troubleshooting."

Therefore, it is the NOS that ties computers and peripherals into a LAN by creating a server computer, which provides the communications center for the network. Let's take a closer look at how the operating system on a network client computer talks to the NOS on the network server.

Client and NOS Interaction

If the NOS makes a computer a server, what makes a computer a network client? For communication to take place between a network client and the network server, client computers must also be outfitted with software that "tunes" them to the network. This software is aptly called *network client software*.

When a standalone computer accesses a file on the local hard drive or prints to a directly connected local printer, this request for service goes to the computer's processor. The processor then makes this request a reality and either opens the specified file or sends a print job to the printer. All this activity is managed locally.

So, how do computers that are designed to access resources locally suddenly become able to access shares on a file server or print to a remote printer on a print server? The network client software that is installed on the client computer actually performs a little "bait and switch" operation that makes the computer think the network resource is still just a local resource.

This process is handled by a part of the network client software called the *redirector*. The redirector intercepts any requests made on the computer, such as a request to open a particular file or to print to a printer. If the redirector finds that the user wants to access a remote file on a server or print to a network printer, the request is forwarded to the network server. If the request is for the access of a local file (on the computer's hard drive), the redirector allows the request to proceed to the computer's processor so that the request can be processed locally.

The redirector can also forward requests from a client machine to servers that supply resources, such as network shares (or shared folders, which are discussed in the next chapter), or servers that supply print services (on small or medium-size networks, this might be handled by just one network server). Requests made on the client computer for remote resources are handled by the network operating system on the server.

Figure 7.1 supplies a diagram of how the redirector directs requests to either the local processor or the network server. The client computer is fooled by the redirector into thinking that all the resources it accesses (whether local or remote) are local.

FIGURE 7.1

The redirector on the client computer determines how requests for services should be routed.

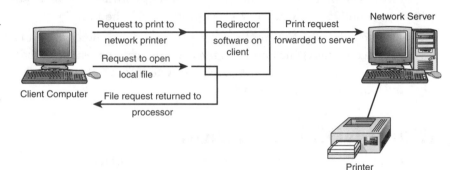

Configuring Network Clients

For a computer to log on to a particular network type, it must be configured with the appropriate network client software. Computers running Windows (any version of 9x, Me, or 2000) provide the necessary client software for different NOS platforms. For example, a computer running Windows Me or Windows 2000 already has the Client for Microsoft Networks built in to the OS, as shown in Figure 7.2.

FIGURE 7.2

Network client software allows a client to communicate with the network server.

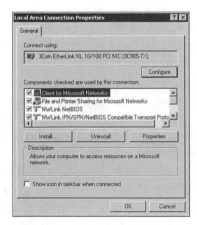

Network client software not built in to an OS (such as Windows) and updates to a network client must be installed on the client computer, just as any other software is installed. For example, although Windows provides a Novell client, a more recent client will probably be available on the Novell NetWare site. It can then be downloaded and installed on your network clients.

Client software provided by an NOS vendor such as Novell will also often include utilities that make it easier for the client to navigate the network and network resources. For example, the latest Novell client (at least the latest when this book was being written) provides the NetWare Connections utility, which allows a user on a client computer to check connections to various servers on the network. The NetWare Connections utility, shown in Figure 7.3, is launched by right-clicking the NetWare Services icon in the system tray. This icon is placed there when you install the NetWare client software on a Windows-based computer.

FIGURE 7.3

Network client software will often include utilities that make it easier for users to view and access network resources.

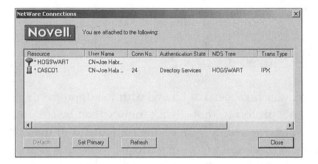

Although this probably goes without saying, computers that serve as network clients must also be configured with network interface cards and the appropriate software drivers for the NICs. Such a computer must then be physically attached to the network using cabling or some other media access strategy.

Configuring Client Computers with LAN Protocols

The network client computers must also be configured with at least one of the network protocols supported by the network server. If you are running a TCP/IP network, both the server and the network clients must be configured for TCP/IP. If you are running clients in a mixed network environment, where resource servers may be running different network operating systems (such as Windows 2000 Server and NetWare, which is discussed in the next chapter), the clients must be configured with all the necessary protocols.

Configuring LAN protocols on a Windows-based client is very straightforward. For example, protocols are added and moved on a Windows Me client using the

Network dialog box, shown in Figure 7.4. You can easily add protocols to the computer's network configuration by clicking the Add button and selecting Protocol.

FIGURE 7.4

The various flavors of Windows make it easy to add and remove network protocols.

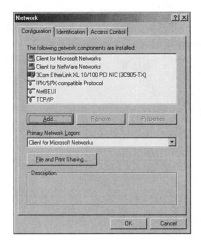

Once a client computer has been configured with the appropriate network client and with the needed LAN protocols, that client computer can be connected to the network. All a user will have to do is turn on the computer and then provide an appropriate username and password to log on to the network (user accounts are discussed in Chapter 16, "A Network Security Primer," in the section "Working with User Accounts"). Figure 7.5 shows the Novell Login screen for the Windows 2000 NetWare client.

FIGURE 7.5

Once the client computer is configured with a network client and network protocols, users can log on to the network server.

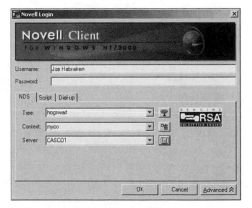

Configuring a Server with an NOS

Although we digressed for a moment to discuss network clients and how they communicate with the network server, we can now get back to our discussion of the NOS. Configuring a computer that will be a network server with a particular NOS is now easier than ever. Veteran network administrators love to recount the days when they were knee deep in NOS installation disks and had to wage a bare-knuckle battle at the command line to get a network server up and running.

As with all software now available, network operating systems ship on CD-ROMs. Nearly all of them provide straightforward installation programs, many of them GUIs, that walk you through the steps of configuring the NOS and the services that it will provide on the network.

Before you actually install the NOS on a computer system, however, you should determine two things: the server's hardware configuration and the client licensing method you will use on your network. These two issues should actually be figured out even before you buy the NOS software. So, let's back up a moment and take a look at these two important aspects of deploying a server on your network.

Server Hardware Configuration

An important part of your "preinstallation research" involves compiling the specifications for your server's hardware configuration so that it will perform correctly when set up with a particular NOS. I'm sure you will agree when I say that the World Wide Web is a great resource. It provides you with a way to quickly research the hardware needs of a particular NOS without even leaving your chair.

All NOS vendors provide a hardware compatibility list. This list lets you know the different hardware devices—everything from NICs to hard drive controller cards—that have been tested and found to be compatible with the network operating system you are going to install. For example, the Microsoft Windows 2000 Server Web site actually provides a search engine that makes it easy for your to not only determine the hardware devices that are compatible with the NOS but also the software. The Windows 2000 compatibility page is shown in Figure 7.6.

Not only do you need to configure your server with hardware that is compatible with the NOS, the server must have enough muscle to actually run the NOS. Each NOS vendor also provides a listing of hardware requirements to run its NOS. For example, the Sun Solaris Unix NOS requires 1GB of disk space and a minimum of 64MB of memory when you run it on an Intel Pentium–based server. If you were to run Windows 2000 Server on that same Pentium computer, you would need 256MB of RAM. Each NOS has its own particular set of hardware requirements.

FIGURE 7.6

NOS vendors supply hardware compatibility lists to make it easier to configure your server's hardware.

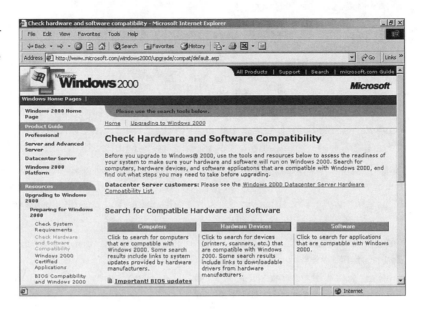

The base hardware configuration for a particular NOS can be found on that particular company's Web site. For example, Novell provides a Web page that supplies both the hardware and software requirements to run NetWare 5.1 (see Figure 7.7).

FIGURE 7.7

The base hardware configuration to run a NOS provides the minimum hardware requirements.

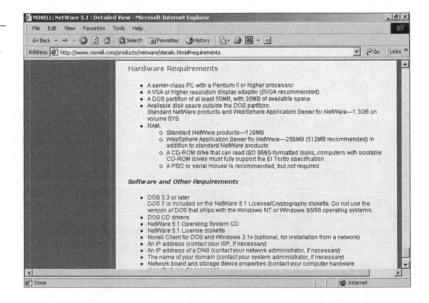

Because the server must be able to handle requests for services from network clients, you don't typically want to skimp on its hardware configuration. If you do, it can quickly become nothing more than a nightmarish, network bottleneck.

One thing that you have to keep in mind is that these basic hardware configurations typically supply just enough muscle to run the NOS on the server. The amount of additional RAM or disk space (or even the number of processors) that you configure your server with will also be dictated by the type of services you provide your users and the number of users on the network. For example, if you are running both file and print services on the same server, you might need to boost the memory or processor speed to handle all the user request calls placed on the server's processor. In Chapter 15, monitoring server hardware performance is discussed in the section "Monitoring Hardware." This is one way to see whether your server hardware configuration is actually working out once you have the server up and running on the network.

Many NOS vendors will also supply white papers and case studies that can help you determine your server's hardware configuration for your particular network situation. For example, let's say that you work for a medium-size company and you plan to deploy your own Windows 2000 Web server and migrate all clients to one particular OS.

No problem—check out `http://www.microsoft.com/windows2000/guide/server/profiles/default.asp`. This Microsoft Web site provides case studies detailing the use of Microsoft NOS products such as Windows 2000 Server. Among the number of case studies is one detailing Starbucks Coffee's use of Windows 2000 Server on its Web server. There is even a case study detailing the use of Windows 2000 Server at Banyan (Banyan actually sold one of the first LAN platforms called Banyan VINES). You will find that other NOS vendors, such as Novell and Sun, also provide examples of how their software products are used by various companies. This information is particularly helpful because these studies will often describe similar configurations to your desired implementation and therefore eliminate a significant amount of guesswork.

NOS Licensing

Once you have the server hardware issues figured out, you need to determine a licensing strategy for the network. Typically, an NOS will require that you have a server license for your server (a separate license for each server) and client licenses for your network clients. For example, you can buy a Novell NetWare 5.1 base package that licenses the server and five client connections. To license more clients, you buy what is called a *connection additive license*. These additive client licenses range from the addition of 5 users to 500 users. Additional server licenses can also be purchased for multiserver networks. Novell offers a number of different volume licensing agreements and price breaks for academic institutions. Take a look at Novell's Licensing site at `http://www.novell.com/licensing/price.html` for more information on the different possibilities.

Microsoft Windows 2000 Server licensing is similar to NetWare's licensing in that you need to license both your servers and your clients. Just because you buy a copy of Windows 2000 Server doesn't mean you can install the software on 50 different computers. Windows Server (NT, 2000, and the upcoming XP version due out late in 2001) actually provides you with two different possibilities for licensing network clients: Per Seat and Per Server.

Per Seat means that you will purchase a license for each network user on the network. Each of these users can connect to any and all the servers on the network. Per Server means that you are licensed for a certain number of concurrent connections to the server. If you have 50 licenses, 50 clients can connect to the server.

Tip

Microsoft's two different licensing options can be a little confusing. Per Seat is probably the best licensing strategy for large networks, especially if network resources are spread across a number of Windows 2000 servers. Per Server is the best choice when you have a small network consisting of only one server. It also works best for networks when only part of your client base is connected to the server at any one time.

All network operating systems supply you with some type of utility that you use to add server or client licenses to the network. Microsoft Windows 2000 Server, for example, provides the Licensing snap-in, which allows you to add licenses to the network. Figure 7.8 shows the Windows Licensing snap-in. This snap-in is used to record client and server licenses that are in use on the network.

Licensing network server and client software is an extremely important part of a network administrator's job. It's important to have the appropriate licenses for all the software running on the corporate network. The legal ramifications of not having the appropriate licenses and getting caught are not pretty at all. Software licensing should be a key part of your overall network plan. Using pirated or unlicensed copies of software is greatly frowned upon in the computer technology world.

FIGURE 7.8

The Windows
Licensing snap-
in allows you to
record client and
server licenses
for your net-
work.

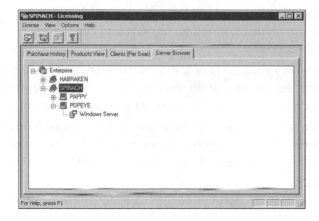

Installing an NOS

Once you've have the server hardware ready to go and have sorted out how you will
license your server and clients, you are ready to actually install the NOS on the
server computer. As already mentioned, most network operating systems ship on
CD-ROMs. Most NOS packages also include some sort of boot disk or provide a utility on the CD-ROM that makes it easy for you to create a set of installation disks.

You can use the boot disk or installation disks to configure partitions on the server's
hard drive or hard drives and also load the appropriate drivers so that the NOS
installation files can be accessed from the CD-ROM drive. You can also forgo using
floppy disks at all and configure the computer's CMOS so that you can boot from
the CD-ROM drive. The CD-ROM, then, supplies you with the appropriate setup
mechanism for selecting and configuring the hard drive on which you will install
the NOS.

Tip

The CMOS is actually the microchip memory that holds the Basic Input/Output System
(BIOS) settings for your computer. These settings include the boot sequence for the
drives on the computer as well as a number of other settings. The BIOS utility that
allows you to control these settings is typically reached by pressing a key such as the
Delete key or the F1 key during the first few seconds of the system's boot sequence.
Each computer manufacturer supplies a slightly different BIOS utility. Most are menu
driven and some even allow you to use the mouse to navigate the various settings. In
most cases some sort of documentation related to the BIOS will come with a new computer. Another source of information on the BIOS utility is typically the computer manufacturer's Web site.

Although installing each of the different network operating systems (and there are
a bunch) will certainly be a unique experience, there are certain tasks you must

perform to get an NOS up and running that are consistent across the different types of network operating systems. Installing an NOS and configuring a server typically require the following tasks:

- *Drive partitioning and formatting.* A drive must be partitioned and formatted so that it can serve as the resting place for the NOS itself. Depending on the NOS, you might need to configure other drives on the server.

- *Server naming.* The server must be given a unique name during the installation process. The ability to access a server by its friendly name is ingrained in just about every NOS. Each NOS will have its own set of conventions for naming the server.

- *Network naming.* The network itself must be identified during the server installation. For example, in the case of a Windows server, the domain (which is the network) is given a name. On a NetWare network, you name the network tree, which again is the network.

- *LAN protocol installation and configuration.* The LAN protocols that will be used for network communication must be installed on the server. Most network operating systems now use TCP/IP as their default network protocol. If you want to use other protocols, such as IPX/SPX and NetBEUI, you can designate that they be included in the server's configuration during the installation process. Configuring LAN protocols such as TCP/IP, where you must provide the IP address and subnet mask for the server, will also be part of the server installation process.

- *Network services selection.* The different services that will be supplied by the server must be designated during the installation process. All network servers will offer file and print services by default, but if you also want the server to provide Web services or other services, such as Remote Access Service, you have to designate this during the NOS installation.

- *Licensing.* The licensing for the server and clients must be configured on the server. Although licensing parameters can be configured once the server is up and running, each NOS will provide you with the option of configuring server and client licensing during the NOS installation. Clients will not be able to communicate with the server until you let the server know that these clients are licensed.

- *Setting the administrator's password.* Regardless of whether the administrator's account is called Administrator, root, or Admin, you must set the password for this administrative account during the NOS installation. Because this account controls the server and the network, you need to select a password that will keep the server secure. Most folks who have done any reading about network operating systems know that the NetWare administrative account is called Admin. Therefore, don't pick a password that can be easily guessed.

■ *Peripheral installation.* Depending on the NOS, peripheral devices such as modems, printers, and other devices can be configured during the NOS installation.

Although the order of these different NOS installation duties will vary from NOS to NOS, you can see that information such as server and network names and even LAN addressing issues pop up during the installation of the NOS. This means that you hopefully had all this information available during the NOS installation because of the network plan that you put together. How servers will be named and the IP addresses assigned to these servers should have been all mapped out long before you sat down to actually install the NOS on the server computers.

Now that we've looked at some general issues related to NOS hardware specifications, licensing, and installing NOS software, let's take a closer look at some of the popular network operating systems in use today. We will start this discussion by looking at Microsoft networking.

Working with Microsoft Windows Server

Microsoft has been in the networking business since the early 1980s, and some of its initial networking efforts, such as NetBEUI and OS/2, were collaborative efforts with IBM. Microsoft LAN Manager was one of Microsoft's first forays into developing an NOS. More important to our discussion of network operating systems is the Server version of Windows. The first version of this NOS, Microsoft Windows NT 3.1, was introduced in 1992. The NT stood for *New Technology*.

An updated (and more stable) version of this NOS was released by Microsoft in 1994, under the name Microsoft Windows NT Server 3.5. Microsoft quickly followed these early releases of Windows NT Server with Windows NT Server 4.0, which was released in 1996. Windows NT 4.0 gained wide acceptance in corporate America (and the world for that matter), making Microsoft a viable player in the NOS market.

Microsoft Windows 2000 Server actually exists in three different flavors: Windows 2000 Server, Windows 2000 Advanced Server, and Windows 2000 Datacenter Server. Windows 2000 Advanced Server is designed for large enterprise networks, and Windows 2000 Datacenter is used for Web hosting environments.

At the time of this book's writing, Windows 2000 Server is the most recent version of the Windows NT NOS; it was released in February of 2000. A new version of Windows Server, Windows XP Server, is due for release at the end of 2001.

Microsoft Windows 2000 Server is a multiplatform NOS and can be run on Intel Pentium hardware configurations as well as RISC processor systems. Windows 2000 Server also supports systems with multiple processors; for example, the Windows 2000 Server product can support up to four processors. Other flavors of the Windows 2000 NOS can support even more processors, with Windows 2000 Datacenter able to support up to 32 processors.

Here is the base hardware configuration for Windows 2000 Server on an Intel Pentium–based computer:

- Processor: 166MHz.
- RAM: 256MB. The minimum supported is 128MB, with a maximum of 4GB.
- Hard drive: 2GB. You need a partition of at least 500MB to install the software.
- CD-ROM drive: 12X.
- Video card: Super VGA.
- Monitor: Super VGA capable of 800×600 resolution.

Note Back in the good old days, the notion of having a super VGA monitor on a server would seem utterly ridiculous. Servers sat in closets, and if they even had a monitor, it was some old monochrome amber thing with dust all over it. However, things change, and because Microsoft Windows Server is a full-blown OS/NOS with a GUI interface, it requires certain video card and monitor requirements to run correctly.

Windows 2000 Server can provide a number of network services, including DNS, DHCP, routing, and remote access (including Virtual Private Networking, which is discussed in Chapter 15). A Windows 2000 Server machine can also function as a communication server, and it supports either Microsoft Exchange Server or Lotus Domino Server (both add-on communication server products), which are discussed in Chapter 9, "Working with Applications on the Network."

Microsoft Network Structure

The basic structure or administrative unit for Microsoft networks running Windows NT, and more current versions of the Windows NOS (such as Windows 2000 and Windows XP), is the *domain*. A domain is a collection of client machines and other network devices that are all managed by the network server, which is referred to as the *domain controller*. The domain controller (typically the first server installed on the network) maintains its own database of user accounts and controls its own resources, such as printers and shared files.

In the case of Windows NT, if the network continues to grow as far as the number of users and client computers, the domain controller, which is responsible for logging on all those users, can be given some help in the form of a *backup domain controller*. These servers, also running the Windows NT NOS, will receive a duplicate copy of the user database from the domain controller and use it to help log in users. Servers with special duties, such as remote access or communications, can also be added to the domain as needed.

A single NT domain (which would include the domain controller and any backup domain controllers) can (according to Microsoft) manage over 10,000 user accounts. If you need to expand beyond the single domain that you created, you can create additional domains, each with its own domain controller and domain name. Then you create trust relationships between these different domains so that they can share network resources (a *trust* is a sort of electronic agreement between domains; it allows users logging on to their own domain to access resources in other domains on the network).

The domain model is considered somewhat flat, however, and does not provide a true hierarchical structure for managing domains, resources, and users. Each domain is kind of a Tupperware container all its own, and sharing resources between the domains means that the network administrator has to spend a lot of time managing the trusts that are set up between the different domain controllers. Figure 7.9 provides a look at how domains running NT servers share resources.

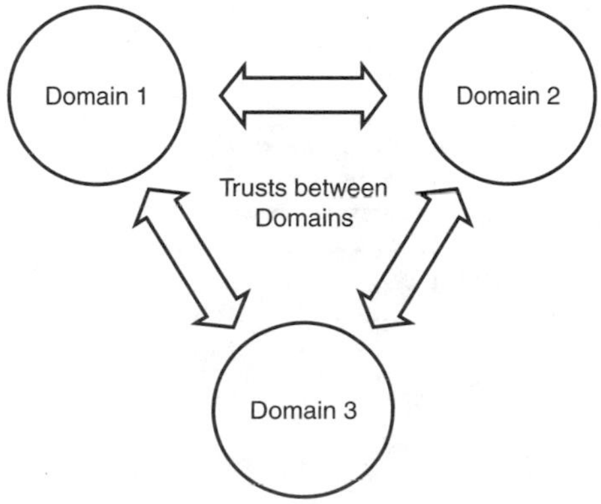

FIGURE 7.9

Multiple domains in a Windows NT environment require trusts to share resources.

Each of the domains shown in Figure 7.9 (Domains 1, 2, and 3) require their own domain controller. Users in the three domains have to be managed at the domain level. This means that an administrator basically manages three different network containers. The only way these three separate containers can share resources, such as files and printers, is to create trusts between the domains. The trusts are represented by the arrows shown in the diagram. The annoying thing about the Windows NT domain structure is that, even if Domain 1 has a trust relationship with Domains 2 and 3, Domains 2 and 3 still can't share resources. The trusts are not transitive. So a trust relationship must also be created between Domains 2 and 3.

The greater the number of domains that are created on a Windows NT network to compartmentalize users and resources, the more trust relationships you have to manage to allow the different domain controllers to share resources. While Microsoft claims the Windows NT environment is highly scalable (meaning, easily expandable), a very large NT network could potentially become an administrative nightmare. There is no administrative utility that will allow you to sit back and manage the entire network. Each domain requires separate care and feeding.

With the release of Windows 2000 Server, Microsoft introduced the Active Directory, a directory service tool used to manage a database of network information that is arranged in a top-down hierarchical manner. The Active Directory basically looks like a tree with branches. The basic unit of the network hierarchy is still the domain (as it is in a Windows NT network) and the first domain created for the network serves as the root of the tree. Additional domains created in the tree are subordinate to the root domain. A user in any of the domains in the tree can access resources anywhere in the tree (see Figure 7.10).

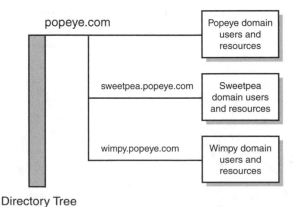

In Figure 7.10, the popeye.com domain provides the root of the tree. This would be the first domain created when the first server on the network is brought online.

Any child domains branching off from Popeye will have access to resources anywhere in the tree, including the Popeye parent domain. This is because there is an implicit trust between all the domains in the same tree.

Notice how the child domains take on the parent's name, such as
sweetpea.popeye.com (Popeye is considered the *root domain*, meaning this domain
sits at the root of the directory tree). This is a Domain Name Service style of naming
items in a hierarchical tree. You find this same type of naming convention on the
Internet (DNS is discussed in the section titled "Understanding DNS," in Chapter 11,
"How the Internet Works").

The Windows Active Directory contains all the objects that make up the network. An
object can be a user, a printer, or a server that provides a particular service. Figure
7.11 shows the Active Directory Users and Computers snap-in, which is used to manage objects on a Microsoft network. (You will find that the Active Directory is similar
to Novell's NetWare Directory Service, which we take a look at a little later in the
chapter.)

FIGURE 7.11

The Active
Directory is the
master database
for the network
objects.

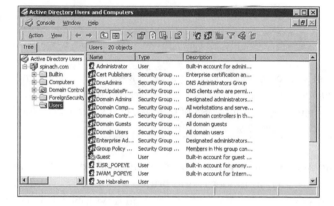

Microsoft NOS Interface

The user interface found on a Microsoft Windows Server computer is exactly the
same as the one found on a Windows client computer. This means that the learning
curve for becoming familiar with the tools and various administrative utilities found
on a Windows server is practically nil. Now, I don't mean that actually learning to
use these tools properly will take no time; it's just that the Windows environment is
so familiar to anyone with a computer that navigating the NOS will be very
straightforward. However, using the various tools correctly and effectively is something that is not going to happen overnight.

With the Windows 2000 version of the NOS, Microsoft has provided a set of snap-ins
that give you access to the various administrative tools that you will use to manage
the network. Because all the tools run in the Microsoft Management Console (MMC),
you work with the same consistent interface (Windows NT actually uses administrative tools that all look a little different). For example, the Active Directory Users and

Computers snap-in shown in Figure 7.11 runs in the MMC, just like the DNS snap-in, shown in Figure 7.12.

FIGURE 7.12

All the Windows 2000 utilities, such as the DNS snap-in, run in the MMC.

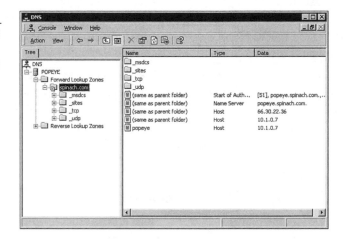

 For a look at setting up and managing a Windows 2000 network, check out *The Complete Idiot's Guide to Windows 2000 Server*, from Que. If you want to consult a heavy-duty reference for Windows 2000 Server, check out *Special Edition Using Microsoft Windows 2000 Server*, also from Que.

Because Windows 2000 Server also embraces the same automatic installation of peripheral devices such as modems and printers—called *Plug and Play*—adding new hardware to a server is no different from adding a peripheral such as a modem to a Windows Me standalone computer that you use in your home.

Windows 2000 also embraces the Control Panel and all the various tools, such as the Add/Remove Software applet, found in the client versions of Windows. The Windows 2000 Server Control Panel is shown in Figure 7.13. As I said before, the Windows 2000 Server user interface is so familiar that you, as the network administrator, can concentrate on running the network rather than trying to figure out how to invoke a particular utility from the command line.

A Final Word About Windows Networking

Although it certainly isn't my intent to bias anyone when selecting an NOS, I thought I should say a few things about the Microsoft Windows NOS related to the marketplace. There are claims that there are more new installations of the Windows Server NOS than any other network operating system. Now, remember, I said *new installations*. There is still a large installed base of Novell NetWare and Unix networks worldwide, and it is hard to get any concrete data on whether Novell and Sun (with its Sun Solaris Unix product) are keeping pace with Microsoft in the NOS arena or are getting totally pulverized.

FIGURE 7.13

The Control Panel, familiar to all Windows users, is provided by Windows 2000 Server.

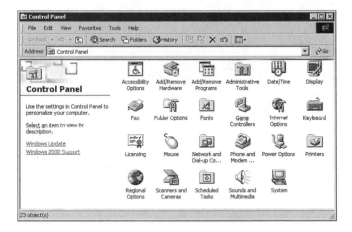

The one observation I would like to make is that network professionals and people trying to break into the IT field are falling over themselves to get certifications related to Microsoft Windows Server products. The Microsoft Certified Systems Engineer certification has become the most sought-after certification in the Information Technology field.

The fact that so many networking professionals are seeking Microsoft certification seems to me to be a fairly good indicator that the Microsoft Windows NOS is definitely selling well. Now having said that, let's take a look at another one of the big LAN NOS players: Novell.

Working with Novell NetWare

Novell certainly was and is one of the major players in the NOS market. Interestingly enough, Novell started out as a PC manufacturer but under President Ray Noorda reinvented itself and concentrated on network software development. Although the first version of NetWare, which was made available in 1983, only ran on a Novell proprietary PC using a Motorola 68000 processor, Novell quickly saw the advantage of supplying a multiplatform NOS. In 1989, Novell marketed a version of its NetWare NOS that actually provided for the sharing of data and printers among IBM/compatibles, Apple Macintoshes, and Unix-based computers.

NetWare provides an excellent example of a client/server networking environment. Clients must be configured with NetWare client software to communicate with the NetWare server.

Novell NetWare has gone through a number of different versions. In version 3.0, released in 1989, support was added for 386 processors, allowing NetWare to run in 32-bit mode. One of the most important updates of NetWare was version 4.0, released in 1993, which provided the first version of the Novell Directory Services (NDS), a hierarchical database used to manage network objects, such as users and network resources (NDS preceded Microsoft's Active Directory by seven years). We will discuss NDS in more detail in the next section of this chapter.

Note The original version of NetWare was designated as NetWare 4.0. In 1985, Novell released a new version of NetWare called *Advanced NetWare* and set the version number to 1.0. All subsequent versions, such as Novell NetWare 5.1, are the offspring of the 1985 1.0 release.

The current version (as of this book's writing) is NetWare 5.1. Here is the base hardware configuration for NetWare 5.1:

- Processor: Pentium II or higher.
- RAM: 128MB. On servers running the WebSphere Application Server for NetWare, it's 256MB (512MB recommended).
- Video Adapter: A VGA or higher-resolution display adapter (SVGA recommended).
- Hard drive: DOS partition of at least 50MB, with 35MB of available space. (1.3GB is required if you're running WebSphere Application Server.)
- CD-ROM drive: ISO 9660–compatible CD-ROM drive (which is just about every 2X-or-better drive available).
- Video card: VGA or better.
- Monitor: VGA or better, with the ability to support a resolution of 800×600.

NetWare is also interesting in that it uses its own proprietary LAN protocol stack, IPX/SPX, for network communication (for more about IPX/SPX, refer back to Chapter 5, "Network Protocols: Real and Imagined"). Because of the necessity of Internet connectivity, NetWare now embraces TCP/IP as the default protocol stack.

NetWare is not a complete standalone OS; therefore, the computer must have DOS 3.3 or better installed on it. NetWare 5.1 ships with DR DOS 7.02, which can be installed on the computer from the NetWare Licensing disk or the NetWare installation CD-ROM (if you can configure your computer to boot from the CD-ROM).

The installation of NetWare 5.1 on a server is every bit as straightforward as installing Windows 2000 Server. Just be sure your server hardware is on NetWare's hardware compatibility list. When you install NetWare on your server, a volume is created called SYS. A *volume* is a partition or a number of partitions that are perceived as one container on a NetWare server. Each volume is assigned a name. You are also given the option of creating additional volumes during the installation process. This is a good idea, and it allows you to create the areas on the server's disk drives that you will use for file storage and sharing.

NetWare can provide network services, such as remote access, and function as a Web or FTP server. Novell is positioning NetWare as an Internet-based application server and has built in the IBM WebSphere Application Server software to the NOS. This Java-based development environment provides a lot of muscle for the creation of Web-based applications.

NetWare does not provide DNS or DHCP services. These network services, if required on the network, must be provided by a server running some other NOS.

NetWare Network Structure

Versions of NetWare prior to the release of 4.0 used a flat database structure called the *bindery* to manage users, server volumes, and resources on the network. Each NetWare server had its own bindery (not unlike a Windows NT domain), making it more difficult for users to access resources on different network servers. As already mentioned, with the release of version 4.0, a hierarchical database called the *Novell Directory Services (NDS)* provides a tree structure that allows for the integration of all network resources and objects into one branching structure.

Hierarchical network-management structures such as NDS provide you with a highly scalable network. New containers or objects can easily be added to the tree (the same is true for Windows Active Directory).

The NDS tree has a root, which is created when you configure the first NetWare 5.1 server for the network. Additional servers, providing additional resources, can be added to the NDS tree as branches. Figure 7.14 shows the NDS tree for a NetWare network as seen in the NetWare Administrator (a Windows utility used to manage NDS objects; we will discuss NetWare Administrator in a moment).

When you create the root of the NDS tree, you must supply a name for the tree (in this case, the tree is called Hogswart). You must also create a context for the network tree when you create the NDS root. The context describes the position of an object within the NDS tree. The context for the NDS tree in Figure 7.14 is "myco." The context of the tree might typically be specified by the name of your company.

FIGURE 7.14

The NDS tree holds all the users and other objects found on the network.

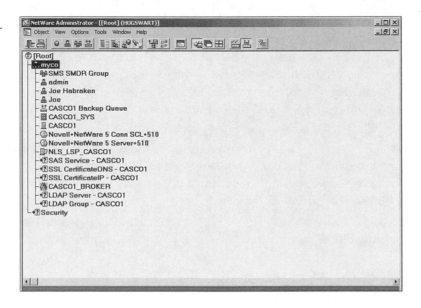

NetWare NOS Interface

NetWare servers have historically been managed using a number of different menu-driven utilities that are run on the server. For example, to manage printers and print servers, you would use the PCONSOLE program.

Although NetWare now provides a couple of different GUI tools for managing and monitoring the network, you still need to have a good understanding of DOS and DOS commands to really be able to manage the server.

Although all the DOS-based utilities are still available on a NetWare 5.1 server, you might find it easier to manage network objects such as users or printers using the Windows-based NetWare Administrator (NWADMIN) program. The NWADMIN program can be accessed from any Windows 9x, NT, or Windows 2000 client computer on the network. You must log on to the network using an account with administrative privileges (such as the Admin account) to start the NWADMIN utility.

NWADMIN is actually started by double-clicking the NWADMIN32 icon in the WIN32 folder on the NetWare server (see Figure 7.15). WIN32 is a subfolder of the PUBLIC folder found on your server's SYS volume. You can create a shortcut for NWADMIN by dragging the NWADMIN32 icon onto your Windows desktop.

FIGURE 7.15

NWADMIN can be started using the icon in the server's WIN32 folder.

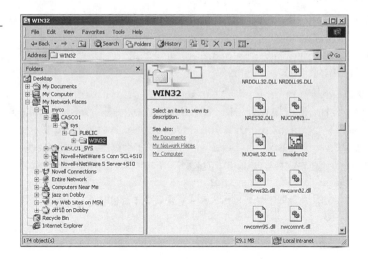

NWADMIN can be used to create new users and volumes, manage printers, and view objects in the NDS tree. All the different management features are accessed using the same types of dialog boxes that anyone who has worked on a Windows client is familiar with. For example, Figure 7.16 shows the Create Volume dialog box, which is used to create a new volume (such as a volume that can be used to store data needed by users).

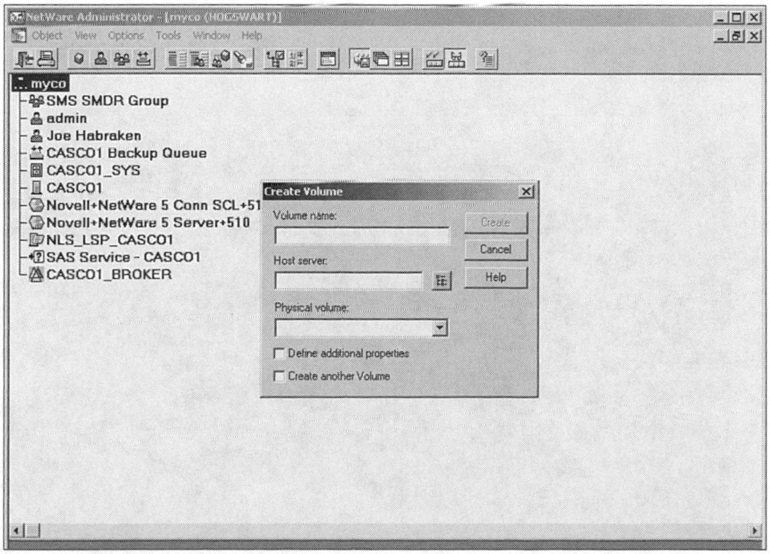

FIGURE 7.16

Administrative tasks, such as the creation of a new volume, are handled in typical Windows dialog boxes even though you are creating the volume on the NetWare server.

Another option for managing the NetWare network is the NetWare Management Portal, which is a new set of management utilities provided by NetWare 5.1. These utilities allow a network administrator to access and manage the server from any computer with a Web browser.

As I've already mentioned, the Management Portal on the NetWare server is reached using a Web browser. All you have to do is type `https://name of server:2200`, where `name of server` is the name that you gave to the server during the installation of the NetWare software. Also, 2200 is a well-known port used to contact the portal software. You can go with the default, 2200, or select another port number if you wish. Note that `https` is used rather than `http` to connect to the server because this is a secure connection, which is supplied by the Hypertext Transport Protocol Secure (or `https`) command.

> In cases where you don't have a DNS server on your network but are still running TCP/IP on the NetWare server (a requirement if you are going to use the Management Portal), you will have to provide the IP address of the server rather than its name in the `https://ip address:2200` address typed into the Web browser's Address window.

Once you are connected to the Management Portal, you can add new users and groups and can view the contents of the NDS tree using the NetWare Management Portal. Figure 7.17 shows the General Administration window of the Management Portal. Users and groups can be managed using this particular feature.

FIGURE 7.17
Users and groups can be managed using the Management Portal.

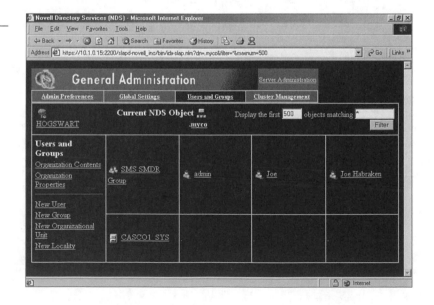

The Management Portal also provides you with the ability to monitor and troubleshoot hardware devices such as drive controllers and network cards. Figure 7.18 shows the Hardware Adapters window provided by the Management Portal.

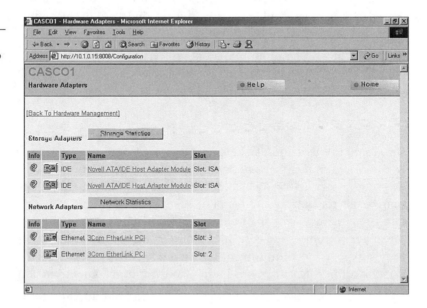

FIGURE 7.18
Hardware devices can also be monitored using the Management Portal.

As you can see, NetWare provides a fairly user-friendly set of GUI tools for managing the network. Although using these tools might get you a sneer from a veteran NetWare administrator, the NWADMIN and Management Portal provide you with all the management options found in the NetWare DOS-based management utilities.

A Final Word About Novell Networking

Although NetWare certainly does not enjoy the market share that it did in 1992 when it controlled 65% of the NOS market, it still has a presence in many companies and institutions. NetWare has always provided an excellent environment for networks requiring file and print serving. However, NetWare has been slightly behind the curve when it comes to providing TCP/IP services such as DNS and DHCP, both of which are available in the Windows Server NOS.

Novell is now positioning NetWare as the NOS of choice for Internet-enabled businesses. With the integration of IBM WebSphere into NOS, NetWare 5.1 does offer a very powerful platform for developing and delivering Web-based applications. So, it is really up in the air as to who will win the battle of the network operating systems in the long term.

Other Network Platforms of Note

Our discussion of network operating systems wouldn't be complete without a look at Unix and Linux. And as far as Unix administrators and Linux aficionados are concerned, this chapter would be pretty much complete after the discussion of these two classes of network operating systems.

Unix and Linux are similar in a lot of respects. Linux is actually a Unix clone developed by Linus Torvalds in 1994. Let's take a look at Unix and then its younger stepbrother, Linux.

Unix

Unix is a multiuser, multitasking operating system that provides a client/server networking environment on a wide variety of hardware platforms. Unix was developed by programmers in the AT&T Bell Labs in the 1970s. Since AT&T's release of the source code for Unix, a number of different versions of the OS were developed in the late 1970s. Unix, a cross-platform marvel, became the standard for workstations, servers, miniframes, and even mainframes, particularly at universities (even the Cray supercomputer ran Unix). This is mainly because Unix was distributed to universities for free; Bell Labs was prohibited by antitrust laws from charging for the OS.

Early versions of Unix provided a DOS-like command interface (or is it that DOS provided a Unix-like command interface, because DOS came after Unix), which provided a constant source of migraine headaches to network end users. Although the Unix command-line interface is still there, different graphical user interfaces—such as the X Window System—have been developed to help users navigate their Unix-based systems and Unix-based networks.

Unix is alive and well in the marketplace and is still one of the most popular operating systems in the world. For example, Sun Microsystems's Solaris, which touts itself as the leading Unix environment, runs on both Intel and SPARC hardware platforms and provides support for multiple processors.

While Microsoft is just rolling out its first 64-bit version of the Windows NOS in 2001, a number of 64-bit versions of Unix already are available. Unix 64-bit operating systems, such as IBM's DYNIX, Hewlett-Packard's HP-UX, and Compaq's True64 Unix, provide a high-performance network environment for application servers and database servers. These operating systems are also widely used for Web hosting.

These 64-bit operating systems do not run on your standard PC or even a more powerful computer that you might consider a server-class machine. For example, True64 Unix is designed to run on a server with multiple Alpha RISC processors (processors that run in excess of 600MHz), gigabytes of RAM, and extremely large hard drives.

Although these 64-bit monster operating systems are still Unix, they typically provide some type of GUI management utility—for example, True64 Unix provides a Web-based management tool accessed using a Web browser. The Unix command-line is still there—the network administrator just doesn't necessarily have to use it.

Linux

Linux was created by Linus Torvalds when he was a student at the University of Helsinki. Linux is an open-system OS/NOS, and because the source code is freely available, a number of Linux flavors have popped up in the marketplace. Linux is similar to Unix in many respects and uses a similar command set.

Linux servers can offer file and print services as well as more complex services, such as Web hosting. The Apache Web Server software is a popular Web hosting add-on for Linux servers. Linux servers can also provide services to non-Linux clients. For example, a Linux computer running Samba can function as a Windows peer computer or as a Windows NT domain controller. Linux and Samba were discussed in Chapter 6, "Configuring Peer-to-Peer Networks."

Because a number of companies—including Red Hat, Caldera, and SuSE—have developed versions of Linux for the consumer market (meaning people other than Linux hackers), some fairly friendly user interfaces have been developed. For example, the KDE interface for Linux provides a Windows-like environment, as shown in Figure 7.19.

FIGURE 7.19

GUI interfaces have been developed for the Linux environment.

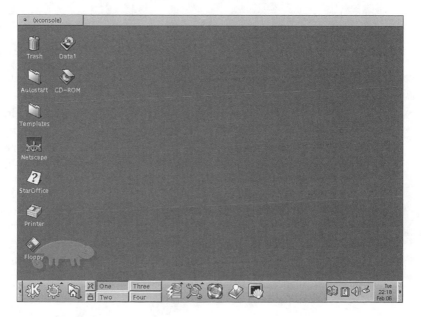

Although the Linux environment can provide low-cost proxy server, firewall, and Web server functionality, the Linux OS can also function as a client operating system. Although Linux is lacking the incredible range of software available for a desktop OS such as Windows, end-user applications are being developed for Linux. Sun Microsystems has developed an application suite package called StarOffice. StarOffice not only runs in the Linux and Unix environments, but it will also run on Windows machines.

StarOffice boasts a word processor, spreadsheet, and database application. Figure 7.20 shows the StarOffice Calc application (yes, it does look a lot like Excel).

FIGURE 7.20

StarOffice provides productivity software such as the StarOffice Calc spreadsheet program.

Although Linux aficionados would love nothing more than to see Linux gain greater mass appeal, it is certainly too early to tell how Linux will fit into the overall network puzzle of the next few years. Network operating systems have come and gone, so it will be interesting to see what the Open Systems folks do to place Linux on the list of viable network operating systems.

Linux offers a lot of possibilities as a cheap way to deploy Web and proxy servers. For more information on Linux, check out *Special Edition Using Linux, Sixth Edition* or *Practical Linux*, both from Que. Unix is used by a number of companies for Web servers and network servers. There are probably more Unix installations out there in the world than any other NOS. For a good introduction to Unix, check out *Think Unix* from Que.

A Final Word on Network Operating Systems

Although this chapter certainly isn't an exhaustive study of network operating systems, I think you can see that there are quite a number of choices. Each NOS definitely has its own set of pros and cons.

You need to do your research before you select an NOS. Take a look at your network needs, your user base, and also your budget. If you are looking at a basic network with file and print services, you have a number of options, including NetWare, Windows 2000 Server, Linux, and Unix. If you want DNS and DHCP to run on the same server that provides file services, you've narrowed your choices to Windows, Linux, and Unix. If you are looking at Web hosting and using Web applications, NetWare jumps back onto the list and provides an alternative to Unix.

So, I think you get the picture. Figure out what you need and then research the possibilities. And most of all, choose wisely. You're the one who is going to be stuck with the NOS you select.

Chapter Summary

- A network operating system, or NOS, is software that allows a computer to "serve up" resources to network clients. The NOS also provides the central access point for a network and requires users to log on.

- An NOS such as Windows 2000 Server is a full-blown, self-contained OS. Novell NetWare is an add-on NOS and requires that a computer be running DOS 3.3 or better as its underlying OS.

- Networking computers requires that both an NOS be running on a server and that client software be running on client computers.

- Calls for resources on the network are handled by the redirector, which is part of the client software. It actually fools the client into thinking that remote shares and printers are actually connected locally.

- Network clients must be configured with the appropriate client software for the NOS. Clients must also be configured with the appropriate LAN protocols that will be used on the network.

- Each NOS product has been tested on a variety of hardware. Hardware that works with the NOS will be found on the network operating system's hardware compatibility list.

- The base hardware requirements for an NOS might not supply enough muscle for the server to provide resources appropriately in all networking situations.

■ Licenses are required for both servers and clients on a network. Each NOS handles licensing agreements in its own way. You must be sure you have enough licenses to cover all your clients and servers.

■ Microsoft Windows 2000 Server is an NOS that provides file and print sharing and a variety of other services, such as DNS, DHCP, remote connectivity, and Web management. Windows 2000 uses the Active Directory to arrange network users and other objects in a hierarchical tree.

■ Novell NetWare 5.1 provides file and print services on the network and is also designed to provide Web services, such as Web applications. NetWare uses NDS to arrange network users and other objects in a hierarchical tree.

■ Unix is available in a number of different flavors and provides an NOS and client environment that can be run on a number of different hardware platforms. Unix servers can provide file and print resources and other services, such as DNS, firewalls, and remote access. Unix is available in a number of 64-bit flavors for use on high-end, high-speed multiprocessor servers.

■ Linux is a Unix clone. It is an open-system NOS and client OS. The source code for Linux is freely available and therefore has lead to a number of different flavors of Linux. Linux can function both as an NOS and as a client OS, and it can provide file and print services as well as services such as remote access, Web management, and proxy servers.

SHARING RESOURCES ON THE NETWORK

In this chapter

- Understanding network shares
- Controlling share access
- Working with Windows shares
- Working with NetWare shares
- Mapping shares to logical drives
- Working with proxy servers
- Sharing printers on the network
- Managing shared printers

If you put garbage in a computer, nothing comes out but garbage. But this garbage, having passed through a very expensive machine, is somehow ennobled and none dare criticize it.

–Anonymous

In Chapter 6, "Configuring Peer-to-Peer Networks," we took a look at how resources are shared on a peer-to-peer network. In the peer environment, each resource can potentially have a different password. Peer networking also does not provide for any centralized control of network resources or, for that matter, centralized control of access to the network itself. A centralized approach to providing resources on the network requires a server computer running an NOS.

Chapter 7, "Working with Network Operating Systems," provided an overview of network operating systems, including NOS hardware requirements and NOS installation. We also took a look at some of the different network operating systems that are currently the frontrunners in the NOS market. In this chapter, we take a look at how resources such as files and printers are provided to network users by network servers.

It certainly is no surprise to anyone that the actual mechanics of sharing files and printers will differ depending on the NOS you are using on your network. In some cases, you may even be using servers on your network that run different network operating systems. We will take a look at how users can access network resources even on a mixed network running more than one NOS.

Let's begin our discussion of sharing resources on the network with a look at the network share. We can then look at sharing other network resources, such as printers.

What Is a Network Share?

A *network share* is a drive or folder on a server that is made available to users on the network. Shares cannot consist of individual files.

So, how does a network share differ from a share provided by a peer computer on a peer-to-peer network? Whereas a peer share can be created by a user on his own computer (which actually can be any computer on a peer network or a server-based network where file and print sharing has been turned on), network shares located on a network server can only be created by network administrators or other users who have the administrative rights to create shares. For example, on a Windows 2000 Server machine, the Administrator account is used to manage server resources such as shares. On an NetWare server, the Admin account has all the power.

As just mentioned, other network users can be given the administrative rights to create shares on network servers. This means that the network administrator can delegate some of the administrative tasks related to shares to certain responsible users on the network. For example, on a Windows 2000 Server machine, this includes any user who is a member of the Administrators group, the Server Operators group, or the Power Users group.

So, what is a group? A *group* is a logical administrative and security container. Security rights and access levels to objects on the network, such as shares, can be assigned to groups. This means that any user who is made a member of a particular group will also be supplied the same rights and access levels that have been assigned to the group.

A network administrator can create his own groups or take advantage of groups that are built in to the NOS. Windows 2000 provides a number of built-in groups, such as Administrators, Print Operators, and Server Operators. Figure 8.1 shows some of the built-in groups found on a server running Windows 2000 Server (groups are located in the Active Directory Users and Computers snap-in). Using a built-in group, an administrator can quickly raise the permission levels for a particular user by making that user a member of a group. More information on groups and security issues related to share rights and permissions is provided in Chapter 16, "A Network Security Primer."

FIGURE 8.1

Groups are security containers that can be used to quickly provide users with certain rights and permissions.

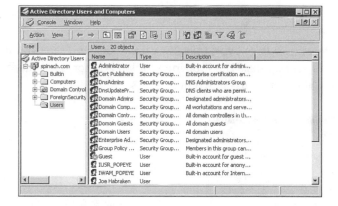

Note   Assigning a user administrative rights on a NetWare 5.1 server can actually be accomplished without making the user a member of a particular group. You can go into the Details dialog box for that particular user and set the Security Equal To option to Admin. This makes the user's account as powerful as the Admin account when it comes to accessing and controlling network resources, including user accounts. Therefore, assigning rights to a number of users using this option probably isn't a very good idea. You can use it to promote your own user account to Admin level, however, so that you can log on to the NetWare server remotely using a tool such as NetWare Administrator.

Sharing Folders and Drives

So, it takes a user who has administrative rights to share a folder (or *directory*, depending on the NOS you are working with) or drive on a network server. Actually creating network shares certainly isn't rocket science. As a network administrator, you can create shares directly on the server (where you have logged in locally with an administrative account) or from a remote client computer (where you are logged on to the network with an account that has administrative rights). Let's look at two different network operating systems to illustrate the creation of shares locally on the server and remotely from a network client.

Sharing Windows 2000 Server Folders

As an administrator logged on to a server running Windows 2000 Server, you can create new folders on the server using Windows Explorer. These folders can then be filled with the files that will be shared on the network. Once the folder has been created, you only need to share the folder (you can also share an entire drive, if you wish).

To share the folder (or drive), you right-click the folder and select Sharing from the shortcut menu that appears. The Properties dialog box for the folder will appear, providing the Sharing tab, as shown in Figure 8.2.

FIGURE 8.2

Options for Windows shares are configured in the folder or drive's Properties dialog box.

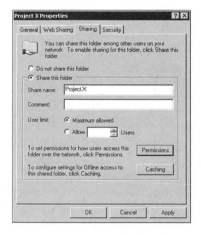

The share must be provided with a name. Other options can also be set in the Properties dialog box, such as the number of connections allowed to the share at any one time.

The Permissions button provided on the share's Properties dialog box is used to designate the different levels of access or permissions that are provided to the various users on the network. By default, everyone on the network is provided with full access to the share. If the shared information needs to be used and edited by everyone on the network, the default setting is just fine. However, in most cases the only way you can protect network resources such as shares is to assign different permission levels. Permission levels and security issues related to users on the network are discussed in more detail in the section "Understanding Share Permissions" in Chapter 16.

Once the various parameters for the share have been set and the Properties dialog box has been closed, the folder will be designated as a share in the Windows Explorer, and a small "share hand" will appear holding the folder, as shown in Figure 8.3.

FIGURE 8.3

Shared folders, such as the Project X folder shown here, are marked with a share icon.

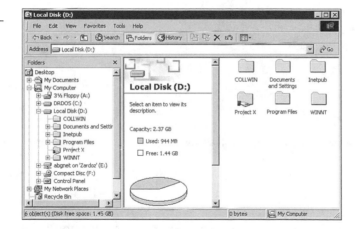

By default, Windows server shares are available to everyone who logs on to the network (this is because a group called Everyone, which has all users as members, is granted access to the shares). Security for the shares (as discussed in Chapter 16) must be configured either on a user or group basis.

Sharing Directories on a NetWare Server

Shared folders (as they are called on a Windows network) or directories (as we still call them on a NetWare server) can also be created by an administrator logged on to the server remotely. For example, as a NetWare administrator using the NWADMIN program, you can log on to the network server from any Windows client computer. You could then create a new directory on any of the server's volumes. This is done by right-clicking any of the available volume icons in the NDS tree and then selecting Create from the shortcut menu.

The Create Directory dialog box appears, as shown in Figure 8.4. All you have to do is supply a name for the directory and then click Create. The new folder will appear in the NDS tree (in the volume that you specified).

FIGURE 8.4

New directories can be created on the server by the administrator from a remote client.

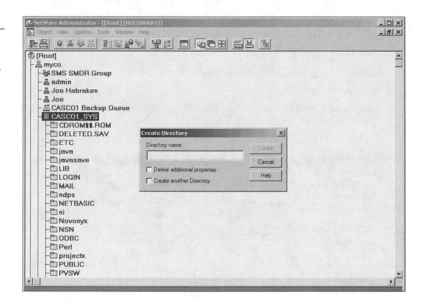

The next thing you need to do is to actually assign users the right to access the directory on the network. NetWare doesn't have a mechanism like the Share feature found in Windows that immediately shares the resource with all the users on the network. On a NetWare network, you must create trustees for the directory. These trustees can then access the directory (their access levels will depend on the rights assigned when they are made trustees).

The easiest way to create the trustees for a NetWare directory using the NWADMIN program is to right-click the directory in the NDS tree and then select Details from the shortcut menu that appears. A dialog box will appear containing the various settings for the directory. To add trustees for the directory, be sure that the Trustees of This Directory tab is chosen, as shown in Figure 8.5.

To actually add trustees for the directory, click the Add Trustee button. A Select Object dialog box will open that can be used to select an individual user, multiple users, or groups of users. Individual permission levels can then be assigned to each user or group as needed.

FIGURE 8.5

FIGURE 8.5

Trustees specified
for the directory
will have access
to the directory
on the network.

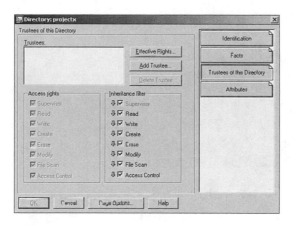

Working with User Directories

So far we have been looking at shared folders and directories as repositories of data
that will be accessed by a number of users on the network. Another type of directory
found on network servers is called a *home directory* or *folder* (again, depending on
the NOS you are using). It is a share configured for one particular user. It supplies
that user a private directory on the server to store important files.

Tip

Setting up home directories for users makes a lot of sense. Home directories supply
users with a place to keep their data (rather than locally on their computers), which
makes the data a little more secure. Also, encouraging users to save their files in their
home directories on the server makes it easy for you to back up users' data when you
back up the server. Backing up a server is discussed in Chapter 14, "Protecting Network
Data," in the section "Backing Up Data."

A home directory can be created for a user when you create the user's account. For
example, Figure 8.6 shows the Create User dialog box, which is accessed using the
NWADMIN program. Notice that an option is provided to create a home directory
for the user.

Once you have named the user and specified the home directory name and path (by
default, the directory name will be the same as the user's name), you can click the
Create button to create the new user. The user account will be created and the home
directory for the user will also be created.

Windows 2000 Server also makes it easy for you to create home folders for your
users. All you have to do is create a folder on the server that will hold all the user's
folders and then share it. Then in the user's Properties dialog box, you can specify
the path for the home folder and have it created automatically. You can also map
the home folder to a drive letter that can easily be accessed by the user from a client
computer.

FIGURE 8.6

Creating a home directory for the user supplies them with space on the network to save their files.

Figure 8.7 shows the Profile tab of a Windows user's Properties dialog box. Notice that the home folder will be mapped to the Z: drive. More importantly, look how the location of the home folder has been specified in the To: box.

FIGURE 8.7

Home folders can be specified for users using the UNC to refer to the server and share using friendly names.

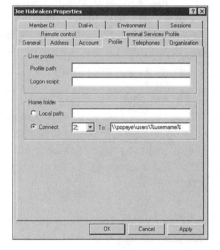

The folder for the user is to be created in a share on the server called *users*. But what's the Popeye stuff? What you are seeing here is called the *Universal Naming Convention (UNC)*. It is a system that uses "friendly names" to refer to resources on a network. The UNC for a share on a server takes the format `\\server name\share name`. So, in the case of Figure 8.7, the share "users," located on the server Popeye, will hold the home folder for the user (and all your users). One last thing: The %username% notation is a way to have the Windows Server automatically create the name for the user's home folder (which, remember, is a share just for that user) using the user's login name.

You can view your various user folders by opening the shared folder that you specified as the container for the home folders. A user can access his home folder by browsing the network or by opening the logical drive that was mapped to the folder. Let's take a look at how users would find network shares and map logical drives to these shares.

Locating Network Resources

Once you have created shared folders or directories on your server, users can access these shares from their client computers. One way to access a network share is to browse for all the shares available and then open the appropriate one. It's worth noting that if the aforementioned share permissions have been implemented, users may see shares on the network that they do not have access to.

Browsing the network with a Windows client (which is the predominant client on both NetWare and Windows networks) is pretty straightforward; for example, on a Windows 2000 Professional client, all the user has to do is double-click the My Network Places icon on the Windows desktop. The Entire Network icon in the My Network Places window can then be used to browse the networks that the client can connect to. For example, Figure 8.8 shows the Entire Network browser window for a client that can connect to both a Microsoft Windows network and a NetWare network (the client computer is configured with both client software for both network types).

FIGURE 8.8

The Entire Network window provides a portal to the servers available on the network.

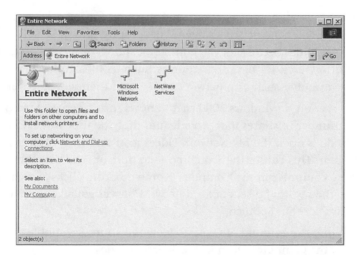

For this particular client to view the Windows Server domains available on the network, the user would double-click the Microsoft Windows Network icon. NetWare servers and shared directories on these servers would be accessed by double-clicking the NetWare Services icon (and a couple of extra double-clicks in either case to actually view the shares available on a particular server). Figure 8.9 shows the shares available on a Windows domain controller named Popeye.

FIGURE 8.9

A user can browse for a particular share on a network server.

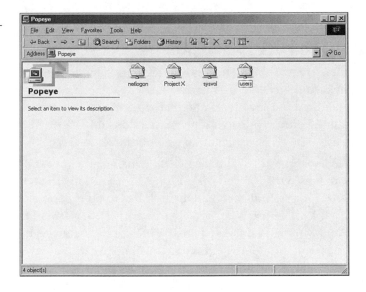

Searching for Network Resources

Browsing for network resources can be intimidating for network users who don't have a good feel for the network's overall geography and get lost looking for a particular shared folder because of the number of shares or servers on the network. Users can also search for network resources, such as files and folders, as well as for a particular computer, such as a network server, and then view the resources it offers.

Let's say a user on a Windows 2000 client knows that a server named Popeye is the host for a number of shares that provide files that the user would like to use. All the user has to do is open the My Network Places icon and then click the Search button on the toolbar. This causes the Search pane to appear. The user then provides the name of the computer in the Computer Name box and clicks Search Now. Figure 8.10 shows the result of a search for a network server called Popeye that is part of the Windows domain Spinach.

Once the computer is found, it's easy to view the shares available on the server. Just double-click the computer's icon in the Search window.

FIGURE 8.10

You can search for network resources, such as computers, files, and folders.

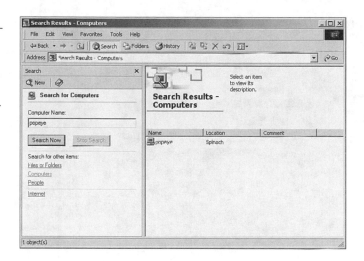

Mapping a Network Drive

Because browsing the network can be tedious and searching the network won't be that successful for some users (especially if they are not that familiar with where specific network shares are located), the best way to give a user easy access to a network share is to map a logical drive to the share. The mapped drive can then be accessed by users directly as if the drive were located locally.

Mapping a network drive in a Windows-based client (which has to be the most widely used client OS on the planet) is equally easy in any of the NOS environments, such as Windows Server and NetWare. All a user has to do is search or browse for a specific share. Then the share can be mapped by right-clicking the share and selecting Map Network Drive from the shortcut menu. The Map Network Drive dialog box then appears (see Figure 8.11). It allows a user to select the drive that will be mapped to the share.

Once the share is mapped, it appears in the user's Windows Explorer, as shown in Figure 8.12, as if it were a local drive. Mapping the drive makes it much easier for users to access files held in a share when they are using application software. All they have to do is access the logical drive and then quickly open a particular file.

Note

Depending on the NOS you are using, logon scripts can be written for users that connect them to shares on the network and create a drive mapping. Logon scripts can do much more than just map shares for users; they can also configure environment settings for the local client workstation. It makes sense to learn at least a little bit of the scripting language that is embraced by the NOS you will use on your network.

FIGURE 8.11
Shares can be mapped as logical drives on a Windows client using the Map Network Drive dialog box.

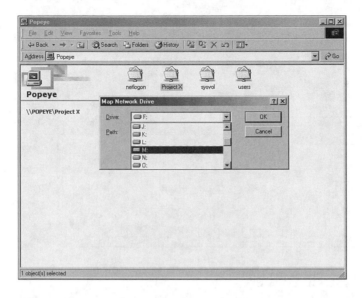

FIGURE 8.12
Mapped shares will appear as logical drives that can be accessed just like any local drive.

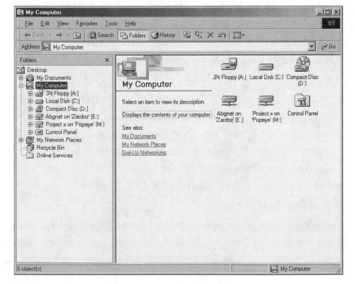

Sharing Printers

Printing has an interesting place in the seemingly long history of PC networking (although it has only been a little more than 20 years); the ability to share printers, along with file sharing, was one of the key reasons personal computers were networked in the first place. A *shared printer* on a network is a printer that accepts print jobs from more than one computer.

When you connect a printer to a server on the network and configure it to share print resources with users on the network, it is referred to as a *print server*. Different terms are also often used to designate where the printer is actually located on the network.

A *local printer* is a printer that is directly attached to a server. The printer is only local, however, in relation to the server that it is attached to. This server will, obviously, serve as the print server for the printer.

A *remote printer* is a printer attached to a computer other than your server, which can be pretty confusing because the computer that the printer is attached to would consider the printer local. Whether a printer is local or remote will depend on which computer on the network you are using as your reference point.

A third type of network printer also exists: the direct connect printer. A *direct connect printer* is a printer that contains its own network interface, processor, and memory for print serving. These printers are typically attached directly to a network hub using twisted-pair cable, just like any computer on the network.

Printers without direct connection hardware can be attached to devices (made by a number of vendors), such as the Hewlett-Packard JetDirect external print server, and then connected directly to the network. The external print server provides at least one parallel port for connecting the printer and a CAT 5 Ethernet port for connection to the network hub. Figure 8.13 shows a Hewlett-Packard JetDirect Ex Plus single-port external printer server.

FIGURE 8.13

Devices such as a Hewlett-Packard JetDirect external print server allow you to directly connect a printer to the network hub.

However, a server or other client computer will still have to be configured as the print server for the printer to manage print jobs. This role does not require the RAM or processor resources from the computer that would be required if the printer were directly connected to the server, however, because the printer has its own hardware to handle the spooling and queuing of print jobs.

You don't necessarily have to use a dedicated server as a print server. Client operating systems such as Windows Me and Windows 2000 Professional can also be used on computers that will provide print services to the network. They work fine as print servers in situations where you don't want to spend the money for another server license just to provide printing.

How Network Printing Works

Before we take a look at how you would configure a network print server, let's discuss how network printing actually works. We have already talked about how communication between a client computer and a server is handled by the network client software and the server's NOS.

When a user prints a document from a network client using application software to a network printer, the redirector on the client machine sends the data out onto the network to the print server computer that controls the particular network printer.

The print server uses software called a *print spooler* to accept the print job and place this job in its *print queue*, which is just some of the computer's memory used to hold print jobs until they can be sent to the printer. When the printer is free to accept the print job, it is released from the print queue.

Several printers can be configured to be part of a *printer pool*, which is basically a group of printers (identical printers that use the same driver software) that is seen by the network as just one printer. Because multiple printers actually make up the one print resource, you have a lot more muscle when it comes to handling a huge influx of print jobs from network users. The various print jobs will be parsed out to the printers in the pool as the printers become available.

Configuring a Print Server

The specifics of configuring a server computer to be a print server will depend on the NOS you are running. However, certain tasks must be accomplished in every network

operating system environment for clients to be able to print to the printer that is
hosted by the print server:

- *The printer must be physically attached to the print server.* Typically this attachment will use a parallel printer cable that attaches the printer to a parallel
  port, such as LPT1, on the computer. Printers with their own print server software will be directly connected to the network via a hub.

- *The appropriate printer driver must be installed on the print server.* Every NOS
  comes with a database of printer drivers. If you've just bought a state-of-the-
  art printer and are installing it on a network that has been running for a
  while, the printer will come with a disk or CD-ROM that supplies the appropriate printer driver for your NOS. Windows 2000 Server makes installing a
  printer extremely easy. Any Plug and Play printer attached to the server will
  be automatically recognized, as shown in Figure 8.14.

FIGURE 8.14

Printers attached
to a Windows
2000 Server
machine are
automatically
recognized by
the Plug and
Play feature.

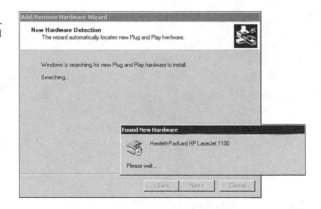

- *The printer must be shared on the network.* How this is accomplished will
  depend on the NOS. On a Windows 2000 Server machine, any directly connected printer will automatically be shared once the appropriate driver has
  been configured. On a Netware server, the printer is available once it has
  been added to the NDS tree.

Once the printer is available on the network, client computers must be configured to
print to the printer; this is really just a matter of connecting to the remote printer
and having the appropriate printer driver installed on each client computer.
Windows clients can actually search or browse for printers on the network.

Once the printer is located, the user can connect to the printer by right-clicking the
printer and selecting Connect (some older Windows client versions require users to
drag the Printer icon from the Network Neighborhood into their Printers window to

connect). Then all the user has to do is provide the appropriate printer driver. A Windows 2000 Server machine functioning as a print server makes the process even easier because a number of different printer drivers for network clients can be stored on the server, as shown in Figure 8.15.

FIGURE 8.15

Printer drivers for different network clients can be stored on a Windows 2000 print server.

Note

In the Windows and NetWare networking environments, printers are published to the Active Directory tree and the NDS tree, respectively. This makes it easy for clients on the network to locate a resource such as a printer in the network's hierarchical catalog (meaning the directory services database).

Managing a Network Printer

Managing a network printer is more than just making sure the printer has a full toner cartridge and is loaded with paper. The network administrator has the ability to pause printing, delete certain print jobs, and even clear the entire print queue.

By default, the administrator account on the print server will have the ability to manage the print queue. You, as the administrator, can also provide certain users on the network with the ability to manage printers. This allows you to delegate some of the workload related to printer and document management.

The degree to which a user can interact with a printer (through the print server) will depend on the permissions or rights that user has been assigned in relation to the printer. Printer permissions or rights are very similar to the permissions or rights you assign to a user in relation to a network share.

For example, on a Windows 2000 Server machine that serves as a print server, the Everyone group (which includes all the users on the network) is provided with the ability to print. Figure 8.16 shows the Properties dialog box for a network printer.

FIGURE 8.16

Different levels of access to the print queue and the printer can be provided to certain users or groups of users.

The actual management of the printer and the print queue will vary from NOS to NOS. In the NetWare environment, an administrator can log on to the print server remotely and view the print queue using the NetWare Administrator utility (the administrator can also log on to a server and use the Console GUI to view and manage documents in the print queue; any printer on the network can be monitored in the NDS tree). On a Windows network, an administrator can also monitor printers and their print queues remotely from a network client (outfitted with the proper administration tools) or directly from the server.

Working in Mixed Network Environments

It is not uncommon to have a network that is not completely homogenous. For example, a Windows 2000 Server network may still have users in a particular department who need to access file or print resources on a NetWare server. Perhaps some users on a NetWare or Windows 2000 Server network are using Macintosh computers to run desktop publishing software but still need to access network resources just like any other network user.

Although in the early days of networking it almost seemed that the different network operating systems made it a point to be as incompatible as possible, platform interactivity has become the rule rather than the exception. It is now fairly common for an NOS to not only support a variety of client operating systems but also provide the ability for different network operating systems to talk to each other on the network.

This means that resources on a mixed network will be served up by servers running different network operating systems. For example, you might have a network where your various Web services are provided by a Solaris Unix server, users are authenticated to the network by a server running Microsoft Windows 2000 or XP Server, and some print and file services are provided by a server or servers running NetWare.

Obviously, serving as the network administrator for a mixed network means you will need to have a working knowledge of more than one NOS. You are probably thinking that trying to get different network operating systems to basically behave and play well together is a nightmare, but, actually, it's not as bad as you might think. In the example mentioned previously, you could actually get all the network operating systems to talk to each other. Because the Windows server is managing user authentication, you only need to install services on the Windows server that will allow it to talk to the Solaris and NetWare servers running on the network.

The services that provide communication between different network operating systems are referred to as *gateways*. A gateway is a computer that uses software as a communication bridge between incompatible platforms or network architectures.

All you have to do is install a network file system gateway on the Microsoft Windows server (which is an optional service available in the Microsoft Windows NOS). This allows for communication between the Windows server (and all the clients it manages) and the Solaris Web server.

For the Windows server and the NetWare servers to communicate, you would install Gateway Services for NetWare. This allows users on the Windows network to access print and file services on NetWare servers on the network. Figure 8.17 shows Gateway Services for NetWare being installed on a Windows server.

FIGURE 8.17

Gateway services can be used to promote communication between different servers running different network operating systems.

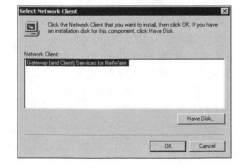

Certainly, having a network that only uses one network operating system on its servers is the ideal situation. You will find, however, that because of the different strengths and weaknesses of the different network operating systems, most larger networks will embrace different NOS platforms.

Chapter Summary

- A network share is a drive or folder on a server that is made available to network users.

- Group membership can be used to assign users different levels of access to shares on the network.

- Home folders or directories can be created for users to provide them with private shares on a network server.

- Windows clients can browse or search for network shares on the network.

- Network shares can be mapped to logical drives, making it easier for users to access the files on a particular share.

- Printers can be shared on the network. This shared resource is managed by a print server.

- Print jobs sent to network printers are accepted by the print spooler software and placed in the print server's print queue.

- A print server is configured by physically attaching the printer to the server computer and installing the appropriate driver for the printer on the server.

- Different access levels can be granted to users in relation to shared printers. Some users can be designated to help manage printers and the print queue.

- In a mixed network environment, embracing more than one NOS gateway software can be used to allow communication between the different NOS platforms.

9

WORKING WITH
APPLICATIONS ON THE
NETWORK

In this chapter

- Deploying user applications on the network
- Understanding groupware
- Working with Lotus Notes
- Deploying Exchange Server
- Working with shared databases

A program is a spell cast over a computer, turning input into error messages.

–Anonymous

So far we have concentrated on how networks actually function: We've discussed protocols, the OSI model, peer/client operating systems, and network operating systems. We've also taken a look at sharing resources such as folders and printers in both peer-to-peer networking environments and on server-based networks.

Our next area of focus is the application. Application software provides us with the various productivity tools we use to actually get work done. Users on a network can take advantage of all sorts of applications; although we usually think of word processing and spreadsheet software as typical applications, other client applications are used to access special servers. These applications provide communication services and access to special databases. Let's begin our discussion of applications with a short discussion on how selecting the software to be used on your network should be approached. We can then look at specific productivity software, such as Microsoft Office and Sun's StarOffice.

Selecting Application Software

Before you can deploy application software either directly on client computers or over the network (both of which are discussed in the next section), you must first select the applications that will allow your various users to get their work done. The process for selecting software for end users should not only revolve around the features provided by the software but also the overall usability of the interface that the software provides.

While in an ideal world, cost would not be an issue in choosing the best software for your company or home office, we, of course, do not live in an ideal world. So, you will have to weigh software features and the user-friendly factor in light of the cost of the software.

Before selecting new software, you should test the software. This might mean buying a copy or two of the software package and testing it in a "mock" network setting to get a picture of the overall usability of the software and how it performs in a network setting. Since, on a small network, buying "test" copies might be prohibitive, take advantage of the fact that most software vendors do provide limited-use demo copies of their software either in the form of shareware or trial versions. Usually the cost of a trial CD is limited to shipping and handling. Testing the software first can save a lot of headaches in the future.

Ideally, setting up an end-user focus group to test the software and then comment on its strengths and weaknesses can help you determine the overall usability of the software. Using this information, along with other factors such as cost and licensing issues, can help you decide whether or not the software will be appropriate for your network (and your users). Many software vendors also supply white papers and various case studies that allow you to see how other companies have deployed and used the software.

Having worked in the computer networking field for a number of years, I have sat in meetings and presentations on a number of occasions where I have heard network administrators and information systems managers say the following:

"I see no compelling reason to deploy or upgrade to that particular software product."

Now, reading between the lines this statement can mean a number of things. It can mean that the network administrators have not done their homework and know nothing about that particular software product. It can also mean that the features provided don't outweigh the overall cost (both in terms of the time needed for configuration and deploying the new software and the budgetary hit) that will be required to deploy the software on a company-wide basis.

Corporate executives will often (unless there is a real budget crunch) want to have the latest and greatest software running on their networks. It almost seems to be a status thing, so that they can say they are running "Super Software 2002" on their network when they are playing racquet ball or golfing with their executive buddies.

Network administrators must do their homework and also exercise great diplomacy in guiding corporate officers into making the right decisions in regards to selecting software for end users. Keep in mind that you will have to support software on the network and poor software selections will only reflect on you, because you have to keep them up and running.

When selecting software, use the following list of questions as a starting place:

- How much will it cost for the software and software licenses necessary to deploy the software on the network?
- How many administrative hours will be required to deploy the new software?
- Will client computers or servers on the network need to be updated to run the new software (and what will be the cost)?
- Will end-user training be required for users to get the most out of the new software?
- Does the new software supply features and functionality that are not currently available using software already available on the network?
- Is the software compatible with software currently running on the network?

When choosing new software, go slow, do your research, and get as much input from your user base as possible. And don't reject new software versions outright, just because it will mean more work for you. Having a network that runs well but doesn't provide the proper productivity tools for end users will eventually come back to haunt you.

Using Application Software on the Network

In the pre-Windows days of the PC revolution, applications such as Lotus 1-2-3, dBASE, and WordPerfect were the primary productivity tools for business users of the PC. Over time, the single application has been displaced by the application suite, which provides an integrated group of applications that share a common interface.

Suite products, such as Microsoft Office, Sun's StarOffice, and WordPerfect Office, provide a word processor, spreadsheet, database, and variety of other applications (depending on the application suite you are using). Suite products also typically offer versions that run on different operating systems. Microsoft Office is available for both Windows and the Apple OS. StarOffice runs on Windows PCs as well as Unix and Linux workstations. WordPerfect Office provides multiple-platform support and is even available in a platform-independent Java-based version.

Note | Selecting the appropriate suite product for your network users should revolve around issues such as features, cost, your network operating system, and the OS running on your client computers. You should also carefully weigh other issues, such as product support and the user learning curve, when you select an application suite for your user base.

The network administrator (meaning you) must make a major decision related to end-user applications: Should they be installed on each client machine or run over the network? Both of these scenarios have pros and cons. Let's take a look at each.

Client-Based Applications

Installing end-user applications on client PCs requires that the PCs have the appropriate hard drive space to accommodate the software files. You must also purchase a separate copy of the software for each client PC or purchase a license for each client.

Having the software files for the application suite actually residing on the client machines can make them more vulnerable to "accidents," such as end users who decide to clean up all those "unneeded" files on their PCs. Applying updates and other fixes to the software can also be a hassle because the update files will have to be placed on every client computer.

So far I've been emphasizing the downside of installing applications on your network clients, but there are some compelling issues on the upside. First of all, running applications locally on client computers does not put additional stress on network servers or eat up a lot of network bandwidth. Running applications locally also means you won't have the added cost of deploying an application server. Another plus of installing applications on the client computers is that the users can continue to work even if the network goes down.

Network-Based Applications

As mentioned in the previous section, running applications from a network application server can result in network slowdowns. However, providing software applications from a network server means that only a subset of the applications' files need to reside on the network clients, meaning you don't have to deploy client computers with large hard drives.

Keeping applications on the network also makes it easier for you when updating the software, and you can protect the actual application files from "accidents." Licensing network clients to use applications running on a server can also (in some situations) be cheaper than licensing the software for installation on each client.

As is the case with every other deployment issue we've discussed in this book, you need to do some research before you select an application suite for your network users. It also makes sense to do some testing (and some research to find case studies) to see whether running an application from a server is a better way to go than installing the application on each client computer.

Working with Groupware Products

In Chapter 1, "Computer Networking Overview," a brief discussion was provided of the communication server. Its purpose is to offer different avenues for user-to-user communication on the network. This type of server provides services such as electronic mail, shared scheduling, and discussion groups (for the posting of messages).

A communication server operates in a true client/server fashion, where client applications are used to communicate with different communication services on the server. The client/server software run on a communication server is often referred to as *groupware*. Groupware is best described as a suite of client communication software used to communicate with a communication server package.

Groupware applications are designed for user communication and collaboration. They offer such services as the following:

- *Electronic mail system.* The groupware communication server serves as the mail server for internal e-mail systems and/or Internet e-mail.
- *Group scheduling.* A centralized scheduling system is maintained on the communication server.
- *Discussion groups.* Users can read and post messages to a discussion database. Discussion groups can be created for the discussion and development of projects by users on the network.
- *Information databases.* Databases such as an employee handbook and a centralized employee address book (including e-mail and phone extension information) can be hosted by the communication server.
- *Task automation.* Forms can be developed that allow users to order office supplies online and invite users to a meeting.

The fact that all these communication resources are centrally held on the communication server means any user on the network can access a particular service, such as e-mail or the calendar/scheduling service. Even remote users can log on to the network through an RAS service and access the services on the groupware server.

Groupware products run on top of an existing NOS on a network server. These communication packages can experience a large number of user connections at any one time. Not only does a server used to run a groupware product need the appropriate muscle to run the underlying NOS, but it also needs to be able to process numerous requests and store a number of online databases. Large hard drives (or multiple drives in a stripe set), generous amounts of memory, and perhaps even multiple processors are typical hardware needs for a communication server. Because information stored on the server hosting the groupware applications can change by the minute, it is also important to perform a daily backup of the communication server (for information about server backup strategies, see the section "Backing Up Data" in Chapter 14, "Protecting Network Data").

A number of groupware products are available on the market. Two of the most widely used groupware environments are Lotus Notes and Microsoft Exchange Server. Let's take a look at both of these groupware environments individually.

Using Lotus Notes

Lotus Notes provides a client/server groupware environment that can be run on a number of different network platforms. Although this groupware product is generally referred to as *Lotus Notes*, it actually has both a client and a server side. The client side is referred to as Lotus Notes and the server side is called Lotus Domino Server. The Lotus Notes client software can be run on a number of Windows clients (95 or better) and the Mac PowerPC (Mac OS 9.0 or better). Figure 9.1 shows the Lotus Notes (Release 5) client software interface on a PC running Windows.

FIGURE 9.1

The Lotus Notes client software provides users with easy access to communication services on the Lotus Domino Server.

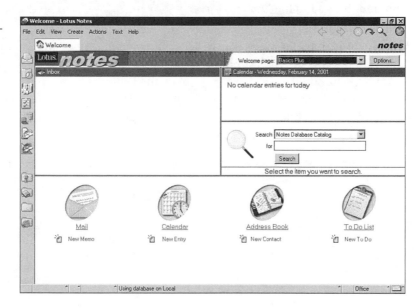

The server product is called *Lotus Domino Server*. It is an add-on communication server that is compatible with Windows Server, NetWare, and Sun Solaris. Lotus Notes supports communications using a number of different network protocols, including TCP/IP, NetBEUI, and IPX/SPX. Figure 9.2 provides a look at Lotus Domino Server running on Windows 2000 Server.

FIGURE 9.2

Lotus Domino Server runs on top of an existing NOS.

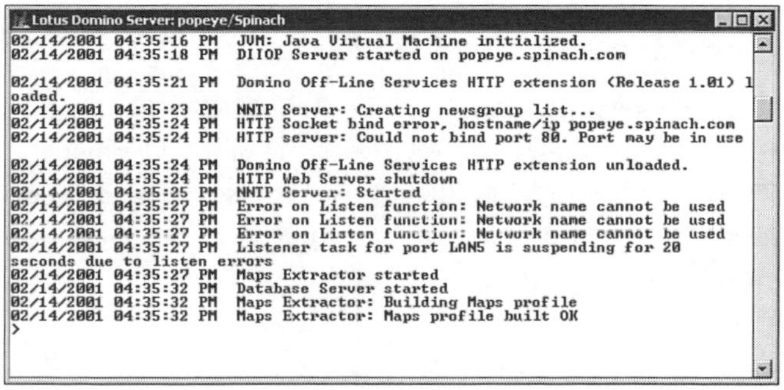

Lotus Notes Administration

As you can see from Figure 9.2, Lotus Domino Server is monitored and controlled using a command-line interface. Fortunately, Lotus provides an administrative tool—the Domino Administrator—that has a fairly easy-to-use interface for monitoring and managing the Domino server.

The Notes administrator (who could be the network administrator or someone assigned the duties of managing the communication server) can monitor, manage, and add resources to the Domino Server. The Domino Administrator software can be installed on any network client to manage the Domino software remotely (much like the NetWare Administrator). For example, the Notes administrator can use the Domino Administrator tool to view the different communication servers on the network and the resources they provide (see Figure 9.3).

FIGURE 9.3

Domino servers and the resources they offer on the network can be monitored using the Domino Administrator.

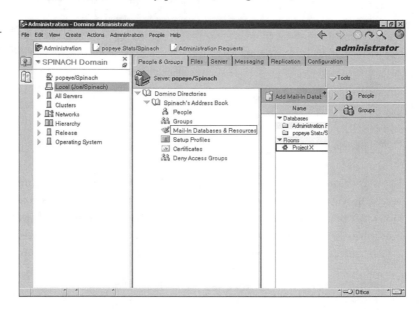

The Domino Administrator software can also be used to create new resources on the Domino Server, such as a discussion database. Figure 9.4 shows the creation of a new discussion database on a Domino Server. Users provided access to this database (resource security is another aspect of managing the communication server) will be able to read and post messages in this database.

FIGURE 9.4

A discussion database, as well as other types of new resources, can be created using the Domino Administrator software.

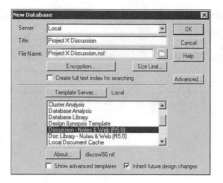

Although the Domino Administrator software's easy-to-use interface might make it easy to manage the communication server running Lotus Domino Server, the actual management tasks required to properly control the Notes/Domino groupware environment—such as creating user accounts and creating new Notes databases—are not. As with any NOS or special network service, it is important that you get the training or have the experience necessary to provide network users with a stable and consistent network resource.

Lotus Notes Client Operation

Because the Notes/Domino environment provides communication services, the Notes client provides a network user with the tools to send e-mail messages, set up meetings, schedule appointments, and read and add information in different Notes databases.

For example, a Notes client can send e-mail to a user or users on the network. If the Domino Server has been configured to handle Internet e-mail, the Notes client can also send e-mail to anyone with an e-mail address. Figure 9.5 shows the new message screen used to compose e-mail with the Notes client.

Users on the network access resources on the Domino Server using the Notes client. The Notes client provides access to all the different communication services provided by the Domino Server, such as e-mail (which was already mentioned), a calendar, a global address book, and discussion newsgroups. For example, Figure 9.6 shows the Notes calendar feature.

FIGURE 9.5

The Notes client provides an e-mail tool for composing new messages.

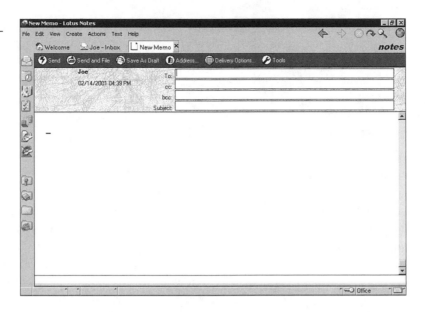

FIGURE 9.6

Users can set up appointments and meetings using the shared calendar feature.

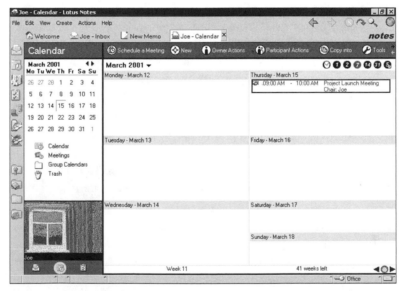

One thing to remember about a groupware platform such as Notes/Domino is that all data related to a particular user is stored on the Lotus Domino Server machine. This makes it possible for the communication server software to verify whether a particular employee is available for a meeting. It also allows users to temporarily have their e-mail inboxes managed by other users when they are away. User collaboration is the theme of groupware such as Lotus Notes.

Using Microsoft Exchange Server

Microsoft Exchange Server is Microsoft's take on groupware. Microsoft Exchange Server runs on a server-class computer that is configured with the Microsoft Windows 2000 Server NOS. Microsoft Exchange is tightly integrated with the Windows 2000 Server (or Windows XP Server) Active Directory. This means that not only are certain Exchange Server administrative duties handled from the Active Directory, but information in the Active Directory database, such as users and groups, is shared with Exchange Server.

Exchange Server offers e-mail services, discussion groups, and shared calendars—all the communication services that you would expect from a groupware product. The client application used to communicate with Exchange Server is Microsoft Outlook. Outlook is part of the Microsoft Office suite.

Exchange Server Administration

Exchange Server administration is actually handled by two different tools on the server: the Active Directory and the Exchange System Manager. Because the Active Directory is used to manage user accounts and other objects on the network, it's no surprise that new e-mail accounts for users are actually created in the Active Directory Users and Computers snap-in (see Figure 9.7).

FIGURE 9.7

Exchange e-mail accounts for network users are created in the Windows Active Directory.

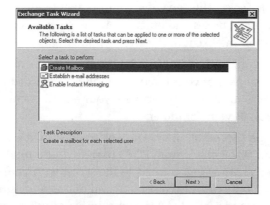

Administrative functions related to Exchange Servers on the network and different global address lists are handled using the Exchange System Manager. This utility can also be used to view user folders (such as the Inbox, calendar appointments, and so on) stored on the Exchange server. Figure 9.8 shows the Exchange System Manager (this is the manager used in version 5.5 of Exchange Server).

FIGURE 9.8

The Exchange Server environment is managed using the Exchange System Manager.

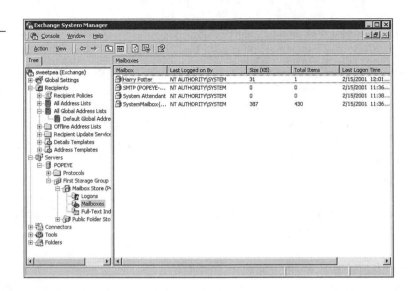

Outlook Client Operation

Microsoft Outlook can be used as a standalone product or as a client for Microsoft Exchange Server. Outlook supports a number of different e-mail services, including the following:

- *Microsoft Exchange Server.* This type of account makes Outlook an Exchange Server client, and mail boxes and other resources, such as shared public folders, are managed on the Exchange Server computer.

- *POP3.* POP3 is a protocol that allows a POP3 e-mail server to function as a mail drop. This means that your Internet e-mail is forwarded to the POP3 server and sits there until you connect with your e-mail client (Outlook) and download the mail to your computer.

- *IMAP.* IMAP is a protocol that allows Outlook to download e-mail from an IMAP mail server. IMAP differs from POP3 in that your e-mail is not removed from the mail server when you connect to the server with your e-mail client (Outlook); you are only provided a list of saved and new messages, which you can then open and read. IMAP is particularly useful when one e-mail account might be accessed by more than one computer (or other remote devices), allowing the same messages to be available from more than one device.

■ *HTTP*. The Hypertext Transfer Protocol is the set of rules that allows you to browse Web sites using a Web browser. HTTP e-mail is accessed via a Web site, and your inbox actually resides on a server that is hosted by the provider of the e-mail Web site, such as Microsoft (in the case of Hotmail) or Yahoo! (in the case of Yahoo! mail). Outlook can be configured to act as your e-mail client for HTTP mail such as Microsoft Hotmail.

When Outlook is used as an Exchange Server e-mail client, users are afforded special abilities not available when Outlook is used as an Internet e-mail client. Sent messages can be given expiration dates, and messages that have not been read can even be deleted from a recipient's mail box or updated with new versions of these messages.

Using Outlook on an Exchange server also provides users with access to the global address book, making it easy to send e-mail to other users on the network or to create distribution lists for messaging, as shown in Figure 9.9.

FIGURE 9.9

Outlook can access address books, such as the global address book, on the Exchange Server.

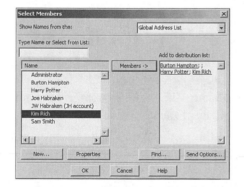

Outlook provides easy access to a user's Inbox, calendar, contacts list, and other communication/organizational tools (see Figure 9.10, which shows Outlook 2000). An Outlook user can create meetings that automatically invite the participants, as well as create tasks that are assigned to other users on the network. Outlook and Exchange Server provide a fairly user-friendly groupware environment that enables network users to collaborate with each other.

FIGURE 9.10

Outlook pro-
vides personal
informational
management
tools that can be
used by network
users to collabo-
rate with each
other.

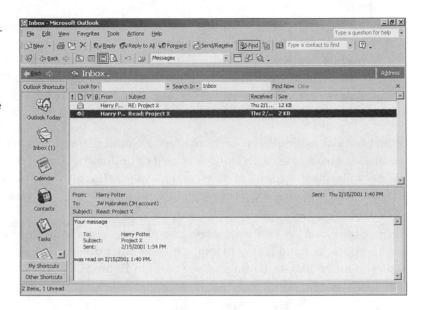

Understanding Client/Server Databases

Another client/server environment found on corporate networks is the *shared data-base*. Shared databases allow users to access information that is held centrally on a database server. This central database may hold customer information, employee information, or data related to a particular project.

The centralized database is certainly not a new concept to computing; large data-base systems were an integral part of early mainframe and miniframe environ-ments. Oracle Corporation's powerful Oracle client/server database environment started out as a product for the miniframe environment but has evolved into a mul-tiplatform client/server system that can also be run on Pentium-based LAN servers.

Client/server databases require both a dedicated server and a client front end. The database server software, also referred to as the *database engine*, is designed to accept requests for information (a request to a database for information is called a *query*) from clients on the network. The actual query is made by the client software on the user's computer. Because the exchange of data between the database server and the database client is transparent to the user, the features and functionality provided by the database client will be the same as if the database resided locally on the user's computer.

An excellent example of a client/server database system is Microsoft's SQL Server (SQL stands for *Structured Query Language*; it is the language used by the database client software to send queries to the database server). SQL Server is an add-on prod-uct that runs on an existing Windows server.

The client front end used to query SQL Server is Microsoft Access. Microsoft Access is a powerful standalone database software application in its own right. It provides all the tools needed to create complex relational databases. Figure 9.11 shows an Access window and an open Access/SQL project.

Note
SQL databases accessed by Access are called *projects*. All the familiar Access objects, such as tables, forms, queries, and reports, are used when working with a SQL database project. This provides any end user with some experience in Access an easy-to-use front end for creating queries, entering new data, and printing out reports as he or she communicates with the database server.

Client/server technology has been changing by leaps and bounds because of the Internet and the desire of companies to try their hands at e-commerce. Any time you book an airline reservation online or order a book from an online bookstore, you are taking advantage of client/server database technology. We will talk more about e-commerce in the section "The Internet and Your Corporate Presence" in Chapter 13, "Hosting a Web Site."

FIGURE 9.11
Shared databases need a client front end, such as Microsoft Access.

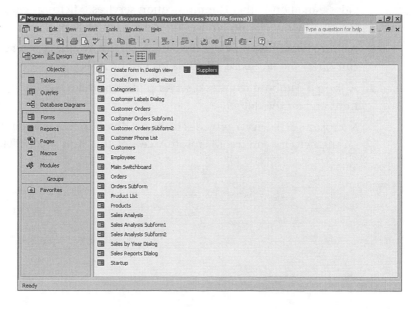

Chapter Summary

- Software suites have replaced standalone applications as the primary productivity tools for end users.

- Applications such as Microsoft Office can be installed on client computers or run from a network server.

- Running applications from a server provides greater control over software updates and provides more security for the software files.

- Applications installed on client computers may run faster than applications run from servers, which can eat up a lot of network bandwidth.

- Groupware products provide communication tools for network users. These tools include e-mail, discussion groups, and shared scheduling.

- Lotus Notes is a groupware product that provides the Lotus Domino Server software for the communication server and the Notes client for client computers.

- Microsoft also provides a groupware platform. Microsoft Exchange Server provides e-mail and other communication services. Microsoft Outlook is used as the client for accessing services on the Exchange Server.

- A shared database provides a client/server environment where network users can query the database, which is located on a server.

- A shared database requires a server platform and a client that can act as the front end for the database.

- Microsoft's SQL Server provides a shared database environment where users on the network can use Microsoft Access as their front-end client.

PART

EXPANDING YOUR NETWORK

EXPANDING A LAN WITH WAN TECHNOLOGY

In this chapter

- Defining the wide area network
- WAN technology and the Plain Old Telephone System
- Working with asynchronous and synchronous modems
- Understanding the T-carrier system
- Differentiating between Circuit and Packet Switching WAN technologies
- Working with Remote Access

A complex system that works is invariably found to have evolved from a simple system that worked.

–John Gall

Our exploration of networking has, so far, centered primarily on the local area network (LAN). LANs, however—even the largest—are isolated; they can only connect computers and other devices in a fairly small geographical area. Large companies and institutions that span multiple sites need to be able to connect all their LANs into one large network. Wide area networks (WANs) are networks made up of a number of LANs. So, a *wide area network* can be defined as a collection of LANs that extend over a wide geographic area.

> You might be wondering what the difference is between an internetwork and a WAN. An internetwork is a network of networks, but it doesn't necessarily span large geographical areas. An internetwork can exist at one site of a large company and is more about ways of expanding a LAN or LANs and still conserving network bandwidth or getting different network architectures to talk to each other on the same network. A WAN is a network that makes use of some of the same devices as an internetwork, but it exists primarily because of the need to connect LANs at different physical locations.

To connect LANs at different locations, some sort of technology must be used that can move data across great distances but still have it arrive at its final destination intact. A number of different technologies exist that can be used to move data from physical site to physical site.

This chapter will concentrate on the different WAN technologies that are in use today. Now, although you might think of the Internet as a collection of networks at different geographical locations, the Internet isn't really a WAN, it is an internetwork (although it does use some WAN technology). When you send data such as e-mail over the Internet (say, an e-mail to France), you aren't using a WAN technology that directly connects your site (your office or home) with the destination site in France. The e-mail goes from your computer to your local e-mail server and then starts a circuitous route that allows the data to hop from server to server until it reaches its destination. We will discuss the Internet and how it works in Chapter 11, "How the Internet Works."

I am making this point because this chapter really concentrates on technologies that are used by larger companies and institutions (although they don't have to be huge companies; they just have to be able to afford the technology). WAN technologies have actually been around since the days of the mainframe. Much of our discussion will revolve around technologies that take advantage of something that we all use: the *Plain Old Telephone System (POTS)*.

Working with the Plain Old Telephone System

The telephone system in this country has been around for more than a hundred years. And when you think about the actual physical infrastructure that makes up the POTS, you can see why it made sense and still makes sense to take advantage of the miles and miles of copper wire to connect computers at different sites.

> The telephone system is also often referred to as the *Public Switched Telephone Network (PSTN)*.

The telephone system is a switched network. This means that as a connection is established on the telephone system's network, it can be switched along different paths. For example, when you make a phone call, your voice communication does not necessarily move along the same route, even though you dial the same phone number when you call a particular person.

> The POTS actually started out as a system where the switching was handled by humans operating plugboards (everyone has seen an old television show or movie where the operator is actually switching the calls by physically connecting wires to a plugboard). The system progressed from human switching to electromechanical switching; switching on the POTS is now handled by digital technology.

As far as the transfer of data is concerned, the telephone system offers more than one possibility for moving information from source to destination. This includes dial-up connections, dedicated lease lines, and different packet-switching technologies. One of the newest technologies for data transfer over the POTS is Digital Subscriber Line (DSL). This technology allows for digital communication over existing phone lines and is fast becoming a viable choice for data transfer by home users (such as for high-speed connection to the Internet) and companies who can't justify the cost of some of the other data communication possibilities.

Before concentrating on the different possibilities for data movement on the POTS, we need to take a look at some terminology related to the physical infrastructure of the telephone system. If you have ever dealt with your local phone company, just in terms of voice telephone service, you know that you're typically responsible for the wiring and equipment inside your house (unless you purchase some kind of special service contract from your local phone company). The lines outside your house are the phone company's responsibility.

In the business world, the phone or LAN equipment inside the company would be called the *customer premise equipment (CPE)*. The place where the CPE ends and the phone company's line begins is called the *demarcation*. The actual physical wires that connect the business to the nearest phone company switching station is called the *local loop*. Figure 10.1 provides a diagram showing these different areas.

FIGURE 10.1
The CPE is connected to the phone system by the local loop.

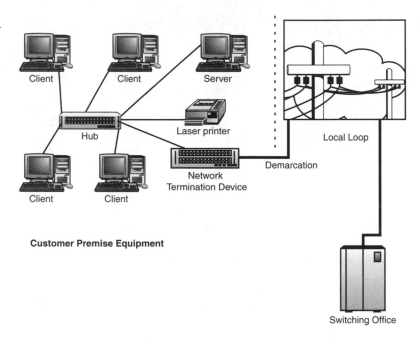

The customer premise equipment will be terminated by some kind of device, such as a router or a digital service unit. We will talk more about the different types of equipment used to connect a company's LAN to the local loop when we discuss specific LAN technologies, later in the chapter.

Working with Dial-up and Dedicated Connections

As already mentioned, the POTS offers more than one alternative for connecting LANs at different locations. Two of these options relate to dial-up connections using modems and connections that used dedicated lines.

In both of these connection strategies, you will run into a device called a *modem*. Two types of modems exist: asynchronous modems and synchronous modems. Let's take a closer look at how modems are involved in dial-up and dedicated connections over the POTS.

Asynchronous Modem Connections

The simplest and least expensive type of dial-up connection uses a modem to connect two computers. Because computers work with digital information, the digital data—that is, the ones (1) and zeros (0)—must be converted so that it can be carried by the analog phone line. This conversion from digital information to analog information is called *modulation*. When analog information is received on the modem connected to the destination computer (such as a server that is configured with a modem to allow dial-in connections), the data must be converted from analog back to digital. This process is called *demodulation*. You can see that the name for these devices, *modem*, is taken from *mod*ulation and *dem*odulation.

An *asynchronous modem* is designed to move data over a regular analog voice-grade telephone line, and it is asynchronous modems that most of us are familiar with. They are used to dial into a network server for telecommuters and are also used by millions of people to connect to the Internet.

Modems used for dial-in connections to Internet service providers and networks using TCP/IP typically use the Point-to-Point Protocol (PPP). PPP provides a secure connection and also provides for error checking. PPP is now used for most dial-in connections to remote access servers (discussed in Chapter 17, "Networking on the Run," in the section "Understanding Remote Access") and to Internet service providers.

An asynchronous modem uses start and stop bits as the way to let the receiving modem know when a particular packet of data starts and stops. Beyond the start and stop bits, many modems incorporate some type of error checking to ensure that the data is sent correctly across the telephone line. The simplest method of error checking involves including a *parity bit* when transmitting each byte. Essentially, parity checking works like this: The sending modem counts how many 1s are in the data stream. If the number is odd, the parity bit is set to 1. On the other end, the receiving modem also counts the number of 1s and determines whether the number is odd or even. The receiving modem then compares its results with the parity bit. If the results match, the data is probably okay and is sent on for processing. If the parity bits don't match, the data is rejected and the destination computer requests a resending of the data.

Modems are generally available for either internal or external connections to a computer. An internal modem plugs into an expansion slot on the motherboard of your computer and provides an *RJ-11 jack* (a four-wire telephone jack) from which you can connect a standard telephone cable between the modem and your wall telephone jack.

An external modem is a separate box that is connected to your computer by way of a serial cable (known as an *RS-232 cable*). External modems have an RJ-11 jack for your connection to your telephone and normally have lights to indicate various status conditions. Figure 10.2 shows a U.S. Robotics 56K external modem. External modems have a slight advantage over internal modems in that you can reset an external modem (turn it off, and then on) without having to reboot the computer.

FIGURE 10.2

External modems can easily be connected to a computer's COM port.

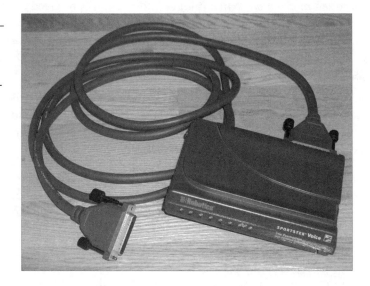

Modem speed is measured in terms of the number of *bits per second (bps)* that can travel across the phone line. As shown in Table 10.1, the International Telecommunications Union has developed the so-called *V series* of standards for modem speed. Note that some standard designations contain the words *bis* or *terbo*. These designations have nothing to do with speed and are merely the French words for second and third, respectively, indicating that these are revisions of earlier standards.

Table 10.1   ITU Standards for Modems

Standard	Bps	Year Introduced
V.22bis	2400	1984
V.32	9600	1984
V.32bis	14,400	1991
V.32terbo	19,200	1993
V.FastClass (V.FC)	28,800	1993
V.34	28,800	1994
V.42	57,600	1995
V.90	57,600	1997

There is some confusion between the bps rate and the baud rate of a modem. *Baud* is an older term that refers to the oscillation of a sound wave on which one bit of data is carried, whereas *bps* refers to the actual number of bits transmitted each second. In early modems, the baud rate and the bps rate were equivalent. For instance, an early 300bps modem did, in fact, have 300 oscillations of sound waves each second. However, as technology evolved, engineers developed methods to compress information and manipulate analog signals to send multiple bits with each sound wave oscillation. These improvements rendered the baud rate obsolete as a measurement of speed. For instance, a modem transmitting at 28,800bps might in fact be transmitting at only 9,600 baud.

When reading through the specs for a particular modem, you might find it described as "Hayes compatible." In the early 1980s, Hayes Microcomputer Products, Inc. introduced a modem, called the Hayes Smartmodem, that included advanced features such as the capability to automatically dial phone numbers. These features and the command set used to initiate the features were soon incorporated into modems from rival manufacturers. Over time, the Hayes-compatible command set became the de facto standard for all modems.

Synchronous Modems

A *synchronous modem* doesn't use start and stop bits; instead, the sending and receiving modems actually use synchronization bits to set up the timing for the transmission. Because synchronous modems do not need the start and stop bits used by asynchronous modems, they can achieve much higher data transfer rates than asynchronous modems. However, because synchronous modems are not designed for communication over regular phone lines, they are generally only found in use with dedicated leased lines.

Dedicated lease lines provide a full-time connection between two networks through the POTS or another service provider. Lease lines are typically digital lines and provide much more bandwidth than analog lines and are also less susceptible to the line noise and interference found on voice-grade connections.

Digital lines commonly used for data transfer include digital data service (DDS) lines and the T-Carrier system, which provides a range of line types for different data rates (T-Carrier lines are discussed in the next section). A *DDS line* can provide bandwidth of up to 56Kbps and supply your network with a permanent, full-duplex connection (data can be sent and received at the same time).

DDS line connections are actually becoming a thing of the past and are fast being replaced by other WAN technologies. Cheaper T-Carrier rates and other connection possibilities, such as DSL connections (discussed later in "Digital Subscriber Line") and even broadband cable connections, are also making the use of DDS lines a thing of the past.

The T-Carrier System

The *T-Carrier system* is a telecommunication technology that consists of high-speed digital lines made up of multiple channels. It is another one of the communication possibilities provided by the POTS. The T-Carrier system can be used for the high-speed transfer of voice, video, and data. Each *channel* on a line can provide 64Kbps of throughput. By combining a number of channels into one line, different elements, such as voice and data, can be moved at the same time over the same line (with each carried by a different channel).

The device that combines signals carried on these separate channels (when data must be sent over the digital line as a single data stream) and that also has the ability to split a received data stream into the appropriate channels is called a *multiplexer* or *MUX*. A multiplexor actually works along the same lines as a cable-ready television or VCR. A single data signal comes into your home from the local cable television provider, and your cable-ready television or VCR contains a multiplexer that breaks the data feed down into the 100+ television channels that you are constantly surfing (no one ever said that more channels would provide better programming). That's what broadband transmission is all about—multiple channels on a single feed.

The number of channels on a T-Carrier line obviously defines the amount of bandwidth that the line supplies, and different T-Carrier lines are available. The T-1 line is the basic unit of the T-Carrier system. It provides 24 64Kbps channels, which can be combined to provide a total transmission bandwidth of 1.544Mbps. Several other T-Carrier lines exists that can provide a large number of channels and extremely high data rates. Table 10.2 provides a summary of the different T-Carrier lines available.

Table 10.2 The T-Carrier Lines

Carrier Line	Channels	Total Data Rate
T1	24	1.544Mbps
T2	96	6.312Mbps
T3	672	44.736Mbps
T4	4032	274.760Mbps

The T-1 line is the basic unit of the T-Carrier system. All the other T-Carrier lines available can actually be thought of as simply particular multiples of T-1 lines. A T-2 line, for example, consists of four T-1 lines, a T-3 line consists of 28 T-1 lines, and a T-4 line consists of 168 T-1 lines.

The cost of leasing T-Carrier lines has actually dropped in recent times. However, for most companies, even a T1 line can seem a bit pricey. Many companies lease one T1 and use some of the channels for data and others for the company's phone systems. Many local phone providers also have begun offering *Fractional-T connections*, where a company only leases a specified number of channels on a T1 line.

Using T-Carrier lines as a way to connect LANs at different locations requires a couple different pieces of equipment. We've already mentioned the multiplexer (MUX), which actually combines multiple channels into one stream of information or breaks the data stream back down into the individual channels. A piece of equipment called a *Channel Service Unit/Digital Service Unit (CSU/DSU)* actually sits between the LAN multiplexor and the connection to the local loop.

Understanding Switched Networks

Another WAN alternative for moving data between different LAN sites is switched network technology. A *switched network* allows multiple users to take advantage of the same line. This makes the overall cost of this WAN technology cheaper than dedicated leased lines.

On a switched network, your LAN (or your multiple LANs at different locations, if your company is connecting multiple sites) is connected to the wide area network by a switched network service provider or the POTS. Data leaving your LAN through the WAN connection enters the switched network and then makes its way to the final destination. The path that the data takes, however, can be different each time. This means that many different users can take advantage of moving data on the switched network almost simultaneously.

When selecting a provider for WAN connections, you will find that there are a large number of possibilities. This is due to that fact that regional phone companies are not operating out of their original areas of operation due to mergers and deregulation. Companies other than the Baby Bells—such as Sprint—also have their own WAN infrastructures, meaning your choices even extend beyond the typical services provided by the POTS.

Switched networks make it easy for companies to expand because additional remote sites can be connected to the switched network at any time. Switched networks come in two different flavors: circuit switching and packet switching.

Circuit Switching

Circuit switching establishes a circuit (a *circuit* being all the phone lines used to connect the sending and receiving devices) during the communication session between sender and receiver. This means that, temporarily, the lines are dedicated to that communication session. Then, when the session is over, the circuit is immediately "torn down" and becomes available for another communication session.

Every time you pick up the telephone and make a phone call, you are taking advantage of circuit-switching technology. A circuit is established during your phone call. However, the circuit might be different (meaning different phone lines are used) each time you call the very same person. Two important WAN technologies that are circuit switched are ISDN and DSL. Let's take a closer look at each.

ISDN

ISDN is available from local phone providers and takes advantage of digital phone switching systems. The cost of an ISDN connection will be dictated by how often the line is used for data transfer. Your usage charge is determined by the connection charge (and there is also often a recurring monthly charge for being connected to the service). ISDN moves data on different channels like the T-Carrier system. ISDN comes in two flavors: Basic Rate ISDN (BRI) and Primary Rate ISDN (PRI).

ISDN is actually a suite of protocols defined by the ITU-T (International Telecommunication Union-Telecommunication Standardization sector) that provides digital communication over existing phone lines.

Basic Rate ISDN uses three channels. Two data-carrying channels, called *B channels*, each provide 64Kbps of bandwidth for data transfer. The third channel, the D channel, is not used for data transfer and, operating at 16Kbps, is used exclusively for setup and control information used during the communication session. BRI can be used for both voice and data communications by dedicating a B channel for each. Typically, however, the two B channels are combined in BRI to provide a data transfer speed of 128Kbps.

For ISDN BRI, your LAN will be connected to the local loop by a router containing a special BRI interface or a device called an *ISDN modem*. It is actually not a modem but an ISDN terminal adapter that is used to connect the LAN to the POTS local loop.

For businesses with a need for more bandwidth, there is *Primary Rate ISDN*. PRI uses a T1 line and provides 23 B channels (each operating at 64Kbps). One D channel is also necessary (as with BRI) to handle setup and to control the connection. All or any number of the 23 B channels available can be combined for data transfer. Some channels can also be used for voice communication.

Digital Subscriber Line

ISDN is rapidly being eclipsed (particularly in the BRI arena) by *DSL (Digital Subscriber Line)* connections. DSL offers voice and data communication over the regular phone lines with speeds of up to 7Mbps (in research situations, connections of 50Mbps have been realized). The great thing about DSL in the small office environment is that the data and voice communication can take place simultaneously over the very same phone line. DSL shares the line with the analog voice signal by using a different frequency for the digital data (that is sent and received using the line). This means you can make a phone call while sending data over the line.

 Note A DSL connection is usually cheaper than an ISDN BRI connection (and offers more bandwidth). This is because DSL charges are typically a flat fee, whereas BRI charges can be based on the amount of time the BRI connection is used.

One of the problems with DSL is that there are several different flavors: ADSL, HDSL, IDSL, SDSL, and others. They are often referred to as *xDSL*. The most common DSL service for home and small business use is *Asymmetric Digital Subscriber Line (ADSL)*. ADSL gets its "asymmetry" from the fact that it supplies three different avenues (or pipes) on a single phone line. Each pipe provides a different level of bandwidth (and is therefore asymmetrical). One of the pipes is called the *POTS pipe*, and it takes care of the analog traffic on the phone line, such as telephone calls. The second pipe provides a medium-size upstream pipe, and the third pipe provides a large downstream pipe.

The fact that a standard has not been chosen by the baby Bells and other providers of DSL means that the equipment used to connect a home or company to the provider's network and the bandwidth available will vary from place to place. Figure 10.3 shows a Cisco DSL router used to connect to the QWEST (formerly U.S. West) DSL network. As already mentioned in this section, DSL providers typically offer more bandwidth downstream (meaning you get a very fast connection to another network, such as the Internet) and less bandwidth upstream (it will take longer for you to send data than receive it). This, again, depends on the service provider you use.

A customer premise device, such as the Cisco 675 ADSL Router, is used to connect the LAN to the DSL provider's network.

Note

At the time that this book was written, DSL was not available in all areas of the U.S. In most areas where it is currently available, it's being used primarily as a way for homes, small businesses, and medium-sized businesses to connect their networks to the Internet. DSL, however, offers much greater possibilities, such as video on demand and networked applications. This means that although it is now primarily used as a way to connect to the Internet, DSL can also be used to connect different corporate sites into one large WAN. For example, High Bit-Rate Digital Subscriber Line (HDSL) is being used in some markets as an alternative to T1 dedicated lines.

As with the other WAN technologies we've discussed, DSL requires a device (such as the Cisco ADSL router, as shown previously in Figure 10.3) to connect your LAN to the provider's switched network. This device is considered *customer premise equipment* (this means you have to buy and maintain this device, although some providers have been giving these devices away to get customers to subscribe to their DSL services). The availability of DSL is also determined by the distance between the provider's nearest switching station (also called the *central office* or *CO*) and your home or company's location. In many cases, the limit is currently two to three miles (although in some markets five miles is the limit).

The big question is this: How does the DSL provider take the numerous client connections and move that data on the provider's switched network? This task is handled by a *Digital Subscriber Line Access Multiplexer (DSLAM)*. Typically located at the provider's central office, it receives signals from multiple customer DSL connections and puts the signals on a high-speed backbone using multiplexing techniques (meaning that all the data is multiplexed into a single signal, just as we discussed in relation to T-Carrier channels). The high-speed backbone can use technology such as ATM (Asynchronous Transfer Mode), which is discussed later in this chapter.

Although DSL is currently marketed as an avenue for high-speed Internet connection, it can be used to connect telecommuters and different corporate sites by using Virtual Private Networking (VPN). We will discuss both remote access and VPN in Chapter 17. Because DSL provides a constant connection between your network and the provider's network (and therefore the Internet), security issues arise. We will discuss firewalls and other network security issues in Chapter 16, "A Network Security Primer."

Packet-Switching Networks

In WAN connections that use *packet switching*, the data is divided into packets. The small packet size used in packet switching provides fast and efficient delivery of data.

Each packet has its own control information and is switched through the network independently. This means that data packets can follow different routes through the WAN cloud and reach the destination out of sequence. Sequencing information included with the packet (it is placed in the packet's header) is used by the receiving device to reassemble the data in the appropriate order.

Packet-switching networks take advantage of virtual circuits when transferring data. A virtual circuit establishes a defined route across the service provider's network so that all the data packets move to the destination along the same route (remember that this route is shared by packets from a lot of other users because switched networks use shared lines). The use of virtual circuits in packet-switching networks can improve the overall performance of your data transfers.

A number of packet-switching technologies exist, such as X.25, Frame Relay, and ATM. The *X.25 standard* was actually originally developed for connecting mainframe computers at different sites. By today's standards, X.25 (which became available in the late 1970s) is considered slow because it does a great deal of error checking (due to the low quality of phone lines available at the time it was developed). Despite the fact that there are faster technologies such as Frame Relay and ATM (two packet-switching technologies that we discuss in a moment), X.25 is still used by some companies.

Packet-switching networks have been available since the late 1970s when X.25 became available. The lower cost of packet-switching networks (when compared to dedicated leased lines) led to a fairly rapid evolution of packet-switching protocols such as Frame Relay and ATM. Although the X.25 protocol seems older than the hills now (when compared to Frame Relay and ATM), it is still used by some companies and institutions for WAN connections. It is, however, rapidly being replaced by other packet-switching alternatives.

Frame Relay

Frame Relay is the successor to the X.25 protocol and is faster because it has shed some of the error-checking functions that slowed the packet-switching capabilities of X.25. Frame Relay operates at the Data Link layer of the OSI model (look back at Chapter 5, "Network Protocols: Real and Imagined," for more about the OSI model) and uses permanent virtual circuits for communication sessions between different points on the WAN.

A *permanent virtual circuit (PVC)* is actually created between two points on the WAN by configuring devices such as routers (that terminate a LAN that is connected to the WAN) with a number that is provided by the service provider. This number, the Data Link Connection Identifier (DLCI), designates the PVC that will connect the two LANs via the WAN. Logical addresses such are IP addresses are then mapped to the PVC, providing a path through the WAN for the movement of data between the connected LANs.

The odd thing about Frame Relay is that it places the data in packets of varying sizes (this is like moving envelopes of different sizes through the same mail slot). This does not significantly impede data flow, but it does introduce some latency into overall throughput. *Latency* is a fancy word for lag time; the different size Frame Relay packets take some additional time to process by WAN switches, thus the latency. ATM, which we discuss in the next section, actually uses fixed-size packets to increase the potential throughput.

The Frame Relay protocol was originally developed for use over ISDN connections. It is now used over T-Carrier and Fractional-T connections.

Asynchronous Transfer Mode (ATM)

Asynchronous Transfer Mode (ATM) is a WAN packet-switching technology that uses a 53-byte packet called a *cell* to move data such as voice and video across public networks (such as the POTS) and private WANs. The ATM protocol stack consists of protocols that reside at the Data Link and Physical layers of the OSI reference model. ATM networks support the multiplexing of information, meaning that several channels of information can be contained in one data stream.

ATM uses a virtual channel as the connection between a sending and a receiving device. A *virtual channel* is basically equivalent to a virtual circuit (refer to the preceding section on Frame Relay). If a company wants redundant virtual channels connecting sites, several channels can be bundled together. This bundle of virtual channels is referred to as a *virtual path*. Virtual channel numbers and virtual path numbers are supplied to the customer by the service provider. These numbers are then used to configure devices such as routers that sit between the LAN and the provider's switching station (connected by the local loop).

ATM is typically run over high-speed fiber-optic networks. For example, *Synchronous Optical Network/Synchronous Digital Hierarchy* (or *SONET*, as it is typically known) is one of the Physical layer specifications for ATM. SONET can provide a throughput of 155Mbps over fiber-optic cabling. ATM backbones are widely used in the telecommunications industry. Many providers of DSL actually connect their DSL customers to the WAN using a high-speed fiber-optic backbone that uses the ATM WAN protocol.

To make things a little confusing, ATM is now being used as a LAN protocol. ATM switches that are used on a LAN use LAN Emulation (LANE) to emulate a LAN on top of the ATM network. This is accomplished by the LANE protocol, which can emulate either an Ethernet or token-ring network. In simple terms, this means that ATM is able to provide a high-speed environment over twisted-pair wire by pretending to be either an Ethernet or token-ring LAN. LANE is an advanced topic related to switching devices (switches are discussed briefly in Chapter 3, "Networking Hardware"), which we won't get to in this introductory book.

A Word Regarding Remote Access

While many of the technologies that we discussed in this chapter are related to expanding LANs beyond a particular geographical location, some of the technologies such as modems, ISDN lines, and DSL connections are also commonly used by remote users to connect to the corporate LAN. Not every company or business—especially small businesses and home offices—will make use of WAN technology to expand the range of their LAN. However, even the smallest of businesses (including a home business) might need to allow users to dial into the local area network and access resources on the LAN as if they were directly connected to the network.

For remote access to work, both the remote user and a special server on the LAN, called a *remote access server*, must be outfitted with some sort of WAN communication strategy. And while modems have been commonly used on both remote access client computers and on remote access servers on the LAN, other technologies—such as ISDN and even X.25 connections—can be used.

Remote access servers that handle numerous dial-in connections are often outfitted with multiple phone lines and multiple modems. A collection of modems on a remote access server is called a *modem pool*.

While expanding the LAN through remote access must certainly be considered a deployment of WAN connectivity (as shown in Figure 10.4), the use of dial-up connections certainly isn't as glamorous as many the WAN technologies that we have discussed in this chapter, such as the T-Carrier system and ATM. However, managing remote access is an important aspect of being a network administrator. We will discuss setting up remote access servers and remote access clients in Chapter 17.

FIGURE 10.4

Dial-in connections allow the LAN to be expanded beyond its physical boundaries.

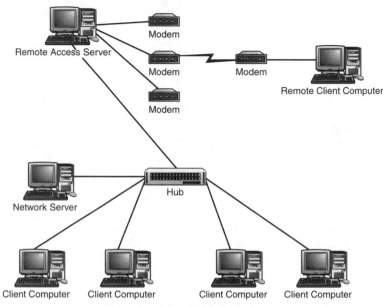

Local Area Network

Chapter Summary

In this chapter we had an opportunity to take a look at the different WAN technologies used to connect LANs at different locations. Some of these technologies—such as modems, ISDN, and DSL connections—are also used by users who connect to the network remotely.

- The POTS (Plain Old Telephone System) provides a number of different strategies for WAN connectivity.

- Dial-up connections over regular analog phone lines using modems provide a relatively inexpensive method of expanding a LAN.

- Asynchronous modems move data over regular phone lines. Synchronous modems are often used on leased digital lines to provide WAN connectivity.

- The T-Carrier system provides high-speed digital lines that can transfer voice, video, and data.

- T-Carrier lines supply a number of channels that can carry voice and data simultaneously on the same line.

- A multiplexer is used to combine or split the different channels available on a T-Carrier line.

- ISDN and DSL are WAN technologies that allow for the transfer of data on regular phone lines.

- Frame Relay and ATM are both packet-switching WAN technologies that provide for the high-speed movement of data over switched networks.

- Remote access is another method of expanding the LAN beyond its geographical boundaries. Remote users can connect to the LAN and access the same resources as local users.

HOW THE INTERNET WORKS

In this chapter

- Figuring out where the Internet came from
- Understanding the FTP protocol
- Working with Internet e-mail addresses and protocols
- How HTTP and HTML make the Web work
- Understanding Internet newsgroups
- What happened to Gopher?
- Getting familiar with the Internet's Domain Name Service (DNS)

The Internet is like a giant jellyfish. You can't step on it. You can't go around it. You've got to get through it.

–John Evans

Now that you are pretty well rooted in LAN technology and have had a chance to peruse some information on WAN connectivity, it's time to take a look at the biggest network in the world—the Internet. In the last chapter we took a look at how the POTS (Plain Old Telephone System) plays an important role in connecting LANs to LANs using different wide area network strategies. I think just about everyone has some feel for how telephone technology was developed (by such technology innovators as Alexander Graham Bell) and how the phone system in this country has evolved over time.

The Internet, however, is another story. Until the early 1990s (when the World Wide Web was born), many people were not even aware of the Internet's existence. Although we will concentrate on looking at how the Internet works in this chapter and explore the various utilities and protocols used on the Internet's infrastructure, we will start with a look at the innovations that led to the birth of this mega-network.

Where Did the Internet Come From?

The Internet's origins in the United States began in the 1960s. The Advanced Research Projects Agency (ARPA) of the Department of Defense was doling out a great deal of research money to universities and other research centers around the country. ARPA quickly realized that having some sort of data network that would connect the various research sites would make it much easier for research scientists and ARPA officials to share information.

A great deal of theory related to packet-switching networks was developed (much of this early research was done at MIT) and then tested by ARPA by the late 1960s. Two issues that were of supreme importance in developing the packet-switching network envisioned by ARPA scientists were the protocol that would provide the rules and transmission scheme for data on the network and the devices that would actually switch the data along a particular path as it moved from a sending to a receiving device.

The development of the hardware switches, called *Interface Message Processors (IMPs)*, actually preceded the finalization of the network host-to-host protocol, and these switches were tested as early as 1969. The IMP was actually the precursor to the router. In 1970 work was completed on the host-to-host protocol that would be used on the ARPA network, now called *ARPAnet*. This protocol, the *Network Control Protocol*, was further developed and eventually rehabilitated into the much more robust TCP/IP protocol suite.

As mentioned in Chapter 5, "Network Protocols: Real and Imagined," TCP/IP is actually a stack of protocols that each serve a particular purpose in the overall communication scheme. Some protocols, such as FTP and HTTP, supply the user interface and network connection, whereas other protocols in the stack, such as TCP or UDP, actually provide the mechanism for transporting the data packets on the network.

The number of computers on the ARPAnet grew rapidly in the 1970s, as the ARPAnet infrastructure was expanded throughout the United States. Networks designed to serve research and higher education institutions such as BITnet (used to send out electronic postings using listserv software), Usenet (a huge electronic bulletin board full of newsgroups, still in use today and discussed in this chapter) and NSFnet (developed by the National Science Foundation) were developed, thus further expanding the range and number of devices on the packet-switching network that began as ARPAnet.

With the expansion of the Internet backbone by for-profit companies beyond the infrastructure built for educational and research facilities, the Internet has become as integral to business and personal communication as the telephone. You would have to go a long way to find a company of any size without a connection to and a presence (a Web site) on the Internet. The number of home connections to the Internet is growing daily at a very rapid pace worldwide.

On a personal level, most people use the Internet to send and receive e-mail and to browse information on the World Wide Web. As far as companies and institutions go, e-mail is also important to corporate communications, as is the presence of companies on the Web. We will talk about issues related to companies and their Internet presence in the next chapter. We will also look at other uses of the Internet for corporate communications, such as Virtual Private Networking (VPN), which provides a way to tunnel private corporate data through the public Internet.

One thing you should keep in mind as you read through the information in this chapter is that the technology developed to make the Internet a reality is also often used on private networks that do not allow public access. This use of Internet protocols and Internet technology to provide networking services on a private network creates what is called an *intranet*. Therefore, an intranet would be the private equivalent of what we see on the public Internet. A company simply uses the TCP/IP protocol, Web servers, FTP servers, and Internet e-mail to exchange information on the corporate network.

Let's take a look at some of the different Internet services available, such as FTP and the Web, and also discuss how each of these different onramps to the Internet is used for data communication. We can then discuss DNS, the Domain Name Service, and its importance related to how devices on the Internet (such as computers) are actually able to locate each other on the internetwork.

Working with the File Transfer Protocol

The oldest of the protocols used on the Internet is the *File Transfer Protocol (FTP)*. FTP is used to send and receive files over a TCP/IP network, regardless of the operating systems used on the computers sending and receiving the data.

FTP supplies the user interface and the various functions of the Application, Presentation, and Session layers of the OSI model. Although FTP is considered a protocol in the TCP/IP stack, it is also a full-blown application used on the Internet to send and receive files.

FTP uses TCP (which we discussed in Chapter 5, when we looked at the entire TCP/IP stack) at the Transport layer, so a real-time connection is set up between the sending and receiving computers on the Internet. IP addressing provided at the Network layer of the OSI model by the Internet Protocol provides the mechanism used by FTP to identify different nodes on the Internet (DNS plays a role in identifying computers on the Internet and is discussed in "Understanding DNS," later in this chapter).

To use FTP to send and receive files on the Internet, you need two things: an FTP server and an FTP client. FTP is a good example of a client/server environment, where the software needed to transfer files is split between the server and the client. Let's take a look at FTP on the server side first.

FTP Servers

An *FTP server* is a computer that allows other computers on the network to connect to it. Therefore, FTP servers can be large network servers found on corporate networks and the Internet that have been configured with server software that allows them to shares files with computers using an FTP client (FTP servers were extremely important to the ARPAnet for sharing files between different sites). FTP servers can also be client computers that are running some kind of FTP server software.

A number of different software packages are available for FTP servers on company networks or the Internet. Microsoft ships Internet Information Server with Windows NT and Windows 2000 Server. This extension of the network operating system allows you to quickly configure an FTP site (it also provides Web site and news server functionality). Figure 11.1 shows the Internet Information Services snap-in tool that is used to configure and monitor Web sites, FTP sites, and newsgroups on a Windows 2000 Server.

Other network operating systems also provide the software and tools to configure an FTP server, including the various Linux clones and Novell NetWare/IntranetWare. Some client operating systems, such as Windows 2000 Professional and the Mac OS, also provide you with the ability to configure an FTP server.

FIGURE 11.1

Windows 2000
Server provides
a utility for con-
figuring Web
and FTP sites.

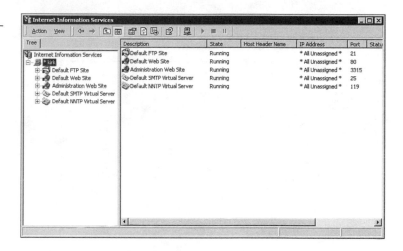

A number of third-party software companies provide FTP server software, which can be used to turn just about any computer running any software into an FTP server. These add-on software products are just fine for setting up an FTP server that will be used to share files with co-workers or with friends over the Internet.

In production environments (a fancy way of saying on a large corporate intranet or a server on the Internet), FTP sites can experience a large number of "hits." So, in most cases you will want to run your FTP site on a server machine (a computer with all the hardware muscle typically found on a server) rather than a client computer.

Once the FTP server software is installed or the FTP service built into the NOS is activated, the directories that will be accessed by users need to be created. Figure 11.2 shows the FTP root directory for a Windows 2000 Server FTP site. Any directories (or in Windows lingo, *folders*) that were used by users to either upload (send) or download (receive) files would be subdirectories of the root directory.

Anonymous FTP

FTP provides a file-sharing environment that can control access to the file server by requiring a logon name and password. This means that the FTP server must validate a user and her password before she can access files on the server.

On the Internet, many public FTP sites allow an anonymous logon. This means that anyone can log on to the FTP site using a username of "anonymous." The password for an anonymous logon is often your e-mail address. A site allowing anonymous logons is often referred to as an *anonymous FTP site*. Figure 11.3 shows Apple's anonymous FTP site, which has been accessed using the Internet Explorer Web browser.

FIGURE 11.2

Directories on the FTP server are placed in the FTP root directory.

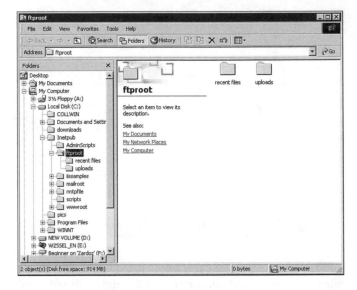

FIGURE 11.3

Anonymous FTP sites are quite common on the Internet.

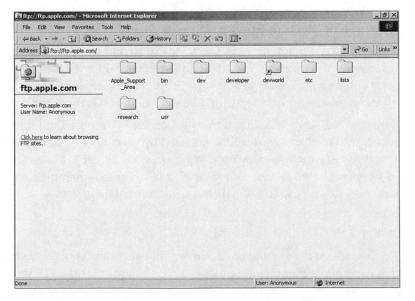

Notice that on a Windows-based computer the directories on the FTP site appear in the Internet Explorer window the same as local directories would. You are potentially accessing files that reside on a computer clear across the world, but the computer's connection to the Internet makes the directories and files appear as if they are local.

FTP client capability is built into Web browsers such as Netscape Navigator and Microsoft Internet Explorer. You can download files from and upload files to FTP sites. These sites are usually referenced by a link on a Web page. Most of these sites are also anonymous FTP sites.

FTP Clients

As you've already read in the discussion of anonymous FTP sites, Web browsers such as Netscape Navigator and Microsoft Internet Explorer can act as FTP clients. You can actually download files from an FTP site by locating them in the browser window and then using the copy command. Files can also be uploaded to an FTP site (that is, if the site allows uploads; many sites are "read only," meaning you can copy files from the site but cannot upload files to the site).

You can also use an FTP client to connect to FTP sites. There are FTP clients for just about any operating system. FTP clients can take the form of add-on software, such as WS_FTP, which is shown in Figure 11.4. The local drives and directories are shown on the left side of the FTP client window, and the remote or FTP directories are shown on the right side.

FIGURE 11.4

FTP clients provide a way to move files from a local computer to an FTP site, and vice versa.

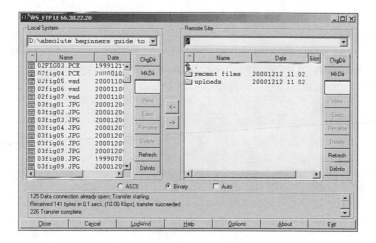

Many FTP clients can be downloaded from sites on the Web, such as TUCOWS (The Ultimate Collection of Winsock Software). Both freeware and shareware versions of clients for a number of different operating systems are available on the TUCOWS site at http://www.tucows.com/.

Many operating systems, such as Microsoft Windows and Linux-based systems, also allow you to connect to an FTP server from the command line. Figure 11.5 shows the command-line commands used to connect to a local FTP server (on the company intranet) from a Windows 2000 Professional client computer.

FIGURE 11.5

Connections to an FTP server can also be established using command-line commands.

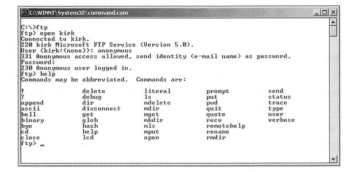

The actual connection to the FTP server is established either by specifying the IP address of the FTP server or by using the fully qualified domain name (FQDN), or *friendly name*, of the server. The role of FQDNs is covered when we take a look at DNS later in the chapter.

Once the connection is established, file directories on the FTP server can be viewed by the client. Files can then be downloaded or uploaded as binary files or in ASCII text format. One of the most compelling reasons for using FTP is that it supplies you with the ability to move files easily between different types of operating systems.

> **Note**
>
> *ASCII (American Standard Code for Information Interchange)* is the basic character set used by most computer operating systems.

Understanding Electronic Mail

Electronic mail (e-mail) was not actually part of the plan when ARPA began to build the data communications network that would eventually evolve into the Internet. However, after being introduced to the ARPAnet in 1972, electronic mail quickly became the most-used application on the network.

It can also be safely said that, on the Internet, e-mail is one of the most widely used applications. Internet e-mail has a client side and a server side, just like FTP and the Web (this is discussed in the section "Working with the Web," later in this chapter).

On the client side, there are a large number of different Internet e-mail clients. Web browsers such as Netscape Navigator and Microsoft Internet Explorer have built-in or associated e-mail clients. A number of different e-mail clients, including some freeware clients, can be downloaded from numerous sites on the Web.

The ability to receive Internet e-mail has also been integrated into popular Personal Information Managers such as Microsoft Outlook and Lotus Notes (both of which are considered groupware products, as discussed in Chapter 9, "Working with Applications on the Network"). Figure 11.6 shows the Microsoft Outlook window and the Inbox with the highlighted message in the preview pane. Multiple views and options exist with such e-mail clients providing a reasonable level of customization.

FIGURE 11.6

A number of different clients, including Microsoft Outlook, are available for e-mail.

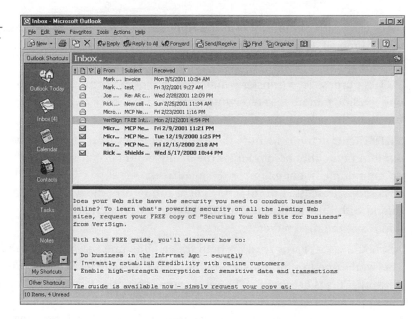

E-mail Addresses

E-mail addresses take the form of *name@domain.suffix*. For example, if I worked at a company named SureFire Fireworks, my e-mail address might be joeh@surefire.com.

The first part of the address is the mailbox or e-mail username. In the case of the preceding example, joeh would be used to specify a particular user and the mailbox in which a mail item addressed to joeh@surefire.com should be placed on the SureFire Fireworks e-mail server.

The second part of the address (in this case, surefire.com) is the Internet domain name of the company and is used to specify the mail server. Domain names are covered in more detail later in the chapter when we take a look at DNS.

In developing an understanding of how e-mail servers on the Internet (or an intranet) work, one needs to remember that the sending and receiving of e-mail on the Internet or a company's intranet is tightly woven into how data is moved from one location to another by the different protocols in the TCP/IP stack (discussed in Chapter 5). The three TCP/IP protocols that we need to discuss in terms of e-mail are the Simple Mail Transfer Protocol (SMTP), the Post Office Protocol 3 (POP3), and the Internet Message Access Protocol (IMAP).

SMTP

SMTP is a protocol that works at the Application, Presentation, and Session layers of the OSI model. It uses TCP at the Transport layer for connection-oriented transport of packets.

SMTP's purpose is to transfer e-mail from a sending computer (for example, someone sending e-mail) to a receiving computer (the SMTP e-mail server). So, SMTP functionality is built into the e-mail client and the e-mail server software.

SMTP clients actually identify the location of a particular e-mail server by using the domain name that accompanies the actual e-mail account name. For example, the domain name in our example joeh@surefire.com is surefire.com. With the help of a DNS server (discussed shortly), the client can resolve the domain name information (along with the fact that it is looking for an SMTP mail server) to the actual IP address of the mail server.

At one time SMTP was used for both the sending and receiving of e-mail messages. This works fine in situations where the clients and the mail server are on the same network. This is because SMTP uses a connection-oriented strategy for moving mail messages (as was already mentioned). However, the Internet isn't necessarily the type of environment where all the computers that use this internetwork are online all the time. Therefore, some sort of strategy had to be developed in which e-mail could be held on a mail server until a particular user logs on to the Internet to retrieve his mail. This is where POP3 comes in.

POP3

POP3 is a TCP/IP stack protocol used by e-mail clients to connect to a POP3 e-mail server. The POP3 mail server basically functions as a mail drop.

The POP3 mail server will have a persistent connection to the Internet, allowing it to accept and hold e-mail intended for the clients that use the server. When a client connects to the Internet, it can use a POP3 e-mail client to connect to the POP3 server and download any available mail.

The client's logon name and a password are used to access the appropriate mailbox on the POP3 server. Once the client connects, all the mail is removed from the server and downloaded to the client computer.

You will find that most e-mail server software supports both SMTP and POP3. So, many companies or Internet service providers will have one server that provides SMTP and POP3 functionality.

Note

You should keep in mind that all the protocols in the TCP/IP stack use IP addresses to identify the source or destination of data packets or datagrams such as e-mail messages. IP addressing is managed by the IP protocol, which operates at the Network layer of the OSI model. To make a long story short, I think you can see that protocols in the TCP/IP stack operate at different layers; to maintain communication between these protocols at different OSI layers, each protocol has been assigned a *well-known port number*. For example, SMTP uses port 25, and POP3 uses port 110. When a port number is combined with an IP address, a socket is created, which actually provides the communication conduit between the applications. Port numbers also serve as an avenue for hackers and crackers to break into your network or computer. See the section "Protecting a Network from Outside Attack" in Chapter 16, "A Network Security Primer."

IMAP

IMAP is an e-mail transport program that provides an alternative to the POP3 protocol. IMAP mail servers do not immediately dump all the available mail from the server to the IMAP client when the client connects. Rather, the server sends a listing of waiting messages. The messages themselves are kept on the server. This allows a user to view both saved messages and new messages on the IMAP mail server.

IMAP is particularly useful when one e-mail account might be accessed by more than one computer or device. For example, a user with a computer and an e-mail–enabled cellular phone or a Personal Data Assistant, such as a Palm Pilot, that is outfitted to connect to the e-mail server might access his e-mail from more than one device, depending on whether he is in the office or on the road.

Because the mail is maintained on the server, even after it has been read, the status of each message can be viewed each time the user logs on to the IMAP mail server, regardless of whether he accesses the server with his personal computer or e-mail–ready cell phone. This is useful when you're on the road because you would see the status of messages as you left them after accessing mail on your office computer, meaning e-mail messages will not be replied to more than one time, and even read messages can be accessed from any e-mail–ready device.

Most e-mail clients support SMTP, POP3, and IMAP. E-mail server software such as Microsoft Exchange and Lotus Domino (the server for Lotus Notes) also supports these different e-mail protocols.

Working with the Web

The software bells and whistles for the World Wide Web (WWW) didn't actually surface until 1991. Scientists at the CERN research laboratory developed the *Hypertext Markup Language (HTML)* so that they could exchange information about their projects over their TCP/IP network.

HTML is the file format used to create documents that can then be read by a Web browser such as Microsoft Internet Explorer or Netscape Navigator. HTML consists of tags that are used to format a document so that it can be viewed in a Web browser. HTML offers a rich environment for creating documents that can include graphics, sound, video, and links to other HTML documents, such as other Web sites.

Hypertext Transfer Protocol (HTTP) is the TCP/IP stack member that provides the connection between an HTTP client (a computer outfitted with a Web browser) and server (which would be a Web server, in this case). A Web client sends a connection-oriented request using HTTP, which uses TCP for the connection, to a particular Web server, typically using the *Uniform Resource Locator (URL)* for the Web server, which is the DNS name of the server. To make a long story short, the URL is the name that you type into your Browser address windows. DNS handles the resolution of the URL to an IP address.

The Web server holding the HTML documents or Web site requested by the Web client will respond to the client with a connectionless HTTP communication that uses UDP at the Transport layer of the OSI model. This allows the Web client to access the actual Web site.

I think just about everyone is familiar with the different Web browsers (clients) available. As far as Web servers go, in the Unix/Linux world, the Apache Web server is quite popular. Netscape offers the Netscape Enterprise server, which can run on Windows, Linux, and Unix operating systems. Microsoft bundles Internet Information Server with Windows NT and Windows 2000 Server.

Your choice of Web server software will depend on the NOS you run on your Web server. We will take a look at hosting a Web site in Chapter 13, "Hosting a Web Site."

Other Internet Onramps

Although e-mail and the Web predominate user access to the Internet, other tools can be used to access various information repositories on the "Net." One of the earliest TCP/IP protocols used for connecting one computer to another was the Telnet protocol. Very useful in the Unix environment, Telnet can be used to connect to another computer and access resources on that computer. Although Telnet is still used a great deal to configure and monitor routers and switches on large internetworks, it isn't used all that much to access the Internet.

Two other protocols that can be used to access Internet information are NNTP and Gopher. These two protocols are discussed in the sections that follow.

Newsgroups

Newsgroups have been around since 1979, when newsgroup servers were set up at Duke University and the University of North Carolina. *Usenet*, a network of news servers connected to the Internet, is still around today. Most news servers are run by educational institutions and large companies. Internet service providers also typically have their own news servers, and they choose which of the newsgroups available on the Internet to carry on their servers and offer to their subscribers. Information on news servers is broken into categories. Each subject area is called a *newsgroup*. Figure 11.7 shows the Xnews newsgroup client window. Xnews is a freeware newsreader.

FIGURE 11.7

Thousands of newsgroups are available on Usenet.

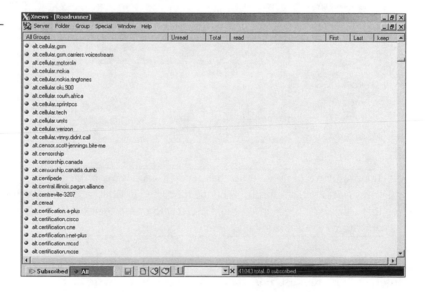

Newsgroups are kind of like an electronic bulletin board, where users can post or read messages. As with other information services on the Internet, newsgroups have a client and a server side. The TCP/IP protocol that allows the exchange of information from a newsreader (the client-side application) to a news server is the Network News Transfer Protocol (NNTP).

NNTP uses TCP to negotiate a connection between the client newsreader and the news server. The client lets the server know which articles in a particular newsgroup it has already viewed, and only a list of new or unread articles will be provided to the client.

Each posting in a newsgroup contains a header that provides the subject of the news post. It is the headers that are downloaded by the client from the server. When the header for a particular article is selected, the entire message is then uploaded from the server to the client.

Users can respond to messages listed in a newsgroup or create new posts. Figure 11.8 shows a new message being created in Outlook Express.

FIGURE 11.8

Newsreaders allow you to create and post messages to a news group.

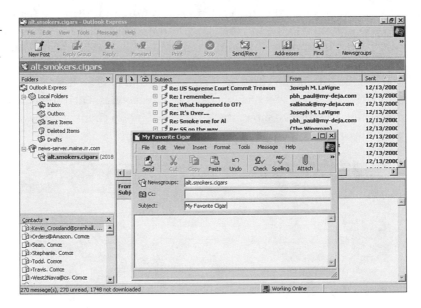

The usefulness of newsgroups has certainly caught on in the corporate world. Both Lotus Notes and Microsoft Exchange (discussed in Chapter 9) offer newsgroup features that allow employees involved on projects to create their own discussion groups, which operate very much like the Usenet newsgroups.

Many different news clients are available. Outlook Express, the e-mail companion to Internet Explorer, also has the ability to act as a newsreader, as does Netscape Navigator. The Apache Server software available for Unix/Linux platforms can act as a news server, as can Internet Information Server, which is a service provided with Microsoft Windows 2000 and NT Server. A number of standalone news server products also exist, such as the DNEWS Server.

Gopher

Our discussion of Internet resources wouldn't really be complete if I didn't at least mention Gopher. *Gopher*, which originated at the University of Minnesota (the school mascot is the gopher), is a client/server system that allows a gopher client to access data on a gopher server (or servers) using a hierarchical directory much like an index. The gopher protocol operates at the upper layers of the OSI model, as do FTP and HTTP. Gopher would have to be characterized as the first user-friendly application available for the Internet.

Gopher servers—at one time there were many worldwide, and there are still Gopher servers out there—are accessed using a Gopher client. As the number of Gopher servers increased during the early days of the Internet, the indexed information provided to the Gopher client could become quite overwhelming. Two search engines, Archie and Veronica, were developed to scan the indexed information provided to the client by the Gopher network.

Gopher clients and Gopher server software (both freeware and shareware) can still be downloaded from sites such as TUCOWS.com on the Web. Gopher has definitely seen better days, however. Gopher capability is built into Web browsers. Figure 11.9 shows the root Gopher directory for the Library of Congress. Note in the figure that there is a message to the fact that the Gopher index is no longer being maintained by the Library of Congress.

FIGURE 11.9

Gopher servers can be accessed using most Web browsers.

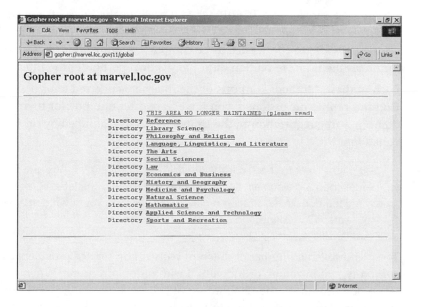

Understanding DNS

Now that we've taken a look at some of the different ways information is accessed on the Internet, we need to take a look at the mechanism that allows users accessing the Web or an FTP server to use friendly, text names. You already know from Chapter 5 that all computers and other devices on a TCP/IP network are identified by their IP addresses. But, how often do you actually type an IP address into a Web browser or FTP client window? The answer is "not very often," and the reason why is DNS.

The *Domain Name Service (DNS)* provides the structure and the strategy that is used to refer to computers on a TCP/IP network, such as the Internet, by "friendly names." This means that you don't have to know the IP address of a particular computer to connect to it. For example, when you type a friendly name such as Microsoft.com into your Web browser, DNS provides the mechanism where the friendly name (Microsoft.com) is resolved to the IP address of the Microsoft Web site.

A DNS-friendly name is referred to as a *fully qualified domain name (FQDN)*. DNS servers (computers running the DNS protocol, which resides at the Application, Presentation, and Session layers of the OSI model) supply the actual mechanism for resolving FQDNs to IP addresses. Typically, each company, organization, or Internet service provider will maintain its own DNS servers that provide FQDN-to–IP address resolution.

All the DNS servers on a TCP/IP network (such as the Internet) use each other as resources as they handle requests for FQDN-to–IP address resolutions from computers on the network. In effect, each large company, organization, or service provider manages the name resolution duties for its own portion of the Internet.

Each of these "portions" or parts of the Internet is referred to as a *DNS domain*. Domain names are assigned; you have to register and pay for them. At one time all domain name registration in the United States was handled by an organization called *InterNIC*.

You might want to check out the InterNIC site at http://rs.internic.net/index.html before choosing a domain name registration provider. The InterNIC site supplies a list of accredited domain registration organizations. Getting your own domain name is covered in Chapter 12, "Connecting a Network to the Internet."

Today, however, a number of different registration service providers can supply a company, organization, or individual with a domain name. When a company registers a domain name, the IP addresses of two DNS servers that will handle the name resolution duties for that domain must be provided. This means that the company will provide two DNS servers that are connected to the Internet. In the case of individuals who register a domain name, the DNS server addresses are typically provided by your service provider.

Servers maintained by InterNIC provide the mechanism for a local DNS server to resolve an FQDN to an IP address on a remote portion of the Internet. Because the InterNIC servers hold a database that provides a listing of all domain DNS servers and their IP addresses, the local DNS merely queries the InterNIC server for the IP address of the DNS server that services a particular domain (using the friendly name). Once the local server receives the IP address of the remote DNS server, the local server can query the remote server directly for the resolution of the remote FQDN to an IP address.

The Domain Name Space

For the Domain Name Service to work, all the FQDNs (or friendly names) of computers and other devices on the Internet (or other large TCP/IP networks) must be unique. The actual structure or scheme used for DNS names is called the *domain name space*. The domain name space is basically an upside-down tree in which the different domains branch out from a central branch or root. Therefore, a *domain* would be considered one division or compartment in the domain name space tree. This hierarchical tree structure for the domain name space also provides for the naming of individual computers that are within a particular domain. Figure 11.10 provides a look at the DNS tree.

FIGURE 11.10

The domain name space defines how domains and computers in domains are named using FQDNs.

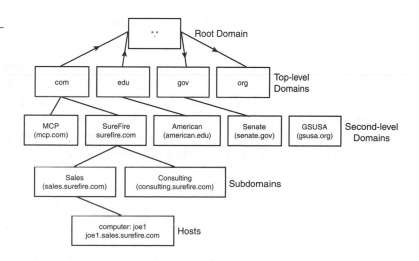

At the base of the DNS tree is the root domain. The Internet's root domain is represented by a period (or *dot*). This is why top-level names, explained next, are always preceded by a dot, as in "dot com." Below the root domain on the inverted DNS tree are the top-level domains. The top-level domains consist of the suffixes .com, .edu, .gov, and so on. Table 11.1 describes the different top-level domain types.

Table 11.1   The Various Top-Level Domains

Top-Level Domain	Description
com	Used by commercial organizations. For example, mcp.com is the domain name for MacmillanUSA.
edu	Reserved for educational institutions. For example, american.edu is the domain of the American University.
org	Used by noncommercial organizations and institutions. For example, gsusa.org is the domain name of the Girl Scouts of America.
gov	Reserved by the United States for governmental entities. For example, senate.gov is the domain for the U.S. Senate.
mil	Reserved by the United States military.
net	To be used by companies involved in the Internet infrastructure, such as ISPs. For example, mninter.net is the domain name of an Internet service provider.
Country names	Two-letter country code for a country's top-level domain (outside the United States). For example, .bs for the Bahamas and .ga for Gabon.
int	Used by registering organizations as defined by international treaties. You don't see too many .int domains.

Below the top-level domains are the second-level domains; these secondary domains consist of company, institutional, and private domains that are commonly used to access a Web site, such as mcp.com (Macmillan Computer Publishing's domain name) and american.edu (the domain name of the American University in Washington, D.C.). Under the second-level domains are found *subdomains*. These subdomains are typically used to divide a larger secondary domain into geographical or functional units.

For example, the fictitious company SureFire Fireworks (from the previous discussion of e-mail addresses) can also be used in relation to DNS FQDNs. Let's say SureFire has a registered FQDN of surefire.com and that Surefire has two distinct divisions—a consulting division and a sales division—each of which operates as its own subdomain. In the DNS tree, these two subdomains (branches off of the surefire.com top-level domain) might be called consulting.surefire.com and sales.surefire.com (as shown in Figure 11.10).

As far as FQDNs for individual computers go, the computer's name is actually tacked onto the beginning of the domain or subdomain name. For example, if you have a computer with the DNS name `joe1`, and it is in the DNS subdomain of `sales.surefire.com`, the FQDN for the computer would be `joe1.sales.surefire.com`. This machine-level designation is referred to as a *hostname*.

How DNS Works

For DNS to actually work on a network, there has to be a local DNS server that handles requests from computers on the network that need to resolve an FQDN to an IP address. A *DNS server* is any server (or any computer on the network for that matter) that runs a DNS service. A number of network operating systems provide DNS functionality—Microsoft Windows 2000 Server, Unix, some Linux clones (such as Sun's Solaris), and Novell's NetWare (version 4.11 and newer), to name a few.

DNS servers basically maintain a database that includes records that map FQDNs to IP addresses. Figure 11.11 shows the DNS utility provided by Windows 2000 Server. Most DNS servers require that the network administrator enter records for each host computer on the network. Windows 2000 actually uses a dynamic form of DNS, and the computers actually work with the DNS server to create their own DNS lookup records.

FIGURE 11.11

A DNS server holds a database of records that resolves FQDNs to IP addresses.

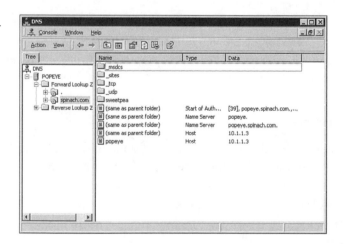

Note

A DNS domain will actually consist of at least one zone. For example, `surefire.com` could be the primary zone for SureFire, although a DNS domain can be broken up into more zones if a network needs to have more DNS servers because of high network traffic. Records held on the DNS server will be held in a zone folder. Zones that resolve FQDNs to IP addresses are called *forward lookup zones*. Zones that resolve IP addresses to FQDNs are called *reverse lookup zones*.

It's the communication between a particular computer on the TCP/IP network and the DNS server that actually initiates the process of taking an FQDN and resolving it to an IP address. The host computer making the request uses a *resolver*, which is software built into an application such as a Web browser. When you type an FQDN or URL (such as www.microsoft.com) into a Web browser, the resolver queries the network's primary DNS server (when you configure TCP/IP on a computer, you specify the local DNS server's IP address).

If the local DNS server doesn't have the information in its DNS database that resolves the particular FQDN to an IP address, the server will contact the next DNS server that is upstream in the DNS tree. If that server has the appropriate information, it relays that information back to the requesting DNS server; otherwise, the upstream server may use some help from other DNS servers on the Internet.

Once the information is returned to the primary DNS server originally queried by the host computer, the server will pass the IP address that has been resolved from the FQDN to the requesting host computer. Obviously, this process happens very fast. Just think how quickly your Web browser is able to resolve an FQDN name that you enter in the browser's address window.

| Note | There are currently seven root DNS servers for the entire Internet. Considering the increased traffic on the Internet, many discussions have taken place related to increasing the number of root servers. |

I think you can probably now see how DNS is an important and integral part of how TCP/IP networks operate. DNS will pop up again in the discussions related to connecting to the Internet in Chapter 12 and creating a Web site in Chapter 13.

Chapter Summary

In this chapter we sorted out the Internet and some of the different TCP/IP protocols that were developed to access information on the Internet. Key points covered are as follows:

- ARPA began the planning and building of the ARPAnet in the 1960s.
- ARPAnet eventually evolved into the public TCP/IP network we call the Internet.
- FTP is used to send and receive files on a TCP/IP network, such as the Internet.
- FTP operates in a client/server environment. Client FTP software provides the interface for the user.

- Anonymous FTP sites are common on the Internet. They allow any user to connect to a site and access the files there.

- Internet e-mail uses the SMTP protocol to move mail from a mail client to the SMTP mail server.

- E-mail clients come in the format *username@domain.suffix*. The username is actually the e-mail mailbox for the user, and the other information specifies the domain name of the company or institution.

- E-mail clients use the POP3 protocol to retrieve mail from a POP3 mail server. All the mail on the server is uploaded to the client computer.

- IMAP is an e-mail transport program that retrieves a list of e-mail on the server without downloading the mail. This means that a user can connect to the IMAP server from different devices and view the same e-mail messages and their status.

- HTML is the coding language to create Web site pages.

- The Web uses HTTP as the transport mechanism between Web browsers and Web sites.

- Usenet provides newsgroups in a bulletin board environment where users can read and respond to messages.

- Gopher was the first user-friendly interface for Internet content, but it has now faded into the background. You will occasionally stumble upon a Gopher server when searching for particular information using a Web browser.

- DNS provides the strategy for resolving friendly FQDNs to IP addresses on the Internet.

- The DNS name space is an upside-down tree, with the root of the DNS name space being the dot (yes, the same dot as found in "dot com").

- DNS clients use a resolver that queries the primary DNS server for help with resolving FQDNs to IP addresses.

- DNS servers maintain a database of records that map FQDNs to IP addresses. When a DNS server cannot find the information in its database, it will query other DNS servers on the Internet.

CONNECTING A NETWORK TO THE INTERNET

In this chapter

- Selecting an Internet service provider
- Working with an Internet access provider
- Understanding the Internet backbone infrastructure
- Connecting a network to the Internet
- Understanding cable modems
- Working with proxy servers
- Using network address translation

It shouldn't be too much of a surprise that the Internet has evolved into a force strong enough to reflect the greatest hopes and fears of those who use it. After all, it was designed to withstand nuclear war, not just the puny huffs and puffs of politicians and religious fanatics.

–Denise Caruso

In the last chapter, we took a look at how the Internet has evolved over the last 30 years from a government-funded project in packet-switching technologies to the very public global network that we are familiar with today. We also discussed some of the different protocols that have come and gone (and stayed) as programmers developed different avenues and interfaces for accessing the Internet.

In this chapter, we discuss issues related to getting your company online. We will take a look at sorting out the different possibilities for connecting to the Internet and how you would go about creating a presence for your company on the Internet. Let's begin our discussion with issues related to connecting your LAN to the Internet.

Connecting to the Internet

Our discussion of networking thus far has been fairly company centric, meaning we have talked about LAN and WAN technology in terms of providing a network infrastructure for a single company or institution. Even our discussion of wide area networking was a look at providing data communication avenues between remote sites and the company's central LAN.

Another important aspect of networking the enterprise involves providing users with a conduit to the Internet. Although the rationale for connecting a company to the Internet can at times seem to be based on nothing more than a high-placed corporate officer shouting "Everyone else is doing it" at a board meeting, it falls on the network administrator or the administration team to determine the best way to connect the company's network infrastructure to the Internet backbone. This usually means researching local Internet service providers (ISPs) and different WAN technology options for the connection between the corporate network and the ISP (with the ISP providing the onramp to the Internet backbone). Before we talk about ISPs and some of the issues related to selecting a connection type (we discuss the various WAN technologies used to connect to the Internet in Chapter 10, "Expanding a LAN with WAN Technology"), let's take a look at how the Internet backbone is structured to provide communication among Internet service providers.

Accessing the Internet Backbone

When ARPAnet was first being developed, its creators wanted to create a packet-switching network that provided redundant paths for data transfer. ARPAnet was to serve as an internetwork (a network of networks) connecting government and educational institutions that could still move data even if sites or network paths became disconnected from the network backbone (that is, destroyed in a nuclear holocaust). As the ARPAnet evolved into the Internet, however, businesses and individuals wanted connections to the Internet backbone. This is where the *Internet service provider (ISP)* or *Internet access provider (IAP)* comes in.

Although the terms ISP and IAP are often used interchangeably when referring to companies that provide Internet access, for our discussion, I'd like to differentiate between the two. ISPs typically serve the little guy, such as a home user or small business, who wants to connect to the Internet and take advantage of Internet e-mail, the WWW, and other Internet services. So, let's say that ISPs (because of the word *service* in the name) provide Internet connections to users and companies and offer services such as Internet e-mail, Web browsing, FTP, and newsgroups—all the typical Internet services. They may even provide some space on their Web servers for user Web pages and may also provide the DNS servers required for connection to the Internet.

An ISP doesn't have to be a monster organization that is directly connected to the Internet backbone. An ISP can actually lease its connection to the Internet from an IAP.

So, what's an IAP? An IAP would be a communications company that only provides a connection to the Internet. The companies served by an IAP (usually larger companies and even ISPs) would be responsible for their own DNS servers, mail servers, and so on. The IAP only provides the onramp to the Internet and actually connects to the Internet backbone via a *network access point (NAP)*. An NAP is a public exchange facility that provides connections for any number of IAPs to the Internet backbone.

So, now you are probably wondering how these different network access points are connected. The different NAPs are actually connected by a set of trunk lines (which are part of the Internet backbone). Sprint is an example of a company that operates a NAP.

Each of the NAPs rests on one of the Internet trunk lines, and these trunk lines allow the Internet access providers to communicate with each other (the end result of their communications is the movement of data over the Internet). An Internet trunk line (and there are currently seven in the United States) is referred to as a *metropolitan area ethernet (MAE)*. The first MAE line was created in Washington, D.C., and is referred to as *MAE East*. The MAE that primarily serves the Silicon Valley is referred to as *MAE West* (kind of figures, doesn't it?).

Note The MAE network is managed by the MFS Communications Company. This company was awarded the contract to manage the MAE backbone by the National Science Foundation.

So, to make a long story short, unless you are a very large company, you probably won't be directly connected to the Internet backbone by an NAP. Your connection will be downstream of the backbone and provided by the linking of your ISP to larger IAPs or companies that have NAP connections.

Choosing an Internet Service Provider

It really goes without saying (although I'm going to say it anyhow) that you should carefully research the different ISPs available for connecting your company to the Internet. Depending on where your business is located, there might be as many ISPs to choose from as used-car dealers. You should also exercise the same caution in choosing an ISP that you would when buying a used car.

While selecting an ISP for a home network or small office isn't as crucial as selecting an ISP for a large corporate network (home networks and small companies can usually switch ISPs fairly quickly if they are not satisfied without that much disruption to the business), you should be sure that you select an ISP that provides good support in case you have problems configuring your network computers to connect to the Internet. You should also look for an ISP with a good track record and one that supplies you with extras such as additional e-mail accounts at a reasonable fee.

Obviously, how your company or small business is planning to use the Internet will color how you choose your ISP. For example, if your Internet connection is extremely important to how your company does business, you will want to select an ISP that can ensure a consistent connection. The following list of questions provides some issues that you will want to explore when selecting your ISP, particularly in situations where you are connecting a larger company to the Internet:

- *Is the ISP redundantly connected to its upstream link?* It's important for you to know how many redundant links the ISP maintains with its "big brother" IAP. Redundant connections assure you of a more consistent connection through your ISP to the Internet backbone.

- *Who will supply the equipment for the ISP/LAN connection?* You need to find out if the ISP provides and configures necessary equipment, such as routers, as part of the connection cost or if you will have to purchase and maintain your own WAN connectivity devices.

- *Can the ISP provide you with a pool of IP addresses for your network and obtain your domain name for you?* Having your own pool of IP addresses to work with provides you with flexibility in bringing new clients onto the network and configuring Web servers or DNS servers that require fixed IP addresses. It's certainly not that difficult to obtain your own domain name (as discussed later in this chapter), but if the ISP will do it for you and maintain the DNS servers required, this is one less thing you have to worry about when building your IP network.

- *Will the ISP help you secure your IP network?* You need to know what the ISP is willing to do to help protect your LAN from invasion over the Internet connection. Find out if the ISP offers firewalls (we discuss firewalls in Chapter 16, "A Network Security Primer," in the section "Understanding Firewalls").

- *What kind of technical support is offered by the ISP?* Find out if the ISP offers 24/7 technical support or if it's closed every time there is a local Star Trek convention.

Although this list doesn't take into consideration any special requirements or your actual Internet connection needs, you probably get the picture that your choice of ISP shouldn't be based totally on price (the same goes with used cars). You need to take the time to be sure the ISP has the experience and connectivity muscle that will assure you of a consistent and cost-effective connection to the Internet. Don't be afraid to ask an ISP for references. Taking the opportunity to talk to other clients of the ISP might prove to be the most valuable research you do when selecting an ISP.

Choosing a Connection Type

Your connection to your ISP can take advantage of any of the different WAN connectivity strategies we discussed in Chapter 10. The connection type you choose should provide enough bandwidth to handle the movement of data between your network users and your ISP. For example, a small business might be able to get away with a 640Kbps DSL connection. A larger business might require a fractional T1 or a full T1 carrier line to provide the appropriate data transfer pipe.

During your initial dialogue with a prospective ISP, you need to find out how much experience it has with the different WAN possibilities for connecting your company to it. An ISP with a proven track record of providing connections for businesses can also provide you with information on the type of connections it is providing to other clients.

One connection type that we didn't take a look when we discussed the various WAN technologies in Chapter 10 is the cable modem. It provides an alternative for small companies looking for a connection to the Internet in markets where DSL isn't available or in situations where ISDN just doesn't provide enough bandwidth. Cable companies such as Time Warner offer cable modem connections.

Cable modem connections take advantage of the cable TV infrastructure. Data is moved on different frequencies (or *channels*, if you prefer). Upstream and downstream data typically require separate frequencies. Although cable modem technology and the methods for allocating bandwidth are still being developed, bandwidths in excess of 2Mbps (with the possibility of speeds up to 30Mbps) can be experienced using the technology (the more bandwidth you want, the more you pay the provider). Because a cable company that offers broadband cable modem connections also serves as the ISP for these connections, a small company that wants a connection to the Internet, but does not necessarily consider the connection to be mission critical, might want to consider broadband as a possible connection.

A number of cable television providers, such as Time Warner, now offer cable modem connections for home networks, small businesses, and even larger businesses. Different connection packages are available that supply varying amounts of bandwidth. The cable modem itself supplies the connection between the ISP (the cable company) and its Internet gateway server. The cable modem is connected to a regular television coaxial cable outlet. You can then connect the cable modem to your router, switch, or hub using CAT 5 twisted-pair cabling.

In many regional cable markets, even the basic home cable modem package will provide dynamically assigned IP addresses and enough bandwidth for five networked computers. It is a very good way to share an Internet connection in a home or small office situation.

Regardless of the technology you choose for your connection to your ISP, you need to be sure you understand that particular WAN technology and how to secure IP traffic between your network and the ISP. The use of firewalls and other security strategies such as IPSec (discussed in Chapter 16) should also play a part in your overall planning of the connection of your network to the Internet.

Getting Your Own Domain Name

For your company to have a presence on the Internet, you need a domain name. The domain name is the friendly name that is used to locate your Web site or FTP site and to label e-mail messages to or from your domain. Domain names can often be procured for you by your ISP (and this works well in cases where the ISP will also host your domain). Alternatively, you can apply for your domain name yourself.

You apply for domain names that end in .com, .org, or .net by contacting a domain name registration provider (sites ending in two-letter country codes are handled by other providers). For example, the InterNIC Domain Services, a registration provider at `http://internicdomainservices.com`, can be used to register your domain name (this is just one of many providers and is only being used as an example, not as a recommendation). InterNIC Domain Services also supplies a search engine you can use to determine whether the domain name you wish to use is already taken. For example,

I searched for Habraken.com and found that the domain was already taken, as shown in Figure 12.1.

FIGURE 12.1
Registration providers supply search engines you can use to see whether your desired domain name is already taken.

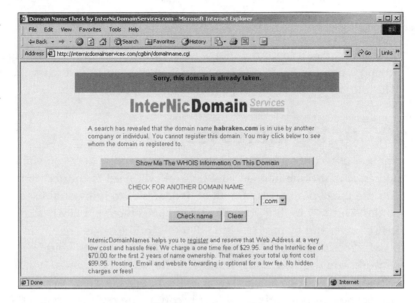

When you apply for your domain name, you will also need to know how DNS services will be handled for your domain (DNS is covered in Chapter 11, "How the Internet Works"). This means that you will either deploy your own DNS servers or use DNS servers provided by your ISP.

Note

In the not-so-distant past, all requests for domain names were made directly to InterNIC, an organization entrusted by the U.S. government to handle domain name registration. InterNIC also initially handled the allocation of IP address pools. A new organization (which has absorbed InterNIC), the Internet Corporation for Assigned Names and Numbers (ICANN), now handles domain name registration. You can check out a list of ICANN-accredited domain name providers at `http://www.internic.net/`.

The cost of a domain name is fairly nominal when you consider that it can help to greatly increase the visibility of your company when used to establish your presence on the Web with a Web site. To register a domain name using InterNIC Domain Services, you pay $29.95 up front. There is also a fee to keep your domain name active. For the first two years, InterNIC Domain Services charges $70. Believe it or not, the fees for registering and maintaining your domain name will vary among domain name registration providers. You should do a little research before you select a provider. Also be advised that ICANN limits the leasing of a particular domain name to 10 years.

You certainly don't have to have a domain name just to connect your small business to the Internet (and don't let an ISP tell you that you do). If having your own domain is going to enhance your business or if your business is going to revolve around e-commerce, you will want to have a domain name.

Just keep in mind that not everyone needs to have a domain on the Internet. If you have a very small company that is establishing its client base through other means, having a domain name and company Web site (which is discussed in Chapter 13, "Hosting a Web Site") might be nothing more than a luxury.

Getting Your IP Addresses

Another aspect of connecting to the Internet involves how you will get the IP addresses that computers on your network will need to connect to the Internet. Many ISPs use the dynamic assignment of IP addresses to individual users and small companies. This means that your client computers receive their IP addresses from a DHCP server run by the ISP. Using dynamic addresses is fine if you have a small peer-to-peer network, but in cases where you are running your own servers on the network, you will need some static IP addresses. For example, Windows 2000 servers, NetWare servers, and Solaris servers all require static IP addresses to operate properly. Servers need a static IP address because many of the services that they provide to client computers find that service using that particular IP address.

You can lease static IP addresses directly from your ISP. Charges vary from ISP to ISP, but based on my experiences with leasing additional static IP addresses for my own small business network, I have found the cost to be around $20 to $30 per month for each static IP address.

Note | You can forgo directly connecting all the PCs on a small network to the ISP by using a proxy server or a host computer running an OS such as Windows Me or Windows 2000 Professional (Windows 2000 Server also supports Internet connection sharing). This means that only the computer providing the Internet connection will need an IP address that is statically or dynamically assigned by your ISP. So, how do the other computers on the network get an IP address? We will discuss that later in the chapter when we look at Internet connection sharing.

If you work at a large company and need a large pool of IP addresses, you can go to the actual source of IP addresses, the American Registry for Internet Numbers (ARIN), to lease your addresses. ARIN is a not-for-profit organization established to register (and administer) IP addresses for North America, South America, the Caribbean, and sub-Sahara Africa.

IP addressing for the rest of the world is managed by two other organizations. The RIPE Network Coordination Centre handles Europe, the Middle East, and the parts of Africa not serviced by ARIN. APNIC (Asia Pacific Network Information Centre) handles the Asian Pacific region.

The minimum number of addresses that can be leased from ARIN is 4,096, which costs $2,500 per year. So, unless you work for a very large company, you will have to acquire IP addresses from your ISP. For more information about ARIN, check out its Web site at http://www.arin.net/.

Sharing an Internet Connection

For a very small business or a home-based business, where the use of the Internet by employees is somewhat minimal, you can choose to not connect all the computers directly to an ISP. Instead, one computer can be connected to the Internet via an ISP and then this connection can be shared with other computers on the network.

Actually setting up the Windows OS to share the connection is very simple. You right-click the connection that is to be shared (such as a network or modem connection listed in Network and Dial-up Connections) and then select Properties on the shortcut menu that appears. Figure 12.2 shows the Sharing tab of a connection's Properties dialog box that is used to configure the sharing of an Internet connection. Notice that it's really just a matter of selecting a check box.

FIGURE 12.2

Windows 2000 Professional provides an Internet connection sharing feature that allows you to share one Internet connection on a small network.

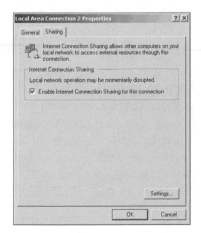

On first inspection, sharing an Internet connection using an OS such as Windows Me or Windows 2000 Professional looks extremely easy. However, there are some hardware issues related to sharing an Internet connection that must be dealt with, and you need an understanding of how IP addressing is going to be handled on the "internal" network to get this whole thing to work properly.

Hardware Required for Sharing an Internet Connection

To accomplish Internet connection sharing using an operating system such as Windows Me or Windows 2000 Professional (or the new Windows XP Personal or Professional), the computer that shares the connection will need two connections: one to the ISP and one to the other computers on the network. In cases where the computer is connected to the ISP using a modem, the connection to the rest of the network will be provided by the computer's NIC (sharing a modem connection is going to provide a very slow connection when shared among multiple computers, but it can be done).

In cases where the computer that will share the connection is connected to the ISP by a DSL router or a cable modem, a NIC is used to connect to the DSL router or cable modem, and this NIC will have to be configured with either a static IP address supplied by the ISP or configured to accept a dynamically configured IP address from the ISP's DHCP server.

So, how does this computer connect to the rest of the network once it is connected to the Internet? It will require a second network card. This second network card will be connected to the hub that connects the other computers on the network.

IP Addressing for the Computer Sharing the Connection

Now, you are probably wondering where the networked computers and the second NIC (the one connected to the network hub) on the computer sharing the Internet connection are going to get their IP addresses? They actually get their IP addresses automatically, but not from a DHCP server. Windows Me, Windows 2000, and Windows XP all embrace a feature called *Automatic Private IP Addressing*. This feature automatically assigns an address to a computer's NIC using a range of IP addresses from 169.254.0.1 to 169.254.255.254, with the subnet mask 255.255.0.0.

Note | The Internet Assigned Number Authority (IANA) has actually reserved the IP range of 169.254.0.1 to 169.254.255.254 for private addressing. Therefore, these addresses aren't going to conflict with any IP addresses on the Internet.

Automatic addressing only takes place when you configure the IP properties on the NIC so that the computer expects to receive its IP address from a DHCP server. Figure 12.3 shows how you would configure a Windows client to take advantage of automatic private addressing. You actually configure it to get its IP address from a DHCP server.

FIGURE 12.3

Computers running Windows that can't find a DHCP server will use the Automatic Private IP Addressing feature.

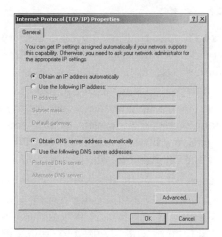

When the computer can't find a DHCP server on the network to supply an IP address, it configures itself with an IP address from the reserved range. Because the computers on the network are constantly talking to each other, they make sure that no two computers use the same IP address.

So, due to the fact that the computers have all automatically assigned themselves addresses from a specific range of IP addresses (actually addresses that all fall into one network range), the computers use these addresses to communicate. They communicate with the computer that provides the Internet connection as well as with each other.

You will also have to configure Web browsers such as Internet Explorer and Netscape Navigator on the computers that will use the shared Internet connection (don't do this on the computer that supplies the shared connection). Oddly enough, for connection sharing to work with the Web browser, you need to be sure that features such as the automatic detection of the proxy server or the use of a proxy server are not selected. You also want to disable dial-up features provided by the browser so that it does not attempt to automatically dial a connection of its own.

When you use the Internet connection sharing feature on a Windows computer, you are basically turning the computer into a proxy server (even though you don't configure Web browsers on computers sharing the connection to use a proxy server, as discussed in the preceding Tip). Proxy servers are the subject of the next section.

Working with Proxy Servers

When you connect your network to the Internet using an ISP or an IAP, you are setting up an environment that provides an unrestricted flow of information between your network and just about everyone else in the world (everyone with an Internet connection). Now, because you know and trust (at least somewhat, hopefully) the users on your internal network and have implemented some security measures on the LAN, you can consider it a *trusted network*. However, because you don't know everyone else in the world and have very little control over security on the Internet itself, you would have to consider the Internet an *untrusted network*.

Every time one of your network users connects to the Web or downloads files from an FTP site, information such as the IP address of the user's computer can be recorded by the Web or FTP site the user connects to. A way to hide important information that can easily be collected (and potentially used to crack into your network) when your users access the Internet is to use a proxy server.

A *proxy server* sits between your trusted network and an untrusted network, such as the Internet (see Figure 12.4). When a user on your network attempts to access the WWW with a Web browser, the request goes to the proxy server. The proxy server strips off the IP addressing information from the data packets that make up the request from the user and affixes addressing information specific to itself. The proxy server then contacts the Web server requested by the user. The proxy server will actually download the requested Web page and then supply it to the user.

Using proxy servers totally hides the IP addressing information on your internal network. Proxy servers can supply additional security by also serving as firewalls (that is, if the proxy server software you use provides firewall features; firewalls are discussed in Chapter 16 in the section "Understanding Firewalls").

Proxy servers can do more than just hide information about the internal, trusted network. Proxy servers can be configured to filter requests made by users on the trusted network to the Internet. For example, you might want to make certain Web sites off limits to your users, and the proxy server can be set up to deny requests for certain types of Web information.

FIGURE 12.4

Proxy servers sit between your network and the Internet and intercept communication requests.

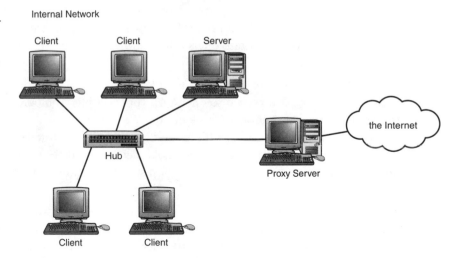

Internal Network

Client   Client   Server

the Internet

Hub

Proxy Server

Client   Client

Proxy servers can also actually speed up requests that are made by your users for information on the Internet. For example, a proxy server can cache Web pages that are accessed by your users. This means that the pages will be readily available (in the proxy server's cache) the next time the user or users access those Web pages.

Proxy server software is available from a number of different vendors, including Microsoft Proxy Server, Netscape Proxy Server, and Sun's iPlanet Proxy Server. There are a large number of proxy servers that exist for small businesses and home offices. Check out www.tucows.com if you want to try out some of these different proxy server packages (we will take a look at a freeware proxy server, called AnalogX Proxy Server, in the section on NAT, which is coming up next).

I've already mentioned the fact that proxy servers can also function as firewalls. Another feature that proxy servers can offer is Network Address Translation (NAT). We'll take a look at NAT next.

Understanding Network Address Translation

Network Address Translation (NAT) allows you to hide a group of computers (such as a network) behind one IP address. In the Unix world, this is known as *IP masquerading*. Basically, your network sits behind the NAT server, which also is typically a proxy server and/or firewall. This means that you only need one "legal" IP address for the server running the NAT software. The IP addressing scheme that you use on the computer network behind the NAT server is really up to you (although there are ranges of IP addresses reserved for this purpose, which we will discuss in a moment).

The Internet connection sharing service provided by Windows Me, Windows 2000, and Windows XP (discussed earlier in the chapter) is really an example of the use of NAT. Windows 2000 Server also offers a full-blown version of the NAT service as part of its Remote Access and Routing features.

Because the purpose a proxy server is to hide a trusted network from an untrusted network, many proxy servers also offer NAT. For example, AnalogX Proxy Server is freeware provided by AnalogX (check out the Web site at www.analogx.com; it offers a number of very useful freeware utilities and applications). AnalogX allows you to connect several computers to one Internet connection. In theory, it works in a fashion that is similar to the Internet connection sharing feature provided by Microsoft Windows.

The AnalogX Proxy Server software is installed on a computer that is outfitted with two NICs. One of the NICs is configured with an IP address provided by your ISP (or receives its IP address from the ISP's DHCP server) and is connected to the ISP. The other NIC is connected to your network and configured with an IP address that is consistent with the pool of addresses you use for your internal network. ARIN has actually blocked out a range of IP addresses in each of the three address classes (A, B, and C), as shown here:

- Class A: 10.0.0.0 to 10.255.255.255, with a subnet mask of 255.0.0.0
- Class B: 172.16.0.0 to 172.31.255.255, with a subnet mask of 255.255.0.0
- Class C: 192.168.0.0 to 192.168.255.255, with a subnet mask of 255.255.255.0

The great thing about using a proxy server with NAT capabilities (or a NAT server) is that you can use as many IP addresses as required internally. For example, you can treat your internal network as if it is a Class A or Class B network, which provides a huge number of addresses. Remember, NAT only requires one "official" IP address for the proxy or NAT server that sits between your network and your ISP.

AnalogX Proxy Server is actually quite amazing in that it provides proxy server caching, NAT, and some firewall capabilities. It also runs on a number of different versions of Microsoft Windows, making it easy to implement for a small office or home business. Figure 12.5 shows the simple interface provided by AnalogX Proxy Server.

FIGURE 12.5

The AnalogX
Proxy Server
software pro-
vides a simple
proxy server
that also pro-
vides network
address transla-
tion.

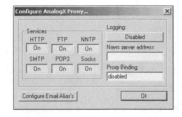

It allows you to toggle Internet services such as HTTP and FTP on and off, and it also allows you to configure e-mail aliases for users on the network. This allows you to use any number of e-mail accounts provided by your ISP (without the need for an IP address for each computer accessing an e-mail account).

Proxy servers and NAT not only provide security and filtering capabilities for large networks, but a proxy server with NAT capabilities can offer low-cost connection options for small companies and home businesses that want to attach more than one computer to a single Internet connection. As with anything else you do associated with networking your business, you need to do research on the options available for the particular client OS and NOS platforms you are running on your network.

Chapter Summary

- The Internet backbone is made up of a number of metropolitan area ethernets (MAEs).

- Connection to an MAE is provided by a network access point (NAP). Communications companies such as Sprint operate NAPs.

- Internet access providers (IAPs) provide connections to MAE NAPs.

- Internet service providers (ISPs) provide a full complement of Internet services, including e-mail and Web hosting.

- When selecting an ISP, you should consider issues such as the ISP's service, redundant connections, and proximity to an NAP.

- Any of the WAN technologies can be used to connect to an ISP or an IAP, including T lines, Frame Relay, and DSL. Cable television companies also offer cable modem connections to the Internet.

- Domain names are procured from domain registration providers.

- IP addresses can be obtained from your ISP or, for large corporations, directly from ARIN.

- Microsoft Windows Me, Windows 2000, and Windows XP offer Internet connection sharing, which allows you to connect a number of computers to the Internet using one Internet connection.

- Proxy servers provide a barrier between trusted networks and untrusted networks. Proxy servers can provide Web page caching, Network Address Translation, and some firewall capabilities.

- Network Address Translation allows you to masquerade a number of computers through one "legal" IP address.

- Proxy servers that supply NAT, such as the AnalogX Proxy Server, provide a way for small networks to connect to the Internet through one ISP connection.

HOSTING A WEB SITE

In this chapter

- Creating your corporate presence on the Web
- Using the Web as a marketing tool
- Selling products on the Web
- Understanding secure online transaction methods
- Hosting a Web site
- Creating a Web site

First we thought the PC was a calculator. Then we found out how to turn numbers into letters with ASCII—and we thought it was a typewriter. Then we discovered graphics, and we thought it was a television. With the World Wide Web, we've realized it's a brochure.

–Douglas Adams

So far, we've discussed what the Internet is (in Chapter 11, "How the Internet Works") and how a company or institution can connect to the Internet (Chapter 12, "Connecting a Network to the Internet"). In this chapter, we take a look at establishing a corporate presence on the Internet in the form of a Web site.

We've also already discussed how you obtain a domain name, but it's how you actually use that domain name in association with your Web site and other services you provide your customer base via the Internet that makes the Internet a positive addition to your business plan.

In this chapter, we discuss issues related to creating a Web page and getting your business on the Web. We look at the options of creating your own Web site or having your Web site created by a company that specializes in Web site development. We also look at how you can use Web pages to enhance communications on a corporate intranet. Let's start our discussion with the reasons why you might want to have a Web site for your business or company.

The Internet and Your Corporate Presence

Although the Internet may have been conceived as a network superhighway with the noble mission of sharing information worldwide, it seems that the Internet has become, particularly in the case of the WWW, an often-congested turnpike littered with thousands and thousands of billboards. Although this might seem a rather cynical view of the Web, I think most people would agree that many (if not most) of the thousands of Web sites on the Web serve as marketing, advertising, and sales mediums for businesses, both large and small.

Regardless of what you think of the Web, most businesses (again, the big and the small) feel compelled to have some sort of presence on the Web. Using the Web as another avenue for advertising or sales should definitely be a part of your business plan. How large of a role the Web should play in your business plan should be determined by the type of business you do.

For example, let's say you run a furniture company that has its own outlet. People travel from all over the region to buy your furniture. But would you like to expand your business range? You might take a look would at the Web and say, "Wow, we can sell furniture right on the Web." Of course, upon further exploration, you realize that the shipping costs for delivering sectional sofa arrangements and oak armoires from your outlet to the customers buying online is roughly equivalent to the Gross National Product of many third-world countries. It might also dawn on you that people like to sit on furniture before they buy it.

So, rule number one for determining how you will use your Web site is to make the Web site fit into your overall business strategy, not turn it upside down. I don't know if you've noticed, but a number of Web-based furniture stores went belly-up in 1999 and 2000.

Your use of the Web should be carefully analyzed the same way you analyze all the other potential sales and marketing avenues you use. If trying to sell directly on the Web requires a support infrastructure that costs a ton of money, you might be better off just using the Web as another advertising venue. The number of "dot coms" that have turned to "dot bombs" in the last couple of years proves that you can't sell just anything on the Web.

Although the Web isn't necessarily the end-all marketing tool or sales platform, it does provide you with the ability to reach very large audiences. Let's take a look at some of the marketing strategies that can used on the Web and some of the issues related to selling on the Web.

Marketing on the Web

The Web provides a large number of content possibilities for marketing your business or company. Information can be presented in a variety of formats, including print, pictures, and even audio and video. All these different content types can then be presented in one place—your Web site.

Here are some of the possibilities:

- *Company mission statement and product offerings.* A business Web site should make it clear who you are and what type of service or product you sell.

- *Testimonials.* Testimonials from satisfied customers can greatly enhance the marketing success of your Web site.

- *Online product lists.* Even if you aren't selling your product on the Web, you can let potential customers know what you sell and why they should buy it from you.

- *White papers.* A white paper allows you to provide a potential customer with background information and case studies related to the product or service that you sell.

- *Frequently asked questions (FAQ).* You can include a list of questions that are typically asked by your customers related to your product or service.

- *Contact information.* Providing potential customers with the ability to ask you questions via e-mail allows them to get answers to questions that are not covered by your FAQ.

- *Downloads.* Downloads can include product catalogs, software demos, newsletters, or other material that will enhance the desirability of your service or product.

- *Video, audio, and interactive content.* The Web offers you the ability to include video and audio content describing your product or service. You can also have interactive content that allows a prospective customer to become better acquainted with your product or service.

To make a long story short, the Web offers more avenues for the delivery of marketing information than any other advertising medium. The Web also provides a platform that can be quickly updated to meet business conditions. For instance, if you can no longer offer a particular service or product, you can remove it from the Web site. Removing a discontinued product or service from a printed catalog would be a lot more problematic than removing the same information from a Web site.

Selling on the Web

Selling on the Web is definitely not for everyone. Not only do you need to have a Web site that provides an up-to-date online catalog, but you also must have the ability to make secure transactions. Web sites that provide online transactions must have some way to track orders and inventory as well as validate customer purchases using various credit cards.

Providing an online store means setting up a fairly complex system of servers. First of all, your Web server will provide the communication interface, such as the catalog and the order form used by the customer. So, the front end for your online store is the Web server that hosts your Web site.

Note

Although you should really research the ins and outs of deploying a Web-based store, software packages are available that you can use to quickly get a Web-based store up and running. These products also offer a pretty high level of security as far as transactions are concerned. For example, there is O'Reilly Software's Web site Professional 3, which allows you to create your online catalog, shopping cart system, and payment system. Web site Professional will run on a number of different operating systems, including Windows 98 and Windows 2000. Depending on the amount of traffic you expect your online store to experience, you don't even necessarily have to deploy the online store on a server-class computer. In the case of small business owners, who don't wish to operate their own Web server, you will find that many Web hosting services can quickly set up an online store for you with a variety of features. An excellent example of a hosting service that also provides you with the ability to choose some of the layout options and features on your site is Microsoft's bCentral at `http://www.bcentral.com/`. This online hosting service provides links that allow you to quickly create any number of different types of company Web sites—even online stores that are then hosted by Microsoft.

On the back end of your online store, an application server will have to provide databases, such as your inventory database, orders database, and customer database. The Web site will provide the interface for customer interaction with these different databases. Figure 13.1 provides a diagram of how different server types are used for online transactions.

FIGURE 13.1
Online transactions require communication between your Web server and an application server.

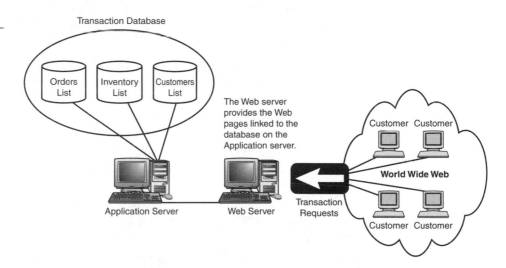

Transaction Database

Orders List

Inventory List

Customers List

The Web server provides the Web pages linked to the database on the Application server.

Application Server

Web Server

Transaction Requests

World Wide Web

Customer   Customer

Customer   Customer

Tip

Not only will you need a Web site designed for online transactions, but you will need a merchant account (which is a special type of bank account) that allows you to except credit card orders on your Web site. There are a number of merchant status providers on the Web, such as InternetSecure at `http://www.internetsecure.com`. These online services can be used to set up your "merchant status." You will find that this is not cheap, however. You must pay an upfront fee and a per-transaction fee. A fairly consistent volume of business would be required to substantiate the expense of becoming an online merchant.

Transaction Security

Not only is the hardware and software infrastructure more intense for Web stores when compared to a simple Web site, your online store must also offer a high-level of security for transactions. Having someone crack your marketing Web site and mess up some of your Web pages is a lot different from having a cracker break in and steal credit card numbers from your customer database. Secure communications on the Web is accomplished using methods such as encryption and digital certificates. A *digital certificate* is basically an electronic identification card. It is used to verify the identity of the sender of an encrypted message.

Here are three of the most popular security strategies for securing online transactions:

- *Secure Socket Layer (SSL)*. SSL was developed by Netscape to secure online transactions. SSL uses a combination of encryption and digital certificates (the certificates are used to verify the merchant's identity) to secure the transfer of information from a Web browser to the Web site store. Popular Web browsers such as Netscape Navigator and Microsoft Internet Explorer support SSL.

- *Secure Electronic Transaction (SET)*. SET is a new standard for securing credit card transactions on the Internet. SET was developed by Visa and MasterCard and provides very strong 128-bit encryption (the more bits, the better the encryption; therefore, 128-bit encryption is harder to decode than 64-bit encryption). SET also uses digital certificates to identify both the merchant and the buyer involved in the transaction. Because SET uses digital certificates (also known as *digital signatures*) to identify a buyer, actual credit card numbers don't actually have to pass between the online merchant and buyer. SET has not been widely implemented because it requires Web shoppers to acquire a digital certificate, and SET requires more bandwidth overhead when compared to SSL.

- *Secure HTTP (SHTTP)*. SHTTP is a superset of the HTTP protocol that provides mechanisms to secure online transactions. SHTTP was developed by Enterprise Integration Technologies and is now the property of Terisia Systems. SHTTP provides for the encryption of transmissions between server and clients. SHTTP also supports the use of digital certificates. Although SHTTP was submitted to the Internet Engineering Task Force (IETF) in 1995 in a request to have it named the standard for secure messaging on the Internet, SSL seems to actually be a more popular method for securing online communications.

Research and planning are important aspects of any network rollout, including a Web site that offers an online store. In the case of Web transactions, it might not be a bad idea to talk to a consultant or company that specializes in transaction security. Keeping customer information secure is a total must for any online sales endeavor.

Remember, also, that running an online store has some of the same pitfalls that you face running a storefront business. There are taxes, insurance, potential liability, and, of course, risks.

Who Will Host Your Web Site?

Before we take a look at the basics of creating a Web page, we should discuss issues related to hosting your Web site. You can choose to deploy your own Web server, or you can choose to have your Web site hosted by an ISP that offers Web hosting as one of its services. Let's take a look at hosting your own Web site, first, and then we can take a look at using a Web-hosting service.

Hosting Your Own Web Site

If you have the budget and the know-how, you can deploy your own Web servers. A Web server can be run using a number of different network operating systems. For example, NetWare 5.1 provides the NetWare Enterprise Web server and even provides the WebSphere application server, which can be used to host back-end applications that interface with your Web site. NetWare's Web server can easily be populated with Web content via NetWare's Management Portal, shown in Figure 13.2. The Management Portal can be accessed by an administrator from any Web browser.

FIGURE 13.2

The NetWare Web server can be managed using a Web browser.

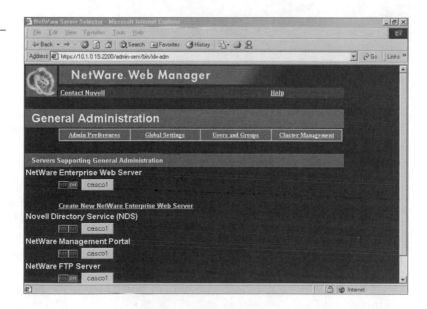

Another popular Web server platform is provided by Microsoft Windows Server in the form of Internet Information Services (IIS) (the version 5 of IIS that ships with Windows 2000 Server is the most recent version of the IIS software). IIS is available in the Windows NT, Windows 2000, and Windows XP versions of the Windows Server software. Microsoft Internet Information Services makes it easy for you to configure Web sites, FTP sites, and NNTP newsgroups (see Figure 13.3). In the Unix/Linux world, the Apache Web server, developed by the National Center for Supercomputing Applications (NCSA) is a popular Web server environment.

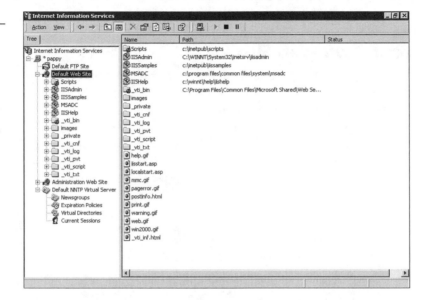

FIGURE 13.3

Microsoft's Internet Information Services allows you to deploy Web sites, FTP sites, and news-groups.

Selecting the NOS and the Web server software for your Web server should be approached as you would approach determining the software configuration of any specialized server on your network. Ease of use, scalability, and compatibility should all be points that you consider when putting together the specifications for your Web server.

Hardware considerations for a Web server are the same as those for any other server on your network. Your hardware specifications need to at least coincide with the minimum for running the particular NOS and the add-on Web server software. Running the Web server with only the minimum hardware requirements, however, will quickly become undesirable. Web servers require a lot of RAM, disk space, and very fast processing to handle the amount of traffic they will experience once they are brought online.

Be advised that hosting your own Web sites on your own Web servers may also require that you deploy your own DNS servers. If your Web site will provide online transactions, you will also have to provide the appropriate application server or servers to manage the transaction databases. Firewalls, proxy servers, and other specialized servers might also be necessary to protect your site from outside attack. Adding Web server management to your network administration duties can stretch one person and even a small staff very thin.

There is a lot more to hosting a Web site than just setting up a Web server and placing Web pages on a computer. Securing the Web site from outside attack and keeping the Web content up to date are also important aspects of managing a Web site. Depending on the size of your company, the management of the Web site is often delegated to a Webmaster. This is an employee who not only understands networking using TCP/IP but also has some design and Web page construction experience.

Using a Hosting Service

An alternative to hosting your Web site on your own Web server is to farm your site out to an ISP or other company that provides Web hosting. Companies offering Web hosting provide a secure environment for your Web site (some more so than others). So, you don't need to worry about security issues related to the Web server. All you have to do is design your site and then upload the Web pages to the Web server.

Rates vary for Web hosting, depending on the amount of space you require on the Web server and the features you require for your site. A Web site designed for online transactions will require more back-end support than a simple site designed as a marketing tool. When choosing a Web host, you should find out what types of features it provides (SQL databases, transaction servers, and so on) and the type of support it provides.

Obviously another key issue in selecting a Web-hosting service is cost. You need to find out how the Web host charges for disk space and if it has additional charges related to the bandwidth that activity related to your site may use.

An excellent source for researching Web-hosting companies can be found at `http://www.hostinglocator.com/`. This Web site allows you to search for Web-hosting services by platform (such as Unix or Windows Server) and also provides some tips on selecting your Web host. Even after developing a "short list" of Web-hosting services based on cost and features, you might want to correspond with each service by e-mail (or even by telephone). Try to get a general feel from the provider to see if customer service is even in its vocabulary.

Because you can upload your Web files to a Web server anywhere on the Internet, you aren't limited to using a local ISP to host your Web site. However, if you have firsthand testimonials from other people or businesses who are familiar with the Web-hosting track record of a local ISP, there might be some very compelling advantages to doing your business locally.

An alternative to working with an ISP that provides Web hosting is to use an online Web-hosting service, such as those provided by Microsoft and Yahoo!. Microsoft's bCentral provides Web-hosting and Web design software to create the Web pages that will populate your Web site. bCentral even gets you your domain name and provide e-mail accounts specific for your domain name. Figure 13.4 shows the Microsoft bCentral Web page that describes its various Web-hosting services. Yahoo! also offers similar services. You can check these out at http://website.yahoo.com/. These online Web hosting services do offer advantages in that it is easy to go online to the actual Web hosting site and change the content on your site using the various Web-based utilities provided by the online service (in the case of an ISP, you need to become familiar with some sort of Web design software, if you are going to change the content of your Web site). Since these services are also offered by large Web players like Yahoo! and Microsoft, the servers used to host your Web site are state of the art and offer quick response to potential clients browsing your site. Not all ISPs can offer Web servers of this quality or speed.

FIGURE 13.4
Web hosting is also offered online by providers such as Microsoft.

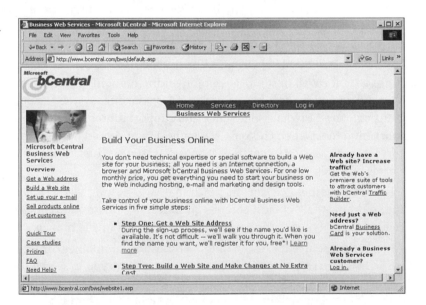

Creating a Web Site

Although the development of the Hypertext Transport Protocol (HTTP) provided the underlying communication structure for the World Wide Web, the authoring language used to create Web pages is the Hypertext Markup Language (HTML). HTML consists of embedded tags that tell a Web browser how to display or act upon information found on a Web page.

Your Web site, no matter how modest, will typically consist of multiple Web pages; the home page, which is the main page for the site, will provide the table of contents for the site. Each additional page on the site will be referenced on the home page by a hyperlink. A *hyperlink* is basically a pointer that allows you to refer to other local Web pages, graphics, and multimedia content on a page. When a hyperlink is clicked in a Web browser window, the user is taken to that page or activates a particular event (such as the playing of video or audio content or the displaying of a picture). Hyperlinks can also be used to refer to remote Web pages or other locations, such as an FTP site.

In the Web's infancy, Web pages primarily consisted of text and hyperlinks. Images were used to provide some respite, but it took some time to develop tools that provided more complex multimedia content on a Web page. Java applets now provide us with applications that can be run directly from Web pages. Also, multimedia plug-ins such as Macromedia Shockwave and Flash, Real Player, and Windows Media Player provide you with the ability to access audio and video content in a Web page.

As far as Web page design goes, your aim is to produce a Web site that is informational, easy to navigate, and aesthetically pleasing. Web site design not only requires an understanding of HTML (and any plug-in technologies that you use), but it also requires an eye for design. Although I'm not saying you need to be an artist or a design expert to create a decent Web site, it certainly doesn't hurt to understand some basic design and layout concepts.

Although we will take a quick look at how you would create a Web site using either HTML or a software design tool, there are many other resources that can walk you through the entire process of Web site creation and help you develop some appreciation for design concepts. In fact, there are probably enough books on Web site design and the various tools for creating Web sites to bridge the Atlantic Ocean between the United States and Europe. If you're looking for a book that is geared toward Web design rather than HTML or a specific software tool for creating Web pages, you might want to check out *The Art and Science of Web Design*, from Que.

Working with HTML

If you want to create your Web pages from scratch, you can use any text editor. As already mentioned, HTML is made up of a system of tags that are applied to text in an ASCII text file. All HTML tags are written in the format <code>, where code would be the actual HTML tag you are using. For example, to center text on a Web page, the HTML code would appear as follows:

```
<CENTER>This text will be centered</CENTER>
```

Note that one tag is used to turn the centering on (<CENTER>) and a very similar tag that includes a slash (/) turns off the centering (the </CENTER> tag). I think you can see that HTML is somewhat intuitive.

When you begin a Web page that you are creating in HTML, the first tag at the top of the HTML document is <HTML>. Other tags follow as needed. For example, the <HEAD> tag is used to specify the part of the HTML document that contains the title for the Web page. The title of the Web page is then specified using the tag <TITLE>. For example, let's say I want to create a simple Web page using Windows Notepad. My HTML code will actually start with the tag <HTML>. To end the page, I use the tag </HTML>. Every "on" tag has a counterpart "off" tag.

Figure 13.5 shows the beginnings of a very simple Web page written in HTML using Windows Notepad. Your text files need to be saved with the extension .htm to be read by a Web browser.

FIGURE 13.5

Web pages can be created directly in HTML using a text editor such as Windows Notepad.

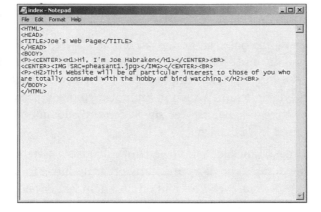

As you work on your HTML documents, you can check your work by opening the file in any Web browser. Figure 13.6 shows the HTML document in Figure 13.5 as it would appear in Internet Explorer.

The Web actually provides some very good resources for learning HTML. For example, check out an online HTML tutorial at http://davesite.com/webstation/html/. A good HTML reference book that will also provide you with some background information on Web design is *Special Edition Using HTML 4, Sixth Edition*, from Que.

FIGURE 13.6
HTML docu-
ments can be
viewed in any
Web browser.
This way, you
can see how
your HTML cod-
ing is working
out.

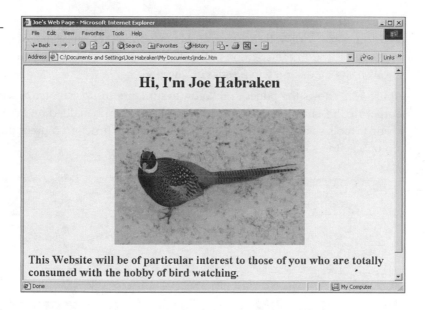

Web Design Tools

A number of Web design tools are available that allow you to create Web sites and Web pages without having to face the laborious task of coding each page in HTML. Examples include Macromedia Dreamweaver and Microsoft FrontPage (and there are many others).

These Web design tools provide a number of different strategies to help you with page design and adding special elements to your Web pages, such as pictures and multimedia content. For example, Microsoft FrontPage provides a number of wizards that can be used to create different types of Web sites (see Figure 13.7).

FIGURE 13.7
FrontPage pro-
vides a number
of wizards that
can be used to
create different
kinds of Web
sites.

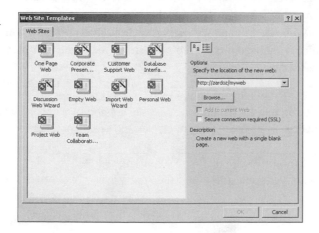

These wizards can create Web sites that range from a corporate-presence Web site, to a customer-support Web site, to a simple one-page Web site. Each of these wizards walks you through the creation of the different pages and objects that will be part of the Web site by asking you a series of questions.

Figure 13.8 shows the pages and Web site structure that is created when you use the Corporate Presence Web Wizard. Each page can then be edited and enhanced as needed. Tools such as FrontPage and Dreamweaver function a great deal like desktop publishing software.

FIGURE 13.8

The Web page structure for complex corporate sites can be created using Web development tools such as Microsoft FrontPage.

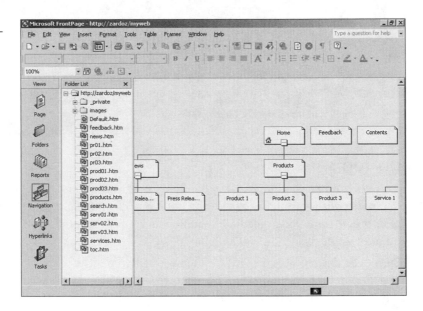

Web design tools certainly make it easier for you to initially create your Web site and update content as required. These tools even provide you with methods for uploading your Web site to your Web server or the ISP server that will host your Web site. For example, FrontPage has a Web publishing feature that uploads your entire site to a specified server.

Note

Although there are a number of design tools available for creating your Web site, there is something to be said for having your Web site created by someone with some Web design experience. There are design companies and seemingly no end of freelance Web designers.

Taking Advantage of an Intranet

Because a network administrator's sphere of influence will vary from company to company, you might find that your company's Web site is either managed by a Webmaster or taken care of by a company that provides Web design and Web hosting. This doesn't mean you can't use Web technology to enhance your internal network, however. Any TCP/IP network can take advantage of Web technology and other Internet-based services. Using Internet technologies on a private network means you are building an *intranet*. You can have Web sites on an intranet just like you find on the Web, but they are private.

Using Web sites in an intranet setting can actually be used for a number of different purposes. You can build Web sites that allow users to easily access data on a database running on an application server. Because just about everyone knows how to use a Web browser, the need for training users to use the front end for the database server is almost nonexistent. Web sites can also be used for the exchanging of files between users, and Web sites designed for specific company projects can be used for discussions between the various participants in a project.

A number of large companies have also found that intranet Web sites can be used to promote company morale. For example, "water cooler" Web sites are provided for employees to post information such as employee birthdays or to invite employees to special celebrations. Providing this type of site can actually cut down on the amount of e-mail used by employees for personal communication with other employees.

Intranets also provide an excellent platform for you to test Web server hardware and your Web site itself. Opening up a Web system to employees on the intranet as a test can allow you to diagnose problems and access overall performance before you actually roll the Web site out onto the WWW.

Chapter Summary

- Your corporate presence on the Web can take the form of marketing Web sites, or you can use the Web as a platform for an online store.

- Web sites make good marketing tools in that they allow you to provide customers with varied content, such as print, pictures, sound, and video. A Web site can deliver more content types than any other advertising medium.

- Creating a Web site that serves as an online store will also require an application server that can manage your inventory and orders databases.

- Online transactions require stringent security. A number of different security strategies exist for online transactions, including SSL, SET, and SHTTP.

■ Hosting your own Web site requires that you have the proper hardware infra-structure, including a Web server and perhaps other servers, such as a fire-wall, application server, and so on.

■ Web server software is available for a variety of the NOS environments. NetWare and Microsoft Windows Server both include Web servers as part of the NOS. Apache Web Server is a popular Web server used on Unix/Linux servers.

■ Web-hosting services can provide the hardware infrastructure and the appro-priate servers to host your Web site and supply a secure Web environment. Online hosting services provided by Yahoo! and Microsoft make it easy for a small business to have a Web site, and these services will even help you get your domain name.

■ Web pages consist of text documents containing HTML tags.

■ A Web page can be created as an HTML text document using a text editor.

■ Web design software makes it easy to create complex Web sites. Web design tools such as Macromedia Dreamweaver and Microsoft FrontPage provide wizards and other features that allow for the creation of Web pages without HTML coding.

■ Building an intranet allows you to take advantage of Internet-based services such as Web pages for internal corporate use.

PART IV

KEEPING THE NETWORK RUNNING SMOOTHLY

PROTECTING
NETWORK DATA

In this chapter

- Working with hard drives
- Understanding hard drive partitions
- Using RAID to protect data
- Backing up network and server data
- Working with different types of backup strategies
- Protecting devices with an uninterruptible power supply

Who's General Failure and why's he reading my disk?

–Anonymous

In previous chapters, we've taken a look at networking hardware and cabling as well as the hardware and software used for network servers and clients. We've also taken a look at how to build a Web site. An important aspect of managing a network, and something that we definitely need to discuss, is how you protect the important data on the network.

Now, I'm not talking about network security issues here, such as strategies for keeping intruders from hacking into your network (these are discussed in Chapter 16, "A Network Security Primer," in the section "Protecting a Network from Outside Attack"). I'm talking about strategies that allow you to protect data in situations where a file server's hard drive fails or an employee accidentally erases an important database file. In this chapter, we will look at strategies that add redundancy to a network. This redundancy can take many forms. It can be a backup of all the important files on the network, or it can be a set of redundant disk drives that contain exactly the same information.

Making sure important computers such as file servers keep running, even during a power failure (at least until you can shut them down correctly), is another issue related to protecting data on the network. The main issue we will look at here is building fault tolerance into a LAN, which is a fancy way of saying we don't want to lose any data, no matter what happens to our servers and other network devices.

Let's begin our discussion with a look at the different data-protection schemes that use redundant disk drives. We'll then take a look at issues related to backing up data on a network, and then we can explore the use of uninterruptible power supplies.

Understanding Hard Drives

Hard drives (or *fixed disks*) store information magnetically. They are actually made up of rigid cylinders and have a read/write head, much like any other magnetic recording device.

Because hard drives have extremely rigid, durable cylinders, they can spin at very high speeds. This means that the data on the disk can be accessed quickly (definitely faster than floppy drives and most removable media drives). Disk speed (or *access time*) is measured in milliseconds and is related to the time it takes a drive to access data. The lower the access time, the faster the drive. For example, an 11 ms drive would be faster than a 28ms drive.

We already talked about the different hard drive types—IDE and SCSI—in Chapter 3, "Networking Hardware." Regardless of which of these drive types you use, the drive typically has to be partitioned and formatted before you can actually install an operating system or other software onto it. Let's take a look at drive partitions and then the formatting process.

Drive Partitioning

Hard drives come in a variety of sizes. Although plenty of hard drives churning away on networks have less than 1GB of drive space, newer computers boast drives with space much greater than a gigabyte (a *gigabyte* is 1,073,741,824 bytes or 1,024MB). As computer operating systems and network operating systems have become more user friendly and more sophisticated at the same time, the hard drive capacity they need in order to operate has grown dramatically.

While drive capacity has grown, drive price has actually dropped in relation to the amount of storage space that you get for your money. The original 10MB hard drive for the IBM PC cost about the same amount as a 40GB drive you would buy today.

A *partition* is a logical portion of a hard drive that is actually read by the computer's operating system as a separate drive (see the following Note). Therefore, you can have a hard drive with just one partition encompassing the entire space on the drive (the maximum size of a partition can be limited by the file system used) or you can partition a hard drive into several different logical drives.

Note

The maximum size you can make a hard drive partition will depend on the file system you format the drive with. The Mac OS supports disk partitioning and sees it as a way to divide a large storage space into more manageable subsets. Partition sizes on a Mac are not limited, however. In the IBM/compatible PC realm, there are actually three different file systems now available for hard drives: FAT16, FAT32, and NTFS. FAT16 (FAT stands for *file allocation table*), the file system used by DOS and early versions of Microsoft Windows, only supports partitions of up to 2GB. With the second release of Windows 95, the FAT32 file system became available. It supplies support for partitions in excess of 2GB (up to 8GB). NTFS (NT File System) can be used on computers running Windows NT and Windows 2000 and provides for partition sizes larger than 2GB. The newest version of NTFS (NTFS 5, available in Windows 2000) also provides an "active disk" format that makes it easier to create and extend partitions on drives.

A number of different tools are available for partitioning drives, depending on the operating system you're working with. For example, Apple OS 8.x (and later) uses Apple's Drive Setup utility.

On the IBM/compatible PC side, partitions have been created on hard drives since the early days of DOS using a utility called *FDISK* (see Figure 14.1). FDISK is a DOS command-line utility that provides a menu system used to create and delete partitions on a hard drive. It is available in all the various versions of DOS and Windows.

FIGURE 14.1

FDISK is a DOS
utility used to
manage hard
drive partitions.

Note

FDISK is included on the boot disk that is provided with the different flavors of
Windows, such as Windows 98 and Me (the disk is in the box with the CD). Insert the
disk and boot the computer. You can then type the "fdisk" command at the command
prompt that appears. Once FDISK is up and running, the menu system it provides makes
it easy to create any number of partitions on a hard drive. More sophisticated operating
systems like Windows 2000 actually provide you with the ability to create partitions and
format them during the installation process. So you can even remove current partitions
on the hard drive and create new partitions as needed.

Operating systems such as the Apple Mac OS, Windows NT, and Windows 2000 provide GUI utilities that you use to create and manage partitions. For example,
Windows 2000 provides the Disk Management utility, which allows you to view the
various partitions on hard drives (see Figure 14.2). This utility also makes it very
easy to create new partitions on a drive.

Drive Formatting

How you format your drive will depend on the operating system you are using.
Every operating system offers some type of utility for formatting drives. When you
format a drive, you completely remove any data that the drive may have held.
Therefore, it's important to be sure you don't need that data before blowing it away.

For example, formatting a drive using a DOS boot disk (such as the installation disk
included with versions of Windows such as Windows 98 or Windows Me) is very
straightforward. At the DOS command line, you type format c:, where C is the letter
of the drive you wish to format.

Formatting a drive is necessary because the appropriate "geography" used by a particular file system for storing and accessing files must be placed on the drive. These
areas in which files will be stored are called *sectors*.

FIGURE 14.2

Some operating systems, such as Windows 2000, provide a GUI drive-management utility for partitioning and formatting drives.

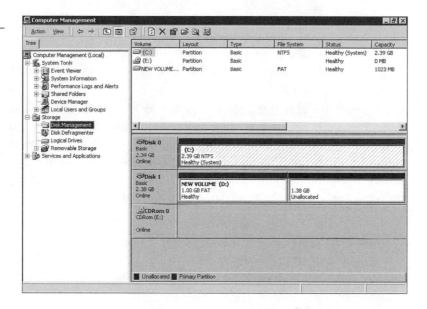

Most operating systems require that you partition and format at least one drive (in cases where the computer has multiple drives, which is typical for servers) before or during the installation of the operating system. Some operating systems, such as Microsoft Windows 2000, also give you the option of changing the partitions on a drive (or drives) and formatting a drive with a different file format during the installation process (such as formatting a FAT drive with the NTFS file system).

Note

You will notice that computer drives are assigned numbers starting with 0. Therefore, your first drive will be drive 0, your second drive will be drive 1, and so on. Because computers (especially servers) can have more than one drive controller, such as multiple SCSI controllers, you could potentially have more than one drive designated as drive 0. Just remember that this is the first drive on a particular drive controller. The controllers themselves will be designated as controller 0, controller 1, and so on.

Working with RAID

Redundant Array of Inexpensive Disks (RAID) is a group of strategies designed to provide fault tolerance for files stored on hard drives. In general, using RAID means that you are placing data on more than one disk; if a disk in the RAID set goes down, you still can get to your data because you either have a complete copy of that data (on another disk in the RAID set) or can regenerate the data on the failed disk from the data and parity information (something we will discuss when we look at RAID 5) on the remaining disks in the set.

In the simplest terms, RAID allows you to take more than one drive and combine them into a disk set (or *array*) that functions just like a single drive. RAID can be hardware supported or software supported. Hardware RAID will be available on a computer where the SCSI controllers found on the motherboard support RAID. Some sort of configuration utility will be provided to set up RAID on a computer that supports hardware RAID. You can also buy add-on boards such as a SCSI controller card.

Large RAID arrays can actually be housed in their own RAID storage cabinets. These special RAID cabinets provide hardware RAID support and also provide bays for a number of disks. For some background information on hardware RAID and a look at some RAID hardware devices, check out Adaptec's site at `http://www.adaptec.com/worldwide/` `product/prodindextech.html`.

With software RAID, the operating system you are running (and this is pretty much limited to network operating system) supports RAID. Windows NT and Windows 2000 Server, Novell NetWare, some Linux clones, and other network operating systems provide support for software RAID.

Understanding the RAID Flavors

RAID comes in eight different flavors, numbered from 0 to 7. The actual types of RAID available with a RAID hardware device or with a network operating system that offers RAID software support will vary. For example, Windows 2000 supports RAID 0, 1, and 5. Before we actually take a look at the different types of RAID, I need to define what a volume is. A *volume*, which in some cases is exactly the same as a partition, is a portion of a hard drive that can function as a separate and discrete drive. In the case of RAID, a volume (which appears to the computer as one drive) is actually spread over two or more drives.

Another piece of information you need before we look at the different types of RAID involves the role parity bits play in RAID arrays. Parity information is extra bits of information included with data that is striped across the drives in a RAID array. These extra bits provide enough information about the data striped across the drives that it can actually be used to reconstruct the data on any one of the drives if one happens to fail. Network operating systems such as Windows NT and Windows 2000 that support RAID sets that use parity bits all have utilities you can use to regenerate any data that is seemingly lost when one of the drives in a RAID array fails (you just put in a new drive and regenerate the entire data library of the RAID set).

Let's take a quick look at the different RAID types. A description of all the RAID flavors, 0 through 7, is provided in Table 14.1.

Table 14.1 RAID Types

Type	Name	Description
0	Disk striping	Data is written across the disks in the array. RAID 0 is not a fault-tolerance method; it's actually used to speed disk access.
1	Mirroring	Two drives (such as partitions or volumes) are mirrored so that each disk in the array is an exact copy of the other disk.
2	A proprietary disk striping method that uses Hamming code error detection and correction	Data is striped across a disk set and parity information is written on a set of parity drives (which are not part of the data set). This requires a minimum of seven drives.
3	Disk striping with a single-parity disk	Data is written across multiple disks in a stripe set with the parity information stored on a single drive that is not part of the data set.
4	Disk striping with a single-parity disk using block parity	This is the same as RAID level 3; however, the parity information is arranged in defined data blocks.
5	Disk striping with distributed parity	Data is written across a striped set of multiple disks with the parity information distributed across the disk array.
6	Disk striping with distributed parity and double-parity bytes	This is very similar to RAID 5: Two sets of parity blocks are created for each block of data stored on the array. However, RAID 6 is slower than RAID 5.
7	Disk striping with a single-parity disk and disk caching	This is a proprietary system, similar to RAID 3 and 4, that is patented by the Storage Computer Corporation. It requires additional hardware and software.

> **Note**
> When you combine the space on multiple disks into a RAID array, the available disk space (the partition or volume) on the drives must be equal.

Now that you've had a brief introduction to the different RAID flavors, let's take a closer look at the RAID types you are most likely to run into. These are supported in hardware RAID systems and by network operating systems that provide RAID software support.

RAID 0

RAID 0 does not actually provide any fault tolerance, even though RAID is considered a strategy for building fault tolerance into servers. It is actually a trick for providing users with faster access to data on file servers and for taking a couple of small drives and combining them to provide more disk space. Because the data is *striped across* (that is, *spread across*) two or more disks rather than one, read and write functions are faster because both (or all) the drives are working simultaneously. Figure 14.3 shows how a RAID 0 array spreads data over multiple drives. Remember that the array of drives would actually be seen by the computer as just one drive with a drive letter designation such as E: (where E: is the actual drive letter).

FIGURE 14.3

RAID 0 is used to stripe data across multiple drives.

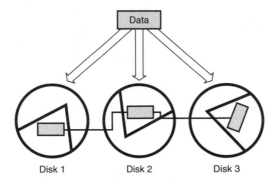

RAID 0 was used a great deal in the days when hard drives were small and slow (not like the incredibly fast gigabyte monsters you can buy now) and there was a need to speed up access to the files on the server and provide an appropriate amount of working storage space. RAID 0 requires at least two hard drives.

Because RAID 0 provides no fault tolerance, when one hard drive in the RAID 0 array goes belly up, so goes your data. In other words, if one drive in the set fails, you lose all your data.

RAID 1

RAID 1, also known as *disk mirroring*, allows you to create an exact duplicate of a drive partition on another disk. This means that the system partition on a server (the partition where all the startup and important NOS files live) could be mirrored onto another drive. If the main drive fails, the mirror-image drive can be used to keep the server running.

Disk mirroring actually allows you to boot a server where the primary drive has failed. Because the mirror provides all the boot and system files found on the drive that the server normally boots to, it can also provide a successful system boot. Although it takes a little work, you typically create a boot disk for the server that specifies that the server should boot to the mirror drive rather than the primary drive. For example, in Windows 2000, you create a boot disk and then edit a text file called boot.ini (on the floppy disk) by changing the location of the drive on which the computer should look for the boot files.

Disk mirroring is supported by a number of network operating systems, including Microsoft Windows 2000 (this would be software RAID supported by the NOS). Windows 2000 actually supplies a wizard called the Create Volume Wizard that makes creating a mirror set very easy. Figure 14.4 shows this wizard, which walks you through the process of creating a mirror set.

FIGURE 14.4

Network operating systems that support RAID typically provide an easy-to-use utility for creating RAID arrays such as mirror sets.

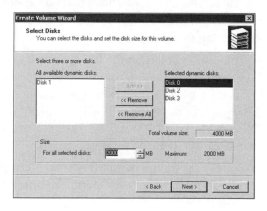

To create a RAID 1 array, you just need to have an extra drive that has at least the same amount of free space as the drive partition you want to mirror. The really cool thing about mirror sets is that if one of the drives in the set fails, you can replace the bad drive and then use the network operating system's disk-management software (or the software that allows you to use a proprietary hardware RAID implementation) to regenerate the mirror set onto a new drive.

> **Note** You can increase the fault tolerance of mirror sets and other RAID arrays by actually having separate drive controllers for each drive you use. This might be considered overkill, but if all your drives (such as SCSI drives) operate off of one controller, that controller's failure can bring down all your drives. Using separate drive controllers on drives in a mirrored set is called *disk duplexing*.

RAID 5

Using disk striping with parity (RAID 5) is considered a good way to build a fault-tolerance safety net for your drive arrays. You need at least three hard drives to configure RAID 5 on a server. A large number of drives can be made part of a RAID 5 array; the actual maximum number will depend on the hardware or software RAID scheme you use. For example, Windows NT Server and Windows 2000 Server (both of which use software RAID) can support up to 32 disks in a RAID 5 array.

RAID 5 works very well on file servers where you have users accessing data all day. The disks in the stripe set actually speed user access time to the data because you don't have a single drive churning away as people open and save files.

When a drive in a RAID 5 set fails, the data on the failed drive is actually regenerated using the data and the parity information that has been stored on the other drives in the stripe set. In cases where a server has hot-swappable drives that are easy to remove and replace, you can regenerate a RAID 5 set with a minimum of server downtime.

RAID 5 arrays require that the same amount of storage space be available in the partitions on the separate drives that will be part of the RAID 5 array. Most network operating systems will not allow you to include the partition that contains the operating system's boot and system files.

When you create a RAID 5 array, all the partitions (on all the drives in the set) are assigned one drive letter and seen by the server (and users accessing the server) as one drive. Figure 14.5 shows a RAID 5 array in the Windows 2000 Server Disk Management utility. Notice that all the partitions in the RAID 5 stripe have been assigned the single drive letter F:.

FIGURE 14.5

RAID 5 allows
you to stripe
data across three
or more disks,
providing fault
tolerance and
faster data
access.

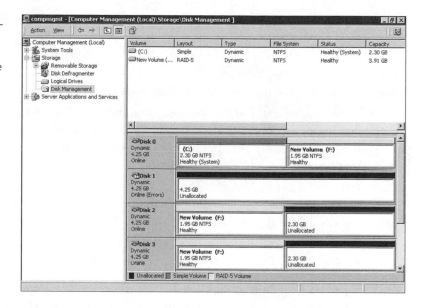

Backing Up Data

Although RAID arrays are pretty cool (network administrators love to sit around and talk about their RAID arrays), the most foolproof of all the fault-tolerance schemes is to simply make a backup copy of important data. Performing regular backups is essential to truly protecting valuable information on the network (and often is considered a foolproof method for keeping your job as network administrator).

When you spec out your network server (some considerations for network server hardware is discussed in Chapter 3), it makes good sense to consider some type of tape backup unit for your server. You can use an internal tape backup drive or an external drive. Backup devices can range from portable units with one drive bay, to backup "towers" that include several tape drive bays and can back up terabytes of data. You even have choices for SCSI tape drives, IDE tape drives, and tape drives that attach to your computer's parallel port.

A number of different hardware manufacturers make tape backup drives, including Seagate, Hewlett-Packard, and Iomega (the list goes on and on). Some of these products come with decent backup software and some don't (you might have to buy the backup software separately). Most network operating systems also supply some type of backup utility. Some are better than others, and you will have to assess whether you can get by with the NOS backup software or you need something more sophisticated. For example, Windows 2000 provides a very easy-to-use backup utility that can be used to back up files in a shared directory (review Chapter 8, "Sharing Resources on the Network," for more information about sharing resources on a server) and back up important system files on the server itself.

Also, a number of different types of tapes can be used in the various backup drives available. Some of the popular tape backup types are as follows:

- *Digital Audio Tape (DAT).* Developed for sound recording, this small high-density tape format can store around 12GB of data per cartridge. DAT has a moderate transfer speed but isn't as fast as some of the others (such as DLT and 8mm).

- *DLTtape (or just DLT).* A half-inch tape format that holds up to 70GB of data and has transfer speeds of 5MB per second (a great Web site that provides all sorts of information on DLTtape can be found at www.dlttape.com).

- *8mm.* Similar to the 8mm video format, these 8mm cartridges can hold around 30GB of data and can transfer data at speeds up to 3MB per second.

You can also back up data to floppy disks (this is probably only practical in peer-to-peer situations where a relatively small amount of data needs to be backed up) or removable media drives, such as the Zip and Jaz drives made by Iomega. You can also copy files to CD-ROM, if you have access to a CD-ROM burner.

One plus related to using backup software is that these software packages use some type of compression scheme that allows you to squish the data you actually back up to a tape. This means that the data takes up less space on the backup media than it actually does on the file server's hard drive. Of course, the only way you can get the data off the tape backup and restore it to a computer is to use the backup software to uncompress and restore the files to the server's fixed disk.

Whichever backup device, media type, or backup software you select, the whole point of backing up data is to restore the data when a drive (or RAID array) on a network server fails. On larger networks, where you must back up a great deal of data, you need to put together some kind of strategy that allows you to back up the most up-to-date copy of each important file. This can be difficult because, on networks with a great deal of users, the data is actually changing by the minute.

Most types of backup software actually provide you with the ability to perform different types of backups, including full (or normal) backups, differential backups, and incremental backups, all of which we will discuss in a moment. Because backing up network data takes time, it's not always practical to back up each and every important file every day. Let's take a look at the different backup types, and then we can take a look at how you formulate a backup strategy that allows you to back up your network on a schedule that supplies you with a recent backup of your data without taking up a lot of your time.

Backup Types

As mentioned earlier, there are basically three different backup methods: full, differential, and incremental. These different types of backups are possible because of file markers. A *marker* is an attribute placed on a file (in other words, the file is tagged). Typically, any operating system you work with will mark or tag a file once that file has been backed up. A file that has changed since its last backup will also be tagged. It is the use of these tags or markers to denote which files have been backed up and which files have not that allows backup software to perform different types of backups. Here's a breakdown of how these backup methods work:

- *Full backup.* This type of backup is also called a *normal backup* or a *daily backup* (depending on the backup software you're using). A full backup takes all the files that you select for backup and backs them up (no matter how the files are currently marked). The files' attributes are then changed to mark the fact that they have been backed up (if you change the file after the backup, the marker will change and indicate that the file has not been backed up since the last changes were made).

- *Differential backup.* This type of backup only backs up the files that have changed since their last backup. The differential backup does not, however, change the marker attribute indicating that the file has been backed up. It leaves the marker alone, meaning the file will still read that it has not been backed up since it was last changed.

- *Incremental backup.* This type of backup backs up only the files that have been changed since the last backup (just as a differential backup does). An incremental backup changes the archive marker on the files that are backed up to identify those files as having been backed up (which differs from the differential backup method).

As stated earlier, just about any backup software will provide you with the ability to do full, differential, and incremental backups. Figure 14.6 shows the types of backups you can perform using the backup utility provided with Microsoft Windows 2000 Server.

 Depending on the backup software you're using, you might run across other backup methods. For example, Windows 2000 offers an additional backup type called Copy. It backs up selected files (even if they have remained unchanged since the last backup) and does not mark them as having been backed up.

FIGURE 14.6

Different backup
types are offered
by most backup
software.

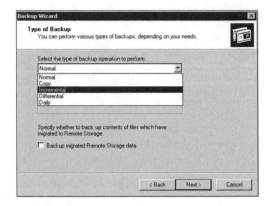

So, we have three different types of backups we can perform. The million-dollar
question is: How do we use these different backup types to be sure we have a valid
backup of our files without spending every waking hour performing backups? The
next section, which explores creating a backup strategy, answers this question.

Creating a Backup Strategy

The type of backup schedule you create for your network will have a lot to do with
the amount of data that needs to be backed up. If the mission-critical files for your
company only take about 20 minutes to back up, you could perform a full backup
every night and always have a fairly recent version of all the important data files
(your backup does not hold any changes that were made to the files during the day,
however).

Note

Backups shouldn't just consist of important data files. It is also important to back up system files on key servers on the network. Therefore, you might typically perform a fairly time-consuming backup on file servers (ones that hold a lot of data) and also do backups on other servers on the network so that their system files can be restored in the event of a problem with these particular servers.

In most cases, however, network file servers hold a lot more data than can be
backed up in 20 minutes. This is why backup strategies will usually consist of a combination of full backups and differential or incremental backups.

Now, before we actually look at using differential or incremental backups in conjunction with full backups, I will say that servers typically don't give you advance
notice when they are going to fail. So, to be in a situation where absolutely no data
is lost, you have to be pretty lucky.

Let's assume that you have a fairly decent size network (a couple hundred users) and a lot of activity as far as data file changes go. One approach to backing up the data would be to do a full backup of the network when network activity is low. This means on Friday night or sometime on the weekend, you would perform a full backup (many backup software packages allow you to schedule a backup where you don't even have to be present for the backup to take place).

So, you now have a complete backup of all the files. On Monday morning, users will begin to access and change those files, making our backup tape out of date. Now you need to find a way to back up the files that have changed without waiting for everyone to go home and then performing another full backup during the night.

One strategy that you can use is to combine incremental backups with a weekly full backup. Remember that incremental backups only back up the files that have changed since the last backup and then mark those files as having been backed up. Therefore, you can run an incremental backup every night using a different backup tape. You would label the tapes Monday, Tuesday, and so on (ending up with tapes for Monday through Friday).

The incremental backups you run each night will be fairly fast (in relation to the full backup you run on the weekend). This is because you will only be backing up the files that have changed since the previous evening.

If the server has a drive failure, you would first restore the full backup tape (from the weekend) and then restore each of the incremental backup tapes for Monday through Friday. Although this seems like a lot of work, you will have lost very little data using this backup scheme. This strategy does require that you have a pretty good pile of tapes handy.

An alternative to the full/incremental backup strategy does exist. It does not provide quite the high level of data security, but it does allow you to use fewer tapes.

You would still perform a full backup on Friday night or sometime during the weekend. Then you would perform a daily differential backup on each night using a second tape. Remember that a differential backup will back up files that have changed since the last full backup (the backup on the weekend), but it does not mark files as having been backed up.

Therefore, you can use the same tape (a tape other than the one used for the full backup) to perform a differential backup each night. This differential backup will take longer as the week progresses because you are overwriting the previous night's files and backing up any file that has changed since the weekend's full backup.

If you need to restore data after having used this full/differential backup scheme, you are only dealing with two tapes. You restore the full backup tape from the weekend and then you restore the differential backup tape from the night before.

You don't necessarily have to back up a network every night as we have discussed. If important files on the network don't change that often, you might be able to back up the data less frequently. The frequency of backups is something that all network administrators must decide for themselves.

On the other hand, having no backup schedule or strategy for a network is pretty much the kiss of death. Yes, I have known network administrators who have been extremely lackadaisical about backups and were extremely lucky in that their networks never had a major data meltdown. It is probably better to be safe than sorry (and unemployed), however, and put together a backup strategy that will allow you to get your file servers up and running when a drive problem occurs or important data is accidentally erased.

You should put your backup procedure on paper and then test it using files that are not mission critical. Perform your various backups over a specified time period and then restore the data. This allows you to take a look at how your backup procedure will actually work when you deploy it on the network.

Working with Uninterruptible Power Supplies

One other fault-tolerance strategy that we should take a look at involves the use of an *uninterruptible power supply (UPS)*. A UPS is a device outfitted with some type of battery that can supply temporary power to a server when there is a power failure. Many UPS devices will also offer surge protection; this will help protect an important device from any voltage surges that may occur during an electrical storm or other power surge problem.

A UPS sits between a server and an electrical outlet. The UPS is plugged into the electrical outlet, and the server is plugged into the UPS. Because the UPS is a peripheral device, it also connects to the computer via a serial cable or a UPS port. The serial cable used is not your typical serial communications cable and will be included with the UPS.

UPS devices also come with their own software that needs to be installed or configured with the appropriate drivers offered by the operating system you are using. This way, they can relay alerts to the operating system related to electrical spikes and brownouts.

A UPS really serves as a silent partner to the server until there is an electrical problem. When power from the outlet is available, the server will be powered by that electricity. At the same time, the UPS is charging its battery.

If the electricity goes out, the UPS will step in and power the server using its battery. This typically supplies the server with 5 to 30 minutes of power. This basically gives you, the network administrator, time to shut down the server properly so that there is no data lost.

It makes sense to use a UPS on servers because most network operating systems can become corrupt or experience problems when they power up again if they have not been shut down correctly. How sophisticated the UPS devices are on your network (in terms of the alerts they can supply and the amount of battery power they can supply) will depend on how quickly you can get to the servers and actually shut them down. Some UPS devices can even be outfitted with a modem and can be configured to call your pager when there is an electrical problem.

You can also use a UPS to protect other mission-critical failure points on your network. A UPS can be attached to switches, routers, hubs, or any other device that you wish to keep up and running for a short period of time when there is a power failure.

Chapter Summary

- Hard drives can be divided into different partitions, each of which function as a discrete drive with its own drive letter.
- Tools such as FDISK, the Apple Drive Setup utility, and the Windows 2000 Disk Management utility allow you to partition fixed disks.
- RAID (or Redundant Array of Inexpensive Disks) is a strategy for building fault tolerance into network servers such as file servers. RAID can be hardware or software based.
- RAID 0 stripes data across multiple disks, which speeds data access but does not provide any fault tolerance.
- RAID 1 allows you to create a mirror set, where two drives contain exactly the same data.
- RAID 5 allows data to be striped across three or more disks; if one disk fails, the stripe set can be regenerated from parity information included on each of the other drives.
- Performing regular data backups is the best way to build fault tolerance into a network and avoid the loss of important information.
- A number of different backup media are available that supply different capacities.

- Most types of backup software can be configured to do a full backup, an incremental backup, or a differential backup.

- A backup strategy that includes full backups and/or incremental and differential backups can help ensure that a fairly up-to-date version of every file on a server can be restored in case of a disk failure.

- An uninterruptible power supply (UPS) is used to temporarily supply power to servers in case of a power failure.

NETWORK TROUBLE-SHOOTING

In this chapter

- Educating your users to work on the network
- Using event logs to determine server problems
- Setting performance baselines for network servers
- Monitoring network traffic
- Checking network connections
- Diagnosing cable problems

The most likely way for the world to be destroyed, most experts agree, is by accident. That's where we come in; we're computer professionals. We cause accidents.

–Nathaniel Borenstein

Much of the discussion in this book thus far has revolved around either a theoretical look at how things work on a network or information on the particulars of how you set up a network, such as configuring client computers or servers. A subject area that we really haven't touched on yet is network troubleshooting.

No matter how well planned and how well implemented a network is, a day will still come when there is a problem—a user won't be able to access the server or users won't be able to print to their default printer. This chapter looks at some of the tools you can use and provides an approach you can take when troubleshooting problems on small, medium, or large networks.

It's Not Always User Error

When users experience problems on a network, the root cause of those problems will almost always boil down to three possibilities: user error, software problems, and physical connectivity problems. Although it is a convenient way to dismiss a problem outright and return to surfing of the Web (okay, so not all network administrators sit and surf the Web all day), not all network glitches can be blamed on user error. Software issues on client machines and servers alike can cause access and connectivity problems on the network. Physical connectivity problems such as shorted-out cables, an unplugged hub, or a router with a bad Ethernet interface can also cause problems on the network, and sometimes physical connectivity snafus can be some of the hardest to track down or troubleshoot.

In terms of user error, one way to limit the damage that your users can potentially do to the network is to have a well-informed and well-trained user base. A little bit of well-planned group training for your users can actually negate a lot of potential problems on the network. Some sort of educational opportunity for your users should be built into your overall plan for your network implementation and management.

Documentation that the users can actually read and refer to as they use the network can also greatly cut down on user error. A brief and concise manual that explains basic network logon and resource access can be a real help to your users. This also gives you an opportunity to establish written policies for network use; for example, you might establish rules such as no software downloads from the Internet and no floppy disks from home. Both of these rules could actually help reduce the risk of virus infection, and no downloads mean that local hard drives remain pretty clean (users can fill up their hard drives with junk pretty fast if they have a high-speed Internet connection and some free time on their hands).

In the case of small business networks or home LANs, the network administrator (this means you) probably wears a number of hats and doesn't necessarily have the time (or, in the case of a home network, the patience) to instruct users on the actual use of the network. In these cases, keep things simple. Don't password protect drives or folders that everyone needs to access and don't make really important files available on the LAN at all. Your best defense against problems on a small network is to regularly back up important files. In the case of teenage users, definitely use some type of antivirus software if an Internet connection is part of your LAN configuration, since they will download music files such as MP3. In cases where you might want to limit Internet access, use a product such as Net Nanny (see www.netnanny.com).

There are other alternatives to written manuals that allow you to document basic network use information for your users or post the "rules of the road" for your network. Company intranet Web sites can provide easy access for users looking for network guidance, and postings in a newsgroup on an Exchange Server or in the Lotus Domino Server environment make it easy for you to update information and provide breaking information such as network status.

Establishing user policies for your company's network not only provides a set of rules for the network users, but it allows you to assume (although users are not always going to follow all the rules) that network client machines will only be running software that is appropriately licensed and correctly configured and that important user files are stored in the appropriate place so that they can be periodically backed up.

Although everyone is aware of the often overused anecdote that accompanies the word *assume* when an assumption proves to be wrong, at least assuming that computers have been configured in a particular "standard" way allows you to concentrate on other issues when attempting to troubleshoot network problems. As I said before, problems on the network (when user error is ruled out) are going to be caused by either software or hardware. Let's take at look at some approaches to troubleshooting software and hardware problems on the network.

You should definitely make your users aware of the fact that only software that has been purchased by the company should be installed on the company's computers (this goes for home networks as well). Allowing users to install unlicensed software is a very good way to bring the Software & Information Industry Association's anti-software piracy folks down on your company. They take software piracy very seriously (as should you). For more information about the Software & Information Industry Association, check out www.siia.net/.

Identifying Network Operating System Problems

All network operating systems provide some sort of utility (or utilities) that you can use to troubleshoot problems related to the network operating system software. These utilities allow you to perform tasks such as seeing whether software drivers for hardware devices such as NICs have loaded correctly (as the system boots up) and whether a particular application has failed.

In the Microsoft Windows 2000 Server environment, a utility called the Event Viewer is provided. The Event Viewer allows you to view three different types of log files: the System Log, the Application Log, and the Security Log (we discuss the Security Log in more detail in the next chapter).

As far as operating system problems go, the log you would want to take a look at is the System Log. The System Log shows information such as driver failures and failed server services. Any events related to server services and system resources will show up in this log. Figure 15.1 shows the Event Viewer's System Log. Note that errors, warnings, and other information are recorded in the Event Viewer's System Log.

FIGURE 15.1

The Windows 2000 Server Event Viewer allows you to view software-related alerts on your server.

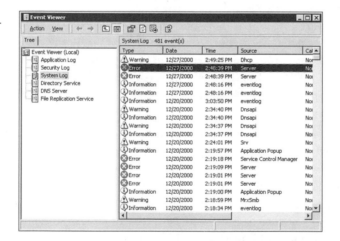

Details on a particular event can be viewed by double-clicking that event. Figure 15.2 shows the properties of an error that has been logged. This error shows that an important folder on the server has either been removed or become corrupt.

Note

For an overview of Windows 2000 Server, check out the book *The Complete Idiot's Guide to Microsoft Windows 2000 Server*, published by Que. It provides information on installing, configuring, and monitoring a Windows 2000 network.

FIGURE 15.2

Error messages on the server allow you to troubleshoot problems before you establish a major server meltdown.

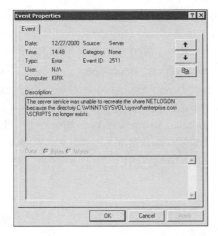

On a NetWare server, errors and server status information are also contained in log files, which are created automatically by NetWare. For example, the SYS$LOG.ERR file lists server errors and general status information related to the server. Another server log file available in the NetWare environment is the CONSOLE.LOG file, which keeps a list of all the alert messages that appear on the server console.

Because all the logs created automatically by the NetWare server are text files, they can be viewed with any text file viewer. You can also view the most recent listings in the SYS$LOG.ERR log file using the NetWare Administrator program. Novell actually provides a lot of information on logging NetWare installations and online help that can help you troubleshoot NetWare problems. Check out Novell's site at www.novell.com. You can search through the product index to find information on the version of NetWare that you are using.

Diagnosing Hardware and Network Problems

It's pretty easy to diagnose a hardware problem once a device has completely died. The fact that a network interface card that has been working is suddenly showing no activity light on the back of the card might be a pretty good indication that the NIC is shot. And when you fire up a server in which a drive has gone belly up or the video card has gone bad, the system BIOS will usually alert you to a major hardware problem and provide a series of beeps as a tip off. An important part of troubleshooting a network is actually avoiding troubleshooting major hardware problems by staying one step ahead of the potential hardware pitfalls.

Most network operating systems will help you keep track of hardware performance. Not only can you monitor hardware devices such as the drives on a server, but you can also discern the relative health of the network itself using various network-monitoring software.

In the Windows environment, you can monitor server hardware performance, such as the processor and RAM, using a tool called Performance Monitor, and network performance can be tracked using a tool called Network Monitor.

Novell provides the Console Monitor, which allows you to quickly view disk requests and service processes on your server. If you are using NetWare 5.1, you can use the NetWare Management Portal to monitor performance statistics on a NetWare Server. The Management Portal can be accessed using any Web browser and the IP address or DNS name assigned to the server. You access the Portal just as you would access any other Web site. Figure 15.3 shows the Server Health Monitor provided by the NetWare Management Portal.

FIGURE 15.3

The NetWare Server Health Monitor makes it easy to view memory and processor usage on a NetWare server.

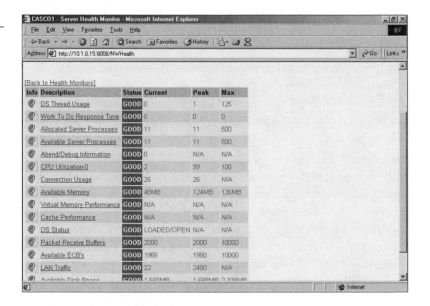

Novell also makes an add-on program called Novell LANalyzer, which can be run from a Windows-based workstation on the network. It provides gauges (it looks a lot like an automobile dashboard) that allow you to view network events such as traffic levels. Other companies also provide a number of add-on programs that can be used to monitor NetWare, Windows, and Unix/Linux networks.

Let's take a look at some of the common practices for monitoring server hardware. Then we can take a look at the basics of network monitoring.

Monitoring Hardware

When you monitor server hardware and server processes' performance, you are trying to identify bottlenecks. A *bottleneck* can be a hardware component on a server, such as the processor or the memory, that is being overtaxed and slowing down overall system performance.

Once your server is configured and your network is up and running, it is important to use your server monitoring software to establish a baseline. A *baseline* is a set of initial readings when the network is fully operational and typically running well. This set of baseline readings can then be used for comparison when you take readings on server performance in the future.

The different server monitoring tools in the different network environments will obviously all operate differently. In the NetWare environment, the Monitor program can be used to track the CPU utilization and requests for services from network clients. In the Windows network environment, hardware and service performance are tracked using Performance Monitor. As an example of how server monitoring tools work, let's take a closer look at how the Performance Monitor works.

On a Windows server, any process that can be measured is referred to as an *object*, and performance objects are added to a graphing system as *counters*. For example, let's say you want to monitor the processor on a Windows 2000 Server. Once you get the Performance Monitor tool open, you need to add a counter to the monitor for processor performance.

 As far as servers go, three areas you should keep an eye on for potential bottlenecks are the processor, the paging file (which helps diagnose memory issues), and the physical drives.

The Windows Performance Monitor provides a dialog box that groups different counters into categories, such as Processor, Physical Disk, and Paging File (which is the virtual memory on your computer; too much access of the paging file shows that the computer could use a little more RAM). Figure 15.4 shows the Performance Monitors Add Counters dialog box.

FIGURE 15.4

Counters used to monitor server performance are easily added to the Windows 2000 Performance Monitor.

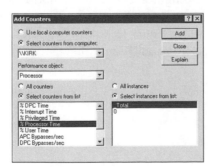

Once a counter is added to the Performance Monitor, the performance of the particular object (such as processor time) can be viewed. Figure 15.5 shows the chart for processor time on a Windows server.

FIGURE 15.5

Processor use on the server can be monitored using the Performance Monitor.

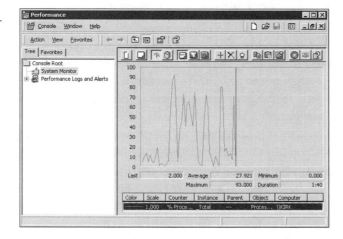

Most performance monitors also provide you with different views of the data. For example, the Windows Performance Monitor provides the chart and histogram views (the histogram view looks like a bar chart). Also, the data can be viewed in a report format.

Once you set up your particular performance monitor with the appropriate counters, you can actually save the data as a log file. This provides you with a baseline you can use to compare with future performance data.

Many of the Performance Monitor tools also allow you to create alerts. An *alert* actually "alerts" you when a predefined threshold has been reached on a particular counter. For example, you might want to create a performance alert that alerts you when a file server's drive (or drives) has reached a certain percent of total capacity. The Windows Performance Monitor actually sends the alert to the Windows Event Viewer's Application Log.

So, for example, if you set up a performance alert in the Performance Monitor to alert you when there is less than 30 percent of free space on a file server, the actual alert would appear in the Event Viewer. Figure 15.6 shows an Application Log alert provided by the Performance Monitor (actually, three different alerts appear in the Application Log).

FIGURE 15.6

Event alerts can
be used to help
you stay on top
of issues such as
the hard drive
space remaining
on a file server.

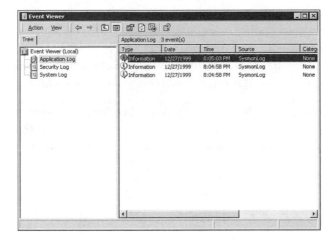

Regardless of the network operating system you use, it is important to set up some
sort of system where you monitor server resources and then compare them against
benchmarks that you have established. When monitoring server performance, try to
build some consistency into your measurements by logging information at times of
peak network use and by consistently measuring the same parameters so that you
have data for comparison.

Monitoring the Network

Network monitoring allows you to monitor the amount of network traffic and take a
look at network processes and events related to network protocols. Many of the network monitoring software packages actually allow you to capture network data
frames and examine them. A software package that can analyze protocol information in a data frame is often referred to as a *protocol sniffer*.

Protocol sniffers and network monitoring software can be a big help in managing a
large network. The problem with these types of software packages, however, is that
they can also be used to actually steal and read information on a network, such as usernames and passwords. Protocol sniffers are often used by hackers to gain information
about networks they wish to steal information from. We will talk more about
hacking/cracking in Chapter 16, "A Network Security Primer."

A number of software companies make network monitoring software and protocol
analyzers. For example, Sniffer Technologies sells a range of network monitoring
software for both the LAN and WAN environments. For the Unix/Linux environment,
a free network analyzer called Ethereal can be downloaded from www.ethereal.com (a
Windows 98/NT version of the software can also be downloaded from the site).

Windows 2000 provides the Network Monitor, which can be used to capture frames (a *frame* being a data packet) and monitor network activity. The Network Monitor provides many of the features that you would find in other network monitoring software packages. Most network monitoring and packet sniffing packages are geared for Ethernet networks because it is the most commonly used network architecture.

> **Note** The version of Network Monitor that ships with Windows 2000 (and NT) is not a full-blown version of the product. You will find that some of the menu choices won't work, and to get all the features you must acquire a copy of the Microsoft Systems Management Server Network Monitor tool. So, no matter what server environment you are working in (Microsoft or Novell), you are probably going to have to buy some type of network monitoring program. The exception to the rule is the Linux environment, where several monitoring tools can be downloaded from the Web for free.

Let's take a quick look at the Windows Network Monitor and how it displays the information that it captures. The Network Monitor window is actually divided into a number of different panes that provide different types of information. Figure 15.7 shows the Windows Network Monitor. This data is collected when you (the network administrator) use the Capture command to begin a capture session.

FIGURE 15.7

Network Monitor provides information on network traffic and can sample data frames traveling on the network.

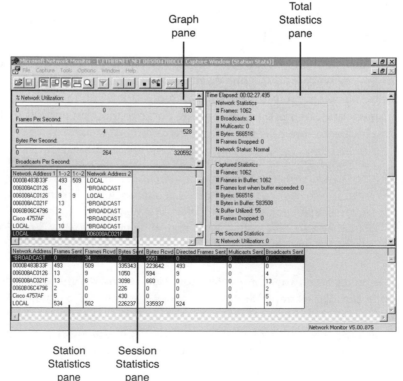

Graph pane

Total Statistics pane

Station Statistics pane

Session Statistics pane

The Network Monitor provides statistics such as the percentage of network utilization and the number of frames per second (this would be the number of frames traveling by the computer running Network Monitor; data is sampled by the computer's NIC). These more general statistics are listed in the Graph pane, which resides in the upper-left area of the Network Monitor window. The Total Statistics pane to the right of the Graph pane provides summary information.

The Session Statistics pane provides information on each session captured (a *session* being communication between two computers or devices on the network). The first column in this pane provides the hardware address (the MAC address of the device's network interface card) of the device that is sending the packets (the packets you are capturing). The second column provides the number of frames (packets) sent to the receiving device from the sending device during the communication. The third column shows the number of frames sent back to the initiating device, and the last column in the Session Statistics pane provides the hardware address of the receiving device participating in the session.

The Station Statistics pane appears below the Session Statistics pane in the Network Monitor window. It provides statistics related to your computer's activity on the network. A number of different columns of information appear in this pane:

- *Network Address.* This column provides the network address that frames were captured from.

- *Frames Sent.* This column provides the number of frames that were sent from the network address appearing in the first column.

- *Frames Rcvd.* This column shows the number of frames received (by the local computer) from the device hardware address appearing in the first column.

- *Bytes Sent.* This column displays the number of bytes sent by the device whose hardware address is listed in the Network Address column (the first column in the pane).

- *Bytes Rcvd.* This column tells you how many bytes were received from the network address listed in the Network Address column.

- *Directed Frames Sent.* This column shows the number of non-broadcast and non-multicast frames that were sent over the network by the device whose hardware address is listed in the first column of the record.

- *Multicasts Sent.* This shows the number of times the address listed in the Network Address column has sent frames to a subset of computers on the network (a *multicast* is a broadcast message to certain computers on the network).

- *Broadcasts Sent.* This column shows the number of times the address listed in the Network Address column has sent broadcast messages to all computers on the network (a *broadcast message* is a message sent to all the devices on the network by a particular computer).

Data collected by monitoring software such as Network Monitor can often be saved to a log file that you can view at a later time. This allows you to capture information related to the network and save it as a baseline. Data collected over time can then be compared to the baseline information. If there is a great deal of disparity between your baseline (or *benchmark*) readings and the new capture information, you know that there must be a problem with the network. For example, if there are tons of broadcast messages from a particular MAC address, a computer on the network might have a malfunctioning network card.

Dealing with Connectivity Issues

Like the other potential server and client computer problems we've discussed in this chapter, problems with connectivity can revolve around software and hardware. In the case of software, many connectivity problems can be caused by incorrect LAN protocol configurations. For example, even on a simple network using the NetBEUI protocol, two computers configured with the same NetBIOS or computer name would actually knock each other off the network.

In terms of connectivity problems related to hardware, networking cables, hubs, network interface cards, and just about any other hardware devices that are important to the network communications can cause connective problems if they are malfunctioning. Although connectivity problems can be difficult to troubleshoot, there are tools you can use to troubleshoot network protocol and hardware issues. Let's take a look at each of these areas individually, starting with some of the tools that can be used to help diagnose network configuration problems. Then we can take a look at some of the devices used to diagnose hardware connectivity problems.

Checking Settings and Connections from the Command Line

Because NetBEUI, AppleTalk, and IPX/SPX pretty much configure themselves as far as computer identification on the network, the protocol stack that seems to offer the most pitfalls as far as configuration goes is TCP/IP. Fortunately, there are commands that allow you to quickly check the configuration of a computer or check the connection between two hosts on the network. Let's take a look at these commands: ipconfig, ping, and traceroute.

Ipconfig

Ipconfig is a command (ipconfig) that can be used on a Windows NT/2000 client or server to quickly check the IP configuration. This is particularly useful when you are using automatic addressing of computers on the network using a DHCP server

(DHCP servers are discussed in Chapter 2, "Different Needs, Different Networks") and want to make sure the client is receiving the appropriate IP settings from the DHCP server. Figure 15.8 shows the results of the `ipconfig` command issued on a Windows client.

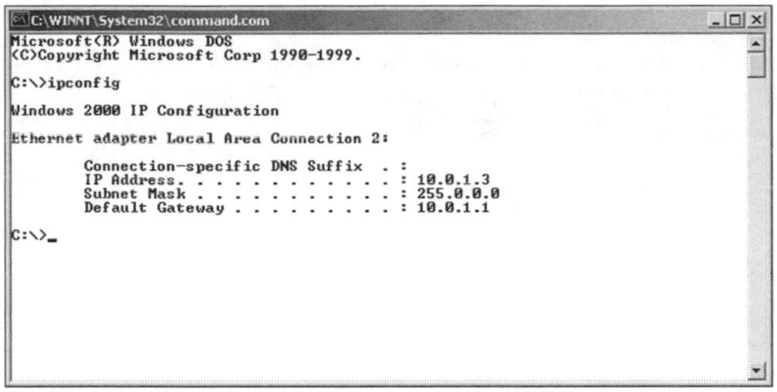

FIGURE 15.8

Ipconfig can be used to view the current IP settings of a Windows NT or 2000 computer.

```
C:\WINNT\System32\command.com                               _ □ ×
Microsoft(R) Windows DOS
(C)Copyright Microsoft Corp 1990-1999.

C:\>ipconfig

Windows 2000 IP Configuration

Ethernet adapter Local Area Connection 2:

        Connection-specific DNS Suffix  . :
        IP Address. . . . . . . . . . . . : 10.0.1.3
        Subnet Mask . . . . . . . . . . . : 255.0.0.0
        Default Gateway . . . . . . . . . : 10.0.1.1

C:\>_
```

Ipconfig comes with a number of different switches that allow you to view more IP-related information or to release or renew the computer's current IP address provided by a DHCP server. In the Windows 9x and Me environments, the command `winipcfg` is launched from the Run box (started by clicking Start, Run). It provides the same type of information that the `ipconfig` command does.

Ping

An excellent way to check the connection between two computers or other devices on an IP network is to use the `ping` command. Ping stands for *Packet InterNet Gopher* and uses ICMP echo packets to test the connection. The command syntax is `ping ip address`, where `ip address` is the IP address of the target device.

> **Note**
> *Internet Control Message Protocol (ICMP)* is a messaging service and management protocol for IP. It resides at the Network layer of the OSI model (the same layer inhabited by IP). ICMP messages are used by both ping and traceroute (we discuss traceroute in the next section).

You can also use the `ping` command using the FQDN name of a computer or other device on the network (DNS provides this capability because it resolves the friendly FQDN to the appropriate IP address). Figure 15.9 shows the `ping` command used to check the connection with a local computer on the network using the destination computer's IP address (10.0.1.1). Figure 15.8 also showed the results of the `ping` command when it is used to check the connection with a remote mail server. The remote server is designated by FQDN, which is converted to the appropriate IP address by a DNS server on the network.

FIGURE 15.9

Ping can be used to check the connection between any two computers or devices on an IP network, including the Internet.

```
C:\WINNT\System32\command.com

C:\>ping 10.0.1.1

Pinging 10.0.1.1 with 32 bytes of data:

Reply from 10.0.1.1: bytes=32 time<10ms TTL=128
Reply from 10.0.1.1: bytes=32 time<10ms TTL=128
Reply from 10.0.1.1: bytes=32 time<10ms TTL=128
Reply from 10.0.1.1: bytes=32 time<10ms TTL=128

Ping statistics for 10.0.1.1:
    Packets: Sent = 4, Received = 4, Lost = 0 (0% loss),
Approximate round trip times in milli-seconds:
    Minimum = 0ms, Maximum =  0ms, Average =  0ms

C:\>ping pop-server.maine.rr.com

Pinging mail.maine.rr.com [204.210.65.65] with 32 bytes of data:

Reply from 204.210.65.65: bytes=32 time=60ms TTL=251
Reply from 204.210.65.65: bytes=32 time=50ms TTL=251
Reply from 204.210.65.65: bytes=32 time<10ms TTL=251
Reply from 204.210.65.65: bytes=32 time<10ms TTL=251

Ping statistics for 204.210.65.65:
    Packets: Sent = 4, Received = 4, Lost = 0 (0% loss),
Approximate round trip times in milli-seconds:
    Minimum = 0ms, Maximum =  60ms, Average =  27ms

C:\>_
```

Traceroute

Traceroute (or *trace*; or on a Windows machine, *tracert*) allows you to actually see the route that data packets take on the network. Traceroute is a tool used for checking data flow on larger networks (internetworks) that include routers; it is very useful in situations where you want to check and see whether a particular router has malfunctioned or whether other equipment is not working properly, causing certain routes to be down on the internetwork. Figure 15.10 shows the `tracert` command used on a Windows 2000 computer to check the route to a remote host on the Internet.

FIGURE 15.10

Traceroute is used to determine the route that packets take from one network device to another.

```
C:\WINNT\System32\command.com
Microsoft(R) Windows DOS
(C)Copyright Microsoft Corp 1990-1999.

C:\>tracert 172.129.70.244

Tracing route to AC8146F4.ipt.aol.com [172.129.70.244]
over a maximum of 30 hops:

  1    10 ms    10 ms    10 ms  ptldme-cmt3-c4-cm-gw.maine.rr.com [10.34.0.1]
  2   <10 ms    10 ms   <10 ms  pos0-1.ptldme-grt2.maine.rr.com [24.25.160.26]
  3    10 ms   <10 ms    10 ms  pos10-1-0.ptldme-brt2.maine.rr.com [24.25.160.38
]
  4    10 ms    40 ms    50 ms  sl-gw7-nyc-6-1-0.sprintlink.net [144.232.172.37]

  5    10 ms    20 ms    10 ms  sl-bb12-nyc-3-3.sprintlink.net [144.232.7.81]
  6    10 ms    50 ms    10 ms  sl-bb20-nyc-6-0.sprintlink.net [144.232.7.121]
  7    10 ms    20 ms    60 ms  sl-bb22-rly-13-0.sprintlink.net [144.232.9.226]

  8    10 ms    20 ms    20 ms  144.232.9.26
  9    20 ms    30 ms    30 ms  208.30.208.2
 10    20 ms    20 ms    30 ms  wc1-dtc-2-P1-0.atdn.net [204.148.98.226]
 11    30 ms    50 ms    30 ms  tot2-dr4-P0-0.aol.com [205.188.168.22]
 12    20 ms    30 ms    20 ms  ipt-fo06.proxy.aol.com [205.188.198.103]
 13   380 ms     *      391 ms  AC8146F4.ipt.aol.com [172.129.70.244]

Trace complete.

C:\>
```

In Figure 15.9, the ICMP packet that was sent to the remote host took 13 hops to reach its final destination (a *hop* is one router on the internetwork). If the `traceroute` command is used in the future to check the route to this same IP address, any change in the number of hops or the intermediary routers would show that something has happened on the network to affect the route that the packets have taken from source to destination device.

Although most of our discussion has been limited to commands used on PCs, both the ping and traceroute commands are often used on other network devices, such as routers, to check connections and the routing of packets between two devices. On a router (such as a Cisco router), the trace command is used to determine the route between two devices. It is commonly used to make sure that routers on the network are working and that the paths you assume are up and running are indeed functional. Figure 15.11 shows the traceroute command (on a Cisco router that command is abbreviated as "trace") being used to check the route between two routers on a network (Alice and sweetpea).

FIGURE 15.11

Traceroute is used to determine the route that packets take from one network device to another.

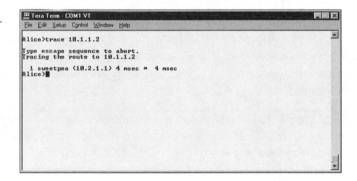

Note

This introductory book to networking can only really provide you with an overview of networking and the various clients, servers, and other devices you would encounter on different-sized networks. Understanding routers and the routing of information on internetworks is definitely a whole story in itself. Cisco Systems actually offers a number of different levels of certification for network administrators who work in routed environments. For a primer on routing, internetworking, and Cisco routers in particular, check out the book *Practical Cisco Routers*, from Que.

Basic Connectivity Troubleshooting Tools

Although commands such as ping and traceroute are very useful for checking network connectivity, there are devices available that can be used to check connectivity problems related to physical cabling. Physical cabling is always suspect when you are experiencing connectivity problems. Network cables can experience disconnections, breaks, shorts, and other problems. Diagnosing these types of problems is done using various tools, ranging from voltmeters to time domain reflectometers (TDRs).

A digital *voltmeter* is a simple device that can be connected to a cable to test the cable for a break or a short. Basically, the voltmeter can tell you whether the cable is bad or not and whether you are looking at a short or break. If the cable has a short, replace it. If there is a break, you must trace the cable (have fun crawling around in the drop-ceiling) to find where the break has occurred.

A *time domain reflectometer* is a more sophisticated device that can diagnose shorts and breaks in a cable, but it can also provide you with information on where the short or break exists on the cable. The TDR actually emits short pulses down the cable and is able to use a timing mechanism that estimates the distance that the pulse has traveled. Many of the software network analyzers, such as Novell LANalyzer, provide you with a built-in cable tester, which allows you to test cables from the LANalyzer workstation on the network.

As I've already mentioned, network cabling is always suspect. For example, people moving furniture can disrupt cable connections, and a leaky roof can cause cabling in the ceiling to become soaked with water (sometimes leading to shorts)—all sorts of weird things can happen to cables that can sever the connections they provide. Always check cables first.

Note A number of companies make time domain reflectometers, such as Agilent Technologies at www.tm.agilent.com. These devices are expensive (I'm talking a couple of thousand dollars or more) and the best way to learn more about how they work is to check out the Agilent product line (their site includes operating manuals) or do a search for time domain reflectomer using your Web browser. Voltmeters are inexpensive devices and can be picked up at just about any hardware or electrical supply store. Any book on home repairs usually includes a chapter on using a voltmeter. You can also find more information about voltmeters and voltmeter manufacturers by doing a search on the Web.

Your Approach to Troubleshooting

Troubleshooting is really an art and definitely an acquired skill. Every network has its own particular quirks (just like a used car), and actually maintaining a particular network is the best way to accumulate the information needed to enable you to troubleshoot that network when problems rear their ugly heads.

One way to make troubleshooting problems a little easier is to keep good documentation related to the network. This includes server configurations, network client configurations, and problems that you have experienced and then solved. Even in cases where you are working with a relatively small network, some sort of map that shows how the network cabling has been run and the addressing of the network devices can be a big help in troubleshooting situations.

When actually attempting to solve a problem on the network, try to use a systematic approach to problem solving. First, identify the problem; then gather facts related to the problem. You might want to make a list of the possible hardware and software failures that can cause a particular problem.

Then, systematically go through your list of possible causes one at a time and troubleshoot the problem. This is a much better approach than the "shotgun" approach, where you run around and change a bunch of server and client settings and physical connections all at once. This never allows you to pinpoint the actual cause of the problem. The problem just kind of goes away (because you fixed it with one of the many solutions you implemented). If the problem appears again, rather than immediately being able to provide the correct solution, you will again have to result to voodoo and run through a whole list of fixes.

As you are working through the list of possible problems, you will find that a good, general approach to troubleshooting is to work from the basic to the complex. Check things that will result in a simple fix; for example, make sure the power cables are connected on computers, hubs, and other network devices before assuming the problem is a complex NOS configuration problem with the server. In many cases a disconnected cable or an unplugged hub, rather than a malfunctioning server, will be causing the problem on the LAN.

Troubleshooting basic issues first also allows you to attempt to fix the network without getting way over your head in terms of software and hardware configurations. If you reach a point as you tick off basic issues that could cause the problem where you are in unfamiliar territory, you might wish to call your software or hardware vendor for technical support. There is no disgrace (even for the seasoned network administrator) to try and get help in solving a network problem.

Chapter Summary

- Most network operating systems provide a logging feature that logs hardware or driver issues experienced on the server. In the Microsoft Windows 2000 Server environment, a utility called the Event Viewer is provided. It allows you to view a System Log that contains any alerts related to system failures. The equivalent log file on a NetWare server is the SYS$LOG.ERR file.

- Monitoring hardware and establishing baselines allows you to determine whether hardware on a server (such as the processor and memory) is being overtaxed and could lead to server failure.

- Disk requests and server processes in the NetWare environment can be viewed using the NetWare Console Monitor.

- Windows NT and 2000 Server provide the Performance Monitor, which allows you to create a baseline log for various server hardware components and monitor hardware usage over time.

- The Performance Monitor allows you to add various counters to the Performance Monitor chart, which allows you to view counter statistics in real time.

- Network usage and traffic can be monitored using network monitoring software such as protocol sniffers. Novell's popular LANalyzer software uses various gauges to provide network usage information.

- The Windows Network Monitor provides you with the ability to view network traffic and capture network frames to examine information such as the sending address on data packets and the amount of traffic generated by specific devices on the network.

- The `ipconfig` command can be executed from the command line to view the IP configuration of a Windows NT or 2000 computer. Other commands, such as `ping` and `traceroute`, can be used with a number of different operating systems to check the connection between two network devices or the route that data takes when moving from a sending to a receiving device on the network.

- Cable connection problems can be checked with devices such as voltmeters and time domain reflectometers.

- Troubleshooting requires good documentation and a logical approach to problem solving.

16

A NETWORK SECURITY PRIMER

In this chapter

- Protecting your network from attack
- Understanding user accounts
- Working with resource permissions
- Using groups to control resource access
- Protecting against computer viruses
- Understanding worms and Trojan horses
- Becoming familiar with the types of outside network attacks
- Understanding IPSec
- Working with firewalls

I think computer viruses should count as life. I think it says something about human nature that the only form of life we have created so far is purely destructive. We've created life in our own image.

–Stephen Hawking

In this chapter, we take a look at network security. The issues related to securing a network have changed dramatically over the last decade, particularly due to the fact that most LANs are now connected (in some way) to the Internet.

Network security was once a study of how to secure resources and information on an isolated network. Security issues revolved around the level of user access to important network resources and protecting systems from virus attacks (often spread initially from computer to computer by an infected floppy disk). Network security also dealt with the actual physical violation of the network, such as the stealing of data by a person with unauthorized access to the building who, using an unattended computer on the network, transferred important data to a floppy and runs with it.

Security really revolved around possible attacks from the inside. Sometimes an attack would be an error by a user or administrator rather than a malicious attack on network resources. For example, a user might inadvertently be assigned the wrong access level to an important network resource and then destroy it by accident.

Today, due to the fact that most networks are connected to the Internet and that many companies maintain a Web presence in the form of a Web site, network security also revolves around attacks from the outside. These attacks take the form of direct attacks by *crackers* (the press often refer to crackers as *hackers*, a notion that the hacking community takes issue with, considering hackers define themselves as extremely knowledgeable computer aficionados and not criminals who break into computer systems) and viruses, particularly viruses spread by Internet e-mail. Network administrators and computer security experts have had to develop new strategies for protecting their networks. A number of new products, such as proxy servers and firewalls, have evolved over the last few years to deal with these latest security threats.

Administrators and Users

Even a pack of wild dogs will have a leader—the alpha dog. The alpha dog serves as the leader of the pack and determines the pack's administrative pecking order. Although most network administrators do not resort to growling or the baring of fangs to maintain control on a network (although I know some who do), the network administrator is the alpha dog and determines all the conditions for user access to the network.

There are really two different aspects that an administrator deals with when working with network security and user access: user authentication and access permissions. *User authentication* is handled by assigning a user a logon name and a password. Other parameters, such as when a user can log on and whether a user can log on using a remote connection, are also configured by the administrator when he creates the user's account. We will discuss user accounts and different logon issues in a moment.

Access permission involves the level or the rights that an administrator assigns a user in relation to a particular resource on a network. For example, a user may have the ability to open and read files in a particular share on the network but not edit those files. We discussed network shares in Chapter 8, "Sharing Resources on the Network," and will discuss access permissions in more detail in this chapter after we spend some time sorting out user accounts.

| Note | In a nutshell, users gain access to the network by being authenticated by their username and password. Their actual ability to access a resource on the network will be related to the permissions they have been assigned for that particular resource. |

Working with User Accounts

A user can't log on to a network without a valid username and password. Therefore, user accounts are really the network administrator's first line of defense as far as network security is concerned. When a user logs on to the network from a client computer, her username and password are used to generate an access token. This access token validates the user to the network (allowing the logon) and also is used to determine the access level that the user will have to resources on the network.

The access token, which is a concept that you run into no matter what NOS you are using, is kind of an electronic identification card, not that different from an ATM card, really. An ATM card validates you to your bank's ATM network and allows you to access certain resources, such as your checking or savings account. The access token generated in relation to your username is also used to determine the resources that you can negotiate on the network and the degree of access you can have.

The network administrator is responsible for creating user accounts. Every network operating system provides a built-in administrator's account that is used to create and modify network user accounts and manage the resources on the network. This administrator's account is given different names in different operating systems, such as root, Admin, and Administrator (Linux, NetWare, and Windows, respectively).

Each network operating system also offers some sort of utility that is used to create new user accounts. Figure 16.1 shows the Create User dialog box used in the NetWare Administrator to add a new user account.

Every network operating system shares some common rules for governing usernames. These rules are as follows:

- *Each and every username must be unique.* Although this rule is a no-brainer, it is important to keep in mind.

- *Usernames are limited to a specific number of characters.* Although the number of characters that can be used to create a username will vary from NOS to NOS, every operating system has naming conventions that you should be aware of before you create your user accounts. For example, Windows provides you with 20 characters for a username. NetWare NDS usernames can be up to 64 characters.

- *Certain characters cannot be used in usernames.* Typically, characters such as the slash (/), backslash (\), and other special characters cannot be used in usernames. Some operating systems allow spaces to be used in the usernames, and others do not. Again, you need to know your network operating system's naming conventions before you create usernames.

Although each network operating system will supply you with conventions that control the creation of usernames, it also makes sense for you (as the administrator) to create a plan related to the creation of usernames. This plan should include the naming conventions you will use when you create the usernames for your various users. For example, if your basic naming convention for usernames is to use employees' first initial and last name, you need to be consistent and use this convention for all usernames you create. Your plan should also include how you will differentiate two users when they have the same first initial and last name.

This user account plan should also include your strategy for how you will assign passwords to your users. Network operating systems allow you to stipulate a password that cannot be changed or assign an initial password that must be immediately changed by the user. Let's take a closer look at passwords and why they are important to network security.

User Passwords

Because user authentication requires a valid username and a valid password, your strategy for assigning passwords to your users will have a lot to do with how secure your network is. A lot of network administrators in the networking industry use first initial and then last name as their basic format for usernames. This means that if someone knows my name is Joe Habraken, it wouldn't be that hard for him to guess that my username on the network is probably jhabraken.

Therefore, it is really the password component of the user account that builds some security into the logon process. This means that you need to make an effort to keep user passwords secret.

Network operating systems provide you with a number of choices related to assigning passwords to your network users. For example, Figure 16.2 shows the New Object - User dialog box used in the Windows 2000 Server Active Directory to create new user accounts on the network. Notice that a series of check boxes provides you with different possibilities related to the user's password.

FIGURE 16.2

Network operating systems such as Windows 2000 Server provide you with different options for assigning passwords to your users.

You are given the option of allowing the user to change the initial password you have supplied the first time she logs on to the network. Alternatively, you can set up the password so that the user can never change it. You are even provided with the option of having the password never expire.

Let's use the different options shown in Figure 16.2 as some food for thought as we discuss some different possibilities for ensuring that password protection remains a security asset on your network. Here are some general thoughts:

- *You can allow users to control their own passwords.* Allowing users to create their own passwords can be particularly useful in situations where you have set an expiration time limit on passwords and require all users to change theirs.

However, if you are going to put users in charge of their passwords, you need to educate them that using their first name or just the word *password* as their password probably isn't going to provide the level of security you are after.

- *You can completely take control of user passwords.* You can assign passwords for your users that they can't change. If you have a lot of users, however, this is going to require a lot of work. This is especially true if you plan to have the passwords expire every so often. What's more, thinking that you can supply a devilishly complex password that no one will ever guess never seems to work, because users often will write down difficult-to-remember passwords on sticky notes and attach them on their computer monitors.

- *You can require that passwords be changed at a defined interval.* It is definitely a good idea to have some sort of password-cycling strategy. Having passwords that never expire only gives people intent on breaking into your network plenty of time to guess the password that goes with a particular user account. Periodically changing passwords makes your network more of a moving target.

People who are intent on breaking into your network certainly aren't limited to imprecise techniques such as guessing usernames and passwords. In Chapter 15, "Network Troubleshooting," we discussed protocol sniffers that can be used by crackers to actually view network traffic. Being able to capture data packets means that information such as usernames and passwords can be also be learned because they are transmitted as text. Strategies involving encryption are used to make it more difficult to take captured information and use it to break into a network. We will discuss encryption later in the chapter.

In essence, you need to come up with some sort of plan for password assignment that is easy for you (the administrator) and your users to deal with and also provides some security for the network. Certainly how you assign passwords to your network users will be colored by the number of users and the importance of the resources on the network.

Other options related to user accounts can also help you build some security into the overall login process. Let's take a look at some of these options, such as logon hours and the user's ability to create more than one concurrent connection to the network.

Other User Account Options

As far as security is concerned, there are some additional measures you can take to keep unauthorized folks from accessing your network using your users' accounts.

Although each NOS will provide different tools for configuring these options, nearly all the network operating systems provide you with the following options:

■ *Logon hours.* You can control when a user can log on to the network. For example, you may choose to allow the user access to the network from 9 to 5 on workdays (meaning during those times when you know the person is at work and needs to access the network). Weekend access or late-night access both could be denied. This would keep someone nasty from using the account to break into the network during non–business hours. Figure 16.3 shows the Windows 2000 Server Logon Hours dialog box, which is used to set the logon hours for a particular user.

FIGURE 16.3

You can limit the logon hours for users in a Windows 2000 network in the hopes of making the network more secure during nonworking hours.

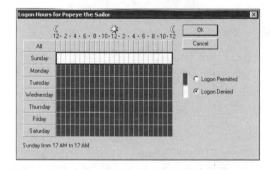

■ *Concurrent connections.* A single username and password can often be used to make concurrent (or simultaneous) connections to the network from different client computers. Limiting the number of concurrent connections can help negate the unauthorized use of a user account. If the user is already logged on to the network and you are only allowing one concurrent connection for that user, no unauthorized attempt can then be made to use that same user account to access the network. Figure 16.4 shows the Login Restrictions settings in the NetWare Administrator. Note that concurrent connections have been limited to one concurrent connection.

■ *Disabling user accounts.* Another option available to the network administrator is the ability to disable a user account. Not only is this useful in cases where you think an account is being used to illegally access the network, but it is also useful in cases where a user has left the company and you know that the position will soon by filled by a new employee. Rather than creating an entirely new account for the new employee, you can change the name on the existing account so that the new employee will have the same access to network resources that were available to the employee who has left. This is because certain permissions have been made available to the account (permissions are discussed in the next section). If you look back at Figure 16.2, you will see that Windows supplies you with a check box that can be used to quickly disable a user account.

FIGURE 16.4

You can limit the number of concurrent connections to the NetWare network to minimize the possibility of unauthorized access.

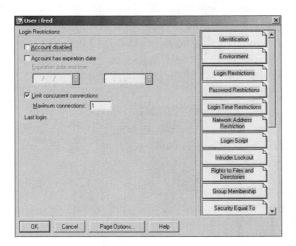

Other options related to user accounts can be used to help secure your network. For example, you can specify the client computers that users can actually use to log on to the network. You might want to only allow users to log on to the network using their own PCs (which means local files stored on the computer are not at risk) or, if a user works throughout your corporate building, you might want to make it easy for him to check e-mail by being able to log on to several different computers throughout the building.

You can also specify whether particular users can log on to the network through remote connections, such as a dial-up connection using a modem. We will discuss remote access and dial-up connections in Chapter 17, "Networking on the Run."

How you use these various options to help secure your network should be part of the plan you create when you sit down to figure out how you will assign usernames and passwords. Having some sort of defined plan to work with allows you to be consistent as you build the accounts for your users.

Understanding Share Permissions

Once users have gained access to the network, they will need to access network resources. We already discussed network shares and print resources in Chapter 8.

However, an important aspect of sharing information on the network is keeping highly sensitive or proprietary data secure as it is shared. This means some users will have access to the information and some won't. It also means that your users will have different levels of access to the data.

Access level to shares on the network is handled by permissions. A *permission* is the access level for a resource that you assign to a user or group of users (we will talk about user groups later in the chapter). Because you can potentially assign a different permission level to each user for every resource on the network, you can really fine-tune the access security for important information on the network.

> Microsoft Windows uses the term *permission* to define the different access levels given to a user for a particular network resource. In the Novell NetWare environment, permissions are known as *rights* (just different terms for the same resource security strategy).

In the Windows network environment, when you create a new share, it is basically wide open to any users on the network because the Everyone group (more about groups in a moment) is given Full Control rights to the new share, as shown in Figure 16.5.

FIGURE 16.5

On a Windows network, new shares are automatically made available to all users on the network.

This means that the network administrator has to determine whether the share's security needs to be "upgraded" in terms of who has access to the data it holds. All permissions can be negated for the Everyone group and then different access levels can be assigned to individual users or certain user groups. Figure 16.6 shows the dialog box used to add users to the Permissions dialog box for a share. The level of permission can then be designated for each user.

FIGURE 16.6

Specific users or groups of users can be added to the Permissions dialog box for a Windows share so that you can assign different permission levels to users or groups of users.

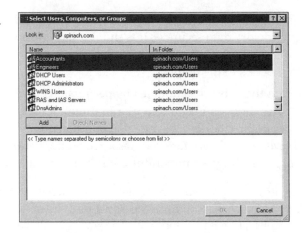

Note   Microsoft Windows networks running Windows NT, Windows 2000, or the upcoming Windows XP Server product also provide you with the ability to secure resources right down to the file level. This is because NTFS (NT File System) provides different access levels to files, folders, and drives. Because a folder on a Windows network can be both protected by share permissions (as we've discussed here) and NTFS permissions, figuring out the actual rights that a user has to a particular resource can become quite a brain-teaser. For example, if a user is giving full access to a folder due to the share permissions set on that folder, but is assigned an NTFS permission of no access, the user will not be able to access the folder. These two different permission systems combine so that the most restrictive access provided is realized by the user. For more detailed information regarding access permissions on a Windows network, check out *Special Edition Using Microsoft Windows 2000 Server*, from Que.

The NetWare environment also provides administrators with the ability to assign different rights to users in relation to resources such as folders shared on the network. Users can be assigned rights, such as Read, Write, Erase, and Modify, to the share. Figure 16.7 shows the NetWare Administrator tool, which is used to specify the rights (or permissions) that a user will have to a resource such as a folder on the network.

Once a user has been assigned permissions (or rights) to a particular resource on the network (such as a folder), those permissions will dictate how the user can interact with that resource. For example, if the user has only been assigned the Read permission for a folder on a server, he won't be able to add any files to that folder or delete items in that folder.

Figure 16.8 shows a Windows client attempting to create a new file in a folder where only the Read permission has been provided (the client is a Windows client and the server is a NetWare server). Note that a message appears letting the client know that the appropriate access level to create a new item in the particular folder has not been assigned.

FIGURE 16.7
Users in the NetWare environment are assigned different rights to a resource such as a network folder.

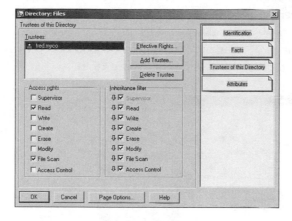

FIGURE 16.8
Permissions dictate the level of access a user will have to a particular resource.

Using Groups to Provide Access Levels

If you have a large number of users on your network, assigning different permissions (or rights) to these users can be a gargantuan task. Network operating systems allow you to place users into groups. A *group* is a logical administrative container that holds a collection of user accounts.

Placing users into groups makes it much easer for you to assign permissions to your users. For example, if you have a shared folder where 20 users need to be able to add and delete files in the folder, you could place all these users in a group and then assign the appropriate permissions to that group. If another subset of your users only needs the Read permission for files in that shared folder, you could create a second group and assign the appropriate permission level.

Groups really become security containers that allow you to provide permission levels by group membership. For example, if a new employee joins your company and needs a certain access level to a resource, all you have to do is make him a member of the appropriate group.

Most network operating systems make it very easy for you to create groups and then assign these groups different permission levels related to network resources. For example, in the Windows network environment (I'm talking about servers running Windows 2000 Server or newer versions of the NOS that use the Active Directory to create new groups), new groups are created as objects in the Active Directory (which we discussed in Chapter 7, "Working with Network Operating Systems") using the New Object - Group dialog box, as shown in Figure 16.9.

FIGURE 16.9

New groups can be added to the Windows Active Directory.

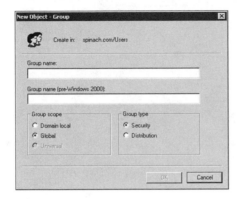

Once the new group has been created, users can be added to the group. Assigning different access levels to the group is handled in the same way permissions or rights are assigned to individual users (as discussed in the previous section).

Keeping track of the permissions you have assigned to a few groups rather than a ton of users makes a great deal of sense. As with all the other aspects of building a network infrastructure, you should probably sit down and plan out how you will use groups in relation to resource access before you start banging away at the particular server utility that allows you to create groups.

Note

Educating your users as to the importance of network resources and providing some training to your users on how to use the network should also negate some of the network implosions you face as a network administrator. Keeping an eye on your network using the tools we discussed in Chapter 15 can also help you pinpoint potential security problems, such as users trying to access resources they shouldn't be playing with. You can also audit logon attempts by users if you suspect a user account is being used to access the network by someone other than the user. Auditing user logon attempts can be monitored in all of the different NOS environments. For example, on a Windows network (using Windows NT, Windows 2000, or Windows XP), logon auditing is turned on using a security feature called Group Policy. Once auditing is enabled, unsuccessful logon attempts for your various users are compiled in the Event Viewer (discussed in Chapter 15).

Fighting Against Viruses

Another threat to your network's security is the virus. A *virus* is a self-replicating piece of software code. Because a virus can copy itself, it can easily (and unfortunately) be spread from computer to computer.

 Note | Although many viruses are actually executable programs that, when launched, replicate and damage your computer system, there are other types of viruses (such as macro viruses) that can hide in a document or spreadsheet rather than an executable file. If you open the file containing the virus, you infect your computer system.

Viruses can be spread on floppy disks and other removable storage media. If you take an infected disk out of a computer and place it in another computer, you have spread the virus. Computers can also become infected with a virus that spreads over the network because of infected shares.

The Internet also serves as a source of virus infection. Viruses can inadvertently be downloaded from the Internet. Viruses can also be spread via e-mail messages.

Interestingly, many viruses do little more than copy themselves; not all are designed to format your hard drive or corrupt a certain file type. A lot of the viruses you run into are just elaborate jokes (although this does not make them any less annoying).

One of the first viruses I remember dealing with, back in my college days, was the Brain virus. Brain was (and still is) a boot sector virus that can load itself into the computer's memory (we will discuss the different types of viruses in a moment). Well, to make a long story short, Brain quickly spread to nearly every floppy disk being used on the college campus (this is in the days of 360KB, 5 1/4" floppy disks). However, it was very easy to find the infected disks because the virus would change the volume name on the floppies to BRAIN. The virus really didn't do much more damage than that.

Although everyone fears viruses, many viruses don't do a whole lot more than replicate and spread. However, as the network administrator, it is your job to destroy viruses with impunity, whether they are just jokes or are designed to wreak havoc on your network data.

Now, I don't want to understate the fact that viruses can do a lot of damage to a computer system. Viruses can delete programs and files, and they can completely overwrite a hard disk. Viruses can be backed up along with the files that you routinely back up on the network (say, from a file server). This means that in the case of a disaster, you only have infected data files to restore to your file server.

Viruses can even find the administrator's password and pass it on to someone outside the network. This person can then log on to the network as the administrator and do all sorts of damage. So, although many viruses are just annoying and take time and money to clean up, some viruses can pose a very large security risk to the network.

| Note | "Hip" computer terminology seems to propagate faster than a computer virus. Viruses, worms, and other types of software designed to mess up your computer (and everyone's computer, for that matter) are often called *malware* (malicious software). |

Types of Viruses

A number of different virus types have evolved over the years. These different types of viruses have been classified based on how they infect a computer:

- *Boot sector viruses.* Some of the first viruses were boot sector viruses. A boot sector virus typically spreads through infected floppy disks or other removable storage media. Boot sector virus infections are helped along by user forgetfulness. If I place a boot sector virus–infected disk in my computer, nothing will happen unless I reboot the system (meaning turning it off for the day and then turning it on the next morning) and have forgotten to remove the infected disk from the floppy drive. On boot up, the boot sector virus is loaded into the computer's memory (because the computer will try to boot from the floppy). The virus can then infect the hard drive or any disks you place in the floppy drive once the computer is up and running. The Brain virus, discussed earlier, and the Exebug virus are both examples of boot sector viruses.

- *File viruses.* Although fairly uncommon now, file viruses actually infect an executable file such as an EXE or COM file (and you know that your operating system is made up of a bunch of executable files). When the infected file is run, the file virus is loaded into the computer's RAM. It can then infect other executable files as they are run on the computer. A form of the file virus is the overwriting virus, which actually overwrites the executable file that it infects. Another form of the file virus is the companion virus. This virus will masquerade as a COM file with the same name as an EXE file on your system. When you run the program, the macro will run first because COM files take precedence over EXE files. The virus will do its thing and then the actual EXE program will run. This means you may not notice that the virus is actually on your system. Examples of file viruses are the Dark Avenger virus and the KMIT virus.

- *Macro viruses.* The macro virus is a fairly recent virus type. Macro viruses are typically written in Visual Basic code and can infect documents and spreadsheet data files rather than executables. When an infected document is loaded into an application such as Microsoft Word, the virus code runs just like any other macro would in that particular application. Another scary thing about macro viruses is that they are not operating system specific. Because Microsoft Excel can run on a Macintosh and a Windows-based PC, the macro virus can actually be spread between the two platforms if the infected Excel worksheet is shared. Macro viruses are also not confined to Microsoft applications and have popped up in other office suites, such as Lotus SmartSuite. An example of a macro virus is the famous Melissa virus, a Word macro virus that automatically spread itself via e-mail.

- *Multipartite viruses.* A multipartite virus has the characteristics of both a boot sector virus and a file virus. It can spread from the boot sector of a drive to another drive, and it can also attack executable files on the computer. Some multipartite viruses can even infect device drivers (such as the drivers for your network interface card). An example of a multipartite virus is Pastika. This virus is only activated on certain days of the month (typically the 21st and 22nd of the month) and can actually overwrite your hard drive.

The actual number of viruses in the "wild" (meaning those found on business computers and networks) at any one time varies, but in general the number is increasing. The number of macro viruses is definitely on the rise. Let's take a look at some other malware that can be a threat to your network's security and resources, and then we can take a look at some strategies for protecting against virus infections.

For a great site containing information on viruses currently found in the wild, check out `http://www.f-secure.com/`. F-Secure, who hosts this site, provides a range of network security products. Another good place to look for information related to viruses is the SANS institute. The SANS, at `http://www.sans.org/newlook/home.htm`, provides information on viruses and other network security issues.

Worms and Trojan Horses

Not all software-based threats to the network come in the form of viruses. There are also two other wonderful products from those demented folks who brought us computer viruses—worms and Trojan Horses.

A *worm* is a program that spreads itself from computer to computer on a network. It doesn't need to be activated like a virus. It just spreads all by itself. A worm can be potentially devastating on a worldwide network such as the Internet because it can quickly spread itself throughout the entire network. Worms typically are platform specific and exploit some weakness in a particular operating system. For example, the Linux.Ramen worm only spreads itself among computers running Linux Red Hat 6.2 or 7.0.

A *Trojan horse* (or just Trojan as it is often referred to), on the other hand, is a program that appears to be perfectly benign, such as a screensaver or a game. For example, the HAPPY99.EXE Trojan horse, when executed, provides a nice little fireworks display on your screen and then immediately uses mail addresses found in your computer's e-mail client to send off copies of itself to these addresses (this is similar to how the Melissa virus is spread).

One of the earliest Trojans was the AIDS Information Disk Trojan, which was actually a disk sent out to medical establishments as an AIDS-awareness product. After being executed, it created a hidden directory on the computer's hard drive and eventually encrypted the entire contents of the hard drive, making it unusable.

One of the biggest threats related to Trojans is that some are actually able to invade a computer and create a portal that allows complete access to the infected machine. This means that the cracker that controls the Trojan actually can do anything he likes with your computer. He can even use it to perpetrate a denial of service attack using your computer to help generate excess traffic that is focused on a particular Web site. Denial of Service attacks are discussed later in the chapter, in the section "Protecting a Network from Outside Attack."

Virus Protection

Protecting a network against viruses, Trojans, and worms really requires two major efforts on the part of the network administrator. First, you need to have some sort of virus protection plan. Then, once the plan has been created, it can be implemented.

Any anti-malware plan should include a list of rules that your users need to follow to keep the network safe from virus infection. These rules might include no disks from home and no personal e-mail on the company's e-mail system. Also, you might have to forbid file downloads from the Internet.

Although these rules might seem a little harsh, many companies have even more draconian behavior guidelines for their computer users. What's more, many companies have very harsh punishments for employees who don't follow the rules, including dismissal (which is probably because giving an employee a good flogging just isn't an option anymore). What a user does on his home computer is his business. But when you have users on a network, where the very lifeblood of the company is the data stored on the network, you really have to lay down the law as far as the rules for network computer use.

You also need to educate your users and provide them with a general overview of what a virus is and what it can do to the network. If users worldwide would have been a little more savvy, the Melissa virus might not have been able to spread so quickly across the entire globe. Although educating your users about the threat of viruses might lead to some employees crying wolf every time their computers slow down a little, having an aware user base might help to nip virus infections in the bud before they become a huge problem.

Your plan also needs to include the installation and maintenance of virus protection software. There are a number of companies that provide anti-virus software: Symantec, McAfee, Norton, and Dr. Solomon's, just to name a few.

Antivirus software can be configured to protect client computers and network servers from infection. Most antivirus software can be configured so that a disk placed in a floppy drive is checked for viruses the moment a user slides it into the drive.

Because many antivirus companies provide their software in trial and shareware versions, you should test the different possibilities to make sure they will work for your particular network implementation. Setting up a test lab before implementing any type of new software is a good idea.

Antivirus software can come in a standalone version that must be installed on every computer or in a network version that runs whenever a computer boots up to the network. Figure 16.10 shows InoculateIT, an antivirus program from Computer Associates, checking a computer for viruses.

FIGURE 16.10

Antivirus software checks a computer's drives and memory for virus infections.

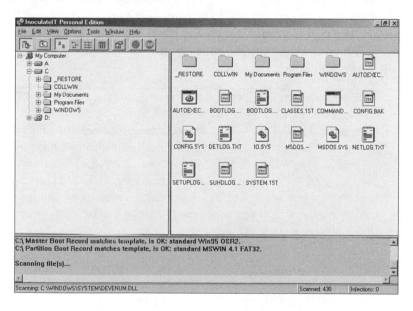

Because new viruses and other malware are popping up all the time, your antivirus software has to be able to deal with the latest and greatest virus threat. This is done by downloading updates that allow the antivirus software to recognize new viruses and repair the damage they have done. Periodically checking for virus updates to your antivirus software should be part of your overall antivirus plan.

Viruses seem to pop up almost as fast as new computing platforms. Even handheld computers, such as those running the Palm OS, are not free from possible computer virus infection. A number of antivirus software manufacturers, including Computer Associates, now offer antivirus software for the Palm OS. For more about handheld computers, see Chapter 18, "PDAs and the Network."

Protecting a Network from Outside Attack

Another security risk for your network involves direct attack. Connecting your network to the Internet provides a nice wide conduit for folks who want to try to crack your network security and gain access to valuable network resources.

Direct network attacks can take different forms, and many of them are possible because of the way the TCP/IP protocol stack operates. Each protocol in the TCP/IP stack communicates on a particular channel, called a *well-known port number* (port numbers are discussed in Chapter 11, "How the Internet Works"). For example, HTTP operates on port 80, and FTP operates on port 21. There are, in fact, over 1,000 well-known port numbers, and each of these ports is a potential path for an attack on your network. Firewalls provide a strategy for blocking these ports, and we will discuss firewalls later in the chapter.

All the ins and outs of network security, particularly those associated with outside attacks, could fill an entire book—and have actually filled a number of books. Companies lose a lot of money and time dealing with network attacks, both on the intranet (the private network) and on the Internet. For some big-picture information on network security, check out *The Concise Guide to Enterprise Internetworking and Security*, published by Que. If you like graphs and are into facts and figures and would like to take a look at some of the more infamous network break-ins and read tales of corporate espionage, check out *Tangled Web: Tales of Digital Crime from the Shadows of Cyberspace*, also from Que.

Another way that direct attacks are engineered involves important information such as login names and passwords being discerned by a cracker using snooping software such as protocol sniffers, which are discussed in Chapter 15. A cracker can sit outside your network on the Internet and intercept data transmissions that can provide enough information for a direct attack on the internal network.

A number of different kinds of attacks can be made on an IP network. A brief description of each follows:

- *Eavesdropping.* Also known as *sniffing* or *snooping*, eavesdropping is the ability to monitor network traffic because it is in an unsecured format. The eavesdropper basically listens in using some kind of network-monitoring software.

- *Password attacks.* These attacks are typically a result of eavesdropping. Once a snooper is able to find a valid account (because this information is not always protected on the internal network), the attacker is able to gain access to the network and discern information such as valid users, computer names, and resource locations. This can lead to the modification, deletion, or rerouting of network data.

- *IP address spoofing.* An attacker is able to assume a legal IP address and gain access to the network.

- *Man-in-the-middle attacks.* The attacker is able to monitor, capture, and control data between the sending and receiving devices.

- *Denial-of-service attacks.* The attacker gains access to the network and then sends invalid data to network services and applications, which causes these network services to operate erratically or to terminate. This type of attack can also materialize as a flood of data directed at a particular service or computer, which results in overload and shutdown. This type of attack has been used repeatedly to take down Web sites on the Internet.

Network administrators use all sorts of strategies to prevent these types of attacks. Secure routers provide one way to protect the internal network, and so do firewalls (discussed in the next section). Another method involves implementing Internet Protocol Security (IPSec), which is a suite of cryptography-based protection services and security protocols that can be used to secure internal networks, networks that use WAN solutions for connectivity, and networks that take advantage of remote access solutions (such as Virtual Private Networking, which we discuss in Chapter 17).

Note   IPSec uses all sorts of protection methods to secure network data. *Cryptography* is the coding or encrypting of data into an unreadable format. IPSec can also use certificates to protect data, where the data can only be read by a receiver with the appropriate certificate credentials. Obviously, implementing IPSec requires a very good understanding of the TCP/IP protocol stack and IPSec itself. For information on IPSec and securing a Windows 2000 Server network, check out *Microsoft Windows 2000 Security Handbook*, from Que.

Securing a network of any size will probably require more than one strategy. This means you need to create a security plan for your network. Once you have a plan, you can implement it with the appropriate hardware or software security tools. Network security is certainly a very hot topic and a very important aspect of any network administrator's job. Securing a network isn't easy, however. Even the big boys, such as Yahoo! and Microsoft, get hammered occasionally by network attacks. Let's end our discussion of network security on a high point with the discussion of a truly marvelous invention: the firewall.

Understanding Firewalls

Firewalls are designed to sit between your network and the Internet and protect the internal network from outside attack. A firewall will examine data leaving and entering the internal network and can actually filter the data traveling in both directions. If data packets do not meet a particular rule that has been configured, the data is not allowed to enter the internal network or leave the internal network. This means that firewalls not only protect a network from outside attack, but they can also control the type of connections made by users on the internal network to the outside (meaning that employees can be restricted from connecting to certain Web sites).

Firewalls are typically a combination of hardware and software, and they really don't look that much different from other connectivity hardware, such as hubs and routers. Firewalls are manufactured by a number of companies, including Cisco, 3Com, and Ascend Communications. Firewalls come in a variety of models that have been designed to protect different size networks. For example, 3Com manufactures the OfficeConnect firewall line as a security tool for small companies. For larger enterprise networks, 3Com offers the SuperStack 3 firewall. The SuperStack 3 firewall is designed to control large numbers of VPN connections (we discuss VPN, or Virtual Private Networking, in Chapter 17). This firewall also provides support for IPSec.

Software-only firewalls do exist. Many of these products are designed for personal use to protect a PC that has a persistent connection to the Internet through a DSL line or a cable modem.

Before we get into a discussion of the different types of firewalls, let me make a compelling argument for how important a firewall can be to network security. I briefly mentioned in the last section that TCP/IP ports provide avenues used by crackers to break into networks and computers. Now, depending on the size of your business and company network, you may think, Why would anyone waste his time trying to break into my network? But thinking that crackers only go after big networks such as Microsoft and the Department of Defense is a very wrong assumption.

I'm not sure why anyone would waste his time trying to crack into networks, but there are a lot of people out there who do try to crack into networks and even personal computers connected to the Internet. For example, check out Figure 16.11. It shows an alert provided by a software firewall, ZoneAlarm, that I have installed on a computer. The computer is attached to a cable modem, so it is always connected to the Internet through my service provider.

FIGURE 16.11

Firewalls can provide alerts when someone attempts to connect to a computer or the network.

The alert shows that someone tried to ping (using the `ping` command) my computer. This means that they know my IP address. The ZoneAlarm firewall blocked this ping attempt. I get at least a half dozen alerts a day on this computer from the firewall software. Some are people trying to ping my machine using the `ping` command (which isn't all that horrible). Others are trying to actually connect to my computer via different ports. My computer is just one of thousands of computers connected to my Internet service provider, yet its TCP/IP ports are probed on a regular basis.

When you set up a computer connected to the Internet with a firewall such as ZoneAlarm (for more about ZoneAlarm, a really great personal firewall, see `http://www.zonealarm.com/`), some of the alerts that you receive will be probes and attempted connections from your service provider. So, not every connection attempt is a "bad guy."

Plenty of people out there are looking for computers and networks they can probe and then connect to. As a sort of hands-on epiphany of your own related to the importance of firewalls, check out `https://grc.com/default.htm`. This site is maintained by Gibson Research Corporation and provides a link to a special site that it has created called Shields Up. The Shields Up site shows how vulnerable computers running the Windows operating system are to outside attack.

Make sure you click the link for Shields Up on the GRC home page. If you are not running a personal firewall on the computer, you will be surprised to find that the Shields Up Web site will greet you using the NetBIOS name of your computer. To make things even more scary, scroll down on the Shields Up page and click the Test My Shields button.

When I ran the shield test on a Windows computer configured for file and print sharing, the output screen from the shield test provided a list of all the folders and printers being shared on the computer. When I ran the probe port test, which is also accessed from the Shields Up page, a number of ports, such as HTTP, Telnet, and NetBIOS, were also shown to be wide open.

Then I installed ZoneAlarm on the computer and reran the tests. The shield test showed that the computer was now operating in "stealth" mode and no information about the computer, such as the NetBIOS name and shared resources, was available. When I ran the port probe test, all the ports had been closed to the outside by the firewall. Figure 16.12 provides the results of the port probe. All ports are now unavailable as a potential route for someone trying to access data on the computer over the Internet.

FIGURE 16.12

Firewalls protect TCP/IP ports.

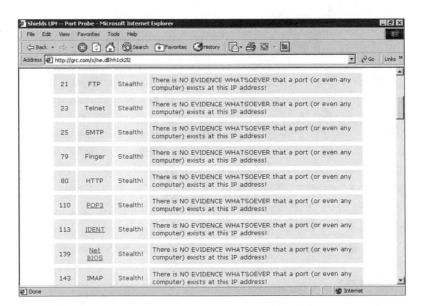

So, firewalls really do work. Let's take a look at the different types of firewalls available for protecting corporate networks.

Types of Firewalls

Firewalls are categorized as different types based on how they deal with network traffic and the layer of the OSI model at which they operate (if you need a refresher on the OSI model, take a look back at Chapter 5, "Network Protocols: Real and

Imagined"). The higher the layer of the OSI model at which the firewall operates, the more sophisticated the firewall. Here are some specifics:

- *Packet filter firewall.* This type of firewall uses a set of rules to determine whether outgoing or incoming data packets are allowed to pass through the firewall. The rules or filters designed to control the data traffic allowed by the firewall can be based on the IP address of the sending device and the particular port being used by the protocol that originated the data packet. A packet filter firewall moves data quickly and is the simplest type of firewall. It operates at the Data Link and Network layers of the OSI model. A router that uses access lists (rules for allowing or disallowing connections based on IP addresses) to filter data traffic can be considered a packet filter firewall.

- *Circuit-level firewall.* This type of firewall is similar to the packet filter firewall (in that it filters packets based on a set of rules), but because circuit-level firewalls operate at the Transport layer of the OSI model, they have greater functionality. A circuit-level firewall can make packets sent from the internal network to a destination outside the firewall appear as if they originated at the firewall. This helps to keep information relating to hosts on the internal network secret. Circuit-level firewalls also can determine whether a connection between a network host and a computer on the other side of the firewall using the TCP protocol has been established appropriately (see Chapter 5 for more about TCP). If the connection has not been established appropriately, the firewall can terminate the connection. This cuts off any connection that has been hijacked by an outside attacker trying to sneak past the firewall.

- *Application-gateway firewall.* This type of firewall operates at the Application layer of the OSI model. Application gateways use strong user authentication to verify the identify of a host attempting to connect to the network using a particular TCP/IP Application layer protocol such as Telnet or FTP. This type of firewall can also actually control the devices that an external host can connect to once the firewall has authenticated that particular user. Application gateways are even effective against IP spoofing (discussed earlier in the chapter) because they do not allow the connection to proceed inside the firewall unless the user can truly be authenticated to the network.

Note Many firewalls also have proxy server capabilities and use Network Address Translation (NAT) to protect the internal network. For more about proxy servers and NAT, take a look back at Chapter 12, "Connecting a Network to the Internet."

You will find that some firewall products are actually a hybrid of the types of firewalls discussed here. For example, a firewall might combine circuit-level capabilities with application-gateway services.

The deployment of firewalls and the development of new firewall products are both proceeding at seemingly breakneck speed. Major news stories on the cracking of big corporate and government networks has only lead to a rise in the purchase of firewalls and the manufacture of more secure firewall products.

A Final Word on Network Security

Securing a network and its resources is certainly the greatest challenge a network administrator faces. Even office politics can seem like a stroll in the park compared to the scramble that takes place when the internal network security has been breached by someone with mischief in mind.

Although this chapter certainly is not intended as the ultimate treatise on network security, I hope that you take a couple things away with you after reading it. First, assess the possible security risks to your network. Second, develop a security plan.

Every network needs a security plan that catalogs the possible threats to the network and the measures you plan to take to negate these threats. If the biggest problem on your network is users messing up important files, your security plan needs to lean toward user education. If you have highly sensitive data on your network, such as the cure for the common cold, your network may face attacks from employees bent on stealing corporate secrets and crackers on the outside who want to break into the network and steal your valuable data. This means you need to come up with a security strategy that can fight against internal and external attacks.

So, take my word for it: You need a security plan. Having a plan also makes it easier to justify the purchase of expensive pieces of equipment such as firewalls.

Chapter Summary

- Network security involves the protection of network resources from attacks that originate both inside and outside the network.
- The first line of defense for network security is user authentication. Users cannot access the network without a valid username and password.
- Each username must be unique.
- User passwords can be controlled by the network administrator or by the network users.
- User account options such as logon hours allowed and the number of connections allowed for an account can be used to increase network security.
- Share permissions or rights are used to supply different levels of access to users in relation to a particular resource on the network.

- User groups can be created on the network and then assigned permissions for various network resources. Any user added to a group will also have the same access rights as those assigned to that group.

- A virus is malicious program code that can replicate and spread from computer to computer on the network.

- A worm is malware that spreads itself from computer to computer without activation by a user (which differs from a virus). A Trojan is malware masquerading as a regular software program, such as a game or screensaver.

- Antivirus software can scan storage devices and computer memory as it seeks out and destroys computer viruses.

- A number of different types of attacks can be launched from outside a network connected to the Internet. These attacks include eavesdropping and IP spoofing.

- IPSec, a suite of IP security protocols that provide encryption and authentication methods, has been developed to help negate malicious attacks on IP networks.

- Firewalls are hardware and software devices that can control the flow of data packets between an internal network and an external network such as the Internet.

- Network security is best implemented when a network security plan has been developed. This plan should identify possible security risks to the network and the methods that will be used to minimize these security risks.

17

NETWORKING ON THE RUN

In this chapter

- Understanding laptop computer screen technology
- Working with laptop expansion cards
- Using a docking station
- Understanding remote access
- Configuring dial-up access
- Working with Virtual Private Networking

We must open the doors of opportunity. But we must also equip our people to walk through those doors.

–Lyndon B. Johnson

In this chapter, we take a look at business on the run—mobile computing. With increasing numbers of employees either working on the road or telecommuting from home (for at least a portion of the work week), the ability to connect these remote users to the corporate network has became an important aspect of managing network users and resources.

We have already taken a look at WAN technology in Chapter 10, "Expanding a LAN with WAN Technology." A number of different technologies were discussed, ranging from dial-up connections, to leased lines, to packet-switching technology such as Frame Relay. For telecommuters and employees working on the road (such as the corporate sales force), connecting to the company's network usually revolves around using dial-up connections or accessing the corporate network through the Internet using a Virtual Private Network (VPN). Both these connection types have their pros and cons, and both have different security issues to deal with.

Let's start our discussion of computing on the run with a general look at the evolution of mobile computing devices. We can then concentrate on laptop computers and remote connectivity strategies.

The Evolution of Mobile Computing Devices

The need for road-ready portable computers has been recognized since the early days of the PC revolution. Computer manufacturers followed fairly quickly behind the launch of the IBM PC with a number of different types of portable computers.

Compaq launched the Compaq Portable in 1982. This DOS-based IBM PC clone provided a 5.25-inch floppy drive and a built-in 9-inch amber monitor. These suitcase-size computers (which weighed almost as much as a desktop PC) could run the same applications as an IBM desktop PC. The desire for mobile computers was proven by the fact that Compaq sold over 50,000 units in the first year.

 Note | The first "luggable" PC was created by Osborne. The Osborne 1, which actually predated the IBM PC, was a suitcase computer that was introduced in 1980. The Osborne had 64KB of memory and a disk drive. It also came with bundled software, including WordStar (a word processor) and SuperCalc (a spreadsheet). Obviously, because you don't have to worry about networking Osborne portable computers (most people don't even know that they ever existed), the Osborne is just another one of those computer history footnotes.

Other companies, such as Osborne and Tandy, went their own direction and produced portable computers that did not provide compatibility with DOS-based business computers. Tandy probably should get the award for one of the first truly mobile computers—the Model 100. The Model 100 was introduced in 1983 and had a small LCD display (less than 3 inches high and 6 inches across). The Model 100 ran a built-in version of BASIC and came equipped with a simple text editor. ROM chips were also available for these lightweight portables (they weighed less than 3 pounds) that contained productivity software, such as word processing, spreadsheet, and database applications. These portables also shipped with a built-in 300-baud modem.

Apple also entered the portable computing market in 1989 with the Macintosh Portable. This 16-pound portable computer, which ran the Mac OS, provided a faster processor than Macintosh SE and boasted a 40MB hard drive. This portable computer eventually evolved into the Macintosh PowerBook.

Portable and laptop computers have evolved as rapidly as desktop PCs, and in the last decade, laptop technology has advanced to the point where a 5-pound laptop computer can pack the processing and storage power found on a much larger business computer. Let's take a closer look at some of the laptop technologies, including screen design and networking capability, found on today's portable computers.

Although the laptop computer is still by and large the mobile "workhorse," handheld computing devices such as Personal Digital Assistantsand even cellular phones are rapidly gaining capabilities that make them viable options to lugging a portable computer around. Wireless communication options are also changing how we compute on the run. Handheld computing devices are discussed in Chapter 18, "PDAs and the Network."

Working with Laptops

The laptops that we now drag along with us on business trips are very different from early portable PCs, such as the Compaq Portable. Advances in processor technology (such as processors built specifically for mobile computing) and motherboard design have lead to a much smaller form factor for the modern laptop.

For those of you who require a definitive reference for PC hardware, including laptops, checkout *Upgrading and Repairing PCs*, from Que. At more than 1,000 pages, this book provides information on every aspect of PC hardware.

Two areas of laptop design that are particularly interesting in light of technology advances are the laptop screen and the expansion cards used in laptop PCs. Let's take a brief look at both of these hardware items.

The Laptop Screen

Because laptops can be configured with the processing power, storage, and memory capacity of a desktop PC, one of the big differences between the two (other than the keyboard) is the screen. Laptop screens use liquid crystals sandwiched between two electrodes. This is why laptop screens are referred to as *liquid crystal displays*.

The liquid crystal diodes are placed on a fine matrix of wires. When a portion of the LCD display must be activated to show output from the computer, the diodes on that portion of the display are supplied current. Each diode serves as a pixel, and all the "turned on" pixels provide you with an image.

Two basic LCD screen types are available for laptops: passive matrix and active matrix.

Passive matrix displays merely hit the liquid crystals with current at a prescribed refresh rate. Active matrix screens, on the other hand, use transistors to control each of the diodes. This means that active matrix displays are brighter and easier to view at different angles than passive matrix displays.

This also means that active matrix displays are more expensive and raise the price tag of the laptop. Active matrix screens also drain a laptop's battery faster than a passive matrix screen. Figure 17.1 shows an active matrix display on a Gateway laptop.

Because the network administrator is in charge of creating the specifications for the laptops used in the field, it is up to you to determine whether your laptops need active matrix displays or passive matrix displays. Although cost is certainly a concern when budgeting, you also need to take into account how your mobile users will be using their notebook PCs and where they will be using them. If the laptops will serve as the primary computers for mobile users (such as your sales force), an active matrix display will certainly cut down on eye strain and be more readable in a larger variety of lighting situations (such as on airplanes or in the parking lot of a client).

PCMCIA Expansion Cards

One of the reasons notebook computers don't weigh a ton and can provide a fairly small form factor is the type of expansion slots they use. In the 1980s, the *Personal Computer Memory Card International Association* (or *PCMCIA*, which was originally made up of a number of computer memory vendors) sought to establish a standard expansion card specification for portable computers. The result was the PCMCIA card, which is now typically called the *PC card*.

FIGURE 17.1

Active matrix
LCD screens pro-
vide a brighter,
crisper screen
than the passive
matrix alterna-
tive.

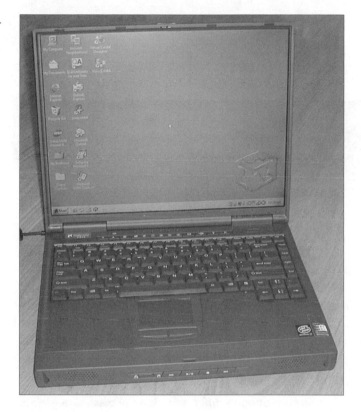

The PC card is about the size of a credit card (although slightly thicker) and allows
for the addition of memory and peripherals, such as modems and network interface
cards, to a notebook computer. PC cards are actually designed to be "hot swap-
pable" and can be removed or added while the computer is running (depending on
the OS you are running on the laptop).

PC cards come in three different flavors or types: Type 1, Type 2, and Type 3. One
difference you will find as you examine each of the card types is that they get pro-
gressively thicker. This is because each PC card type was designed for certain types of
add-ons. Here's a description of each PC card type:

- *Type 1*. Used to expand the RAM on a portable computer. Type 1 cards have
  also been available as ROM memory cards that actually contain specific software applications.

- *Type 2*. This type of PC card will typically be a modem or network interface
  card that fits into an internal slot on the portable computer.

- *Type 3*. The Type 3 PC cards have been designed to allow support for devices
  such as removable hard drives and CD-ROM drives.

Figure 17.2 shows a PC card slot on the side of a Gateway Solo notebook. Notice that this particular laptop is configured with both a modem and a NIC. The modem uses an RJ-ll connector (the same as a telephone) and the NIC uses an RJ-45 connector (the type of connector found on twisted-pair network cabling).

FIGURE 17.2

PC card slots provide a way to add peripherals to notebook computers without taking up a lot of space.

The Personal Computer Memory Card International Association continues to create standards for portable device peripherals and has been involved in the development of standards for SmartMedia cards (if you have a digital camera, you probably have a SmartMedia card). The booming PDA and cellular phone industry has also lead to PCMCIA standards for miniature card technology, such as memory upgrade cards for handheld computers.

Notebook Docking Stations

Before turning our attention to different remote access strategies, one more subject that I want to discuss related to portable or notebook computers is the docking station. One of the dilemmas of the network administrator who deals with employees who spend some of their time in the office and also spend time on the road is that outfitting their office with a PC and also supplying them with a notebook computer seems to be somewhat of a redundant effort. Unless the employee who has the two computers is savvy enough to transfer files between the two devices, he is constantly going to be scrambling around (and begging for your help) when he needs to find and print that important report he typed up in his hotel room when he was at a Las Vegas business convention last week (first of all, as the network administrator, you should definitely be highly skeptical of anyone's claim that he did work while in Las Vegas).

A way to negate the need for two computers for one employee is to use a docking station. A *docking station* is basically a cradle that a notebook computer can be placed in or attached to. Even the simplest docking stations provide port replication, which means that printer ports, serial ports, and monitor ports are replicated on the docking station. This means that a monitor can be attached to the docking station, as can input devices such as a keyboard and mouse.

Some docking stations also provide you with the ability to add additional storage devices and connect the notebook (when it is in the cradle) to the company network. Using a docking station means that the notebook doesn't have to be configured with certain peripherals, such as a network card. Also, because devices such as external monitors and keyboards are connected to the docking station, the employee can disconnect the laptop from the docking station and he is ready to hit the road.

Understanding Remote Access

Although wireless technology will definitely change our options for connecting to a network from a remote location in the next few years, the asynchronous modem still serves as the typical connection device and uses the public phone lines as the communication conduit. Any desktop PC or laptop computer can be outfitted with a modem. Almost all client operating systems also provide a dial-up client that can be used to connect to a network using a modem. Millions of people use modems and dial-up clients to connect to their Internet service providers so that they can check their e-mail and browse the World Wide Web.

For a user to be able to connect to a corporate network from a laptop (or any computer) using a modem, there has to be a computer at the company that will accept the call and allow the user to log on to the network. This type of computer is called a *remote access server*.

The Remote Access Services (RAS) server must be running an NOS that allows remote access, and it must be configured to allow dial-in connections. Communications hardware such as an analog modem (or several modems in a modem pool to allow a number of connections from users), an ISDN modem, or some other connectivity device is required so that the RAS server can field the incoming calls.

Microsoft's Windows 2000 Server, Novell's NetWare, Sun Microsystems's Solaris, and the various Unix/Linux platforms—all the big players in the NOS market—offer remote access. Remote access servers use a technique called *tunneling* in which packets from your network, which are encapsulated into a particular frame type by the network protocol you are using (such as TCP/IP or IPX/SPX), are moved across the public switched telephone network in a virtual tunnel that is hosted by a particular wide area networking protocol or access protocol, such as the Point-to Point Protocol (which we discuss later in the chapter).

Setting up remote access really is a two-part process. First, you must install and configure an RAS server. Once the RAS server is up and running and can accept an incoming call, you need to configure the remote client computer (or the user must be walked through the process of configuring the remote client). Let's take a look at the server side or the RAS equation first.

Configuring an RAS Server for Dial-Up Access

Depending on the size of your network, the RAS server can be your primary network server or an additional server on the network that is specifically charged with handling remote access connections. Configuring a server for remote access involves the following tasks:

- *Installing network protocols on the server.* You must install the network protocols on the server that will be used by the remote hosts to access network resources and services. For example, Microsoft Windows 2000 Server allows remote clients to use TCP/IP, IPX/SPX, AppleTalk, or NetBEUI to connect to network resources.

- *Installing connectivity hardware.* Before you can configure the Remote Access Service on the server, you must connect your modem or other connectivity device to the server and install the appropriate software drivers for the device (meaning the modem or other device needs to be functional before you can configure the Remote Access Service on the server).

- *Configuring the Remote Access Service on the server.* Each network operating system will supply a utility for configuring the Remote Access Service server. For example, Windows 2000 Server uses the Routing and Remote Access (RRAS) snap-in, shown in Figure 17.3, to start and configure the RAS server. A Novell NetWare server uses the NIASCFG utility, which is started at the NetWare server prompt using the load niascfg command. NetWare 5.1 also provides the NetWare Management Portal, shown in Figure 17.4. It allows you to configure services such as the Remote Access Service using the Web browser on a network client computer.

Note

As we discussed in Chapter 7, "Working with Network Operating Systems," NetWare servers can be configured using different DOS-based utilities, such as NIASCF. These various utilities are loaded at the SERVER prompt (when the server is running) using the LOAD command. In the most recent version of NetWare (version 5.1), various services, including the Remote Access Service, can also be configured using the NetWare Console 1 GUI (on the server) or the NetWare Administrator, which is run from a client computer connected to the server. In addition, there is also the NetWare Management Portal, which is accessed using a Web browser on a network workstation.

FIGURE 17.3

NOS utilities such as the Windows 2000 Server RRAS snap-in are used to configure a remote access server.

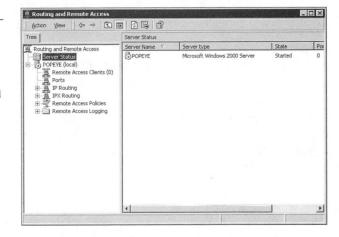

FIGURE 17.4

NetWare 5.1 provides a Web-based utility that can be used to configure your NetWare server.

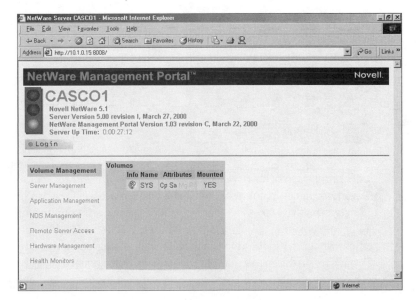

Note

When remote access servers are configured, another issue that pops up is authentication. Different authentication protocols can be used that must be negotiated by the remote clients for them to connect to the remote access server. A number of different authentication protocols are available. Some authentication protocols provide greater security than others. For example, the Password Authentication Protocol (PAP) uses clear text login names and passwords (*clear text* means that the login and password are transmitted over the line as text), which makes it easier for hackers to steal logon and password information. Other protocols, such as Challenge Handshake Authentication Protocol (CHAP), use encryption and other methods to provide a more secure environment when the clients negotiate access.

Once the RAS server is configured, user accounts must also be enabled for dial-in. On a Novell Netware 5.1 network, the Netware Administrator utility is used to specify dial-in client properties for each user who will be given dial-up privileges (there is a remote access tab on the user's details window). On a Windows 2000 Server network, user accounts are enabled for dial-in using the Windows Active Directory. Figure 17.5 shows the Properties dialog box for a user account. The Dial-In tab is used to enable remote access for the user.

FIGURE 17.5

User accounts must be enabled for remote access.

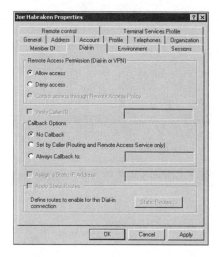

 Configuring a server for remote access makes it convenient for remote users to get at network resources, but it also opens up a possible avenue for unauthorized access to the network. If you take a look at Figure 17.5, you will find that some security measures can be implemented to help control user access. For example, the remote connection can be configured so that the server will hang up after authenticating the user and then call back the user's phone number to reestablish the connection. This is one way of keeping out unauthorized users who have stolen a username and password.

Configuring an RAS Client

Once the RAS server has been set up and configured for dial-in connections and the user account of the individual who will dial in to the RAS server has been enabled for remote access, you need to configure the client computer. The client computer must be configured with a LAN protocol or protocols that match those supported by the RAS server and the network.

The client computer must also be outfitted with a device that allows it to remotely connect to the RAS server. In most cases, this means that the remote client must be configured with a modem.

Once the client computer has been set up with the appropriate LAN protocols and a modem, the client computer must be configured with a dial-up connection that is used to dial the RAS server. Most types of client software have built-in dial-up clients. Windows clients, such as Windows 2000 Professional, even provide a connection wizard that can be used to set up the computer to dial in to a remote access server.

In Windows 2000 Professional, the dial-up connection is created using the Make New Connection icon in the Network and Dial-Up Connections dialog box. Figure 17.6 shows the Network Connection Wizard dialog box. The wizard can create dial-up connections to private networks (meaning to an RAS server). This wizard is also used to enable connections to a remote network over a Virtual Private Networking connection (which we discuss later in this chapter).

FIGURE 17.6

Windows 2000 provides a wizard to create the dial-in access to the remote server.

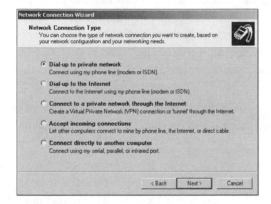

Once you select the Dial-Up to Private Network option, all you have to do is provide the phone number for the RAS server and then supply a name for the dial-up connection. An icon for the connection is placed in the Network and Dial-Up Connections dialog box.

When the user double-clicks the connection icon in the Network and Dial-Up Connections dialog box, the Connect dialog box opens, as shown in Figure 17.7. All the user has to do is supply the correct password and then click Dial. The phone number of the RAS server will be dialed and a connection will be made to the server.

Once clients are connected to the RAS server, they can access the company network and its servers and printers. The network resources that clients can access will be determined by the privileges or rights that have been assigned to the users (just like any other users on the network, including those who log on to the network from computers that are on the LAN).

FIGURE 17.7

The Windows Connect RAS Server Dial-Up dialog box is used to dial up the RAS server.

Understanding Access Protocols

For the dial-up connection to work between the remote client and the RAS server, a protocol must be used that takes the data packets exchanged between the client and the server and encapsulates them for movement over the POTS network. *Encapsulation* is just a fancy term for taking a particular frame type (such as an Ethernet frame) and placing it in a sort of electronic baggy. The frames can then move across the alien public phone network and still maintain their integrity as a particular frame type.

This electronic bagging or encapsulation of frames for movement across the phone network is handled by an *access protocol.* Two common access protocols are SLIP and PPP.

The *Serial Line Internet Protocol (SLIP)* is an access protocol that was developed primarily to allow PCs to connect to the Internet using a modem. It operates at the OSI model's Physical layer and allows data to flow across the telephone line to a remote system. SLIP provides no data compression or error checking and only supports connections to TCP/IP networks. The use of SLIP has all but evaporated because of the introduction of PPP.

The *Point-to-Point Protocol (PPP)* provides a reliable connection between computers, and PPP supports multiple network protocols, such as IP, IPX, and NetBEUI. PPP also provides compression and error checking and is therefore more reliable than a SLIP connection. PPP also supports password encryption, which allows for a more secure connection between the remote client and the RAS server.

You only really need to remember SLIP in terms of its historical significance; it was the first remote access protocol used for dial-in connections. PPP is used by default by most network operating systems and client operating systems. Whether you set up RAS for a NetWare network or a Windows network, PPP will be used as the access protocol for dial-up connections. PPP supports TCP/IP, IPX/SPX, and even NetBEUI. This means that the RAS client and the remote server can use a variety of LAN protocols to communicate over the PPP tunnel.

Managing Remote Connections

Once the user is attached to the remote access server and the network, the remote access software that you are using on your server will provide you with the ability to monitor that remote connection and any other remote connections on the server. This means that you can monitor the activity of the remote client in terms of the number of bytes that are sent and received and the time that the client has been logged on to the network.

On a Windows 2000 remote access server, dial-in connections are monitored and managed using the Routing and Remote Access tool, as shown in Figure 17.8. Not only can the connection be monitored, but the connection can be terminated by the network administrator. This allows you to sever unattended connections and free up modems for other dial-in connections. Hey, the network administrator giveth, and the network administrator taketh away.

FIGURE 17.8

Remote access connections can be monitored.

Obviously there is much more to managing remote access than monitoring connections and occasionally knocking a remote user off the network. A plan must be developed that allows remote users to get at the network resources they need to get their jobs done. Remote access should not become a way for remote users to connect to the network and thus gain free access to the Internet. You will have to make sure that only a subset of your users is configured for remote access and that the dial-in connections are used for business purposes. This might not make you the most popular employee at your company, but it will allow you to provide remote connections for the users that truly need them.

Working with Virtual Private Networks

Another possibility for remote connections to the company network involves the use of a *Virtual Private Network (VPN)*. A VPN is a secure, dedicated, point-to-point connection over a public IP internetwork, such as the Internet. Using a VPN means that you don't have to configure the RAS server with a modem pool or other WAN connection type. The RAS server just needs to be connected to the Internet, and the remote client will connect to the company network by tunneling through the Internet.

> A VPN can also be used to create a connection between a branch office and the main corporate office. As long as the branch office can connect to the Internet, data can be securely routed over a VPN tunnel to and from the corporate network. This can actually be a cost-saving measure because a dedicated line, such as a leased phone line or some other WAN connection, doesn't have to be maintained between the branch and main offices.

A VPN connection has both a client and server side (as do remote access dial-up connections). The *tunnel server* provides the server side of the connection. Most network operating systems provide support for VPNs in their remote access software. The VPN client is referred to as the *tunnel client* and will need remote access software configured to connect to a VPN tunnel server. The actual connection between the server and the client is referred to as the *tunnel*.

VPN connections or tunnels are managed by the *Point-to-Point Tunneling Protocol (PPTP)*. PPTP is an extension of the PPP protocol and provides for the encapsulation of the data that moves between the remote client and the RAS server over the Internet. Basically, your data frames (such as Ethernet frames) are encapsulated by PPP and then encapsulated again by PPTP. This means that any frame types can be transmitted over the Internet between the remote client and the RAS server. When encapsulated data frames reach their destination, they are "unencapsulated," meaning the PPP and PPTP "baggies" are stripped from the data frames.

Configuring a Tunnel Server

Windows 2000 Server (and its more recent incarnation, Windows XP Server), Novell NetWare 5.1, and a number of other network operating systems provide support for VPN remote access. In many cases, the Remote Access Service that is configured for remote dial-up connections can also be configured for VPN. For example, the Windows 2000 Server Routing and Remote Access snap-in provides a wizard (just like it does for dial-up connections) that can be used to quickly configure the VPN.

Figure 17.9 shows the Windows 2000 Server wizard for configuring VPN. The NIC that provides the connection to the Internet for the server must be specified as the connection for incoming VPN connections.

FIGURE 17.9

Network operating systems such as Windows 2000 Server also provide remote access to the network via VPN.

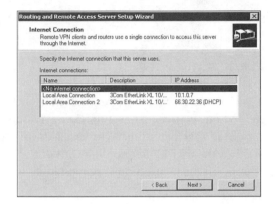

The remote access server can also be configured to supply IP addresses to VPN clients that connect to the RAS server (or the RAS server will allow the network DHCP server to assign appropriate addresses). Such an IP address is actually assigned to the PPP virtual adapter that is created on the tunnel client (once it has been configured for VPN). This assigned IP address does not mess up the IP address that has been assigned to the client's dial-up adapter by the ISP used by the client to connect to the Internet. The client will actually be simultaneously connecting to two different IP networks because of the VPN tunnel (one network being the ISP's network; the other being the Windows network that the client is connecting to via the VPN).

Configuring a Tunnel Client

Once the tunnel server is configured on the network (and connected to the Internet), the tunnel client needs to be set up. The client needs to be outfitted with a modem or some other connectivity medium and have an account with an ISP for a connection to the Internet.

The tunnel client is configured using the dial-up client software provided by the client's operating system. For example, on a Windows 2000 VPN tunnel client, the VPN connection (and the addition of PPTP to the computer's protocol list) is handled by the Network Connection Wizard (in the same manner as a dial-up connection is created). During the configuration process of the client, the IP address of the tunnel server (the RAS server on the network) must be specified, as shown in Figure 17.10.

FIGURE 17.10

FIGURE 17.10

The IP address of the tunnel server must be specified when the tunnel client is being configured.

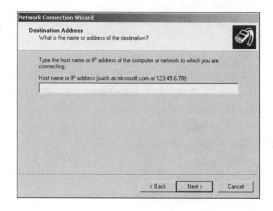

Once the tunnel client is configured, it's just a matter of double-clicking the VPN connection icon that is created during the client setup. Figure 17.11 shows the initiation of a VPN connection from a VPN icon in the Windows Network and Dial-Up Connections window. Note that the username and password of the tunnel client are verified by the tunnel server when the connection is requested by the remote client.

FIGURE 17.11

The username and password are verified by the VPN tunnel server when a VPN connection is requested by a remote client.

Monitoring VPN Connections

Once the tunnel client has connected to the tunnel server, the VPN connection can be used to move data between the two computers. In essence, the tunnel client is now connected to the network just like any other LAN clients are connected. The user will have access to any network resources that she has the appropriate privileges for.

Remote access servers that provide VPN support also supply you with the ability to monitor remote connections. Figure 17.12 shows the Windows Routing and Remote Access snap-in; note that there is currently one remote connection to the server.

FIGURE 17.12

The number of remote connections can be viewed on the server's remote access utility.

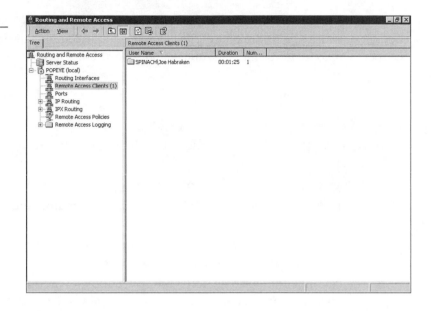

Because VPN and dial-up connections both take place over virtual ports—either supplied by a modem for dial-up or IP virtual ports for VPN—you can also monitor the number of active ports on a remote access server. The details of the connection on each virtual port can also be viewed. Figure 17.13 shows the connection statistics for a PPTP virtual port used for a VPN connection.

FIGURE 17.13

The connection statistics for a remote connection, such as a VPN tunnel, can be viewed on the remote access server.

Tip

RAS servers supplying dial-up or VPN connections can also control these remote connections. As the network administer, you can actually close a connection if you wish. You can also monitor connection time and the amount of data that has been moved on a remote connection.

Both dial-up and VPN connections allow you to expand your network beyond the confines of your LAN infrastructure. This allows you to accommodate employees on the road, employee telecommuters, and employees working at remote corporate sites.

Chapter Summary

- Portable computers quickly followed on the heels of the PCs introduced in the 1980s.
- A notebook screen is made up of an LCD display.
- Notebook LCD displays come in two flavors: active matrix and passive matrix.
- Active matrix screens control the LCD diodes with transistors, making them brighter and crisper than passive matrix screens.
- The Personal Computer Memory Card International Association developed an expansion card standard for notebook computers. The result, the PC card, provides expansion modules not much bigger than a credit card.
- A docking station provides an easy way to connect a notebook to the network and increases the functionality of a laptop to nearly desktop status.
- Remote access servers supply remote clients with the ability to connect to the network using either dial-up or VPN connections. Most network operating systems support remote access.
- Dial-up connections are controlled by an access protocol such as PPP or SLIP. PPP is now used in most cases and provides encryption and compression for the connection.
- A Virtual Private Network (VPN) allows remote clients to connect to the LAN over the Internet. The remote connection is accepted by an RAS server configured for VPN.
- VPN connections are managed by the Point-to-Point Tunneling Protocol (PPTP). This protocol provides an additional layer of encapsulation for the data moved through the VPN tunnel.
- Dial-up and VPN connections can be monitored and controlled from the RAS server.

PDAS AND THE NETWORK

If it keeps up, man will atrophy all his limbs but the push-button finger.

–Frank Lloyd Wright

In the last chapter we took a look at mobile computing and the different strategies available for connecting a remote user to a local area network. In this chapter we'll take the concept of mobile computing one step further and concentrate on Personal Digital Assistants (PDAs).

So, what is a *Personal Digital Assistant*? A PDA is basically a handheld computer, and for the purpose of this chapter we will limit our discussion of PDAs to devices that actually have processing power (meaning you can manipulate data, even send and receive data, on the PDA without being attached to a PC). This means that the PDA must have a processor and an operating system.

Let's begin our discussion of PDAs with a look at some of the devices available. We will then take a look at the two operating systems that dominate the PDA market: the Palm OS and Windows CE (which is now known as *PocketPC*).

The Personal Digital Assistant

PDAs started out as a handheld devices that made it convenient to take information such as addresses, phone numbers, and appointments on the road. These devices were really just electronic organizers with a limited amount of memory; however, these early PDAs still provided a user with the ability to sync with Personal Information Managers (PIMs), such as Microsoft Outlook and Lotus Organizer (or PC-based programs included with these handheld devices that provided address book and calendar features).

Information on the PDA was also held on the PC in a program such as Outlook. When the PDA and a program like Outlook are synchronized, the different address records and appointments are reconciled. Any records not on the PC are downloaded from the PDA and any records not on the PDA are downloaded from the PC.

An important distinction between the early PDAs and those available on the market today is that the forerunners of the current devices did not provide you with the ability to add applications to them; the calendar, address book, and other utilities on the devices were embedded in their ROM firmware chips.

Note PDAs have certainly come and gone; one of the first devices available was the Newton MessagePad, which was released by Apple in 1993. Texas Instruments also took a crack at the PDA market with a line of organizers that are now no longer available.

The current wave of handheld devices are truly small PCs. They boast a decent amount of memory and pretty powerful processors. These devices also allow you to add applications to their configurations. Most current handhelds also provide you the ability to beam information to other PDAs using infrared ports on the devices.

Note With cellular technology evolving at a rapid pace, a number of cellular phones are now available that are Web ready. They can be used to view Web pages and to send and receive e-mail. This type of cellular phone is basically a PDA and a telephone all wrapped into one unit.

PDAs come in a variety of sizes and price ranges. For example, the Palm Pilot (which, as of the writing of this book, is certainly the most popular of the PDAs) provides several different devices that vary in functionality and price. The entry-level Palm Pilot, the Palm m100 (which sells for around $140), provides 2MB of memory and a Motorola processor (running at 20MHz). The high-end Palm Pilot, the Palm VIIx, provides 8MB of memory and wireless technology that allows for remote connection to the Internet (the VIIx sells for around $450).

Other PDAs are available that run the Palm OS. For example, Sony makes a PDA called the Clié. Handspring (a company started by some of the architects of the Palm OS) offers the Visor in a number of different models. Figure 18.1 shows a Handspring Visor Deluxe, which provides 8MB of memory and an expansion port for add-on devices, such as a modem and a cellular phone.

FIGURE 18.1

PDAs such as the Handspring Visor are pen-based, handheld computers.

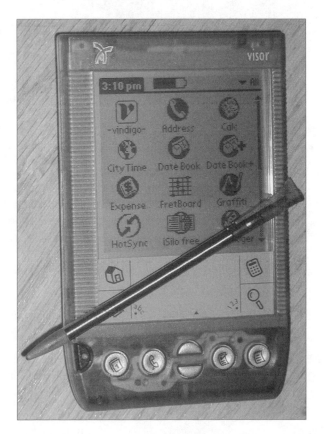

Windows-based PocketPCs also come in a variety of models (and price ranges). For example, the HP Jornada 548 is a Windows-powered Pocket PC with 32MB of memory (16MB RAM and 16MB ROM) and a 133MHz Hitachi processor. The HP Jornado 720 Handheld PC is a higher-end device that offers a 206MHz processor, a built-in modem, and an attached keyboard, making it almost a laptop computer, without actually being called a *laptop* (it runs the Pocket PC Windows CE OS, not the full-blown Windows OS, as a laptop would). Figure 18.2 shows the HP Jornada 720.

FIGURE 18.2

PDAs come in a number of different form factors; the HP Jornada 720 provides a keyboard and a built-in modem (photo courtesy of the Hewlett-Packard Company).

A number of companies have PocketPCs on the market, including Microsoft, HP, Compaq, Casio, and Hitachi. All these devices use the Windows CE operating system. The Hitachi HPW600ETM is certainly one of the priciest units (over $1,000), but it offers a touch screen, a 56K modem, and a 133MHz RISC processor. The Hitachi unit even provides a port for the connection of an external monitor.

As you've probably noticed from the figures provided in this section, PDAs are basically built with two major designs in mind: handheld pen devices and slightly larger units that provide an attached keyboard (although keyboards are available for nearly all the PDAs as add-ons). Before taking a look at how PDAs are used to communicate with PCs and the network, let's take a quick look at the two most popular operating systems used on these devices.

PDA Operating Systems

As I already mentioned at the outset of this chapter, two operating systems—Palm and Windows CE—dominate the handheld computing market. The Palm OS provides a minimalist take on handheld computing and offers a simple interface ideally designed for access with a stylus. Windows CE is a mini-version of Windows and offers the same familiar interface, providing the Windows Start menu and a Windows desktop.

Each of these operating systems provides a basic collection of applications and productivity software, and each provides you with the ability to add additional applications to the device. Let's take a quick look at each of the operating systems and then concentrate on how these devices can be used offline and online in conjunction with a corporate LAN.

You know a new computing device has been accepted by the computing community when hackers actually take the time to develop a virus for it. Viruses for PDA operating systems have actually popped up, and software companies such as Norton are developing antivirus software for the PDA operating systems.

The Palm OS

The Palm OS provides the Application Launcher, which is used to start the various programs held on the device. Figure 18.3 shows the Palm Application Launcher. Any of the programs shown can be started with a quick tap of the stylus on the appropriate icon. Buttons on the bottom of Palm and Handspring PDAs also provide a quick way to launch commonly used programs, such as Date Book, Address Book, To Do List, and Memo Pad (respectively, from left to right on the device). Two scroll buttons (one top and one bottom) located between the four buttons at the bottom of the Palm device can be used to move up and down within any application or in the Application Launcher.

Additional icons appear on a small plastic overlay just above the button area on the device. The Applications icon is used to return to the Application Launcher from any application. The Menus icon just below the Applications icon is used to open any menus that are available for the Application Launcher and individual applications. For example, Figure 18.4 shows the Apps menu for the Applications Launcher. Also available on the plastic overlay area is the Calculator icon, which starts the device's calculator, and the Find icon, which provides a search engine that can be used to find the occurrences of a search string in any of Palm's application files (such as the Address Book application, the e-mail application, or any other application you have installed on your Palm device).

FIGURE 18.3

The Palm OS Application Launcher uses a system of icons to launch the programs on the Palm device.

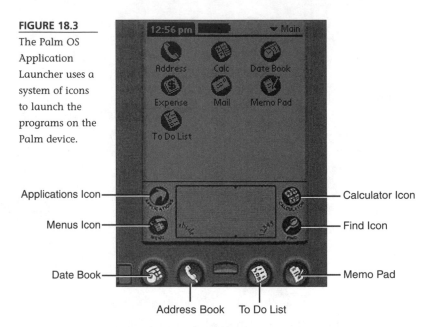

Applications Icon

Menus Icon

Date Book

Address Book   To Do List

Calculator Icon

Find Icon

Memo Pad

FIGURE 18.4

Menus for the various applications and the Application Launcher are opened by selecting the Preferences icon.

This plastic overlay rectangle also provides the Graffiti writing area. Graffiti is a program that provides you with the ability to write with the stylus on the Graffiti writing area. The Graffiti software recognizes your scribbles and places the correct characters into the application area that you are currently working in. The left side of the Graffiti writing area is used to enter letters of the alphabet, and the right side is used to enter numbers with the stylus.

Launching an application on a Palm device is just a matter of tapping the appropriate icon on the Application Launcher screen with the stylus. For example, to start a new memo, using the Memo Pad application, you would tap the Memo Pad icon with the stylus. In the Memo Pad application window, a tap on the New button opens a new memo. You can then enter the memo text using the Graffiti writing area, or you can open the little virtual keyboard by tapping the dot just below the "abc" logo on the left side of the Graffiti writing area.

Figure 18.5 shows a new memo screen with the virtual keyboard open. Once data is entered in an application, this information is stored in the device's RAM, which is *nonvolatile RAM* (meaning you won't lose your data when you switch off the device).

FIGURE 18.5

Data can be entered into an application using the stylus on either the Graffiti writing area or the virtual keyboard.

Windows CE

The Windows CE (or PocketPC) operating system provides you with the familiar look of the Windows desktop (although the overall look of the desktop and the Start menu varies slightly among the different PocketPC devices). Although Palm and Palm clones are currently (as of the writing of this book) on top as far as units sold, it is common knowledge that the Windows-based handheld devices provide more complex applications, such as "pocket" versions of Word, Excel, and Outlook. These devices also provide more hardware power in terms of processing and memory.

Applications on a PocketPC are launched either via the Start menu or by using icons on the desktop. Figure 18.6 shows the Windows CE desktop on an HP color handheld device.

Depending on the actual device, information can be input with the stylus (as in the Palm environment) or via the hardware keyboard (if the device has a keyboard).

Working Offline and Online

PDAs are designed primarily for offline "on the road" computing. However, PDAs outfitted with a modem or cellular connectivity technology can connect to a service provider and access e-mail or the Web (or the corporate network through a Virtual Private Network—discussed in Chapter 17, "Networking on the Run"—or a private Web site) and can even synchronize with a PC through a remote connection.

Now having said all that concerning remote connectivity, in most cases the PDA is still going to be used as a standalone device. Data can be referred to, edited (or deleted), and added to. Then when the device is synchronized with a desktop computer, new information is added to the application database that holds that particular kind of information. For example, a salesperson might sync his handheld device (a Palm, for example) to his e-mail application on his PC. He can then read e-mail messages that he has been unable to get to while on the road.

FIGURE 18.6

PocketPC hand-
held devices pro-
vide the familiar
Windows envi-
ronment.

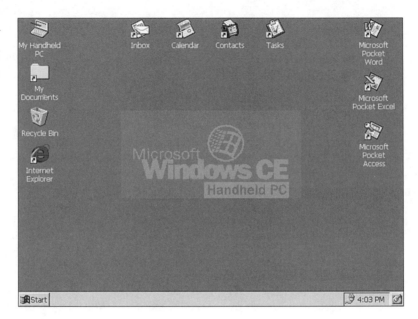

Responses to these e-mail messages or new e-mail can then be stored on the hand-held device until it is again synchronized with the user's PC. For example, on a Palm device, the Mail application is used to read, answer, and create mail messages.

Obviously, if a person is equipped with a handheld device that has all the bells and whistles, such as a modem, the amount of online work that he will do on the hand-held computer will depend on how often he wishes to connect to a particular service, such as the Web. Figure 18.7 shows the pocket version of Internet Explorer accessing the Web on a Windows CE device connected to the Internet.

Synchronizing PDAs and the Desktop

The true power of PDAs is that the applications on them can be synchronized with desktop applications. For example, in the Palm environment, the Mail, Address Book, and Calendar applications can all be synchronized with the different services provided by Microsoft Outlook (Inbox, Contacts, and the calendar). In the Pocket PC environment, the pocket version of Outlook can be synchronized with the desktop version of Outlook on the PC.

FIGURE 18.7

Handheld
devices can
directly connect
to Internet serv-
ices such as the
Web.

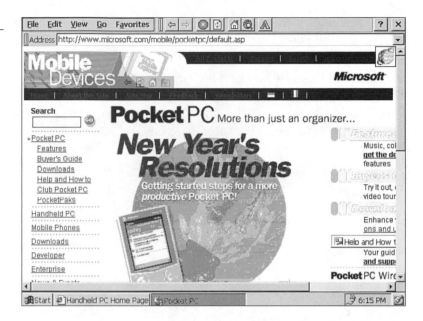

The implication of synchronization is that information temporarily held on the PDA
ends up on the desktop computer. What's more, if the computer is connected to a
network where groupware applications such as Outlook are used to share calendar
information, the PDA information will eventually dovetail with information that
can be accessed by different users on the network (in an environment where groupware applications are being used).

In fact, Palm has developed an Ethernet cradle; Palm devices placed in the cradle
can be synchronized directly on the network using Palm's Hotsync Server software.
This means that a network administrator could allow users to sync their Palm
devices with groupware applications found on a Microsoft Exchange Server or in a
Lotus Notes environment. The Hotsync Server software allows handhelds to be basically managed like any other device on the network.

In the Windows CE environment, Microsoft has developed a Terminal Server client
for Windows-based PDAs. This allows these handheld devices to become mobile network clients that can directly access network applications using a modem or wireless
connection.

The Synchronization Cradle

Although software and hardware for synchronizing PDAs directly to the network are
being developed at a rapid pace, the most common method of synchronizing a PDA
with a PC (whether the PC is on the network or not) requires a simple physical communication connection between the PDA and the PC. All the PDAs available support

serial synchronization, where a connection is made between the PDA and a COM port on the computer. Many PDAs also can be synchronized to a PC or Macintosh computer via a USB connection.

A cradle that holds the PDA and is connected to either a COM port or a USB port on the PC is the most commonly used strategy for synchronizing a handheld device with a desktop computer. Figure 18.8 shows the USB cradle used to sync a Handspring PDA running the Palm OS to a PC.

FIGURE 18.8

A synchronization cradle provides the connection between the PDA and the PC.

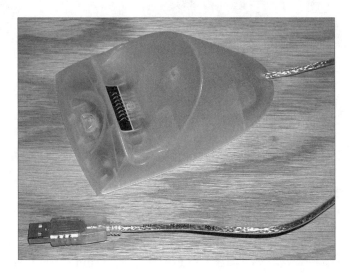

 PDAs are certainly the newest computing toy, and everyone suddenly seems to think he needs one. Therefore, caution is required when selecting a device that will actually best suit a company's needs in situations where you might arm your entire sales force with a particular PDA. This means that PDA deployment should be researched and planned, just like any other hardware or software deployment that you make as a network administrator. You need to find the right device, not only in terms of functionality but also in terms of how it will sync up with the software and hardware you use in the PC environment. For example, if you are running Windows NT Workstation on your PCs, which happen to have USB ports, you won't want to buy PDAs with USB cradles, even though you have USB ports. Windows NT Workstation won't support the USB cradles. Remember, research, test, and then deploy!

Synchronization Software

Once a physical connection is supplied between the PDA and the PC, it's up to synchronization software to actually sync up the data on the PDA and the computer. No matter what type of PDA you are working with or the operating system that it is running, you will be dealing with synchronization software both on the PDA and on the PC.

In the case of both Palm OS–based handhelds and Windows Pocket PCs, the synchronization software is part of the default application installation on the PDA itself. The software that resides on the PC has to be installed and is typically provided with the PDA on a CD-ROM. Figure 18.9 shows the Palm Desktop application's Custom dialog box, which is used to set preferences for the synchronization of a Palm OS device and a PC.

FIGURE 18.9

Software on the PC provides the command center for synchronizing a PDA with the desktop PC.

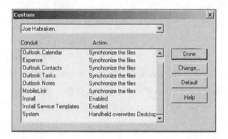

How synchronization proceeds, such as which applications are synced and which data set (on the PDA or the PC) should hold precedence during the synchronization, is configured using the sync software on the PC (again, as shown in Figure 18.9). In cases where you wish to add applications to the Palm device, the applications are first placed on the PC and then downloaded to the handheld device during synchronization.

For example, to add an application to a Palm device (the procedure to add an application to a Windows CE PDA would be very similar), you specify the application that you wish to add to the PDA's configuration during the next synchronization. Figure 18.10 shows the Palm Desktop's Install Tool dialog box. Applications to be installed on the Palm device are added to the installation list. This can include software purchased on CD-ROM or applications downloaded from the Web.

FIGURE 18.10

Additional applications are added to the PDA during synchronization with the PC.

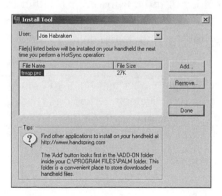

The number of applications that you can install on a PDA will, of course, be dictated by the memory available on the device. Having a bunch of games installed on a PDA for those late-night flights might seem like a good idea until you find that you are running low on storage space for important business contacts or other data.

Probably one of the most seductive aspects of PDAs such as Palm and Windows CE devices is that there are literally hundreds of programs available for them, and many are free. The Web offers a number of sites that provide a huge amount of freeware and shareware for both the Palm OS and the Windows PocketPC/CE operating system. One of the best sites is `http://www.zdnet.com/downloads/`. You can search for applications by specifying Palm or CE as your PDA's operating system.

Synchronization itself can be initiated from the PDA; in many cases, a button on the sync cradle begins the sync process. The sync software residing on the PC can also be used to initialize synchronization between the PDA and the PC. In cases where the PDA is outfitted with a modem or wireless connectivity hardware, synchronization can also be initiated by the PDA over a remote connection to the PC. This typically means that the PC must be outfitted with a modem so that it can respond to the "call" from the PDA.

Introducing Bluetooth Technology

Although the technology for integrating PDAs into a network infrastructure is still somewhat limited, I would like to end our overview of PDAs with some information on Bluetooth, a new wireless technology that shows great promise in connecting mobile devices such as PDAs with PCs and network devices.

In 1998 some of the big players in the PC and mobile computing arenas, such as Intel, IBM, Nokia, and Toshiba, banded together to come up with a new standard for connecting mobile devices. This search for a standard has resulted in Bluetooth, which is an open-specification, royalty-free technology.

Bluetooth is a radio wave technology. A radio transceiver is either installed directly in a device such as a PDA or added to a device such as a PC with an expansion card. Bluetooth is touted as a technology that could greatly reduce the use of physical cabling to connect devices.

Bluetooth is named after Harald Bluetooth, a Viking king. If you would like to read more about Harald and what is going on with Bluetooth technology, check out the Bluetooth site at `http://www.bluetooth.com/default.asp`.

Now, you are probably thinking this sounds a lot like the infrared ports that you find on printers and laptop computers. However, because Bluetooth uses radio waves, it does not require a line-of-site connection between two communicating devices. For example, you could potentially sync up a PDA with your computer the moment you walk into your office using Bluetooth technology.

This technology actually has a lot of possibilities and could provide links between computing devices, mobile phones, and peripheral items such as headsets and keyboards. Bluetooth technology is also being developed for implementation in a full-blown LAN infrastructure.

If Intel, IBM, and some of the other big Bluetooth supporters have their way, you will probably be seeing more implementations of Bluetooth technology in computing and LAN devices. Because the specifications for the technology are royalty free and the technology uses bandwidth that can be used consistently worldwide, this technology may take off like some of the other open-systems technologies available, such as the Linux operating system.

Chapter Summary

This chapter provided an overview of handheld computing and the personal digital assistant. Important points presented in the chapter follow:

- A PDA is a handheld computer that actually provides processing power and data storage.

- The two most popular PDA operating systems are the Palm OS and the Windows CE OS.

- The Palm OS provides a minimalist approach to computing, so Palm devices do not typically have the processing power or memory found on Windows PocketPC devices.

- The Windows CE/PocketPC operating system provides the familiar Windows interface and Windows applications such as Word and Excel.

- Palm devices provide easy access to applications using the Application Launcher, which allows the launching of any installed application with a tap of the stylus.

- The Windows CE environment provides the Windows Start menu and desktop icons that are used to launch applications with either a stylus or from the keyboard found on some PocketPC devices.

- PDAs provide users with the ability to work both offline and online (using a modem or cellular technology). Offline information accumulated is then synced with a PC to reconcile any information changed in applications such as an address book or calendar software.

- To synchronize a PDA with a PC, a physical connection is necessary between the devices, and synchronization software must be present on the PDA and the PC.

- Bluetooth is a new open-systems technology that uses radio signals to connect mobile computing devices with PCs and other network devices.

FUTURE NETWORKS: WHERE IS TECHNOLOGY TAKING US?

In this chapter

- Microsoft and the 64-bit NOS revolution
- Higher speed networks in your future
- Groupware's evolution to Webware
- Here comes IPv6
- Making phone calls on the Internet
- Computing on the run and handheld computers
- Peer-to-peer communication on the Internet

Computers in the future may weigh no more than 1.5 tons.

–Popular Mechanics, 1949

Network technology and computer technology in general continue to evolve at a rapid pace. This book has provided a snapshot of the technologies and possibilities found in the realm of computer networking at a particular moment in time. We have discussed the hardware elements of networking and taken a look at both the theoretical and actual processes that take place when data is transferred over a network. We have taken a look at the physical infrastructure of networking, the types of servers used on networks, and ways to protect and secure data on a network.

Although predicting the direction any industry will take in the future is difficult at best, predicting how we will compute in the future and how we will share data between devices is pretty much a mind-blowing task. Predicting the future of computing can also prove to generate comments that are very, very wrong. For example, at the 1977 Convention of the World Future Society, Kenneth H. Olson, then President of DEC, made the following prediction:

> "There is no reason for any individual to have a computer in his home."

I don't think we need to analyze this particular prediction any further.

The best predictions are probably kept very short and very vague, not unlike those predictions made on the Psychic Hotline. However, I will forgo that advice and take my best shot. In writing this chapter, I've tried to take a look at some of the areas of networking and computer technology that are already sitting on the cusp of change and predict where they are going, at least in the near future. When in doubt, I've used my trusty Magic Eight Ball to guide me.

Network Operating Systems with More Muscle

Sometime in late 2001 (or early in 2002), Microsoft will release the first 64-bit version of its popular network server platform, Microsoft Server. This means that different versions of Windows Server will be available—one that runs on servers with 32-bit processors and one that runs on servers with 64-bit processors. Although there have been a number of 64-bit Unix flavors around for years, Microsoft always has a way of capturing the public's imagination, even when it releases a product that isn't all that original (the case in point is Windows 3.1 and then Windows 95; the MAC OS had done all that GUI stuff years before).

Breaking into the 64-bit market means that Windows XP will run on some of the large, enterprise-size servers built by HP, Compaq, and other server hardware vendors. This means that the proprietary versions of these hardware vendors' 64-bit Unix network operating systems might feel a little heat from Microsoft's 64-bit version of Windows.

The fact that Microsoft is getting involved in the 64-bit NOS market means that Microsoft must see the integration of the corporate network with the Internet and the wider use of application servers and intranet technologies as a signal that network servers are probably going to need a lot of muscle—particularly in cases where the server runs some of the new services related to audio and video on demand that we will see in the near future.

Now, I'm obviously guessing at Microsoft's reasoning for becoming involved in the 64-bit NOS market, but here's my prediction (which is probably less risky than my guess about what Microsoft thinks). Microsoft's 64-bit version of its Windows XP Server platform should actually bring to light the fact that there are 64-bit operating systems out there and that they run on some very fast, high-end hardware. Microsoft may not take over the 64-bit market, but it will highly publicize the fact that the market is there.

With the computer hardware industry in a sales slowdown right now (that is, the first quarter of 2001), pricing should become somewhat competitive on enterprise-level server hardware. This means that hardware and server functionality normally reserved for the big boys may find its way into the medium-size business arena.

Even if this prediction is extremely wrong, I do think it safe to say that server hardware (even 32-bit platforms) will need to provide more muscle in the near future to run the Web-related services software and applications servers that companies desire. This means that multiprocessor servers with very big hard drives (or RAID arrays) and a lot of memory are going to become the rule rather than the exception.

High Speeds Coming to a Network Near You

The Ethernet standard has been around since 1976, and even though Fast Ethernet has been available for a number of years, many networks still run at the original 10Mbps Ethernet speed. Although a gigabit version of IBM Token-Ring is in the works, token-ring networks have been happy to plug along at 16Mbps.

So, one might wonder why faster LAN architectures haven't been adopted with greater fervor. Well, other than the expense, there has not been a huge bandwidth crisis on these networks. Smaller networks seem to have all the bandwidth they need for file and print sharing. Larger networks use switches and routers to conserve network bandwidth.

I would also make the case that there have not been any applications or network services that have put a bandwidth crunch on networks in general. However, things are going to change, and therein lies my next prediction.

High-speed fiber-optic data backbones are being rapidly established in this country and around the world. For example, ATM over a fiber backbone, such as SONET (which stands for Synchronous Optical Network), can provide a huge pipeline for moving large chunks of data quickly, particularly those originating from audio and video applications.

The fact that high-speed backbones are becoming more available to ISPs and uplink IAPs means that faster Internet connections are becoming more available to small and medium-size businesses. As small businesses begin to integrate their network infrastructures with the Internet, particularly the Web, the type of content available on the Internet may start to put some stress on the network architecture.

Therefore, in a nutshell, I think companies will begin to embrace the cost of high-speed hubs, switches, and NICs to upgrade the speed of their core networks to technologies such as Fast Ethernet. This is so that they can handle the data that will bombard their networks from the Internet. With many pundits predicting that the Web is going to become a sort of interactive television, larger amounts of bandwidth needed to handle audio and video will be required of any LAN that is connected to the Internet. Small and medium-size companies taking advantage of intranet technologies on their company networks will also feel obliged to provide their users with as much bandwidth as possible to handle some of the multimedia-based applications that will begin to become available.

Let me also make a second prediction: The use of dial-up Internet connections, at least in the workplace, should decrease significantly over time. So, no matter how you slice it, businesses that have a symbiotic relationship with the Web and use new network applications are going to require more available bandwidth on their networks.

Groupware Becomes Webware

In Chapter 9, "Working with Applications on the Network," we discussed *groupware*, which provides a communications environment for users on a corporate network. Although I certainly think Microsoft and Lotus will remain the big players in this software area, I also think we will see an evolution of groupware products into what I like to call *Webware*. The interface that is provided for the end user will appear more like a Web browser, and it will place discussion groups, e-mail, and other communication avenues into a context that at least mimics what users experience on the Internet (the Web, in particular).

Now, this prediction isn't particularly daring because intranets already use Internet protocols to provide users with different communications options over private networks. My prediction is that groupware software will become the front end for intranets and serve as the primary interface for users as they search a database or even do basic word processing. For that matter, there is no reason why the groupware client will not also become the interface that users work with when accessing resources on the Internet or the Web. Local and remote resources will appear the same to the network user.

A clue that this type of software suite may be on the horizon is that there has already been press on Microsoft's Netdocs, which will provide a communications interface for e-mail, personal information management, and digital media management. Although Netdocs is being touted as an Internet-based productivity suite, there is no reason why this type of communication and productivity package will not evolve for the intranet environment.

IP Addressing Using IPv6

I think anyone who surfs the Web even occasionally is aware of the fact that the incredible number of people and businesses connected to the Internet has all but exhausted the number of available IP addresses. As you know from Chapter 5, "Network Protocols: Real and Imagined," IP addresses currently consist of four octets of information. Each octet holds 8 bits of information, meaning an entire IP address consists of 32 bits. This version of the Internet Protocol is called IPv4, which provides 4 billion unique IP addresses.

Although not every one of the 4 billion unique IP addresses has been used, networks of the near future, particularly in the home market, may include your refrigerator, your television, and maybe even your car. This means that the current address pool will be pillaged in pretty short order. Therefore, a scheme that provides more addresses is required.

This is where IPv6 (or IPvng, ng for next generation) comes in. IPv6 is a new version of the Internet Protocol. It not only provides some enhancements for moving data on the IP network, but it also provides a new IP addressing scheme. IPv6 increases the number of bits in an IP address from 32 bits to 128 bits. This means that IPv6 can supply billions and billions of possible addresses.

IPv6 has actually been around for a number of years, but the cost (and aggravation) of retooling their network IP addressing from IPv4 to IPv6 has meant that companies have avoided the whole issue. ARIN has actually begun providing IPv6 IP addresses, but only a handful of companies have adopted them. Even proponents of IPv6 are sandbagging on the upgrade of IPv4 because it has provided a very stable addressing system and IP protocol.

So, my prediction is that IPv6 is finally going to overcome the ennui that has placed the IT profession in a near coma. IPv6 addressing will begin to roll out in earnest in the next 10 years. Whether the upgrade from IPv4 will go smoothly is another story. IPv6 is supposed to be fully compatible with IPv4 and provide mechanisms that allow IPv4 IP addresses and IPv6 addresses to cohabitate on the same network.

Here Comes IP Telephony

Voice over IP is the current brass ring that a large number of communications firms are grasping for. Time Warner, Nortel Networks, and a number of the Baby Bells are all testing or rolling out IP telephony networks and products for both the commercial and home markets.

For example, Time Warner is now testing an IP telephone system for the consumer market that consists of a telephone connected to a cable modem. All phone calls are handled over the IP network, just like any other type of network data would be moved using the various protocols in the TCP/IP stack.

In IP telephony product demonstrations I have seen (and experienced), there is some lag time between when a caller speaks on one end of the connection and when the voice data is heard by the caller on the other end of the connection. However, faster IP switches and high-speed fiber-optic backbones are now being used to make voice-over-IP telephone calls no different from a phone call made over the public switched telephone network.

As far as my prediction goes, I think the Baby Bells need to watch their backs. Voice-over-IP implementations in the business and consumer markets could allow communications companies who have invested in large IP network infrastructures to begin to take a big bite out of the profits available in the telecommunications market.

Computing on the Run Kicks into High Gear

Although mobile computing has been greatly enhanced by the advent of a number of wireless connectivity strategies, as well as the proliferation of handheld computing devices such as the Palm Pilot and the PocketPC, I certainly don't think this market is even close to approaching maturity. Wireless technology providers are still scrambling to increase their service areas, and applications for handheld computers (and the handheld computers, themselves) are still evolving.

So, in the case of handheld computing on the run, I think we are only seeing the tip of the iceberg. As more wireless providers enter the market, the ability to connect a handheld computer to a network via a modem or some other wireless connection is going to become much more available. Also, I don't think we've seen how far the capabilities of handheld computers can be taken, because we currently consider them little more than electronic day planners and address books.

As companies tie their networks more closely to the Internet or deploy their network services using intranet strategies, accessing company resources may be no different from accessing a Web browser. This means that once a fast and consistent connection is available for handheld devices, users can access data quickly and easily on the corporate network as if they were using a local network client.

So, as far as my prediction goes, I think we will see handheld computers evolve into Web portal devices that can be used to access data on the Internet or on corporate intranets. Faster processors, more memory, and different input strategies will also make it easier to enter and retrieve data on these handheld devices.

I'm not saying that handheld devices will completely supplant laptop computers, but you might see more people on airlines using small collapsible keyboards to enter information on handheld computers than you will see people trying to open their laptops up in such a restricted space.

Peer Computing on the Internet

A concept that will definitely become a reality in the next few years is secure peer computing on the Internet. We've already discussed how a secure connection can be made between a remote client and a network using a VPN (Virtual Private Networking) connection in Chapter 17, "Networking on the Run." Peer-to-peer or P2P communication on the Internet, however, will not only benefit companies using the Internet, but home users and small businesses that wish to share files and communicate within a secure environment.

Systems such as Microsoft's Instant Messaging, and Web sites such as Napster (which at the time that this book was written pretty much had the plug pulled on it by the courts) are examples of peer-to-peer communication on the Internet. Instant messaging allows direct communication between users on the Internet, and sites like Napster allow users to directly share files between computers (in the case of Napster, music files are shared). This concept will be greatly expanded so that Internet users who want to interact in a small group will be able to communicate and share files.

The Internet currently embraces a communication environment where information is broadcasted to a number of users from Web servers; peer-to-peer Internet communication will allow users to both send and receive information and files directly from computer to computer. A number of peer-to-peer projects, such as BrowseUp, are now underway on the Internet. BrowseUp is an add-on utility for Internet Explorer that allows users to publish information on the Web in a collaborative environment. For more information on BrowseUp, check out its Web site at `http://www.browseup.com`.

Another example of peer-to-peer Internet computing tool is FirstPeer, which allows users on the Internet to share files. FirstPeer also allows you to create groups, which allows any number of Internet users to collaborate within the secure confines of the group. For more information about FirstPeer, see its Web Site at `http://www.firstpeer.com`.

Peer computing and collaboration on the Web may be the next step for how we take advantage of the Internet infrastructure. P2P computing may also be a major paradigm shift in how we compute in the coming decade.

Where Will It All End?

The continued evolution of computer hardware and software used to network computers isn't going to slow down anytime soon. So, to make a long story short, the basic trend of computers becoming more powerful and faster and running more complex, yet user-friendly applications is not going to change. Also, the need to network computers so that resources can be shared is not going to become any less important. We are also going to continue to see businesses considering some kind of Web integration in their overall business plans.

For the network administrator, the future holds all sorts of possibilities. Any number of choices for NOS platforms, client operating systems, and server products that provide network applications will be available. This means that the network administrator will have to learn a lot of new technologies and be able to work with a variety of server products.

Although many network administrators see embracing new networking technologies as a curse, I believe it is a benefit of the job. To be able to learn new technologies and solve new problems can only make your job all that more interesting.

Chapter Summary

- With Microsoft's release of its 64-bit version of Microsoft Windows Server, we may see a demystification of and increased interest in 64-bit server platforms.
- With Internet- and Web-based applications demanding more and more bandwidth, we should see a increase in the WAN bandwidth available to companies and institutions, which may necessitate an increase in LAN bandwidth with such technologies as Fast Ethernet.

- The increase in high-speed yet cost-effective technologies such as DSL and cable modems should eventually lead to the demise of the Internet dial-up connection.

- Groupware products will evolve into "Webware." Accessing Internet services such as the Web and taking advantage of services on corporate intranets will be the job of the Webware suite products.

- We are rapidly approaching the day when the lack of available IP addresses will necessitate the adoption of IPv6.

- IP telephony is rapidly developing into a viable alternative to the regular phone system.

- With handheld computers becoming more powerful and wireless technologies becoming more available, computing on the run may be dominated in the future by Palm Pilots and Pocket PCs.

- Peer-to-peer or P2P computing on the Internet will make it much easier for home users and small businesses to share files and communicate in a secure environment using the Internet infrastructure.

PART V

APPENDIXES

GLOSSARY

access permission   The level of access or the rights assigned to a user in relation to a particular resource on a network.

access protocol   A protocol that is used to move network data across a WAN connection. Access protocols provide the encapsulation that creates the virtual tunnel. See also *tunneling*.

access time   Measured in milliseconds, access time is the time it takes a drive to access data. The lower the access time, the faster the drive. For example, an 11-millisecond drive would be faster than a 28-millisecond drive.

Active Directory   This name refers to both the hierarchical tree structure provided in the Windows 2000 network environment and the utility used to manage users, computers, and other devices such as printers in the Windows 2000 network environment.

alert   An alarm or notification you can configure on the Windows Server Performance Monitor that alerts you when a particular threshold for a process, such as hard drive usage, has been reached.

American Registry for Internet Numbers (ARIN)   The central registry for IP addresses used in a number of countries. ARIN is a not-for-profit organization established to register (and administer) IP addresses for North America, South America, the Caribbean, and sub-Sahara Africa.

American Standard Code for Information Interchange (ASCII)   The basic character set used by most computer operating systems.

Anonymous FTP site   An FTP site that allows anonymous logons. FTP typically requires a logon name and password. See also *File Transfer Protocol (FTP)*.

AppleTalk   The built-in networking language (protocol stack) used by the Apple Macintosh OS.

Application layer (DoD)   This layer in the DoD stack is equivalent to the OSI Application, Presentation, and Session layers. This layer provides the user interface for the various protocols and applications that access the network, and it handles file transfer, remote login to other nodes, e-mail functionality, and network monitoring. It also sets up the session between communicating nodes and manages the transport of data between them.

Application layer (OSI Model)   The top and seventh layer of the OSI conceptual model. This layer provides the user interface and services such as message handling and file transfer on the network.

ARPAnet   A internetwork developed by the U.S. government and various universities that provided a redundant, packet-switching infrastructure for the movement of data across wide geographical areas.

asynchronous modem A device designed to move data over a regular analog voice-grade telephone line. See also *modem*.

Asynchronous Transfer Mode (ATM) A high-speed packet-switching WAN technology used on optical networks. ATM is typically deployed on high-speed backbones such as SONET. See also *Synchronous Optical Network/Synchronous Digital Hierarchy (SONET)*.

attenuation The degradation of the data signal over a run of cable or other medium.

Automatic Private IP Addressing (APIPA) The ability of computers running Windows 2000, Me, or XP to automatically assign themselves an IP address when they cannot find a DHCP server on the network.

B channel The data-carrying channels on an ISDN connection. Basic Rate ISDN uses three channels. Two data-carrying channels, called *B channels*, each provide 64Kbps of bandwidth for data transfer. The third channel, the *D channel*, is not used for data transfer. Instead, operating at 16Kbps, the D channel is used exclusively for setup and control information used during the communication session. See also *ISDN*.

backup domain controller An additional server computer used on a Microsoft domain to provide some help to the domain controller for logging on and authenticating network users.

bandwidth The data pipe or conduit provided by a particular network architecture. Bandwidth is the amount of data that can ultimately be pushed along the network medium under ideal conditions.

baseband Data that flows in a single bit stream. Ethernet, token ring, and other LAN technologies use baseband transmissions.

baseline A set of initial performance readings taken on a server or a network and then used for later comparison.

Basic Rate ISDN (BRI) A form of ISDN that provides two B channels for the movement of data over regular phone lines. See also *ISDN* and *B channel*.

baud The oscillation of a sound wave on which one bit of data is carried. Baud was once used as a way to classify modem speeds; it has now been replaced by bits per second. See also *bits per second (bps)*.

bit The smallest unit of data found on a computer; bits are represented by either a one (1) or a zero (0).

bits per second (bps) The number of bits moved per second by a device such as a modem. Modems and other devices are typically classified by bps.

boot sector virus   A virus that is typically spread to a system when an infected disk is left in the floppy drive when a user boots up a computer. The virus then replicates to the boot sector of the computer's hard drive.

bottleneck   A hardware component on a server, such as the processor or the memory, that is being overtaxed and is slowing down overall system performance.

bridge   A internetworking device used to segment networks that have grown to a point where the amount of data traffic on the network media is slowing the overall transfer of information. Bridges use MAC addresses to keep local data traffic on each segment of the network. See also *MAC address*.

broadband   Data transmission where a single line can carry multiple transmissions on different channels.

bus topology   A LAN topology where computers are connected at intervals to a main trunk line or network backbone. Bus topologies typically use a passive network architecture, where the computers on a bus just sit and listen. When they "hear" data on the wire that belongs to them, they accept that data.

cell   A 53-byte packet used by ATM to move data, such as voice and video, across public networks (such as the POTS) and private wide area networks. See also *Asynchronous Transfer Mode (ATM)*.

central office (CO)   The nearest POTS switching station to a company or institution.

channel   One carrier unit on a T-Carrier line. Each channel can provide up to 64Kbps of throughput, and channels can be combined to provide greater amounts of bandwidth. See also *T-Carrier system* and *multiplexer (MUX)*.

Channel Service Unit/Digital Service Unit (CSU/DSU)   A piece of equipment that sits between a LAN multiplexer and the network's connection to the local loop. It provides for the timing of the data transfer. See also *local loop* and *customer premise equipment (CPE)*.

circuit   The virtual path created for a communication session on a circuit-switching network. See also *circuit switching*.

circuit switching   Establishes a circuit during the communication session between the sender and receiver. This means that, temporarily, the lines are dedicated to that communication session. Then, when the session is over, the circuit is immediately "torn down" and becomes available for another communication session. ISDN is an example of circuit switching. See also *ISDN*.

Class A   A category of IP addresses used for very large networks. A Class A network provides over 16 million node addresses.

Class B A category of IP addresses used for large and medium-size companies and institutions. There are 16,384 Class B network addresses available, with each Class B network supplying over 65,000 host addresses.

Class C A category of IP addresses used for small networks. There are over 2 million Class C network addresses available. Class C networks only provide 254 node addresses, however.

client A computer on a network that accesses resources provided by server computers.

connection-oriented transport A protocol operating at the Transport layer of the OSI model that uses a system of acknowledgements to ensure data delivery and defines a static route on the network so that packets are delivered along the same route during the session. This is considered a reliable connection.

connectionless transport A protocol operating at the Transport layer of the OSI model that does not use acknowledgements or a defined route on a network to move data from one node to another. Connectionless protocols do not require the network resources that a connection-oriented protocol does, but connectionless transport is considered an unreliable method of data delivery.

counters The real-time graphs added to the Windows Performance Monitor. Graphs are used to monitor the performance of an object. See also *object* and *Performance Monitor.*

crackers Renegade computer users who attack computer systems and networks; their arsenal includes viruses and a variety of attack strategies, such as denial-of-service attacks and IP spoofing.

crossover cable A twisted-pair cable that has been configured to allow the direct connection of two computers that are outfitted with Ethernet NICs.

crosstalk Interference passed between two closely located data wires.

CSMA/CA Carrier Sense Multiple Access with Collision Avoidance. A network access strategy used by AppleTalk. A device that is ready to send data out onto the network will notify the other network nodes of its intention to place data on the network.

CSMA/CD Carrier Sense Multiple Access with Collision Detection. A network access strategy used by Ethernet networks. If a node sending data detects that there has been a collision, it will wait to resend the data until the line is determined to be free of other data.

customer premise equipment (CPE) The LAN devices and the telephone system inside a company or an institution.

cyclic redundancy check (CRC) A mathematical calculation that is included in the trailer of a data frame. The CRC is calculated on both the sending and receiving computer. If the CRC checks are in agreement, the data contained in the frame is considered to be intact.

data bus The parallel collection of wires provided by a motherboard for the movement of data between devices on the motherboard and the computer's processor.

data frame Data packets moving down the OSI model are encapsulated by particular network architecture, such as Ethernet or token ring, into a frame. The frame makes the data packet compatible with the network architecture's media-access strategy.

Data Link Control protocol (DLC) A mainframe communication protocol that is also used to allow computers on a network to communicate with printers directly connected to a network using devices such as an HP DirectJet box or HP DirectJet card.

Data Link layer (OSI model) Responsible for the movement of data across the actual physical link between computers. It is also responsible for assuring that the data is received error free.

database engine The software on a database server that accepts requests for information from clients on the network.

de-encapsulation The process of moving raw data received by a node up the OSI stack into a format that can be accessed by a network user using a particular application.

default gateway On IP networks that have been divided up into subnets, the default gateway is the router that provides the connection for a subnet to access the rest of the network.

demarcation The place where the CPE ends and the phone company's equipment begins.

demodulation The conversion of data from analog to digital. This data-conversion process is provided by a modem.

Department of Defense (DoD) model A network communications conceptual model that was developed by the Department of Defense in the infancy of the Internet. The DoD model has four layers: Application layer, Host-to-Host layer, Internet layer, and Network Access layer.

differential backup This type of backup only backs up the files that have changed since the last backup. The differential backup does not, however, change the marker attribute, which indicates that the file has been backed up.

Digital Data Service (DDS)   Digital lines supplied by the POTS or other service provider that are used for data transfer. DDS lines include the T-Carrier system. See also *T-Carrier system*.

Digital Subscriber Line (DSL)   One of the newest technologies for data transfer over the POTS, the DSL technology allows for digital communication over existing phone lines.

Digital Subscriber Line Access Multiplexer (DSLAM)   A device located at a provider's central office that receives signals from multiple customer Digital Subscriber Line connections and puts these signals on a high-speed backbone using multiplexing techniques. See also *Digital Subscriber Line (DSL)* and *multiplexer (MUX)*.

direct connect printer   A printer that contains its own network interface, processor, and memory for print serving. Such printers are typically attached directly to a network hub using twisted-pair cable.

disk duplexing   Disk mirroring where separate drive controllers are used on drives in a mirror set. See also *Redundant Array of Inexpensive Disks (RAID)* and *disk mirroring (RAID 1)*.

disk mirroring (RAID 1)   This type of RAID is used to create an exact duplicate of a drive or drive partition. If the main drive fails, the mirror-image drive can be used to keep the server running. See also *Redundant Array of Inexpensive Disks (RAID)*.

DNS domain   A friendly name assigned to a company or institution that has a presence on the Internet. Domain names must be leased by an organization for use on the Internet.

DNS server   A server that resolves friendly domain names (URLs) to IP addresses (and vice versa). There are seven core DNS servers on the Internet.

domain   The basic structure or administrative unit for Microsoft networks running the Windows NT, 2000, and XP network operating systems. Each domain is managed by a server called the domain controller. See also *DNS domain* and *domain controller*.

domain controller   The server on a Microsoft network domain that maintains the database of user accounts. The domain controller can also offer network resources, such as printers and shared files.

domain name space   The actual structure or scheme used for DNS names. The domain name space is basically an upside-down tree in which the different domains branch out from a central branch or root.

Domain Name System (DNS)   The hierarchical, friendly naming system devised for the Internet. DNS servers are used to resolve these friendly DNS names to actual IP addresses.

dotted decimal   The format used to display IP addresses. This format consists of four decimal octets separated by periods.

electronic mail (e-mail)   A network service that allows users to send and receive messages.

encapsulation   The process of moving user data down the OSI stack on a sending node through a number of intermediary formats.

enterprise network   The network infrastructure for a large company or institution that consists of multiple sites across a geographical area, a country, or even the world.

Event Viewer   A utility available on a Microsoft server that allows you to view different event logs related to the server's system and security. This utility is useful in determining whether drivers for devices such as a NIC have loaded correctly on the server.

Fast Ethernet   So named because of its "faster" throughput speed (when compared to the original 10Mbps flavor of Ethernet), Fast Ethernet provides a bandwidth of 100Mbps.

FAT   Stands for File Allocation Table. It is the file system originally developed for use in the DOS environment. It uses a file allocation table to store the name and location of files that have been saved to a disk. The original version of FAT is referred to as FAT16. A newer version of FAT called FAT32 was developed by Microsoft to provide support for larger drive sizes.

fault tolerance   The ability for a hardware system or software to recover from errors or physical problems. Fault tolerance on networks is increased by strategies such as server backups, RAID arrays, and antivirus software.

Fiber Distributed Data Interface (FDDI)   A network architecture that provides high-speed network backbones that can be used to connect and extend the range of LANs.

file sharing   The ability of an NOS or OS to allow network users to connect to files or resources on a server or peer computer on the network. A number of operating systems and all the network operating systems provide strategies for sharing file and drive resources on peer-to-peer and server-based networks.

File Transfer Protocol (FTP)   A member of the TCP/IP protocol stack used to send and receive data between computers on the Internet or an intranet.

file virus   A virus that actually infects an executable file such as an EXE or COM file.

firewall   A device designed to sit between your network and the Internet that protects the internal network from outside attack. A firewall will examine data leaving and entering the internal network and can actually filter the data traveling in both directions.

forward lookup zones Records held on a DNS server that are used to resolve friendly names to IP addresses. See also *DNS server*.

fractional-T connection A connection that uses a portion of the channels provided by a full T-Carrier line. See also *T-Carrier system*.

FTP server A server that provides FTP services to network clients. See also *File Transfer Protocol (FTP)*.

full backup This type of backup can also be called a normal backup or daily backup (depending on the backup software you are using). A full backup takes all the files you select for backup and backs them up (no matter how the files are currently marked).

full-duplex Allows communication between a sending and a receiving device in both directions simultaneously.

fully qualified domain name (FQDN) The complete DNS name for a computer on a TCP/IP network. An FQDN will include the Internet domain name and the name of the computer.

gateway A computer or other device that uses software as a communication bridge between incompatible platforms or network architectures.

Gigabit Ethernet Uses the same IEEE Ethernet specifications and the same data format as other versions of Ethernet. Gigabit Ethernet provides a data transmission speed of 1,000Mbps.

Gopher A TCP/IP protocol developed at the University of Minnesota (the school mascot is the gopher) that provides a client/server system that allows a Gopher client to access data on a Gopher server (or servers) using a hierarchical directory, much like an index.

group A logical administrative container that holds a collection of user accounts.

groupware A suite of client communication software that is used to communicate with a communication server package.

hacker An extremely knowledgeable computer aficionado. A criminal hacker would be a cracker. See also *cracker*.

half-duplex Transmission of data can take place in two directions between a sending and a receiving device, but with half-duplex, data can only be transmitted in one direction at a time.

handshake An electronic communication agreement between two computers exchanging data over a network.

hardware sharing   The ability to share hardware devices such as printers, CD-ROM drives, and hard drives on the network. The ability to share peripherals is built in to many operating systems. Network operating systems also provide the ability for a server to share hardware devices.

hop   Designates the number of routers that packets pass through on an internetwork as they move from source to destination. Each hop would be one router.

Host-to-Host layer (DoD)   Equivalent to the OSI Transport layer, this layer provides flow control and connection reliability as data moves from a sending to a receiving computer. This layer takes the data from the Application layer protocols and begins the process of readying the data for movement out over the network.

hostname   The machine-level designation provided to a computer or other device on an IP network.

hub   A device with typically no active electronics that supplies a central connection point for computers arranged in a star topology.

hyperlink   Basically a pointer that allows you to refer to Web pages, graphics, and multimedia content that are listed on a particular Web page. When a hyperlink is clicked on in a Web browser window, a user is taken to that page or activates a particular event (such as the playing of video or audio content or the displaying of a picture).

Hypertext Markup Language (HTML)   The programming language used to create Web documents that can be read by a Web browser such as Microsoft Internet Explorer or Netscape Navigator. HTML consists of tags that are used to format a document so that it can be viewed in a Web browser.

Hypertext Transfer Protocol (HTTP)   A TCP/IP stack member that provides the connection between an HTTP client (a computer outfitted with a Web browser) and a Web server.

IEEE (Institute of Electrical and Electronics Engineers)   An international organization whose mandate is to develop and share electrical and Information Technology specifications worldwide.

impedance   The resistance of a wire to data transmission. All cable types have impedance, which is measured in Ohms. The greater the impedance, the more energy required to move the signal over the wire.

incremental backup   This type of backup backs up only the files that have been changed since the last backup (just as a differential backup does).

Interface Message Processor (IMP)   A hardware switch that was the precursor to the router. IMPs were used during the initial testing of ARPAnet. See also *ARPAnet*.

interference Signals or noise from nearby devices that interfere with a wire's ability to move a transmission signal.

Internet A giant, global internetwork that connects millions of computers. The current Internet evolved from government-sponsored packet-switching networks such as the ARPAnet.

Internet access provider (IAP) A communications company that provides a connection to the Internet backbone. IAPs typically serve larger corporations that maintain their own DNS servers and other Internet services servers, such as e-mail servers, and only require an onramp to the Internet infrastructure.

Internet layer (DoD) This layer corresponds to the OSI Network layer and is responsible for the routing of data across logical network paths and provides an addressing system to the upper layers of the DoD stack. This layer also defines the packet format used for the data as it moves onto the network.

Internet Message Access Protocol (IMAP) An e-mail transport program that provides an alternative to the POP3 protocol. IMAP mail servers do not immediately dump all the available mail from the server to the IMAP client when the client connects. See also *POP3*.

Internet service provider (ISP) A provider of Internet-based services. An ISP provides an Internet connection to users or companies in addition to other services, such as Internet e-mail, Web browsing, FTP, and newsgroups. An ISP also typically offers space on its Web server for personal or corporate Web sites.

internetwork A network of networks. An internetwork is a collection of LANS that uses different internetworking devices, such as routers and switches, to expand the range of the LANs.

InterNIC The central authority for domain names in the United States.

intranet A private, internal network that uses the TCP/IP protocol stack and different Internet technologies and servers to create an Internet-like environment for the users on the network.

IP Address The unique logical address assigned to every computer and other devices, such as routers, on a network that uses the TCP/IP protocol.

IP Version 6 (IPV6) A new IP addressing system that provides a greater number of bits (128 bits). IPV6 will offer billions more IP addresses than are currently available with IPV4.

IPSec (IPSecurity) A suite of cryptography-based protection services and security protocols that can be used to secure internal networks, networks that use WAN solutions for connectivity, and networks that take advantage of remote access solutions.

IPX/SPX (Internetwork Packet Exchange/Sequenced Packet Exchange)
A proprietary LAN protocol stack developed by Novell. IPX/SPX provides its own unique system for node addressing and was originally developed for LANs using the Novell NetWare NOS.

ISDN   A suite of protocols defined by the ITU-T (International Telecommunication Union-Telecommunication Standardization sector) that provides digital communication over existing phone lines.

ISDN modem   A terminal adapter that is used to connect a LAN to the POTS local loop. See also *ISDN*.

latency   The lag time it takes data to move from one place to another. Some WAN technologies, such as ATM, use fixed-size packets to increase the potential throughput and decrease latency.

Linux   A Unix clone created by Linus Torvalds when he was a student at the University of Helsinki. Linux is an open-system OS/NOS, and the source code is free.

local area network (LAN)   A collection of personal computers and other peripheral devices connected at one location.

local loop   The actual physical wires that connect a business to the nearest phone company switching station.

local printer   A printer that is directly attached to a server. The printer is only local, however, in relation to the server it is attached to.

LocalTalk   The actual hardware devices, such as the built-in ports, on the back of Mac computers and the special shielded twisted-pair cables that make up the physical connection for Apple networks.

Logical Link Control sublayer   This sublayer of the OSI's Data Link layer maintains the link between sending and receiving computers as data is moved across the physical media of the network. See also *Data Link layer (OSI model)*.

MAC address   The hardware address provided by the MAC sublayer of the OSI's Data Link layer. MAC addresses are actually burned into devices such as NICs and router interfaces. Each MAC address is unique. See also *Data Link layer (OSI model)*.

macro virus   Typically written in Visual Basic code, this type of virus affects documents and spreadsheet data files rather than executables. A number of Microsoft Word and Excel macro viruses have surfaced in recent years.

malware   Viruses, worms, and other software that are designed to mess up a computer.

marker   An attribute placed on files by the OS that differentiates files that have been backed up from those that have changed since the last backup.

Media Access Control sublayer (OSI model)   The sublayer of the Data Link layer that provides access with the network media and provides the addressing system used to move data frames on the network. See also *MAC address*.

modem   A device that can modulate and demodulate an analog transmission, providing for data communication over a regular phone line.

modem pool   A collection of modems on a remote access server. The modem pool provides for multiple dial-in connections.

modulation   The conversion of digital information on a computer to analog data carried on a phone line (modulation is handled by a modem). See also *demodulation* and *modem*.

multipartite virus   A virus that has the characteristics of both a boot sector virus and a file virus. It can spread from the boot sector of a drive to another drive, and it can also attack executable files on the computer. See also *boot sector virus* and *file virus*.

multiplayer gaming   A number of PC-based games are designed to allow multiple players to interact during a gaming session on a network. Individuals who set up home-based, peer-to-peer networks can take advantage of a large number of computer games that provide support for multiple players.

multiplexer (MUX)   The device that combines or divides the signals carried on the separate channels of a digital carrier line. See also *T-Carrier system*.

Multistation Access Unit (MAU)   A connectivity device containing an internal, logical ring that is used as the central connection point for computers on a token-ring network.

NADN (Nearest Active Downstream Neighbor)   The computer being passed a token is the nearest active downstream neighbor.

NAUN (Nearest Active Upstream Neighbor)   The computer that passes a token to the next computer on the logical ring is called the nearest active upstream neighbor.

NDS   Stands for Novell Directory Services. It is the logical, hierarchical directory tree used to manage users and devices on a Novell network. NDS became the structure for Novell networks with the release of NetWare 4.

NetBIOS Extended User Interface (NetBEUI)   A simple but fast LAN protocol stack designed for small networks. NetBEUI is a nonroutable protocol and was designed as an extension of Microsoft and IBM's NetBIOS protocol.

network   A group of connected computers that can share resources. Networks can be as small as two computers connected in a peer-to-peer arrangement or as large as global networks, such as the Internet, that use a number of different WAN connectivity strategies, including satellite technology.

Network Access layer (DoD)   This layer is equivalent to the Data Link layer of the OSI model and consists of the protocols that take the packets from the Internet layer and package them in an appropriate frame type.

Network Address Translation (NAT)   The ability to hide a group of computers using IP addresses behind one or more IP address. NAT is often used to hide friendly networks behind a proxy server. See also *proxy server*.

network architecture   The defining strategy for how computers on the network access the network media. The network architecture will also play some part in the network topology deployed on the network. Examples of network architectures are Ethernet and token ring.

network interface card (NIC)   A peripheral device containing a transceiver (a transmitter and receiver) that is able to convert data from parallel to serial, and vice versa. A NIC is the computer's connection to the network media.

Network layer (OSI model)   Responsible for the addressing of packets and their routing on the network.

Network Monitor   A Windows Server utility that allows you to monitor and track network performance and traffic.

network operating system (NOS)   Software that imparts special server capabilities to a computer. A server running an NOS can authenticate users to the network and share network resources.

network share   A drive or folder on a server that is made available to users on the network. Shares cannot consist of individual files.

newsgroup   An electronic bulletin board provided by a news server, such as those provided by Usenet. Information on news servers is broken into categories. Each subject area is called a newsgroup.

node   A client computer, server, or other device (such as a router) that is connected to the network.

NTFS   Stands for New Technology File System. It is a file system available on computers running Windows NT and Windows 2000 that supports the spanning of large volumes and uses transaction logs, making it easier to recover data on a failed disk. NTFS is an improvement over the FAT file system that was originally developed for the DOS/Windows environment. See also *FAT*.

NWLink   Microsoft's clone of the IPX/SPX protocol stack. See also *IPX/SPX (Internetwork Packet Exchange/Sequenced Packet Exchange)*.

object   On a Windows server, any process that can be measured using the Performance Monitor is referred to as an object. See also *Performance Monitor*.

octet   One portion of the four-part IP address. Each octet in an IP address is equivalent to 8 bits of address information. Each IP address consists of four octets (or 32 bits).

OEM   Stands for Original Equipment Manufacturer. It refers to large resellers of computer equipment. Software manufacturers such as Microsoft often supply OEMs with special versions of their software that is highly compatible with the OEM's hardware.

OSI (Open Systems Interconnection) reference model   A conceptual model developed to illustrate how network protocols allow computers to communicate on the network. The OSI model consists of seven layers. Each layer serves a specific function as data moves through several intermediary forms before it is transmitted by a computer onto the network.

packet   A blanket term for data that is being processed to be sent over a network. In theory, a packet is created at the Transport layer of the OSI model when data is segmented into small data packages.

packet switching   In WAN connections that use packet switching, the data is divided into packets. The small packet size used in packet switching provides fast and efficient delivery of data.

parity bit   Extra bits placed in a data stream sent by a modem. The parity bits are used to check for errors in the transmission.

partition   A logical portion of a hard drive that is actually read by the computer's operating system as a separate drive.

peer   In a peer-to-peer network, the computers on the network functions as peers. Each peer has the capability to access and serve up resources such as files and printers.

peer communication   Information placed by a protocol operating at a particular layer of the OSI model in a data packet's header that is intended for a protocol operating at the same layer of the OSI model on the receiving computer.

peer-to-peer networking   A simple, low-cost method for connecting personal computers in situations where you want to share files and other resources, such as a printer. The capability to provide peer services is built in to the OS that is running on the peer computers.

Performance Monitor   A utility available on Microsoft servers that allows you to monitor server hardware performance, such as the processor and RAM.

permanent virtual circuit (PVC)   A connection route set up between a sending device and a receiving device on a public switched network. The PVC is identified by a Data Link Connection Identifier (DLCI). Logical addresses, such as IP addresses, are then mapped to the PVC, providing a path through the WAN for the movement of data between the connected LANs.

Personal Digital Assistant (PDA)   A handheld computing device that provides productivity software for managing appointments, contacts, and other personal information.

Physical layer (OSI model)   This layer defines the actual physical aspects of how cabling is connected on a particular network topology.

PING (Packet Internet Gopher)   A simple diagnostic command that uses echo packets to test the IP connection between two computers on a TCP/IP network.

Plain Old Telephone System (POTS)   The infrastructure of the public switched telephone network in the United States. The POTS provides a number of different WAN technologies.

plug and play   An operating system service that allows for the automatic recognition and installation of peripheral devices such as modems and printers.

Point-to-Point Protocol (PPP)   A TCP/IP protocol that provides a reliable connection between computers. PPP supports multiple network protocols, such as IP, IPX, and NetBEUI. PPP also provides compression and error checking and is therefore more reliable than a SLIP connection.

POP3   A TCP/IP stack protocol used by e-mail clients to connect to a POP3 e-mail server. The POP3 e-mail server basically functions as a mail drop.

Presentation layer (OSI Model)   The converter layer of the OSI model. This layer converts the data into a format that can be read by the receiving computer.

primary DNS server   A DNS server on a network that serves as the premier DNS name–to–IP address resolver on the network. It is called the primary DNS server because client machines are configured to consult it first when trying to resolve friendly names to IP addresses (or vice versa).

Primary Rate ISDN   A faster version of ISDN for businesses. Primary Rate ISDN uses a T1 line and provides 23 B channels (each operating at 64Kbps). One D channel is also necessary (as with BRI) to handle setup and to control the connection. All or any number of the 23 B channels available can be combined for data transfer. Some channels can also be used for voice communication.

print queue   The list of print jobs waiting to be printed. These print jobs are held in the print server's memory or hard drive in the form of a print queue.

print server   A computer used to queue up print jobs and control printer access. A print server typically has a printer directly connected to it.

print spooler   Software on a print server that accepts print jobs from network clients and readies them for printing.

printer pool   Several identical printers that have been configured to appear as one printer on the network. Because multiple printers can accept print jobs sent to the pool, print services are provided faster to network users.

program sharing   Involves applications such as spreadsheets and word processors being run over a network. File servers and special applications servers provide the platform for sharing different applications over a network.

protocol   Software code that provides the rules for how computers communicate on a network. LAN protocols such as TCP/IP or IPX/SPX actually are made up of a number of protocols in a stack. There must be a common protocol for the computers to communicate.

protocol stack   A group of tightly associated protocols, each with its own function, that work together to prepare data for the communication process.

proxy server   A server that sits between your network (considered a trusted network) and an untrusted network, such as the Internet. The proxy server masks the computers that are hidden behind it on the trusted network.

public folder   A folder on a network server that can be accessed by network users who have the appropriate permissions.

query   A request to a database server for information from a network client.

RAID 0   A method of combining several drives into one RAID array that provides for faster access time. RAID 0 does not actually provide any fault tolerance. See also *Redundant Array of Inexpensive Disks (RAID)*.

RAID 5   A method of combining several drives into one RAID array so that the information is striped across the drives. If one drive in the array fails, the data can be regenerated using parity information contained on the other drives in the array.

redirector   Software on a client computer that handles the little "bait and switch" operation that makes the computer think a network resource is still just a local resource.

Redundant Array of Inexpensive Disks (RAID)   A group or array of hard drives that provides fault tolerance on a server and is seen by network clients as a single drive.

remote access server   A server that accepts incoming dial-in connections or virtual connections from remote client computers.

remote printer   A printer attached to a computer other than your server. The computer that the printer is attached to would consider the printer local. Whether a printer is local or remote will depend on which computer on the network you are using as your reference point.

repeater   A device that takes the signal received from computers and network devices and regenerates the signal so that it maintains its integrity along a longer cable run than is normally possible. Repeaters are also referred to as concentrators.

resolver   The software on an application such as a Web browser that contacts a DNS server for resolving a friendly name to an IP address.

resource   A hardware component on a server or a computer. A resource can be the memory, processor, or hard drive space on a computer.

reverse lookup zones   Zones on a DNS server that resolve IP addresses to friendly names. See also *DNS server.*

ring topology   A LAN topology where computers are arranged in a physical circle. The ring topology moves information on the wire in one direction and is considered an active topology. Computers on the network actually retransmit the packets they receive and then send them on to the next computer in the ring.

RJ-11 jack   A small jack that accepts RJ-11 or telephone connectors.

RJ-45 connector   The male end on a twisted-pair cable used to connect to various network devices such as a computer's NIC.

router   A internetworking device used to connect LANs via LAN and WAN connections. The router uses a combination of hardware to route packets between networks.

routing protocol   A protocol used by routers to build routing tables and determine the best path for data on a routed network.

RS-232 cable   A cable used to connect a device such as a modem to a COM port on a computer.

Samba   A Linux add-on program that allows Linux computers to participate in Windows workgroups. Samba derives its name from Server Message Block (SMB). SMB is an important part of the NetBIOS/NetBEUI protocol stack and supplies the data blocks that make requests between client and server or between peers on a Microsoft network.

scalable networks   Networks designed so that any number of clients or additional servers can be added to them. The scalability of a network will often depend on the network operating system being used on the network.

Secure Electronic Transaction (SET)   A system developed to secure credit card purchases on the World Wide Web. SET was developed by Visa and MasterCard and provides very strong 128-bit encryption. The more bits, the better encryption. Therefore, 128-bit encryption is harder to decode than 64-bit encryption.

Secure HTTP (SHTTP)   A superset of the HTTP protocol that provides mechanisms to secure online transactions. SHTTP was developed by Enterprise Integration Technologies and is now the property of Terisia Systems. SHTTP provides for the encryption of transmissions between servers and clients.

Secure Socket Layer (SSL)   A system used to secure online transactions on the Internet. SSL was developed by Netscape to secure online transactions and uses a combination of encryption and digital certificates (the certificates are used to verify a merchant's identity) to secure the transfer of information from a Web browser to a Web site store.

Serial Line Internet Protocol (SLIP)   An access protocol developed primarily to allow PCs to connect to the Internet using a modem. It operates at the OSI model's Physical layer and allows data to flow across the telephone line to a remote system.

serial ports   The communication (COM) ports on a computer. Serial ports are typically used to connect communication devices such as modems to a computer.

serial transmission   Data bits are lined up in a single bit stream for transfer over a network medium such as copper wire.

server   A computer that actually serves up the resources available on the network—everything from files to electronic mail post offices. A server running a network operating system also controls access to the network and authenticates users based on login name and password.

server-based networking   A networking model where user access and the sharing of resources is centrally controlled. Resources and user logon are controlled by a specialized network server.

service   A resource, such as e-mail, newsgroups, or teleconferencing, provided by a communication server.

service access points (SAPs)   Communication channels that are provided by the Logical Link Control (LLC) sublayer of the Data Link layer of the OSI model. SAPs are used so that lower layers of the OSI model can communicate with upper layers in the OSI stack.

Session layer (OSI model)   The layer of the OSI model responsible for setting up the communication link or session between the sending and receiving computers.

share   A resource such as a drive, folder, or printer that is made available to other users on a network.

share-level security   A security scheme in which each resource on a network is managed separately and often requires a unique password for access. Share-level security is typical for the peer-to-peer networking environment.

shared database   A client/server environment where a shared database is held on a database server and is accessed using database client software on network client computers.

shared printer   A printer on a network that accepts print jobs from more than one computer.

shielded twisted pair (STP)   Network-grade twisted-pair cabling that is encased in a protective shielding.

Simple Mail Transport Protocol (SMTP)   A protocol that allows e-mail servers to send and receive messages. This protocol operates at the Application, Presentation, and Session layers of the OSI model.

simplex   A type of transmission in which data can only be sent in one direction between a sending and a receiving device. Your thermostat and furnace are good examples of simplex transmission.

sneakernet   Sharing information from computer to computer by physically passing a disk holding the information.

SQL (Structured Query Language)   A language used to build complex client/server databases. SQL is also used by the database client software to send queries to the database server.

star topology   A LAN topology where each computer or device on the network is connected to a central device called a hub. Each computer is connected with its own cable (typically twisted-pair cable) to a port on the hub. Star LANs typically deploy a passive network architecture.

subnet   A logical division or subset of a large IP network. Each subnet is connected to the other subnets on the network by a router.

supercomputer   A term typically reserved for some of the large mainframe and miniframe computers built in the last few decades. Cray Corporation actually marketed a powerful mini called the Cray Supercomputer.

SWAT (Samba Web Administration Tool)   A Samba configuration tool that can be accessed using a Web browser on a Linux computer. See also *Samba*.

switched network   A WAN connectivity strategy that allows multiple users to take advantage of the same line. Switched networks can take advantage of two different strategies: circuit switching and packet switching. See also *circuit switching* and *packet switching*.

Switches   An internetworking device that can be used to preserve the bandwidth on your network using segmentation. Switches are used to forward packets to a particular segment using MAC hardware addressing (the same as bridges). See also *bridge*.

Synchronous Optical Network/Synchronous Digital Hierarchy (SONET)
A Physical layer specification for high-speed fiber-optic networks. SONET networks typically used ATM as their WAN protocol.

T-Carrier system   High-speed digital lines made up of multiple channels provided by the POTS or other service provider. The T-Carrier system can be used for the high-speed transfer of voice, video, and data. Each channel on a line can provide 64Kbps of throughput.

thicknet   A heavy-gauge coaxial cable that is fairly inflexible and requires special equipment (over and above a simple network card) to connect a computer to the network backbone.

thinnet   A fairly flexible coaxial cable (RG-58A/U) used on Ethernet LANs.

time domain reflectometer   A sophisticated device that can diagnose shorts and breaks in a cable and can provide you with information on where a short or break exists on the cable.

token   A data packet that is passed from computer to computer on a network using a ring topology. Possession of the token is necessary for the computer to transmit data onto the network.

topology   The overall physical layout of a network.

Traceroute   A diagnostic command that can be used to see the route that data packets take between two computers on a TCP/IP network.

translator   A protocol that has the ability to transform data packets from one format to another. Translator protocols typically reside at the Presentation layer of the OSI model and make sure that data will be understandable when received by a computer on the network.

Transmission Control Protocol/Internet Protocol (TCP/IP)   A suite of protocols developed for the Internet. It is a routable protocol stack that is universally embraced by client operating systems and network operating systems.

Transport layer (OSI model)   Responsible for the flow control of data between communicating computers.

trusted network   Another name for the internal or corporate network. It is trusted because of the administrator's ability to control user activity. See also *untrusted network*.

tunnel client   A computer that remotely connects to a tunnel server using a VPN. See also *Virtual Private Network (VPN)*.

tunnel server   A server that provides the network connection for a Virtual Private Network session.

tunneling   Remote access servers encapsulate packets in a frame so that they can move through a virtual route or tunnel across the public switched telephone network. Virtual tunnel encapsulation is provided by the wide area networking protocol or access protocol that is being used to host the connection.

uniform resource locator (URL)   The friendly name of an Internet resource such as a Web server on the World Wide Web. A URL is defined by the registered domain name of a company and the domain name system hierarchy.

uninterruptible power supply (UPS)   A device outfitted with some type of battery that can supply temporary power to a server when there is a power failure.

Universal Naming Convention (UNC)   A naming system that uses "friendly names" to refer to resources on a network. The UNC for a share on a server takes the format *server name\share name*.

Unix   A multiuser, multitasking operating system that provides a client/server networking environment on a wide variety of hardware platforms.

unshielded twisted pair (UTP)   Network-grade twisted-pair cabling that is not encased in a protective shielding.

untrusted network   An external network such as the Internet that will be connected to the internal or trusted network. It is untrusted because the network administrator has no control over the users or activity on the external network. See also *trusted network*.

Usenet   A network of Internet servers that allows users to post and read messages in newsgroups. See also *newsgroup*.

user authentication   The process where the user is allowed access to the network by virtue of his login name and password.

user communication   A term that encompasses any number of different mediums for user communication on a network. These different communication mediums include electronic mail, newsgroups, and video conferencing.

username   The name that a user must provide when logging on to a server-based network.

Virtual Private Network (VPN)   A secure, dedicated point-to-point connection over a public IP network such as the Internet.

virus   A malicious, self-replicating piece of software code. Because a virus can copy itself, it can easily (and unfortunately) be spread from computer to computer.

voltmeter   A simple device that can be connected to a cable to test the cable for a break or a short.

volume   A portion of a hard drive or parts of several hard drives that can function as a separate and discrete drive. In the case of RAID, a volume (which appears to the computer as one drive) is actually spread over two or more drives.

well-known port numbers   Conduit numbers that have been assigned to TCP/IP protocols and are used in conjunction with IP addresses to form a connection between protocols functioning on a sending and receiving computer. For example, SMTP uses port 25, and POP3 uses port 110.

wide area network (WAN)   LANs at different locations connected together using various WAN technologies.

WINS server   A special server on a Microsoft network that resolves NetBIOS names to IP addresses.

workgroup   A group of peer computers that operate in the same logical network space.

workstation   A powerful standalone or network client computer that provides the memory and processing power to run more complex software, such as the design software used by engineers.

worm   A program that spreads itself from computer to computer on a network. Worms are self-replicating and do not require user interaction to spread throughout a network.

xDSL   See *Digital Subscriber Line (DSL)*.

zones   AppleTalk networks can be divided into logical subsets. Each of these subsets is called a zone. Zones are used to group users into logical workgroups, making it easy for them to share network resources.

ONLINE NETWORKING RESOURCES

This appendix provides Web links you can use to further research networking and networking products. The links are placed in categories for easy reference.

Networking Theory and Information

Web Address	Site Name	Resource Type
http://www.hardwarecentral.com/	Hardware Central	Provides tutorials and articles on a number of different networking subject areas.
http://www.utexas.edu/computer/vcl/comptech.html	University of Texas Virtual Computer Library	Provides links to information on Information Technology, operating systems, and a number of other computer technology subject areas.
http://www.nsrc.org/	Network Startup Resource Center	Primarily a resource center for networking in developing countries. This site does provide articles and links to information on networking topics.
http://www.networkcomputing.com/	Network Computing	Online magazine that provides basic and advanced information on networking and network hardware.
http://webopedia.internet.com/	Webopedia	An online dictionary/encyclopedia that provides an online technical dictionary and links to different technology subject areas.
http://www.microsoft.com/technet/	Microsoft TechNet	A site that provides articles and white papers on a variety of networking topics (with a decided slant toward Microsoft products).

Web Address	Site Name	Resource Type
http://www.zdnet.com/	ZDNet	Provides information on networking and a number of computer technology–related subject areas. Also provides buyer guides and links to online versions of *PC Magazine*, *Macworld*, and *eWeek*.
http://americanhistory.si.edu/csr/comphist/	Smithsonian National Museum of American History	Provides pictures and information on the evolution of modern computing.
http://www.computer.org/history/	IEEE Computer Society	Provides a history of computer evolution, including a timeline.
http://www.networking.ibm.com/primer/primerintro.html	IBM Networking Primer	A primer on networking infrastructure and connectivity.

Network Interface Cards (Including Phone Line Networks and Wireless Networks)

Web Address	Site Name	Resource Type
http://www.3com.com/products/nics.html	3Com Network Interface Cards	Provides resources for selecting Ethernet NICs for client computers and network servers. A link is also provided to 3Com's token ring NIC products and home networking products for phone line and USB networks.

Web Address	Site Name	Resource Type
http://www.linksys.com/products/	Linksys Product Information	Provides links to both Ethernet NICs and wireless NICs. Links are also provided for hubs and wireless access points.
http://www.networking.ibm.com/	IBM Networking Hardware	Provides links to Token Ring networking hardware and other IBM connectivity products.
http://www.intel.com/wireless/	Intel Wireless	Provides links to different wireless networking products from Intel.
http://www.proxim.com/products/selector/index.shtml	Proxim	Wireless NICs and other connectivity devices for home and enterprise networks.
http://www.diamondmm.com/	Diamond	Home and corporate networking products, including NICs and modems.
http://www.bluetooth.com/	Official Bluetooth Site	Information on Bluetooth technology and links to Bluetooth-qualified wireless hardware technology.

Network Connectivity Hardware (Hubs, Switches, and Routers)

Web Address	Site Name	Resource Type
http://www.cisco.com/	Cisco Systems	Provides links to white papers on networking topics and links to information on different Cisco connectivity products, such as hubs, switches, and routers.
http://www.3com.com/products/hubs/index.html	3Com Hubs	Links to both home hub products and large network hubs made by 3Com.
http://www.canarycom.com/products/products_frameset.htm	Canary Communications Products	Links and product information in PDF files is provided for Canary hubs, repeaters, and other network connectivity devices.
http://www.alliedtelesyn.com/home.htm	Allied Telesyn International	Provides links to connectivity products such as broadband and DSL routers.
http://www.networkbuyersguide.com/	Network Buyer's Guide	Provides information and links for networking hardware, networking software, and computer hardware devices. This is one of the more complete resources for tracking down network and computer hardware.

Computer Hardware (Drives, Motherboards, RAM, UPS, Tape Backup, and Modems)

Web Address	Site Name	Resource Type
http://www.adaptec.com/ worldwide/product/ prodindextech.html Network Security	Adaptec Product Index	Provides links to hardware storage–related devices, such as RAID arrays and SCSI adapter cards
http://www.lsilogic.com	LSI Logic Corporation	Provides links to different device controllers and RAID hardware
http://www.abit.com.tw/	ABIT	Links to ABIT motherboards
http://www.pinegroup.com/	Pine Group	Links to motherboards, sound cards, modems, and other peripheral devices
http://www.actiontec.com	Actiontec	Links to modems and other connectivity devices, such as DSL modems
http://www.kingston.com/	Kingston	Links to different memory products
http://www.vikingcomponents.com/	Viking Components	Links to memory, modems, and router and server memory products
http://www.maxtor.com/ Maxtorhome.htm	Maxtor	Links to different hard drive and storage products
http://www.westerndigital.com/	Western Digital	Links to hard drive and controller cards
http://www.adic.com	Adic	Links to tape backup hardware and software

Operating Systems and Network Operating Systems

Web Address	Site Name	Resource Type
http://www.microsoft.com	Microsoft	Links to client and network operating systems from Microsoft
http://www.sun.com	Sun Microsystems	Information and links related to the Solaris NOS
http://www.novell.com	Novell	Links to Novell NetWare 5.1 and other Novell networking software products
http://www.linux.org/	Linux Online	Links to information and Linux distributions

Groupware and Shared Databases

Web Address	Site Name	Resource Type
http://www.lotus.com/home.nsf/welcome/lotusnotes	Lotus Notes	Links to Lotus Notes software and information
http://www.microsoft.com/exchange/	Microsoft Exchange Server	Information and links related to Microsoft Exchange Server
http://www.novell.com/products/groupwise/	Novell GroupWise	Information and links related to Novell GroupWise groupware product

Network Monitoring and Security (Including Antivirus Software)

Web Address	Site Name	Resource Type
http://www.hp.com/security/home.html	HP Security Software	Links to firewall, proxy server, and other network security software
http://www.sniffer.com	Sniffer Technologies	Product links, such as Network Protocol Sniffer software
http://www.netscout.com/index1/index1.html	NetScout Systems	Links to different network-monitoring and management systems
http://www.cisco.com/warp/public/44/jump/ciscoworks.shtml	CiscoWorks 2000	Information and links related to the CiscoWorks enterprise network-monitoring software
http://www.ipsentry.com	IPSentry	Information and links related to IPSentry network-monitoring software
http://www.mcafee.com/	McAfee	Links to McAfee antivirus software
http://www.drsolomon.com	Dr. Solomon	Links to Dr. Solomon antivirus software
http://www.symantec.com	Symantec Antivirus	Links to various Symantec antivirus software
http://grc.com	Gibson Research Corporation	Link to the Shields Up Web Site, allowing you to check the security holes in your Internet connection

Laptops and Handheld Computers

Web Address	Site Name	Resource Type
http://www.compaq.com/products/handhelds	Compaq Handhelds	Information and links to information on different Compaq handheld computers
http://www.handspring.com	Handspring	Product information and links related to the Handspring handheld computing devices
http://www.palm.com	PalmPilot	Product information and links related to the PalmPilot handheld computing devices
http://www.hp.com/jornada/	HP Jornada	Product information and links related to the HP Jornada handheld PC
http://www.gatewayatwork.com	Gateway Laptops	Links and information related to Gateway laptop computers
http://www.toshiba.com	Toshiba	Links to information related to Toshiba laptop computers

Index